Back to the Earth

Back to the Earth

AN INTRODUCTION TO ARCHAEOLOGY

JOHN P. STAECK

College of DuPage

Mayfield Publishing Company
Mountain View, California
London • Toronto

Library of Congress Cataloging-in-Publication Data
Staeck, John P.
  Back to the earth : an introduction to archaeology / John P. Staeck.
    p. cm.
  Includes bibliographical references and index.
  ISBN 0-7674-1108-0
    1. Archaeology.   I. Title.
  CC75 .S69 2001
  930.1—dc21

                                                        00-53299

Manufactured in the United States of America
10   9   8   7   6   5   4   3   2

Mayfield Publishing Company
1280 Villa Street
Mountain View, CA 94041

Sponsoring editor, Janet M. Beatty; production editor, Melissa Williams; manuscript editor, Elaine Kehoe; design manager and cover designer, Jean Mailander; text designer, Michael Warrell; art editor, Robin Mouat; artists, Lineworks, John & Judy Waller, and Robin Mouat; photo researcher, Brian Pecko; permissions editors, Matthew Ballantyne and Martha Granahan; manufacturing manager, Randy Hurst. The text was set in 10.5/12.5 Minion by Thompson Type, and printed on acid-free 45# Scholarly Matte by R. R. Donnelley and Sons.

For my family, thank you one and all.

PREFACE

Back to the Earth introduces students to archaeology—*modern* archaeology as I perceive it. I've started with the assumption that students need to learn first what data is and how archaeologists go about generating it. Interpreting data and applying those interpretations to past cultures seem to follow more naturally once students grasp the range of archaeology's fundamental ideological components and field methodologies. Experience has shown me that students are quicker to grasp these concepts when presented with both the personal and professional sides of archaeological research in concrete detail. They also respond well to a variety of case studies, including examples from historical archaeology and "ripped-from-today's headlines" cases that focus on preservation, legal, and ethical issues. By combining these elements in this text, I hope that its readers will not only gain an understanding of modern archaeology but also will be attracted to pursuing more advanced studies in the field.

FEATURES

I've created a number of features to make this a more useful text in contemporary archaeology:

■ *Fundamentals are covered in just enough detail.* I haven't tried—or wanted—to be encyclopedic. I feel strongly that each instructor should have the option to amplify and adapt the text as he or she sees fit.

■ *The text emphasizes Cultural Resource Management throughout and highlights several examples in the last chapter.* It's important that students understand the politics of archaeology, especially in North America, and the need for public education about archaeology and CRM.

■ *Examples of historical archaeology appear throughout the text.* Few introductory texts plumb the richness of the historical record to make fundamental concepts come alive. In addition to the examples from prehistory, students will find fascinating accounts, for example, of recovered ship cannons, artifacts found on the Little Big Horn battlefield, and bottles of early North American patent medicines.

■ *First-hand accounts of archaeological research and interpretation written especially for this text provide lively examples of the research process.* Three particularly compelling examples of archaeological research are included with numerous photographs: Dr. Louis Flam's work with the Sindh Archaeological Project in Pakistan, Dr. Robert Salzer's research on the archaeology and pictographs at the Gottschall site in Wisconsin, and Dr. Marie Selvaggio's study of hominid scavenging niches during the Plio-Pleistocene.

■ *Some issues and concepts appear in multiple locations in order to highlight the interrelationships within archaeological research.* This is particularly the case with archaeometric approaches to studying the past and key issues such as CRM and NAGPRA. This system of cross-references should help to tie issues together in students' minds as well as to provide quick references for further information on the topics at hand.

■ *The text includes strong student helps.* Numerous photos, as well as maps of sites, charts, and graphs provide a visual framework for the concepts. Terms are defined on the page where they first appear as well as in a glossary at the back of the book. Each chapter concludes with a summary and "For Further Information" section. A Bibliography provides further resources.

ORGANIZATION

This book begins with a discussion of what archaeology is and is not. Chapter 1 presents five generalized goals of modern archaeology: finding and recovering the past, ordering finds in space and time, interpreting past human behaviors, educating people about the past, and preserving the past. Readers will be exposed to the basic ideas of scientific reasoning and critical thought in general through a look at pseudoscientific archaeology.

Chapter 2 introduces the three variables that all archaeologists must master: material culture, space, and time. Traditional ideas of seriation, typologies, and culture area approaches are introduced, as are modern methods of integrating such things through geographic information systems and similar technologies. Material culture is introduced and explored in detail, including fundamental concepts such as sites, site localities, features, artifacts, and ecofacts. The chapter takes care to make students understand that the information they are exploring is an essential part of archaeological research that can be approached through a variety of avenues.

Chapter 3 introduces students to a cross section of theories and perspectives in archaeology. This chapter is not designed to be an exhaustive treatment of all archaeological thought but it does cover processualism and postprocessualism in general, while introducing the fundamentals of specific approaches such as human ecology, systems theory, and behavioral archaeology.

Chapters 4 and 5 cover fieldwork. In order to maintain consistency in chapter size and to help students digest a great deal of information in smaller pieces, Chapter 4 primarily addresses survey methods, including remote sensing, while Chapter 5 primarily deals with excavation and dating methods. The section on dating provides an overview of modern relative and chronometric approaches, including basic information on the technological aspects of these methods. These chapters are designed to introduce students to the real worlds of archaeological field research and to some important aspects of archaeometry. This chapter also reaches out to other disciplines in an effort to help students see the relationships and possible career connections between archaeology and other disciplines.

Chapter 6 introduces students to what stone tools are, how they were made, and how they are studied. The chapter provides an excellent opportunity to introduce students to numerous lithic sequences, including the Paleoindian-Archaic-Woodland sequence of eastern North America. Clearly other sequences could be introduced here and the instructor has been given free rein in terms of how best, or if at all, to teach such material.

Chapters, 7, 8, and 9 follow the basic pattern introduced by the chapter on stone tools. These three chapters introduce ceramics, metals and glass, and organic material (in that order) and provide some operational examples of how we study such remains and what we can learn from them. The chapter dealing with organic material also discusses NAGPRA and pertinent issues of working with human remains.

The book closes with Chapter 10 on archaeology today. This section discusses ethics, careers, problems with looting and with site preservation. Several examples of significant looting, its impact, and the legal response to these actions are presented, most strongly in association with Slack Farm and the GE Mounds. This chapter is written with the hope that students will take the notion of stewardship, as well as the legal and ethical ramifications of collecting, with them when they leave the classroom.

SUPPLEMENTARY MATERIAL

The Instructor's Manual includes a test bank of more than 700 multiple-choice and short-answer/essay questions as well as chapter learning goals, suggested activities, and lists of key terms.

A web site allows students the opportunity to explore further. The site will include links to breaking news in archaeology and an online image bank of figures taken from the text that can be downloaded for use on an overhead projector. If you'd like to contribute comments, suggestions, or corrections, please contact me at Staeck@cdnet.cod.edu.

ACKNOWLEDGMENTS

I owe a great many people thanks for their assistance with this work. The authors of the original essays have graciously agreed to provide us with insights into their careers as well as into their personal approaches to, and experiences in, archaeology; thanks go to each of them. Thanks also go to my wife and children for providing support and understanding during the writing of this volume.

I'm also indebted to the reviewers who provided timely and useful comments on the drafts of this manuscript: Sarah Campbell, Western Washington University; Aubrey Cannon, McMaster University; Debra Gold, St. Cloud State University; George Gumerman, IV, Northern Arizona University; Patrick McCutcheon, Central Washington University; Heather McKillop, Louisiana State University; James Skibo, Illinois State University; and Paul Welch, Queens College.

Most especially, though, my warmest thanks go to the staff of Mayfield. The numerous contributions of copyeditor Elaine Kehoe, production editor Melissa Williams, art editor Robin Mouat, and sponsoring editor Jan Beatty are beyond measure. The patience and skill of these editors helped in many ways to convert a vision into a reality. I am certain that I speak for all of them in saying that I hope you enjoy the fruit of our labors.

CONTENTS

LIST OF BOXES

1

INTRODUCING THE PAST

To touch the past is a kind of magic. Without conjurations or sleight of hand, hard work and curiosity reveal a world far more beautiful and real than can otherwise be imagined.

—Anonymous

Archaeology: Mention the word and many people conjure up images of Indiana Jones swinging from a whip and grabbing fabulous treasures. Other people imagine bearded men bedecked in baggy shorts, digging around ancient pyramids in search of mummies. Or, alternatively, we might think of the fabulous treasures associated with the Egyptian pharaohs, Maya kings, or Chinese emperors (Box 1.1). Indeed, a romantic notion of discovering the remains of long-vanished civilizations and exploring the ruins of forgotten places, lost to humanity from time immemorial, is the very fabric of popular ideas about archaeology. Such romantic images of bygone splendors, coupled with the often spectacular creations of past peoples, have attracted millions of people worldwide to attend museum exhibits of archaeological finds and to follow accounts in the news media of archaeological explorations. This interest has also spawned an amazing number of pseudoarchaeological accounts that purport to link past civilizations with everything from space aliens to King Arthur's Camelot. The fascination that modern people have with those who came before has also generated a more sinister effect: a thriving marketplace for grave robbers and looters who steal and sell the past.

Hence, this introductory exploration of archaeology is more than a survey of ancient civilizations and long-dead rulers. In this book, we examine what archaeology is and what it is not. We sample the many and varied ways that archaeologists go about their work, along the way stopping to look at how archaeology functions and at some prominent archaeologists. We do, of course, survey some of the more important archaeological discoveries from around the globe and examine how these discoveries can inform us about different lifeways through time and space. As a matter of course, we should also have fun. Although there is a serious side to archaeology, for professionals and amateurs alike there is always a measure of enjoyment in discovering the past.

WHAT ARCHAEOLOGY IS

Archaeology is literally the study of the old: *archaeo* meaning "old" and *logy* meaning, loosely, "the study of." Literally, then, archaeology is the study of old things, of the past. More than just reading about the past, though, archaeology encompasses the techniques and approaches used to study the past and ways of interpreting past events. The common theme in all of archaeology is that part of our information comes from the material remains of the past, the actual things people made, used, and altered, and then left behind. These remains are collectively called **material culture.** In effect, archaeology has become a discipline that seeks to identify and understand what happened in the past through the things people made and used. This book will help you understand how we go about doing this, from the actual events archaeologists study through the ways that archaeologists recover, analyze, and explain these events.

One of the most common questions archaeologists are asked is, How old does something have to be for archaeologists to study it? The answer is surprisingly complicated and often catches many people off guard. Something brand new can be studied by archaeologists, just as can something tens of thousands or more years old. The common element for archaeologists is that whatever we study helps us gain insights into the past. For example, by studying how people organize their societies today, we can build models that will help us understand how people may have organized themselves in the past. It sometimes seems odd that the behaviors of modern people can provide insights into the lives of past peoples, and it is certainly true that there is no one-to-one or direct correlation between the modern world and the past. Yet people are fundamentally the same now as they were throughout much of the past: They need food, shelter, access to resources, and a variety of tools to help meet these needs. So some of the fundamental problems that confronted humans in the distant past still confront us today, though our technological solutions to these problems have become more sophisticated.

Archaeology, Anthropology, and Culture

material culture The material remains of the past; the actual things people made, used, and altered, and then left behind.

To understand what archaeologists attempt to accomplish, it is necessary to understand where archaeology fits in the broad spectrum of Western education. In general, the curriculum at most Western schools is divided into three main divisions: the natural sciences (such as biology and physics), the social sciences (such as political science, anthropology, and sociology), and the humanities (such as history and languages). In North America, archaeology is usually classified as a subset of the social sciences, and, because of the specific history of the origins of archaeology, it is usually further classified as a subset of anthropology. Archaeology, though, is also part of biblical studies, classics, and even some history programs. For our purposes, we approach the study of archaeology through anthropology. We do this because, fundamentally, archaeology involves the study of things created and used by humans. Because of this, it is appropriate to approach these studies within the broader context of anthropology, which is literally the study of humankind.

Because anthropology studies humanity in both physical and social contexts, it is a very broad discipline that has many subbranches. Scholars usually group these various subbranches into four subdisciplines, **sociocultural anthropology, linguistic anthropology, physical anthropology,** and archaeology. This is sometimes called the four-field approach. According to this idea, each subdiscipline has its own approaches and techniques but shares some important common ideas and interests with the others. Because this approach allows anthropologists to study so many aspects of humankind, we call the approach **holistic,** meaning that it studies everything related to being human.

Sociocultural anthropology studies the rules of being human, such as how we calculate who we are related to (kinship), how we make a living, how we organize the world, and all of the beliefs that are part of religion, science, and the arts. Sociocultural anthropologists usually work with living peoples and emphasize the concept of **culture.** Culture is the term we apply to all of the beliefs and customs that we learn as members of society and that bind members of any given society together. It is the sharing of these customs and beliefs that allows people to anticipate and understand what other people are doing. When two people from different cultures meet, they often have trouble understanding each other. This occurs because each person has expectations about how other people should behave and what to expect. These expectations are not universal, and when different cultures have different expectations, there is usually a communication gap. Culture is also patterned, and this makes it important to archaeologists. The patterns of culture form the mental template that all people use to interact with one another and the natural world. The physical things humans make to accomplish any task, whether simple or complex, reflect cultural ideals and make up what we call material culture. Because archaeologists excavate material culture, we need to understand something about culture as a system of rules. By discovering the patterns reflected by material culture, archaeologists can seek to reconstruct the larger cultural system to which the materials belong.

Linguistic anthropologists study the languages of humans and the rules that make these languages work. Like culture, languages are learned and shared. When two people who speak different languages meet, they may not be able to communicate. The sounds one person produces may have no meaning in the other person's language, or, sometimes embarrassingly, the sounds have

sociocultural anthropology The study of living or historically recorded societies with the goal of understanding the mechanisms of interpersonal and intergroup interaction.

linguistic anthropology The study of the human use of language and how it is both developed by and helps to develop meaning within culture.

physical anthropology The study of humans as biological creatures, including their genetic diversity and evolution.

holism The notion that anthropology encompasses the study of all aspects of human behavior, past and present.

culture All of the beliefs and customs that we learn as members of society and that bind members of any given society together. It is the sharing of these customs and beliefs that allows people to anticipate and understand what other people are doing.

BOX 1-1

1325 B.C.: LOST, ONE PHAROAH;
NOVEMBER 2, 1922: FOUND SAME

November 1, 1922, saw the arrival of another anxious day for Howard Carter. He had been digging in the Valley of Kings for nearly a decade searching for the tomb of a little-known pharoah named at birth Tutankhaten. He was the son of Egypt's great heretic Pharaoh Akhnaten and one of his lesser wives, Kiya. Through the twists of politics and fate, though, Tutankhaten became a "living god" and was ruler of all of Egypt. Under the tutelage of an elder statesman named Ay, the boy reversed the problematic policies of his renegade father and restored the priesthood of Amun to its paramount place in Egyptian religious circles. To mark this event he took the name Tutankhamun, replacing the -aten portion of his birth name, a reference to the disk of the sun as a god, with -amun, who was viewed as the patron of the most potent of the Egyptian priesthoods of the day. The young pharaoh did not long enjoy the thankfulness of this priestly order, for he died before the age of twenty, probably somewhere between his seventeenth and nineteenth years. He reigned as pharaoh less than nine years and left no living heirs. Because of the obscurity of Tutankhamun, Carter and his patron Lord Carnarvon hoped that his tomb remained intact, overlooked by ancient and modern grave robbers alike, as well as by previous archaeologists.

Carter was near the end of his funding and was likely in the last year of his efforts in the Valley of Kings. During the day of November 1, 1922, Carter's workmen began clearing away the remains of the huts of the workers who had helped build the tomb of Ramses VI in 1143 B.C. Carter himself had helped to excavate some of these remains six years earlier while searching for the remains of Tutankhamun's tomb. As the work proceeded, one of the workmen noticed a step beneath the rubble, some ten paces north of the entrance to the tomb of Ramses VI. Carter was encouraged, but the tomb behind the steps, if one existed, had to be a small one. Nonetheless, Carter ordered the stairway cleared. The next day, twelve of the sixteen steps were cleared, and Carter was able to see a wall at the base of the stairway.

It was still partially blocked by rubble, but the plaster coating on the wall seemed intact. In fact, it was intact, and it bore the jackal-head seals that identified at as a royal tomb. Carter had found the apparently unopened tomb of a pharaoh less than fifteen feet from where he had searched six years before!

Carter quickly dispatched a cable to Carnarvon in England. The now-famous document reads simply, "At last have made wonderful discovery in the Valley; a magnificent tomb with seals intact; re-covered same for your arrival; congratulations."

Carnarvon dropped his affairs in England and booked passage to Egypt and the Valley of Kings as quickly as possible; and three weeks later Carnarvon and Carter began the process of clearing the final rubble from in front of the tomb. By November 24, 1922, the entire entrance to the tomb was visible. Both men noticed with concern some obvious damage to the entrance and feared the worst—that the tomb had, in fact, already been looted. Yet the seals themselves were intact, and this suggested that the administrators of the royal burials had resealed the tomb in antiquity. This was the sort of thing that happened in tombs that had been looted. More doubt crept into Carter's and Carnarvon's minds. Perhaps some things yet remained to be discovered, they hoped, but both feared the tomb was empty. After photographing and carefully removing the seals, the entrance was cleared to a sloping passage filled with rubble placed there in antiquity. This, too, suggested an effort made to seal a looted tomb.

After having workers clear the passageway, Carter found another doorway. Like the first, it had been sealed in the very distant past with rubble. Carter carefully began to pry away some stones, Carnarvon waiting anxiously behind him. Once a small opening had been made, Carter inserted a lighted candle to check for dangerous fumes. All seemed well, and Carter peered in to see what his single candle had illuminated. He stood silent for a long moment, much to Carnarvon's disapproval.

"Can you see anything?" Carnarvon asked.

Carter responded quietly, "Yes," he said, "it is wonderful."

In front of Carter rested the antechamber, a storeroom for all of the goods a pharaoh might need in the afterlife. Largely intact were the parts of a chariot, three gold-covered couches, quivers of arrows used by the pharaoh himself, and a host of other goods. Two life-sized gilt statues armed with maces stood silent guard over the material, each facing the other on opposite sides of a door on the far side of the chamber. Another doorway suggested to Carter that the remains of Tutankhamun might lay beyond, still intact. Later inspection revealed that Carter was correct, for the earthly remains of the boy king rested in a series of sarcophagi just beyond the antechamber.

It was with this discovery that archaeology leapt from scientific backrooms to the front pages of tabloids. Photographers, journalists, and wealthy visitors became commonplace at the tomb as workers carefully mapped and packed the priceless remains. The tomb, designated KV 62 (the sixty-second tomb to be uncovered in the Valley of Kings), became the focal point for a series of social and political dramas that were to involve Egyptian authorities, the British government, and the always opinionated Carter. These encounters, which are legendary, helped to further strain relations between the Egyptian authorities and Carter, who once worked for them, and the British museums. Carter had clearly proceeded with his work in the tomb before acquiring the proper permissions and oversight from the authorities, and there were questions about what may have been removed from the tomb before the antiquities officials were able to inventory its contents. This, though, is another story.

Howard Carter (left) and Lord Carnarvon (right) prepare to pack for transportation one of the life-sized statues from Tutankhamun's tomb.

Howard Carter exhibiting material from the tomb of Tutankhamun.

Howard Carter and an assistant examine a portion of Tutankhamun's coffin.

very different meanings. Consider the word *see* in English and the word *sí* in Spanish. When an English speaker makes the sounds for this word, he or she intends the sounds to convey the meaning of visualizing or viewing something. The Spanish speaker, however, makes these same sounds to indicate an affirmative answer, such as "yes." Linguistic anthropologists also study how meaning is conveyed by people and the histories of languages. Because these histories and rules all express aspects of culture, archaeologists can use the information linguists gather to help understand the patterns of culture reflected by material remains.

Physical anthropologists study the human body, how it works, and how it evolved. Some physical anthropologists work with living populations and try to understand the diversity of the human form; others use their skills to identify the remains of the dead; whereas still others study the development of living primates, including humans. Because physical anthropologists deal with the human form and because archaeologists occasionally find the remains of human beings on their sites, physical anthropology and archaeology are sometimes very closely related.

For a modern archaeologist, all of the subdisciplines of anthropology offer information and assistance in deciphering the past. Because we cannot excavate an intact culture, with all of its spoken language and social rules, we must seek to discover these things through the physical remains left to us by past peoples. Therefore, archaeologists rely heavily on their colleagues who work with living peoples and on the things they can discover in order to infer how past peoples may have lived. It is not an easy task; it is challenging and sometimes frustrating. In this sense, doing archaeology is like trying to solve a large puzzle for which we do not have a solved example or perhaps even all of the parts. Nonetheless, with trial, error, and careful reasoning, pieces can be fit together so that a pattern emerges. As the pattern grows and becomes more complete, we can attempt to decipher the final form of the puzzle.

Archaeology and History

In many respects, archaeology shares interests and goals with history, but the two disciplines are fundamentally different. History is primarily the study and interpretation of written records; it is dependent on the presence of texts and/or extensive oral traditions. Archaeology, on the other hand, is principally the study of the material remains of past peoples. Such remains include houses, tools, food waste, and even the remains of the people themselves. Archaeologists certainly welcome the presence of written and oral records, for they help us to understand the events and ideas of a given time period, but such records are not absolutely necessary.

A second important distinction between history and archaeology should be made. Historians are dependent on what people remember and record. Historical documents tend to emphasize the particular points of view and interpretations of those people who record history. Because of this, historical records contain biases, both in what is selected to be recorded and in how the information is presented. Historians are aware of these biases and seek to account for them. For example, the history of American slavery and plantation life is dominated by accounts of the plantation owners and their lives. We can learn a great deal about who plantation owners were, how they lived, where they lived, and how they managed their businesses. Yet we can say little of the slaves themselves. The people who were recording the documents that are available to historians were primarily concerned with the plantation owners, the socially dominant people in the society of the antebellum South. Slaves were only peripherally mentioned in many accounts, and then often only as property or assets that needed to be managed. Hence, because historians tend to work with written documents, they are limited in what they can discover about people who were rarely or only incidentally mentioned in documents or oral traditions.

Archaeologists, on the other hand, have their own perspectives and problems. Because all people use material goods in some form or another, and because many of these materials can be excavated, archaeologists have a means of learning something about all people in all times. Humans have been making and using tools for about 2 million years, long before the development of writing (which occurred in Mesopotamia only about five thousand years ago). Thus, most past human activity is unrecorded and beyond the memory of living humans. Only through the systematic examination of past material remains by archaeologists can we hope to learn about and understand the lifeways of most past peoples.

Archaeology is not without its limitations, though. Not all materials survive in the ground to be excavated. Many archaeological sites have been destroyed by the growth of modern towns and cities, and still other places of archaeological interest have been covered by rising sea levels during the past three to five thousand years. Similarly, material remains are not as precise as historical documents. It is usually impossible to learn the names and life histories of specific individuals through archaeology, although recent advances in method and theory do make it possible for archaeologists to at least sometimes distinguish the material remains of individuals.

Over the second half of the twentieth century, a special relationship has begun to be forged that links history with archaeology. This relationship, usually known as *historical archaeology,* combines the strengths of document-based research with the best of excavation-based research. The problems inherent in history, such as biases in accounts or gaps in data, can be explored and to some extent filled through archaeological exploration, and a level of detail and specificity not usually attainable in archaeology can be achieved through historical research. As we explore later in this book, the alliance between these two disciplines provides us with exceptional resolution, as well as accuracy, when it comes to exploring the past.

Archaeology and Classical Studies

As previously noted, archaeology is also closely allied with studies of the classical world. Often combined under the general heading of *classics,* such disciplines typically emphasize the study of the Greek, Roman, and Egyptian civilizations. Most classics programs developed out of the renewed interest of European intellectuals in classical authors such as Aristotle, Pliny, and Herodotus that developed in the eighteenth and nineteenth centuries. Therefore, classical studies often include a strong language component, usually centering on Greek, Latin, and Hebrew.

Classical studies tend to be similar to history in that a strong emphasis is placed on reading and interpreting the documents of the ancient world, though unlike history there has always been a notable archaeological component within classical studies. In many respects this can be attributed to the rise of **antiquarianism** and early archaeology, alongside the renewed interest in the ancient Mediterranean world. As scholars began to ask more sophisticated questions about the past events recorded by classical-era authors, they began to turn to developing disciplines such as archaeology and art history in order to better obtain answers. The work of pioneering archaeologists and antiquarians, such as Heinrich Schliemann (Box 1.2), demonstrated the utility of archaeological inquiry both in finding information not directly obtainable through examinations of documents and in raising new types of questions that had previously been unasked.

The distinction between classical studies and archaeology is not always easily discerned, though there are indeed differences. Some of these are products of the different histories of the two disciplines, whereas others are specific to the goals and methodologies of each. Classical studies, for example, has been traditionally tightly focused on the high civilizations adjacent to the Mediterranean Sea, whereas archaeology has cast its research interests much farther afield. Such differences are not absolute, though: There are classicists who study other cultures and civilizations, and there are archaeologists who specialize in the study of what have traditionally been defined as classical civilizations. For most beginning students of the past, the most important difference between the two areas seems to lie in the orientation and interests of instructors in the various disciplines. There is little mistaking the gleam in the eye of an instructor who lectures about a favorite subject, nor is there anything amiss when such passion is brought to the classroom. Indeed, especially when students just begin to study the past, such variety of interests as might exist at any typical school can only be viewed as healthy.

Archaeology and Geography

As with both history and classics, there is a natural affinity between some elements of geography and archaeology. *Cultural geography,* for example, emphasizes differences in human cultures through space and sometimes through

antiquarianism Collecting materials made by people of past eras for the sake of possessing, displaying, and/or feeling a connection with the past. Antiquarianism often emphasizes the most spectacular and finest examples of past material culture rather than the everyday material culture used by most people.

time. When time is a major factor in geographic studies of people and cultures, then the studies are sometimes called *historical geography*. Both cultural and historical geography are similar to archaeology in that they organize and study people through space and time. As is discussed later in this chapter, this kind of study is one of the fundamental goals of modern archaeological research.

Yet geographers have developed their own concepts and methodologies for their work. As you might expect, an emphasis is placed on defining the spatial and temporal components of past cultures, as well as perhaps the connection of such things with the physical layout of the world regions in which these peoples lived. Computers have become increasingly important in such work, and geographic information systems (GIS; see Chapter 2) have become valuable tools in undertaking sophisticated spatial and statistical analyses. By entering the volumes of data that geographers have amassed on world cultures into databases linked to maps (essentially the basic description of a GIS), scholars have been able to model the pace and nature of cultural changes through space and time.

Archaeologists are not blind to the benefits of GIS technology, and there has been a strong movement within the discipline to take advantage of computer-based mapping and databases. Archaeologists, though, also work more intensively with the material components of past cultures, and it is often the archaeological research that provides the basic data that geographers use to create their models. In this sense, geography and archaeology form a productive and dynamic dyad, or a pair of points between which information flows. Indeed, the potential connections between archaeology and geography are so strong that some colleges and universities have sought to integrate these disciplines into a single far-reaching program.

Archaeology and the Natural Sciences

Up to this point I have highlighted some of the connections and differences between archaeology and disciplines traditionally identified as either social sciences or humanities. There is much more to what archaeology is and what archaeologists do, though. Although the connection might not be obvious at first, there are strong connections between archaeological research and natural science disciplines such as geology, physics, chemistry, and even astronomy. Because archaeologists work with the material left behind by past peoples and because these materials have form and substance, as well as positions within the earth, it is important for archaeologists to understand what happens to the material that they excavate on a direct, physical level. The combination of natural scientific disciplines with archaeological issues and problems is generally referred to as **archaeometry,** a term that is broad enough to include a great many things yet specific enough to denote the importance of natural scientific disciplines to solving archaeological problems.

Geology is the most commonly utilized natural science within archaeology. Every person who excavates needs to understand the basics of how sedi-

archaeometry The combination of natural scientific disciplines with archaeological issues and problems.

BOX 1.2

HEINRICH SCHLIEMANN: BELIEF AND PASSION IN ARCHAEOLOGY

Heinrich Schliemann (1822–1887) began life as the son of a well-to-do German merchant family. He was raised with the anticipation that he would become a typically well-educated and successful businessman of the era. Like many of his peers, he was taught to read the classic literature of ancient Greece and Rome so that he might understand the roots of Western civilization. Unlike many of his peers, though, his reading kindled an ever-growing fire of curiosity within Schliemann, one that would eventually set ablaze the worlds of archaeology and classical scholarship.

By his mid-forties Schliemann had made a substantial fortune dealing in furs and other commodities across central and eastern Europe. He had become the success that he had been raised to be, and, with his education and fortune intact, he was able to pursue his passion for Homeric epics. Most scholars of the day believed that Homer's writings were largely fanciful, perhaps based on grains of truth but largely representing a Greek tradition of epic fiction. Schliemann, however, believed that these writings were literal histories and that by following the descriptions in Homer's writings he would be able to retrace the steps of such heroes as Agamemnon, Achilles, Helen, and Hector. Scientists of the day cast a dubious eye on Schliemann's proposed research but nonetheless counseled him on where he might begin his search.

In 1871 Schliemann made his way to the area around Hissarlik, a large tell (man-made earthen hill) in Turkey that contained the remains of an unknown number of past villages and towns. It was in this region that Schliemann hoped to retrace the descriptions in Homer's writings and find the city of Troy, allegedly the site of so many great deeds of the Greek and Trojan heroes. Schliemann was meticulous, perhaps even obsessed, with his search. At times he seems to have taken off his shoes and socks and waded up streams, assessing their temperature in order to compare them with Homer's descriptions of warm and cold streams.

Finally Schliemann became convinced that Hissarlik itself must be the site of the fabled city of Troy, and so

he began to excavate. Hiring local workmen and pouring in large amounts of his personal fortune, not to mention his own time and energies, Schliemann began to excavate trenches throughout the site. In all, he uncovered at least eleven different levels of cities, any number of which might represent Troy—if, indeed, Troy ever existed and, if so, if this was the site upon which it existed. Regrettably, Schliemann was not an archaeologist, and his methods were sometimes crude and destructive. His passion for proving that this was the site of Troy drove him relentlessly, yet the proof that he required eluded him.

During one particular afternoon Schliemann noticed that some stones along the side of a major wall seemed out of place. Probing the stones with his knife and hands, he saw the entrance to a covered and sealed chamber. Perhaps he saw even more. He ordered his work crews home early that day, telling them it was his birthday and that he was celebrating. Then he returned to his find and began work. What he uncovered surpassed even his own fertile imagination. Inside a small chamber, Schliemann discovered dozens of precious objects: gold necklaces, armbands, and countless other smaller pieces of treasure. Schliemann removed the material and kept the find a secret. Only later, after the material had been removed from Turkey, did he announce to the world that he had found what he called King Priam's treasure. He had his beloved wife bedecked in the precious jewelry and then photographed. The material itself was set aside for a German museum.

The archaeological world was in an uproar. Schliemann had clearly found a fantastic horde of precious material, but much of it looked too early to date to the era of Troy. It seems that, although Schliemann had found a Trojan city and that this city might even be Troy, he may have inadvertently dug through the layers of that city in his impatience to find such treasures as he eventually discovered. Whatever the case, the site of Hissarlik is still a productive and important archaeological site that continues to be researched by teams of international scholars today, over a century later. Per-

Heinrich and Sophia Schliemann (right) and their associates pose for a photograph before the massive Lion Gate at Mycenae, Greece.

haps in a final twist of fate, though, scholars are still not sure if this site represents Troy and, if so, which layer is the Troy of Homer's epics.

A final, darker side exists to this tale as well. The removal of the treasure, along with other significant materials, to Germany created a lasting international problem that even today has not been resolved. German museum scholars have spent years tracking down the material since its disappearance at the end of World War II. The material was eventually located in Moscow, where it had been moved after the fall of Berlin. The German museum petitioned for its return; after all, Schliemann had given the material to them. The Rus-

sian government, however, is not sure that the material should be returned in light of the damages done to Russian art and civilization during the German invasion of the former Soviet Union. Moreover, the Turkish government has pointed out that Schliemann was supposed to leave the material in Turkey and that he had smuggled it out of the country to begin with. Thus, three countries, each with its own interest, debate the fate of one of the world's most famous finds. An anxious world community can do little but wait for the outcome of the negotiations and hope that the material has survived its time in wartime storage facilities.

ments are deposited, moved, and transformed by physical processes. Because what archaeologists dig up must be recorded in a precise three-dimensional context (called **provenience**), the sediments that surround the material must also be understood. As every student of geology is taught early on, the earth is alive in the sense that it is constantly changing, moving, and reorganizing parts of itself in sometimes obvious, sometimes subtle ways. Later in this book I discuss the importance of *geoarchaeology,* or the study of the archaeological record in a geological context. The relationship of archaeological materials to their surrounding environment is part of what we call context.

Physics and chemistry have parallel roles. Both physical and chemical alterations occur in the soil in which archaeological materials are buried, but it is sometimes forgotten that the materials themselves change according to physical and chemical principles while they are buried. Rust, for example, is a basic process of oxidation that can alter and destroy most forms of iron that archaeologists might come into contact with. Similarly, certain sorts of stone weather or change according to the amounts of water and/or physical pressure that they are exposed to. Argillite, a type of stone that holds a sharp edge when freshly worked into a tool, decays rapidly once left in the ground. When excavated it is sometimes barely recognizable as stone, let alone as a tool. In cases in which this sort of decay, or even potential decay, exists, archaeologists need to understand what has happened so that they can stabilize the material and prevent its ultimate loss. Such work is often the job of conservators, people who specialize in identifying the physical and chemical processes that change material culture and who develop ways to prevent such decay from occurring.

Other physical properties are also important to archaeologists. Many techniques used to determine how old an object is are based on physical and chemical studies. The most common form of these dating techniques is radiocarbon dating, developed in the middle of the twentieth century and based on the half-life of carbon 14. As we will see later, this technique is based on a thorough understanding of nuclear decay, as well as on statistics. Other related and parallel dating techniques that we will encounter include obsidian hydration, potassium-argon dating, and thermoluminescence, though there are many more.

Still other branches of the natural sciences are also important to archaeologists. Ecologists, biologists, zoologists, and a host of other scientists specializing in the study of different plant, animal, and insect life provide us with a wealth of information about the past. Without the work of such people it would be difficult to identify the species or age of animals that past peoples hunted, the time of year when people lived at a certain place, or even the sorts of environments that past peoples had to contend with. Clearly such things are important to archaeologists, and it is useful to have access to people who can help with these sorts of issues. Thus, although not every archaeologist needs to be a nuclear chemist or wildlife biologist, the discipline is better and stronger for the presence of those people who combine the natural sciences with archaeological issues.

provenience The precise three-dimensional location of an object on an archaeological site.

Everything Else and the Kitchen Sink, Too

It would be both naive and misleading to claim that this discussion encompasses all, or even the bulk, of disciplines that can be integrated with archaeology. In general, archaeology borrows from any discipline that can contribute to better meeting the set goals and research questions of an archaeological project. The skills of artists, photographers, engineers, computer programmers, mathematicians, linguists, and countless others can be brought to bear on archaeological problems. In this sense, archaeology, like anthropology, is holistic. There are so many facets of human behavior, both past and present, that almost anything can be of use in studying the past. Creativity and the willingness to both experiment with and verify the accuracy of new techniques are components of modern archaeological research. With this in mind, this book focuses on the fundamentals of archaeological research and material but whenever possible seeks to give you resources and ideas on how to follow additional paths of investigation on your own.

THE GOALS OF ARCHAEOLOGY

Now that we have placed archaeology in the context of other academic disciplines, it is important to identify precisely what archaeology is. Although each archaeologist might define archaeology slightly differently, most would agree that it is the systematic study of the material remains of humans and their anatomical predecessors. Likewise, if we asked each archaeologist to make a list of the goals of archaeological work, it is likely that the following five general points would be on the majority of the lists. Thus, for our purposes here, the goals of modern archaeological research are

1. To find and record the past, preserving a record of it for future generations. This goal can be described as *discovery*.

2. To order, both chronologically and spatially, the remains of the past, so that we may understand the sequence and distribution of past events and peoples. This goal can be described as the *reconstruction of culture history*.

3. To explain how and why the patterns we have identified came to develop. This goal can be described as the identification and explanation of *cultural process and cultural interpretation*. We are essentially interpreting lifeways.

4. To preserve and manage the past because archaeological resources are nonrenewable. Once these resources are lost to development, erosion, or other forces, they are lost forever. Surprising to many students is that archaeologists do not dig up everything that they find. Indeed, archaeologists are ethically and professionally bound to preserve a record of the past for future generations. It is always important, then, for archaeologists to carefully weigh the value of what they might learn by excavating against the knowledge that, once they remove part of a site, they can never put it back. This goal can be labeled *cultural resource management*.

5. To educate living people and future generations about the past. Because archaeologists remove materials from their places in the ground, it is only the records that they keep of their work and the interpretations that they make that preserve the past. Part of the value of this work is to teach people about the worlds of past peoples; part is to educate them about the importance of such things as arrowheads and pieces of pottery that they might find in plowed fields or alongside streams. Many archaeologists have come to the conclusion that only an enlightened and concerned public can truly help to preserve the archaeological record and to stop pothunters and grave robbers, people who literally steal the world's heritage out from under our very feet. This goal is labeled, effectively if somewhat unimaginatively, *education* (Box 1.3).

Goal One: Discovering the Past

Before archaeologists can do any work of any nature, they must first find remains of the past. You may be surprised to learn that among the first and best places to begin are with books like this one and by using the library. Two of the things that make humankind unique in the animal world are (1) our curiosity and (2) our tendency to record and store the results of inquiries into subjects we find interesting. Hence, we create vast storehouses of accumulated knowledge that can be used as starting points for discovery. Libraries and textbooks such as this, then, provide springboards from which we can launch ourselves in the direction of problems and topics that pique our interest.

Once archaeologists find a topic of interest (sometimes referred to as a research problem or simply a problem), they need to find out as much about this topic as they can. It is essential that an archaeologist be conversant with the literature surrounding a topic they are investigating before they ever begin to excavate. For instance, if we were interested in the decline of the Roman Empire, we would need to read the ideas others have had on this topic before we ourselves set out to explore the event. We would want to know a great deal about the geographic and temporal distribution of the Roman Empire, about its political structure, its enemies, its problems, and its assets. We would also like to know something about how the Romans perceived the world in which they lived, because it was ultimately their decisions that led to the collapse of the empire. By understanding the ways the Romans viewed their world, inasmuch as any modern person can understand the ideas of past peoples, we may be better able to interpret the actions of these people and how they led to the ultimate collapse of their empire.

Of course, not all past peoples left as much material behind as did the Romans. Nonetheless, other archaeologists may have undertaken research or produced records that may help a researcher get a handle on her research interests. We can use the reports and notes from such excavations to identify the types of things that were found, the environmental conditions in the area, both past and present, and a range of other data that will help the members of a new research project better understand what they are trying to do and what they will encounter in the field.

Archaeology, though, is still a discipline that thrives on recovery of new information. Much of this information comes from excavations and related field studies. Additional information is generated by examining previously excavated materials with new techniques and in light of new interpretive theories. Still other information is acquired through cooperative studies with colleagues in other disciplines, such as cultural anthropology, geology, physics, linguistics, and chemistry. Indeed, it can be said that the past can be discovered equally well in the laboratory, the library, and the trenches.

Goal Two: Reconstructing Culture History

Once you find the past, a logical question arises about what to do with it. Early in the history of archaeology simply finding the material was sufficient. As time passed, people decided to display and then report on what they had unearthed. This led to a period in which describing the remains of the past was deemed the primary goal of archaeology.

By the end of the nineteenth century and the beginning of the twentieth, researchers were beginning to see more possibilities in the remains of the past. Archaeologists such as William Flinders-Petrie, Augustus Pitt Rivers, and Alfred V. Kidder began to pioneer new ways to order the remains of past civilizations. Ultimately, a new goal was set for archaeologists: to order the remains they unearthed across both time and space. As is discussed later, this led to the development of time-space grids and new classificatory systems, such as the Midwest Taxonomic System. Just as discovering the past is an essential part of doing archaeology, so, too, is organizing the physical remains of the past in order to better understand when and where things happened. Subsequent sections of this text will explain in more detail how modern archaeologists approach this goal.

Goal Three: Explaining Cultural Process and Interpreting Past Cultures

Beginning in the late 1940s and building through the 1950s, a movement developed that sought to push the goals of archaeology even further. Although it had become standard practice for archaeologists of the day to find, describe, and order excavated materials, it became increasingly clear that still more could be done to understand the way past peoples lived. It was not enough to describe what, when, and where—archaeologists now began to ask how and why things happened.

This drive culminated in what has been described as *processual archaeology.* As I discuss in more detail in Chapter 3, this form of archaeology emphasizes scientific methods of explanation. In particular, processual archaeolo-

BOX 1.3

KATHLEEN KENYON: DAME COMMANDER OF THE ORDER OF THE BRITISH EMPIRE

Although archaeology was dominated by men during its formative years, a number of pioneering women also made their mark in the field. One of the most famous archaeologists of her era, Kathleen Mary Kenyon (1906–1978), excavated at important sites ranging from the Roman occupation of Verulamium in southern England to Jericho and East Jerusalem in the Near East. Knighted for her distinguished service and mastery in archaeology, Kenyon built a legacy of meticulous stratigraphic excavation that still stands today.

Kenyon's first field experience came under the direction of Gertrude Caton-Thompson, who led a major expedition to the ruins now known as Great Zimbabwe in the modern state of Zimbabwe (then southern Rhodesia). Kenyon initially served as expedition photographer but quickly added the duties of excavation supervisor to her list of accomplishments. The project demonstrated conclusively that the monuments were constructed during Europe's Middle Ages by Bantu-speaking Africans, a conclusion that did not sit well with the apartheid governments of southern Africa. The excavation also resulted in Kenyon's first published academic article, "Sketch of the Exploration and Settlement of the East Coast of Africa."

In 1930 Kenyon joined the excavation team of the legendary archaeologist Sir Mortimer Wheeler at the Roman site of Verulamium. From Wheeler, Kenyon extracted the concepts of precise stratigraphic excavation, methods she was to use, revise, and expand upon throughout her career. Among her achievements on this project was the unearthing and description of the Roman theater at the site. The find was spectacular and rare. Indeed, it is still the only public monument of its kind in the United Kingdom.

Kenyon's greatest claim to fame, though, was to come as director of the excavations at Tell es-Sultan, the current name for the ancient city of Jericho. Between 1952 and 1958, Kenyon systematically reexcavated the site, which had been explored twice before, once by a German team and once by an American team. The American team had claimed to have found conclusive evidence of the walls said to have been collapsed by Joshua's army in the thirteenth century B.C. Kenyon's initial season of excavations, conducted as always with precise concern for stratigraphic relationships, demonstrated that this assertion was incorrect. The levels identified by the American team as belonging to the era of Joshua were unequivocally dated to the early Bronze Age, almost a millennium earlier. The discovery sent ripples through the *biblical archaeology* community and soon became the center of much debate. Some scholars found it impossible that the Bible was wrong, others argued that the Bible might be right but that the American team was wrong, and still others began a growing movement that questioned whether events in any holy text could be

gists want to know what factors combined to influence past peoples' decisions and lifeways. What type of foods were available for people to eat? Was there enough food available in the natural environment for entire populations to thrive, or were people forced to modify their environments to produce enough food to survive on? How did these factors affect what past peoples did? Why did some populations thrive and grow while others diminished and failed?

As you can see, the first questions remain ones of description, but they feed into more complex questions that emphasize the processes (hence processual) of cultural development and change. It is important to understand that the development of processual questions and research is predicated upon the

documented archaeologically. This movement has become one of the most influential in biblical archaeology today.

Kenyon was not done with her work at Jericho, though. She pursued her excavations more closely and to greater depths than either of the previous teams had. Far beneath the Bronze Age levels, she found pottery dating to the Neolithic era, thousands of years earlier than the Bronze Age community. Still she persisted, until at last she encountered the lowest levels of the oc-cupation. These dated to approximately eight thousand years B.C., making Jericho one of the oldest towns in the world. She also clearly demonstrated that sedentism, the practice of living in one place, and food production predated the advent of pottery by one thousand or more years in the region. This discovery had important ramifications for disproving the provocative notion of a Neolithic Revolution, an idea put forth by the famous scholar V. Gordon Childe (see Chapter 7).

Kathleen Kenyon (right) and C. N. Goodman examine pieces of pottery from the Roman theater at Verulamium.

Kathleen Kenyon and her assistant Douglas Tushingham examine fragments of a Bronze Age embankment.

first two goals of archaeology, discovering and ordering the past. Before archaeologists can ask why things happened in the past, they must first know what existed in the past, where different types of material remains are found, and in what sequence these materials were deposited.

Some interpret part of this goal as developing an understanding of the specific beliefs of past peoples. Because archaeologists can find the past, order it, and explain the processes related to changes in the past, some archaeologists have begun to ask if we could find ways to better understand the full range of past cultures. As you know, culture is a concept anthropologists use to characterize all of the behaviors and ideas that help define the social rules by which humans live. These rules differ by time and space, as do the material products produced as a result of these rules. In effect, what some archaeologists have begun to ask is whether or not they can reconstruct and understand the social rules and ideas of past peoples.

This is a very tricky proposition because archaeologists, for the most part, do not have living members of the societies they study with whom they can verify their interpretations. Because of this, it is difficult and perhaps impossible to be sure that our interpretations of past social rules and ideas are correct. Yet, if we want to really understand the past and how it came to be made, there is little choice but to try. As early as 1948, an archaeologist named Walter Taylor began emphasizing such ideas. His arguments, however, were controversial, and his criticisms of the descriptive archaeology of the era were poorly received. By the early 1960s, though, the first processual archaeologists began to echo many of the same sentiments advanced by Taylor. Still, the process of developing techniques to reconstruct the fabric of past lives has been slow and difficult. Beginning in the late 1970s and progressing to the present time, a new movement has developed in archaeology. This movement has sought to point out and rectify the failures of the processual archaeologists in reconstructing past cultures and has achieved some success in expanding the types of data and approaches employed by archaeologists. The various new approaches that are being attempted in this vein are often very different, but, for lack of a better term and for simplicity's sake, they have been labeled *postprocessual archaeology,* meaning after processual studies. This term and its implications have stimulated many archaeologists to ask new questions and develop innovative research projects while simultaneously generating conflict among some other archaeologists. Yet, in hindsight, we might argue that this conflict is the inevitable result of the growing pains that archaeology is still undergoing.

Goal Four: Cultural Resource Management

Perhaps the single most overlooked aspect of archaeological resources is their fragility. It is hard to imagine that things such as the pyramids of Giza, which have stood for thousands of years, or the mighty Roman Colosseum, which once served as part of the heart of one of the mightiest of the world's civilizations, might be lost. But such structures are being lost. Every year wind, water, man-made pollutants, and even the traffic of tourists erodes such monuments just a bit further. Likewise, sprawling suburban developments adjacent to the world's largest cities daily engulf less dramatic but nonetheless important archaeological resources.

The loss of such resources is enabled and even accelerated by two key factors. First, human population is growing at an unprecedented rate. Within your lifetime it is estimated that there will be over 10 billion human beings alive on this planet, more than double the number present during the last half of the twentieth century. It is important that societies develop places for people to live and ways to produce food to sustain this many humans. Sometimes this means that the past must give way to the future.

Second, many people are unaware of the remains of the past that are under their very feet. Whereas it is hard to ignore such structures as the pyramids of Egypt or temples such as Angkor Wat in Cambodia, it is often easy to miss the smaller remains of the human past. These smaller remains, such as the locations of individual houses or places where people extracted resources from their environments, are at least as important as the large monuments. As we shall see, most people lived in and used such smaller places, and they left less grandiose materials behind. Yet these people made up the vast majority of human history, and it was their labor, support, and myriad contributions that made the construction of large monuments possible. Thus it is important for all of us to recognize that there exists at least a chance that we might live on top of, or right next to, evidence of the human past.

What are we to do in such cases? We cannot stop population growth, nor can we tell people that they can't build new houses to live in or new roads to drive on. Instead, we have to carefully manage the resources that still exist. Much of what archaeologists do today is aimed at identifying and preserving the cultural materials left to us by previous generations. This means that it is the job of archaeologists to assess the importance of each site and recommend to governments, builders, and similar agencies whether or not a given set of resources should be preserved. This might entail changing the path of a roadway or incorporating old earthen mounds into the layout of a modern park, or it may mean excavating these resources as completely and swiftly as possible so that development can continue without the information present on such sites being lost. This is the world of cultural resource management, and all archaeologists, whether they work in the private sector as consultants for developers or whether they work for colleges and universities, need to be concerned about managing the finite resources of the past.

Goal Five: Education

Given what I have discussed here, it is not surprising that many archaeologists have come to the conclusion that the best way to preserve sites is to teach people about their importance. This is difficult because many people have never considered parts of the past important. After all, some people say, what can the dead teach us? Why should we care about such-and-such remains?

The two principal answers to these questions are sometimes hard to explain and harder for some people to accept. First, except in very rare cases, the archaeological record, and the information and stories that it provides us, belongs to the world, to everyone. Certainly individuals may own the property that archaeological materials are found on, and sometimes we might even be able to identify to whom certain objects belonged. Looking at the bigger picture, though, the material from one parcel of ground is related to material from other parcels of ground and so on. It is the pattern rather than the specific item that is most important in understanding the past. Unfortunately, we cannot reconstruct the pattern without finding, examining, and curating the many specific items that we excavate. Thus the first answer to these questions is that it matters little whether a single person is interested in something but a great deal that tens of thousands of others are interested. Certainly archaeologists do not want to violate the rights or privileges of any person or group, but they do very much want to help people understand what they do and why it is so important to keep archaeological resources intact. Hence, in the sense of world heritage, the past belongs to all people and deserves to be shared.

Second, artifacts themselves are not as important to archaeologists as are the places in which they are found and the *precise connection between archaeological materials*. It is this precise relationship that enables archaeologists to ascertain the pattern of the material culture and to interpret that pattern—to, in effect, put a piece of the past back together. The provenience of an item, its precise three-dimensional position on an archaeological site, is most important to archaeologists and to interpreting the past. Thus, taking artifacts out of their original context effectively destroys part of the past, just as does building a high-rise on a site at which archaeological materials are found. Most people believe that the artifacts themselves are the key resources for archaeologists. Thus people may collect, trade, and sometimes even sell archaeological materials. In some cases, such trafficking is illegal and can be punished by heavy fines and prison sentences. Sadly, such laws are too frequently broken and too infrequently enforced.

Before going on, we need to briefly explore the issue of casual artifact collecting. In many parts of the world, farmers, gardeners, or just about anyone who digs into the earth finds evidence of past peoples. In North America this usually takes the form of chipped stone tools or pieces of broken pots. In most cases, it is not a crime to pick up and examine these things. I have yet to meet a farmer in the American Midwest who does not, or whose father or grandfather did not, have a cigar or shoe box full of such material. In a general sense this practice is not terribly destructive, because the material has already been plowed up from its original position. It does become destructive, though, when thousands and thousands of people collect these items without reporting their finds. If we think about a site that is plowed year after year for a century, it is not hard to imagine that the site might be completely destroyed. In fact, recent legislation in Canada has proposed making it a crime even to pick up such artifacts.

Most archaeologists, though, really do not object to farmers picking up these things. Indeed, these people are demonstrating an interest in the past, just as do archaeologists. It would be ideal for the farmers to report to their local community college, university, or state archaeological office about what they are finding. The government will not come out and confiscate the land, nor will it compel farmers to abandon their fields. In most cases, the archaeologists will probably want to come out to the site, record what is there, and assess the likelihood that the site may make unique contributions to our understanding of the past. If such is the case, then the archaeologist may ask for permission to excavate on the land and likely enough will try very hard to compensate the farmer for any losses in crops or other produce brought about by the excavations. As we discuss in future chapters, archaeologists do not always make large holes wherever they dig, and it is often hard to find the specific spots that archaeologists have excavated within a year or two after the work is finished.

Through education, archaeologists seek to let the public know what they have been finding, what these finds mean, and what archaeology really is. In every instance in which education has been tried consistently, the public has taken a liking to archaeology and has generally sought to preserve the resources around their homes and farms. Once people know what archaeologists are looking for and understand that they do not intend to take their land or cause them problems, then a strong positive relationship often develops. It is people like you, the readers of this book, who have the opportunity to become the best educators. When you are shown something a person has found, encourage him or her to contact a professional archaeologist or one of the many avocational archaeological societies that exist, especially in North America.

WHAT ARCHAEOLOGY IS NOT

Now that you have an idea of what archaeology is, let us examine some of the things that it is not. First and foremost, archaeology is not the wanton destruction of archaeological resources through indiscriminate excavation. Every archaeologist must have a reason to dig, and when an archaeologist sets out to excavate, she is committing herself to completing the entire process of research, from background searches through publication. Consequently, archaeologists must be very particular about when and where they choose to allocate their energies.

Second, archaeology is not the search for fancy objects from the past, or "goodies." In this sense the Indiana Jones movies, although a great deal of fun for many, tend to misrepresent modern (though not necessarily past) archaeology as a search for rare treasures to be placed in museums. Although some excavated materials are displayed in museums and made accessible to public viewing, the heart and soul of archaeological research rests in reconstructing how the people who made these material objects lived and functioned. There is nothing wrong with having fun while doing archaeology; many archaeologists of my acquaintance find the Indiana Jones films entertaining. However, they are not manuals on how to do archaeology.

Third, archaeology is not the recovery of past materials for sale and profit. Although archaeologists have encountered everything from precious gems to gold jewelry in some parts of the world, none of this material is sold. In fact, it is important that all of the finds from an excavation be kept together so that they can be properly analyzed and cataloged. In this sense, operations such as the late Mel Fisher's Treasure Salvors in Florida, the group that recovered much gold and silver from the wrecks of Spanish galleons, are not archaeological. Rather, they are commercial or speculative investments that exploit archaeological resources. In the case of Treasure Salvors, their more recent efforts have featured significant components of underwater archaeological research, though the final disposition of the materials recovered in such work remains questionable in the minds of many archaeologists. Simply put, archaeology is done for knowledge and to manage cultural resources, not to recover goodies for resale.

Beyond such commercial enterprises, there is a darker and seamier side to what some people label archaeology. Some unscrupulous people excavate known sites, sometimes on other people's lands or on federal property, in order to obtain artifacts for resale. Many times these people seek out burials or sacred places because such areas are likely to produce the rarest and most valuable materials for resale. These people are thieves, looters, and, sometimes, grave robbers. There is no excuse for their actions; they are a product of both ignorance and greed.

Unfortunately, the problem is not limited to a few isolated sociopaths or hardened looters. An examination of the newspapers in most major cities will periodically reveal the presence of a so-called pre-Colombian art sale. This is a sale, sometimes in the form of an auction, at which archaeological material is bought and sold. Some of the material comes from farmers who have collected boxes of arrowheads or other odds and ends over generations, but a disturbing amount of the material at some auctions is new material—that is, material that has been recently looted from archaeological sites and sent out for resale. Some auction houses refuse to deal in such material, but others are not very careful about reviewing or enforcing the regulations and paperwork for selling items that might have been looted. In the most dramatic cases, the governments of countries such as Peru have sent archaeologists and government officials to major auctions in the United States and requested the return of materials that they identified as stolen from archaeological sites. In almost all cases the official requests have been refused, and the materials were sold for large amounts of money. The situation was so bad in the late 1980s that President George Bush ordered a halt to the importation and sale of questionable antiquities from countries such as Peru. The presidential ban was an effort to stem the flood of stolen materials that were finding their way through the United States into private collections. Unfortunately, other countries have no such bans in place, and **looting** still continues unabated in some parts of the world. Make no mistake: Not only is this theft on an international scale, but it is also a business that has cost an unknown, but doubtlessly increasing, number of lives. It is, in part, the job of archaeologists to make people aware of what is happening and to help preserve the sites that are being looted.

Fourth, archaeology is not speculation. Archaeological research is based on fact, data analysis, and probability. Unfortunately, many bookstores and publishers elect to label speculative works and works based on poor or questionable research as archaeology and market them to the public. A review of bet-

looting The uncontrolled excavation and effective theft of material culture for personal satisfaction or gain.

ter bookstores will usually reveal a section in the social sciences in which the reader may acquire a handful of very good and often very well written texts on archaeological research. Surrounding such works, though, there are invariably a large number of books claiming to have archaeological proof for everything from evidence that space aliens built the Egyptian pyramids to the existence of the lost continent of Atlantis. Indeed, the Indiana Jones movies have proven so popular that some authors have written books that they claim prove through archaeology that the lost Ark of the Covenant has been found and that the Holy Grail exists somewhere between Somalia and Jordan. Although none of these claims can be discounted in total—for to do so denies the possibility of a one in a billion chance at correctness—none of them is close to being substantiated.

Modern authors have not been the only ones to invent such fanciful tales. There have been persistent folktales that ancient Celts colonized North America two thousand years ago, that Irish monks sailed to North America in leather boats, and that African explorers not only discovered Mesoamerica but also colonized it, founding the first civilization there. Archaeological research rejects these tales as unlikely—indeed, as extraordinarily unlikely. Although it is impossible to say that an event never happened, we can determine when there is no legitimate evidence to support the claim that some events ever happened. Thus, when we encounter elements of **pseudoscience,** as such extraordinary claims are labeled, we need to be critical, thoughtful people. In any case, we should consider the evidence that is available on any given topic and then weigh it carefully. As much as we might want to believe something is true, such as a romantic notion that the lost castle of Camelot exists, buried in western England, we need to acknowledge that the evidence does not support this. Indeed, the evidence, when we bother to look at it, often tells much more fascinating and romantic tales about human perseverance and ingenuity.

One final point to note here is that archaeology is not paleontology; they are different disciplines. Paleontology is a subfield of geology and deals with fossil remains, such as dinosaurs. Some paleontologists do work closely with archaeologists and biological anthropologists studying human evolution, but they do so in different ways. To put it bluntly, archaeologists don't dig up dinosaurs, paleontologists do.

SUMMARY

We can see that archaeology is something much more than a simple search for the material remains of the past. Today, archaeology is the search to understand the lives of past peoples. This search encompasses a wide range of approaches and ideas. Many of these approaches and ideas are borrowed from archaeology's sibling subdisciplines; others are borrowed from different fields altogether, such as economics and biology; and some are uniquely archaeological. In the end, archaeologists must view themselves as something more than collectors of past curiosities and something more like anthropologists of

pseudoscience The presentation of untested or untestable statements as fact. Such claims also reject scientific methodology and often emphasize fantastic or overly romanticized notions of natural and cultural behavior.

anthropological archaeology The study of the human past, principally through material culture.

past peoples. We also must remember that we have chosen to study the past and that that choice makes us advocates for the preservation and careful management of the past. Archaeology does not exist just in the library or in the ivory towers of academia; rather, archaeology exists in the trenches, newspapers, and city council rooms of the world around us. And it is here, in these venues, that the past can be brought to life and used to help modern people understand where they came from and how their cultures developed. If we are careful, we may even be able to learn from the mistakes of past peoples and avoid the pitfalls that brought such civilizations as Mesopotamia, Greece, the Maya, and even mighty Rome crumbling to the ground.

FOR FURTHER INFORMATION

Alva, W. 1988a. Discovering the New World's richest unlooted tomb. *National Geographic* 174 (4): 510–14.

———. 1988b. Into the tomb of a Moche lord. *National Geographic* 174 (4): 516–49.

Bahn, P. G., and J. Vertut. 1988. *Images of the Ice Age.* New York: Facts on File.

Feder, K. L. 1998. *Frauds, myths, and mysteries: Science and pseudoscience in archaeology,* 3rd ed. Mountain View, Calif.: Mayfield.

Wheeler, M. 1954. *Archaeology from the earth.* Harmondsworth, England: Penguin Books.

Williams, S. 1991. *Fantastic archaeology: The wild side of North American prehistory.* Philadelphia: University of Pennsylvania Press.

2

ORDER IN THE RECORD
Material, Space, and Time in Archaeology

Take this watch for instance; $10 from a vendor in the street. Bury it in the sand for a thousand years and it becomes priceless.

—*Paul Freeman as Renee Beloch in Raiders of the Lost Ark*

A brief review of the five goals of anthropological archaeology reveals that the first two of these goals, finding and recovering the past and placing the past in a meaningful spatial and chronological order, center on two primary criteria—space and time. Archaeological remains exist in specific spaces within and on the earth, and each artifact or other piece of data was produced at a specific point in time. It is the archaeologist's job to join these two variables, space and time, with the materials that have been recovered so that we can begin to make sense out of what people were doing in the past.

MATERIAL: THE FIRST FRONTIER

When we talk about archaeology, we often talk about material culture. As you know, material culture is all of the physical things left behind by past peoples and includes everything from temples to human excrement. In fact, there are so many different kinds of things that archaeologists divide them up into specific categories.

Artifacts

Artifacts make up the bulk of archaeological material culture. These are things that have been made or deliberately modified for use by humans and their ancestors. Thus a stone spear tip is an artifact, as is a piece of caribou bone that has been specifically cut

FIGURE 2.1

Some attributes of a sample biface.

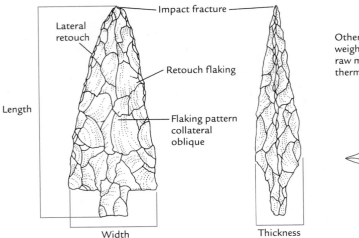

Lateral retouch

Impact fracture

Retouch flaking

Length

Flaking pattern collateral oblique

Width

Thickness

Other attributes:
weight
raw material
thermal alteration

Cross section

and modified so that it can be used to scrape hides. Just the tip of the spear point or a piece of stone knocked off the spear point during its manufacture can also be considered artifacts.

We can step beneath the level of artifacts, though, and talk about their specific **attributes.** These are the individual characteristics of the artifact we might be examining. For example, the spear point we mentioned previously has a certain length, width, thickness, and shape, as well as potential for damage or use wear (Figure 2.1). Similarly, it is made out of a certain sort of raw material and manufactured according to very specific procedures that can be used to identify artifacts made by the same or related peoples. In fact, it is the combination of all attributes that come together to define a specific artifact.

Over the years archaeologists have noticed that some artifacts have very similar attributes. In fact, some have so many attributes in common that they can be considered as a group that represents a people's common ideas about the attributes of such artifacts. When we find such groupings, we call them types. Such types can be compared with other clusters, and archaeologists can create what we call **typologies.** A typology is nothing more than a formal description of all of the attributes that characterize most, if not all, of the artifacts that archaeologists recognize as clustering together. As is shown later in this chapter, typologies can be useful because they are often specific to certain places at certain times. Thus archaeologists who find artifacts that belong to a certain type already have a rough idea about when, and sometimes where, that artifact may have been originally made.

However, one warning about types and typologies is important. In defining a given type, archaeologists are deciding what attributes are most meaningful and which are less so to them. Our assumptions may not conform to the intentions of the people who made the artifacts, so we cannot be sure that our types would be recognized as meaningful categories of artifacts by past peoples. In general, and now with the aid of computers, we can process a great deal of data about various attributes, and we think we can get pretty close to

artifacts The materials deliberately produced by past peoples.

attributes Specific, measurable elements, such as length, width, or weight, that combine to define a specific artifact or feature.

typology The formal description of all of the attributes that characterize most, if not all, of the artifacts that archaeologists recognize as clustering together.

identifying groups of artifacts in the terms in which past peoples may have thought of them, but we can never be absolutely certain.

One important way to double-check our assumptions is to compare **morphological typologies** with **functional typologies.** As is discussed later, archaeologists are sophisticated enough scientists to identify the ways in which many artifacts have been used. Thus we can group the same set of artifacts in two different ways. First, we can organize the type by morphology, that is, by shape and overall appearance (Figure 2.2). This is the older method of forming typologies, and it has enjoyed a great deal of success not only in archaeology but also in related disciplines (Box 2.1).

Once we complete this grouping, we can turn around and classify the artifacts by their functional attributes, that is, the attributes that reflect specifically how a given tool was utilized. For instance, a projectile point or spear tip that has struck something hard with its point often suffers what we call an impact fracture. Its tip blunts or breaks off. Other tools that look identical, though, may be broken across the midsection, as if they were used like a pry bar to separate two things, such as a limb bone from a hip socket. Still others might have faint striations (lines) etched along their sides running adjacent to the edge, as if the tool had been used to saw or pierce something soft. The net result is that morphological and functional typologies do not always correspond. In fact, they often indicate that past humans used their tools in a variety of ways, making multiple use of a single tool that might do one thing very well but that could also be used to accomplish other tasks. We need look no further than our own culture to see how something as simple as a screwdriver might also be used as a punch or an awl or how its handle might be used as a light hammer. The key to using all typologies is to be flexible and to remember that people of the past were inventive, clever, and sometimes in just as much of a hurry as you or I are today.

Features

Sometimes material culture is made up of many different elements or even of sediments that represent the decayed remains of a single piece of material culture, such as a wooden post or beam. A wall, for example, is a human-made structure and therefore is classified as an artifact. Each brick in the wall also can be classified as an artifact, assuming that it has been made or deliberately shaped by people. If mortar was used to link the bricks or stones, then the mortar too could be labeled an artifact. In fact, such compound artifacts and nonportable cultural remains are usually labeled **features.** A feature is usually a nonportable human construction composed of multiple discrete elements, such as bricks, mortar, and the remains of wooden posts (Figure 2.3). As with artifacts, features can also be grouped into typologies based on both morphological and functional attributes.

Features, though, often convey a great deal more information to archaeologists than do single artifacts. First, a feature contains several different forms of materials, and archaeologists can extract some measure of information

morphological typology An archaeological typology based on the shape and related physical characteristics of material culture.

functional typology An archaeological typology based on the manners in which the objects under study were actually employed in the past.

feature A combination of artifacts and/or ecofacts that create a single, definable item, such as a fireplace or burial.

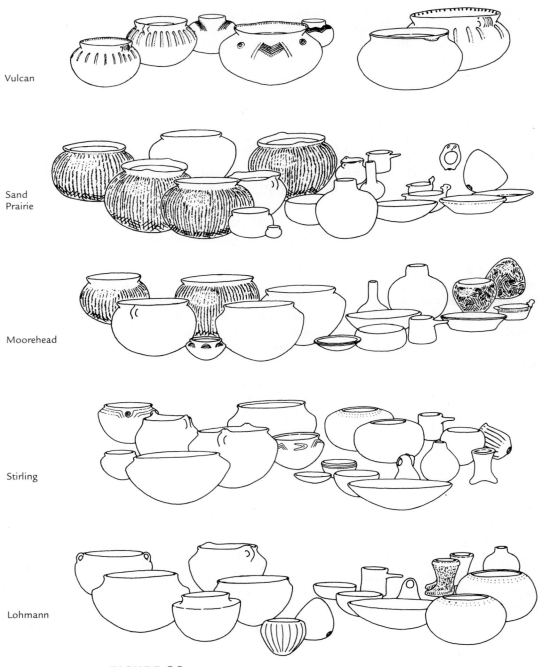

Vulcan

Sand
Prairie

Moorehead

Stirling

Lohmann

FIGURE 2.2

Groups of Mississippian ceramics from the American Bottom organized by vessel form and archaeological phases (Lohmann earliest, Vulcan latest).

BOX 2.1

TYPES, SERIATION, AND THE FORD-SPAULDING DEBATE

An archaeological type refers to a group of material remains that are perceived to be related to each other, usually in either form or function. As demonstrated by the work of William Flinders-Petrie in Egypt, typology and seriation are closely related concepts. By sorting artifacts into types and then following the change in types through time, archaeologists developed a series of chronologies that helped provide order in the archaeological record. Essentially, this is one of the things Flinders-Petrie is best known for. He used these techniques to sort out the sequence of burials at the site of Diaspola Parva by arranging the pots accompanying each interment into a chronological order based on changes in shape, size, and decoration. In the Americas, though, large and often fiery debates raged over how to define types. Because Americanist scholars had few written records to help them date the material they excavated, they were increasingly reliant on building chronologies based on changing styles of artifacts. A natural outgrowth of this process was an attempt to understand exactly what constituted a specific type of artifact.

One of the most influential scholars in exploring this situation was James A. Ford. Ford viewed typologies as heuristic devices, that is, as conveniences applied by modern researchers to refer to groups of materials that they had organized as a type. Such types were valid tools for assisting in exploring the past, but Ford held that they reflected how we saw the shapes and materials used by past artisans more than they reflected how these people themselves saw the materials. Perhaps as a result of this perspective, Ford also argued that seriations could be accomplished using the critical eye of the archaeologist. Similarly, types could be defined based on visual inspection and the subjective classification of an archaeologist. After all, for Ford, types and seriations of both groups of individual artifacts and whole types were imposed on the archaeological record.

In a classic 1952 paper, "Measurements of Some Prehistoric Design Developments in the Southeastern United States," Ford described ceramic types from across much of the Southeast. He argued that styles, and therefore types, changed gradually over time and through space. Further, in this and other publications he argued that types could be used to create chronology only by studying assemblages that reflected brief periods of time (so that the types would be consistent), that it was only possible to seriate types that came from

(continued)

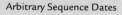

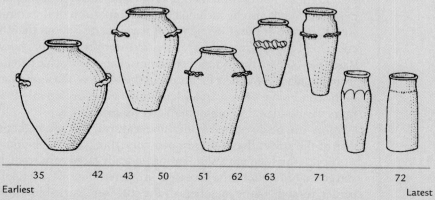

| 35 | 42 | 43 | 50 | 51 | 62 | 63 | 71 | 72 |

Earliest　　　　　　　　　　　　　　　　　　　　　　Latest

Flinders-Petrie's seriation of the ceramics from tombs at Diaspola Parva, Egypt.

BOX 2.1 (continued)

the same cultural tradition, and that these types should also come from the same general area.

A contemporary and no less a luminary than Ford himself was Albert Spaulding, who took sharp exception to Ford's article, responding with a scathing critique the following year. Spaulding saw types and seriation very differently than did Ford. Instead of accepting that types were heuristic devices imposed on the archaeological record by archaeologists, he argued that types could be discovered through careful measurement and statistical analyses. In this sense, Spaulding argued that types reflected the real categories that past peoples themselves established. If this were so, then a study of types and how they change in time could not only help construct chronology, as Ford suggested, but could also enlighten researchers about the way past humans saw their own technology. Moreover, changes in styles of type could be viewed as reflecting social pro-

cesses, as reflecting the ebb and flow of human preferences and, perhaps, of human societies as well. This meant that types not only could be compared across regions and times but also that they should be. Spaulding argued that such research would further archaeological understanding of past human behaviors, as well as culture history.

The debate between Ford and Spaulding captivated and stimulated archaeology for the next several years. In the end, Spaulding's view held sway. Interestingly enough, it is Ford's intuitive classification of types and styles that is still widely used today rather than Spaulding's statistical method, though variants of this method are still to be found. It may be that types can exist on two different levels, one imposed and one discovered. Consequently, archaeologists now tend to be sure to specify how they apply the concept of type and what they are actually using for their seriations.

---

from each form. Second, and more significant, the way the feature's components are assembled to accomplish some purpose conveys a tremendous amount of information about how past peoples conceived of and constructed their world (Figure 2.4). A single grave for a common person might include a small number of tools that the deceased held dear during life, as well as any appropriate ritual regalia. The grave of an elite member of society, however, might contain great amounts of material that was not particularly dear to the person in life but that marked that person's social position. Some personal materials might also be included, but a comparison of the commoner's grave with the grave of the elite might reveal a great deal about their lives and societies. To begin with, many more resources were expended in burying the high-status person than the commoner, and many more valuable items were removed from circulation by their inclusion in the tomb of the elite than were buried in the commoner's tomb. Indeed, the high-status person might be buried with more wealth than the commoner had ever seen in life.

More can be discerned from these features, though. Perhaps the orientation of the graves themselves reveals something about religious beliefs. Early medieval Christian graves in Europe typically faced east, so that the morning sun could be "seen" by the deceased. In Western Europe several thousand years earlier, though, many members of the elite were buried in tombs looking toward the roadways that passed between their expansive burial mounds. Other cultures allowed their honored dead to decay on scaffolds tended by family guards, and, then, when the body had decayed, the bones were gathered to-

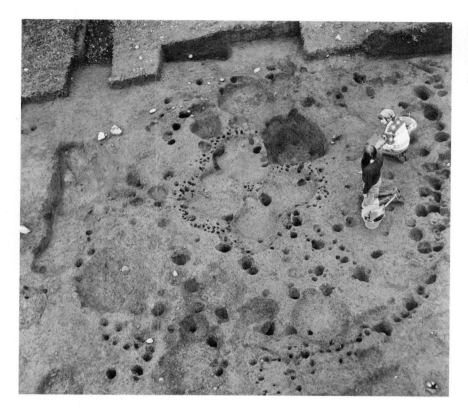

FIGURE 2.3

Excavated postmold features revealing two overlapping structures.

7-20-79   CCSC
FARMINGTON VALLEY
SQUARE S1
DEPTH   60 CM BS
OLD FARMS   VIEW S

FIGURE 2.4

Thermally altered stones mark the base of a pit used as an earth oven. The stones were heated and then placed in a pit, where their radiant heat was used for cooking.

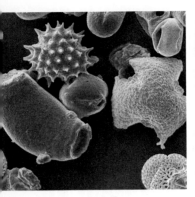

FIGURE 2.5

Pollen grains provide evidence for such things as the seasonal use of sites and the presence of certain key plants, such as maize or squash.

gether and buried in a bundle. The point is that the collection of materials that combine to create any feature, whether it is a house, fence line, or burial, conveys information to archaeologists if they are careful enough to record it and place it within the social context of the people of the past. The latter, of course, is not easily done.

Ecofacts

Not all material things that carry information about the human past were made or modified by humans. Material such as pollen, seeds, and grasses and remains of rodents and even insects can help archaeologists reconstruct such things as the environment in which people lived, the changes that occurred in that environment over time, and, of course, what people ate. Such naturally occurring pieces of data are often referred to as **ecofacts** (Figure 2.5).

One of the most commonly recovered classes of ecofacts consists of rodent remains. In many archaeological sites in which bone is preserved, hundreds, sometimes thousands, of fragments of bones from small mammals such as voles, mice, rats, shrews, and a host of related creatures are recovered. These remains show no evidence of human modification, such as would result from hunting, trapping, or butchering, and seem to reflect portions of the local mammalian population that lived on and near the site. The importance of many of these species is that they are exclusive to certain small-scale environments, called microenvironments. Such microenvironments have specific temperature ranges, plant and insect populations, and a host of other ecological characteristics. Thus the presence of animals peculiar to such environs on archaeological sites indicates that the humans at the site may also have had access to these microenvironments. Moreover, the humans would also have had access to the other plant and animal species specific to such places. Without ever having recovered direct evidence for certain plants, then, archaeologists can postulate their presence and test for them in future excavations. All of this helps archaeologists recreate past peoples' patterns of **subsistence.**

ecofacts Naturally occurring materials such as pollen and phytoliths that can provide information about past human behaviors.

subsistence The means by which people acquire essential resources, such as food.

archaeological record All things left behind by past peoples and preserved in or on the earth.

What Is Lost

Now that I have introduced some of the terms and concepts important to studying material culture, I must note that not everything that past peoples made and used is available to archaeologists. Softer and more perishable substances, such as cloth, often disintegrate very quickly in the earth, especially in soils that are particularly acidic or basic (any nonneutral pH level). Water, burrowing animals, human building activities, and a host of other factors can also accelerate the decomposition of some materials once they have been deposited into the **archaeological record** (the total of all things left behind by past peoples and preserved in or on the earth). In general, only very dense and nonorganic materials tend to persist in the ground for long periods of time, though special conditions such as dryness or coldness can also preserve things for

TABLE 2.1 General Preservation Trends		
Usually Survives	**Sometimes Survives**	**Rarely Survives**
stone	bone	textiles
glass	antler	leather
moderate- and well-fired ceramics	corrosion-prone metals (iron)	flesh
Corrosion-resistant metals (copper, sometimes as salts)	wood ceramics fired at low temperatures	biological waste (feces etc.)
		paper

FIGURE 2.6

The remains of Cherchen Man, a 6'6" male who died in approximately 1000 B.C. The exceptionally dry climate of western China helped to preserve his body largely intact.

very long periods of time (Figure 2.6). So the question is, What sorts of things might archaeologists expect to find in a temperate climate in generally neutral (chemically speaking) soils?

As shown in Table 2.1, things such as stone, glass, well-fired pottery, and metals resistant to corrosion all survive well in the ground. With the exception of the metals, which survive because of their chemical composition, the items in this category tend to survive because they are hard and composed of inorganic material, silicas. These qualities make these items resistant to both biochemical decay and erosion.

On the other end of the spectrum, items such as textiles and leather, which are primarily or entirely organic (although some forms of leather tanning use chemicals such as chromium and add inorganic elements to leather), degrade very quickly. Usually within a century such items have become fragmented and are largely unrecognizable, if they have not disappeared completely. Note that many of the everyday things that we use, such as clothing, are among the first things to disappear. Thus the archaeological record does not represent a complete cross section of daily life. Every archaeologist must be aware of this bias and must try to take steps to account for it when interpreting what was recovered from an excavation.

SPACE: THE SECOND FRONTIER

The finding and description of material culture represents the earliest phase of archaeology. In many respects this is the portion of archaeology's past that was dominated by antiquarianism. In this phase it was the material itself that was considered most valuable, and to possess rare objects was often a mark of status and education. The terms that I introduced in the previous sections have their roots in the shift from the simple possession of the past to more sophisticated issues of organizing and interpreting the past. It is here that we turn to the second dimension of archaeology, that of space.

It seems obvious to most of us that human beings have made different sorts of things in different places. Archaeology teaches us that things differ across time as well. During the age of exploration and colonial expansion of the sixteenth through nineteenth centuries, though, this fact was not always so obvious in a world that lacked sophisticated telecommunications and in which most people were born, lived, and died within an area perhaps no larger than a modern town or small city. Under these circumstances, seeing different and exotic things made by other peoples created a unique set of problems.

Early Assumptions

For centuries Western scholars had relied to varying degrees on biblical explanations of the world. The great debates did not center on whether evolution occurred, for that was an obscure sideline that would not explode into the public eye until the middle of the nineteenth century. Rather, the debate was over whether or not the biblical version of God had created all people at once—after which some people degenerated for failing to follow Scripture—or whether God had created many different sets of people, the greatest of which (according to Europeans, of course) was the western European male. The former version was known as **monogenesis** and the latter as **polygenesis.**

Note that a certain set of assumptions was at work here that was to color inquiries into human society and that still tints them today. First, the implicit point of origin for the entire scheme is that Western males were superior to all other people. Generally, all peoples were marked by skin color (a materially quantifiable component or attribute) and their point of origin, or geography. Second, Europeans assumed that the western European societies must be superior and were therefore closer to God.

Following this logic there was little that could not be done to other peoples and their cultures. Monogenesists could argue that they were saving souls through hard labor, and polygenesists could argue either that they were converting souls (not surprisingly, through hard labor) or that other peoples were less than human and were therefore able to be exploited just as any other animal. It is important to note that Christianity was not the only religion in the world that held similar beliefs. It was, however, the religion professed by the most powerful colonial agencies in the world and by the authors and collectors of many of the things we know of the people first encountered by European explorers.

The net result of colonial expansion was that European scholars organized the material cultures of the different people they were coming into contact with according to their own philosophical biases and assumptions of superiority, which guaranteed that most would classify material from far afield as primitive, though some areas were set aside for special admiration. In general, if the originators of exotic cultures were still alive and were competitive with European colonialism, as were the Aztec, Maya, Inca, and other cultures, then their material culture was considered by Europeans to be perhaps beautiful but somewhat barbaric. If, however, the material culture came from extinct civilizations, especially those that had thrived in areas of current colonial dominance and especially if those civilizations were mentioned in classical

monogenesis The belief in a single divine creation of humankind.

polygenesis The belief in multiple divine creations of humankind.

texts, then such material culture was generally revered as spectacular and very cultured.

Such was the case with ancient Egypt and Mesopotamia, and this particular bias was to lead to the bizarre notions of extreme **diffusionism** that became popular in the nineteenth century. **Heliocentrism,** a form of diffusionism, postulated that all civilization developed first in ancient Egypt and then moved, or diffused, outward. This position, particularly favorable to a small set of English elite, became increasingly untenable, though, as new discoveries were made throughout the world. Evidence of elaborate civilizations came to light in different places across Asia and the Americas. The latter stirred the most controversy because it was difficult to explain how Egyptians could have traveled as far as what is now Guatemala, Mexico, and Peru. By the middle of the twentieth century there were few scholarly adherents to heliocentrism or to extreme diffusionism—that is, the belief that the emergence of one civilization was based solely on the spread of ideas and material from another civilization.

Yet some old ideas die hard. Norwegian explorer Thor Heyerdahl took great pains to prove that it was possible, if very unlikely, for Egyptians to have sailed across the Atlantic. His journey on the *Ra II* (his copy of an Egyptian boat) has helped to keep the idea alive that Egyptians did, in fact, spark Maya and Aztec civilization. In fact, no Egyptian artifacts, bodies, or other sorts of evidence have ever been recovered in the New World in a situation that suggested their arrival other than as materials collected by historic-era travelers. Still, authors such as Ivan Van Sertima have raised the specter of trans-Atlantic contact in order to further their own political, social, or economic agendas.

In the latter half of the twentieth century another sort of diffusionism became popular. Authors such as Graham Hancock and Erich Von Däniken have made significant sums of money publishing books claiming to have evidence for the ancient continent of Atlantis or its parallel (Hancock) or for extraterrestrials (Von Däniken). Both authors have latched onto notions of extreme diffusionism, and both are prototypical examples of pseudoscientists. Although their works are sometimes entertaining, their scientific scholarship is dubious, and their speculations need to be viewed precisely as such. At best their ideas can spark interest in the past; at worst their ideas can spark notions of nationalism and racism and serve to mislead otherwise intelligent and curious people seeking to learn about the past.

Modern Approaches

Archaeologists and geographers have come a long way from the ideas of radical diffusionism. Modern researchers now enlist the aid of people such as ecologists, naturalists, and computer programmers in order to more efficiently and realistically study how people use space. In the late 1920s and early 1930s people such as Alfred Kroeber began discussing what came to be known as **culture areas.** Kroeber and his contemporaries noted that people living in

diffusion The spread of material or ideas from a point of origin into other places.

heliocentrism The belief in an extreme form of diffusionism popular among some English scholars in the late nineteenth and early twentieth centuries, according to which all culture developed in Egypt and spread outward through space and time.

culture area A broad geographic region defined by similar natural resources in which the humans who live there tend to develop related or parallel cultural adaptations to exploit these resources.

BOX 2.2

THE CULTURE AREA CONCEPT

Geographers and anthropologists alike have observed that societies that exist in the same or very similar environments over time often develop similar strategies for survival. These strategies also tend to be accomplished by the development of comparable technologies, thus making the material cultures of some societies functionally similar. Although the items from one society may look stylistically different from materials designed to accomplish the same purpose in another society, the items are functional equivalents.

This was the basic set of observations used by people such as Alfred Kroeber to help define culture areas. A culture area is a broad geographic region defined by similar natural resources in which the humans who live there tend to develop related or parallel cultural adaptations to exploit these resources. The grouping of different societies within a culture area offered early anthropologists and geographers, and later archaeologists, several advantages. First, it enabled researchers to discuss general patterns of behavior across large areas at a time when such behaviors were first being recorded in detail. Second, it allowed scholars to classify and organize societies into forms that enabled research to grow and develop. Third, this idea was to be adopted by W. C. McKern in his Midwest Taxonomic System at the tradition and pattern levels. Fourth, the equation of environment with behaviors was a fledgling step into analyzing human-environment interactions, a topic of study that would dominate some segments of archaeology throughout the remainder of the twentieth century.

The negative aspects of the culture area concept were easily pointed out, though they were not so easily corrected. By grouping different societies together based on common environments, scholars tended to see the environments as causal factors that formed human societies. This view, called environmental determinism, developed into a heated area of debate for several decades before the issue was finally resolved. Rather than dictating behavior and beliefs, environment was eventually seen as a limiting factor in which humans could make a range of choices that ultimately shaped their behaviors and lives. Likewise, environment also came to be seen as something that was, at least in part, shaped by humans. With the development of irrigation, burning programs, and a host of other actions, humans learned to change and manipulate the environment to meet their needs. Thus was born the general field of study of cultural ecology, that is, study of human-environment interactions. This field has given rise to numerous archaeological specialties, including archaeoparasitology (the study of parasites in past human societies), paleoethnobotany (the study of human uses of plants), and zooarchaeology (the study of human uses of animals).

Because scholars have grown more sophisticated in their study of humans and how they are distributed through space, the culture area concept has been abandoned. It survives, though, in general descriptions of archaeological regions, such as the American Southwest or the Eastern Woodlands. In archaeology, such terms reflect as much about people and general perspectives of behavior as they do about geographic locations. For better or worse, this is the legacy of the culture area approach.

---

adaptation The development of specified cultural responses designed to cope with the natural and social environments of a given people in a given place and time.

similar environments often made similar material (and sometimes behavioral) **adaptations** to survive in that climate. For example, Native Americans living in the eastern third of North America, an area dominated by forests and streams, tended to hunt in similar ways, to make use of waterways for transportation, and to share a number of other similarities. Likewise, people living on the North American Great Plains, an area in which forests tend to

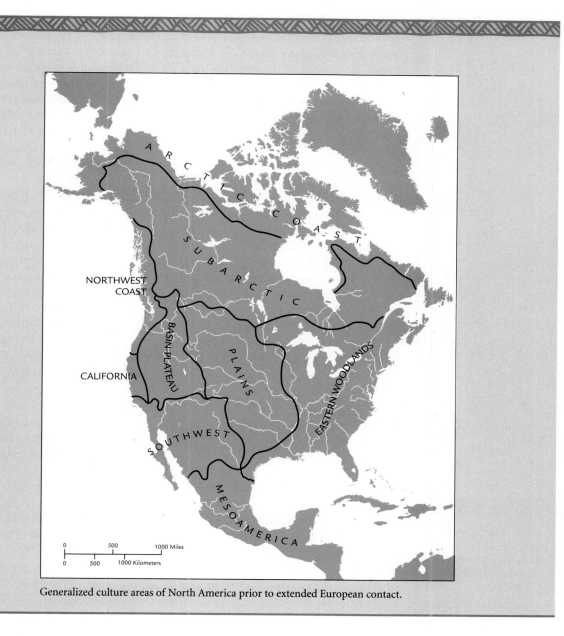

Generalized culture areas of North America prior to extended European contact.

exist only along rivers, tended to have a different suite of adaptations to life. All in all, large blocks of space could be defined in which similarities and differences in human lifeways could be identified and studied. Although the meanings of some of these similarities and differences were open to debate, the operation of defining culture areas was a key step in refining archaeological studies (Box 2.2).

By the mid-1960s the culture area concept was being replaced by a smaller unit of study, the region. In the so-called *regional approach,* archaeologists identify an area that is essentially a discrete environment or series of environments. Regions might be specific river valleys, the highlands overlooking specific lakes, or other territories that were viewed as ecologically discrete places within larger environmental zones. The principal advantage of the regional approach was that archaeologists could focus their research on a relatively small area and therefore better identify the resources and challenges that people of the past confronted in the region. In turn, this allowed archaeologists to study more variables that combined to influence and help structure the lifeways and ideas of past peoples.

A parallel development focusing on political space emerged among geographers. People such as Carl Sauer and his colleagues began experimenting with mathematical and spatial concepts such as *Thiessen polygons,* which are areas overlaid on top of maps and which serve to predict the political space a given town or place might control. Likewise, geographers divided settlements into tiers based on their size and function, thus defining which places were at the center of social and/or economic activities and which were subsidiary. Since desktop computers became popular in the middle 1980s, much of this sort of research is done using specialized databases linked to geographic information.

In this vein **geographic information systems,** or **GIS,** provide a very powerful way to integrate data on material culture with spatial data. Simply put, a GIS reads the same sort of data that are put into standard databases, such as artifact types, numbers, and their locations, and then displays the information graphically. GIS software can then be queried to determine how close certain things are to such variables as water, routes of transportation, or raw material sources. This allows researchers to create predictions and models that show ways in which many of the different variables in the data are related to each other (Box 2.3).

Such work was readily translatable into archaeology, in which scholars used the concepts to predict what archaeological sites were likely to be the most important centers in ancient political, social, and economic spheres. Other applications include plotting precisely where artifacts were recovered from an archaeological dig. Such small-scale maps and records of spatial distributions then allow archaeologists to model the relationship between different clusters of artifacts or features. This is done in much the same way that models describing larger connections, such as those mentioned previously, are created. It is important to understand that such predictions always had to be tested through excavation and research; but the concepts gave archaeologists and their geographer counterparts a framework on which to build hypotheses. As you will see, this framework is essential when undertaking scientific research of any nature.

Although all of these things are important to understanding what archaeology is and how it developed, the two most commonly used spatial concepts in the discipline are those of **sites** and **components.** An archaeological site is

geographic information system (GIS) A database linked to a spatial component capable of displaying data on a projected landscape.

sites Spatially discrete places in which evidence for past human activity is found.

component A single zone within an archaeological site that represents the actions of past peoples, often presumably within a relatively short span of time.

BOX 2.3

GEOGRAPHIC INFORMATION SYSTEMS

The dawn of the information age has provided archaeologists with a variety of tools that enable them to explore the past in ever more sophisticated ways. Computerized databases allow access to and analysis of large amounts of information in a short period of time. Digital imagery allows the accurate display of archaeological features on a site or even on sites on a map. If you put these two concepts together, though, you enter the world of geographic information systems, or GIS.

GIS combines spatial images with data that have a spatial component. In archaeology, material remains recovered from sites, sites themselves, and the geophysical regions in which the sites exist all have spatial components. We can combine these sorts of data with more conventional data about the types, attributes, numbers, and other properties of the material culture that we have excavated. The benefits of this sort of work range from providing outstanding visual references that help convey descriptions and geographic relationships to analysts and viewers alike to enabling researchers to make sophisticated mathematical queries about spatial aspects of archaeological data.

Data are combined by creating a series of layers, each displaying a single theme. For example, we might begin building a GIS project by creating a base map. This could be done by digitizing the contours on a United States Geological Survey (USGS) topographic map or, in the age of the World Wide Web, downloading such a map from the USGS. This layer would provide all of the basic physical elements of the map. We could then add to the terrain another layer displaying the digitized paths of waterways and lakes, another layer containing the boundaries of towns and structures, and perhaps a fourth layer illustrating the course of roads. We might then add a fifth layer showing the location of all archaeological sites known in this region. At any time a researcher can view any combination of these layers.

More important, though, if the databases are sufficiently complete, a researcher could ask a number of important questions. For example, an archaeologist might want to see the relationship of sites from a specific time period, say the Middle Woodland (ca. 500 B.C. to 300 A.D.), to major drainages in the area. The computer program can be quickly instructed to show only these pieces of data. Likewise, the program can also be instructed to determine if people on one site could see across valleys and hills to other sites or if these people could see specific locations on the landscape. Alternatively, the program could be instructed to calculate how far an average person could travel across the landscape in a given day, thus defining the area in which people might be most likely to forage for food. Such questions only begin to explore the uses of GIS in archaeology.

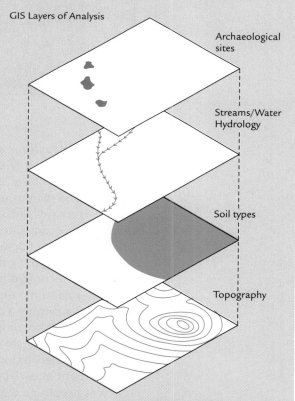

GIS Layers of Analysis

Archaeological sites

Streams/Water Hydrology

Soil types

Topography

Some basic layers of analysis and display within a geographic information system.

FIGURE 2.7

Multiple components on a
single archaeological site.

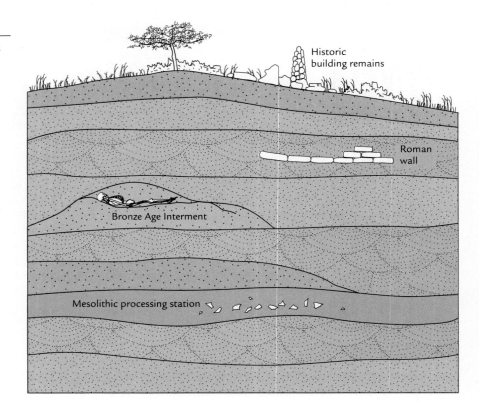

Historic
building remains

Roman
wall

Bronze Age Interment

Mesolithic processing station

simply any place from which we can recover evidence for past human behavior. A site might represent something as large as a city or as small as a place where a lone hunter sharpened a tool. Because of this variation some sites are easier to find than others. For example, large places that are used by many people over long periods of time tend to be places at which more material culture has accumulated. Consequently, these are easier to find than are the dozen or so stone fragments left by that lone hunter sharpening a tool.

As you might imagine, some places have been used by different people at different times or in different ways at the same time. In such cases archaeologists can sometimes distinguish different spatial clusters of materials, each cluster representing a different occupation of the site. Each of these occupations is called a component (Figure 2.7). Because each component is essentially discrete, these spatial clusters are very useful to archaeologists. They allow researchers to look at the behaviors of a specific group of people as a unit, without material from other occupations and therefore perhaps from different people, mixed in. Ideally, components make up the building blocks for examining past lifeways of a particular group of people at a particular place and at a particular time. Though it seldom proves to be simple, identifying discrete components is a very useful task on many archaeological projects.

FIGURE 2.8

A view of Olduvai Gorge, one of the most famous site localities in the world.

Finally, there is something called a **site locality.** These are large areas that contain many different sites. In one sense, a city could be considered a site locality, because it is hard to imagine any archaeologist actually excavating an entire city. More likely, an archaeologist might be able to work within a district or neighborhood within the city, thus making that place a site within the larger site locality. More commonly, though, a site locality is something akin to Olduvai Gorge in East Africa. This is part of the great Rift Valley that runs from the Red Sea southward across entire countries, including Tanzania and Ethiopia. Sometimes people refer to Olduvai Gorge as if it were a single, relatively small site, the site from which the fragments of many important human ancestors have been excavated. Yet, in reality, there are hundreds, if not thousands, of discrete archaeological sites in the gorge (Figure 2.8).

TIME: THE THIRD FRONTEIR

The third major variable in archaeology is time. As we discussed in Chapter 1, one of the major goals of archaeology is to order material culture in time and space. Thus far in this chapter I have defined material culture and examined the importance of space. This leaves the task of looking at time.

In general, archaeologists can look at what they find in two ways. They can examine materials that are of approximately the same age, and they can compare materials through time. The first approach is called **synchronic,** or within time. By comparing artifacts and other finds that are approximately the same age, archaeologists can begin to see the range of technological and behavioral

site locality A large geographic area, such as a valley or gorge, in which many separate sites are clustered.

synchronic Within time or within a limited span of time.

variation that existed at that time. For example, archaeologists could compare the different types of stone tools that existed three thousand years ago. Doing so would reveal a staggering variety of different forms, uses, and raw materials. If we map the variation across space, then we might be able to identify broad trends as represented by culture areas or more narrow trends such as might present between neighboring regions. Indeed, if we were to be more persistent still, we might be able to identify individual variation within a single site or component.

Alternatively, we might look at changes across time. This is the **diachronic,** or across time, approach. In this fashion we can study the changes that take place in the material culture and behaviors of people over extended periods of time. This is particularly useful in conjunction with regional approaches because diachronic studies within a fixed region allow archaeologists to examine how people interacted with their environment, modifying both their own behaviors and the environment in order to survive and thrive.

Because time is one of our key variables, archaeologists have developed a set of concepts that help us to interpret temporal sequences within components and across sites. Archaeologists often have the advantage of being able to see the layering within the earth as they excavate; therefore, this layering can be used to help determine the relative age of material found within each layer. By relative, we simply mean that we are able to determine that one artifact is older than another artifact in a different level or vice versa. Relative dates, as they are called, do not provide ages in years but do help us sort out the sequences in which sites were created.

The use of layers of earth to determine sequences is based on the Law of Superposition, codified by the English geologist Charles Lyell in the middle of the nineteenth century. The Law of Superposition states that layers, or strata (stratum is the singular form) as they are properly called, at the bottom of a geologic sequence are normally older than the layers that form on top of them. An analogy of some use may be that of a layered birthday or wedding cake. The first layer must be placed on the plate before the second is placed on top of it. The second must be in place before the third layer is placed on top of it, and so on (Figure 2.9). Now geology is more complex than making a layer cake, and there are specific ways in which a geologic sequence appears to be inverted, usually because of erosion and redeposition. Still, the study of the layering of the earth, called **stratigraphy** (Figure 2.10), is perhaps the most fundamental and widely used method of establishing chronologies on an archaeological site.

More accurate dating techniques have been developed that can provide archaeologists with more specific age ranges, often within a number of years. Such techniques are called *chronometric,* or time-measured, techniques and include such methods as tree-ring dating and radiocarbon dating. These approaches are typically based on scientific principles that allow researchers to measure some variable, such as the growth rings on trees or the amount of carbon isotope 14 present in material, and then count backward from a known

diachronic Across or through time.

stratigraphy The systematic study of layers of sediments, usually to determine the sequence in which past human acitvities took place.

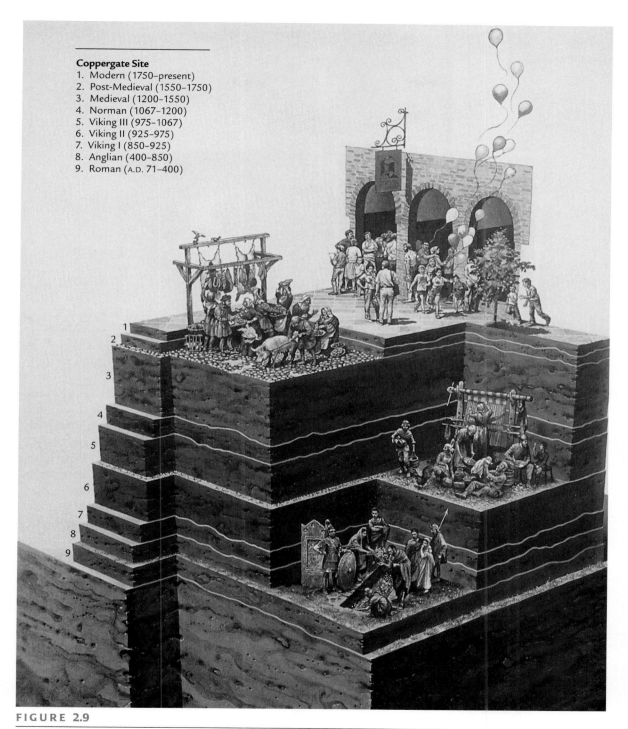

Coppergate Site
1. Modern (1750–present)
2. Post-Medieval (1550–1750)
3. Medieval (1200–1550)
4. Norman (1067–1200)
5. Viking III (975–1067)
6. Viking II (925–975)
7. Viking I (850–925)
8. Anglian (400–850)
9. Roman (A.D. 71–400)

FIGURE 2.9

Multiple archaeological components from the same site illustrated stratigraphically.

44

FIGURE 2.10

historical point. In this way archaeologists can begin to determine how old some item is in standard calendar (solar) years.

Other terms and approaches to dating the past may seem more arcane than stratigraphy, but they are closely allied with it. **Terminus post quem,** or TPQ, and **terminus ante quem,** or TAQ, are particularly useful tools. TPQ refers to the date after which something must have happened. It can be determined when archaeologists recover an artifact that has a known date. For example, if archaeologists excavate a privy (an outhouse) that was abandoned and then used as a garbage pit (which was quite common in many places) and find a coin dating to 1760 at the bottom, then everything above that coin must have been placed there during or later than 1760. It would be unlikely for the coin to have found its way to the bottom after other things had filled in the privy. It is possible that things made before 1760 were discarded after the coin was lost or discarded, but the actual date of the disposal of these items must be 1760 or later.

TAQ is a somewhat more ephemeral concept and has limited applications. It is based on the absence of some item that was widely used at a known time. For example, in a modern home in North America we would expect to find some sort of plastic bottles. We can look at manufacturing records and determine when certain sorts of plastic bottles became common. So, were we future archaeologists excavating a twentieth-century home that had no plastic bottles of any sort, we could infer (but not know for sure) that the house was abandoned prior to the popularization of plastic bottles. More often than not

terminus post quem Refers to the date after which something must have happened.

terminus ante quem Refers to the date before which something must have happened.

we would be correct, because our inference is based on a widely distributed and popular type of material culture. However, we could not be sure that our inference is correct because we may have excavated the home of someone who recycled all of their plastic. Further, some popular items are not preserved in the ground but disintegrate, becoming invisible to archaeologists. More research needs to be done, but at least archaeologists with a TAQ have some data from which to build hypotheses that they can test.

TIME, SPACE, AND MATERIAL CULTURE INTERTWINED

As the preceding sections indicate, archaeologists need to integrate the three major variables discussed thus far—material culture, space, and time. How we have come to do this is important because it fosters a better understanding of precisely what it is that we do today and acknowledges the painstaking hours, years, and, indeed, lifetimes of work that have gotten us this far.

As I noted previously, archaeology developed out of and then alongside antiquarianism. In the 1830s, during this era of mutual development, Christian Jurgen Thomsen, usually referred to as simply as C. J. Thomsen, first formally combined material, space, and time. Although historians had tinkered with the idea for more than a century, Thomsen organized all three so that everyone could see how material culture changed through space and time.

The Three-Age Approach

Thomsen had grown up in a wealthy Danish merchant family, and during his education he developed a fascination first with old coins and then with antiquities in general. In 1816 he was appointed curator of the Danish National Museum, the first person in the country ever to hold such a post. Thomsen brought a businessman's pragmatism to his work and quickly became aware that there was a need to explain to visitors exactly what they were seeing in the museum. This led to a reorganization of the museum's collection and, in 1836, to a guidebook that described how Thomsen had ordered the exhibits and the formation of what became known as the concept of museum ordering.

What Thomsen had done was to group his museum's antiquities collections by material. He formed three broad groups: items made of stone, those made of copper and bronze, and finally those made of iron and steel. Thomsen reasoned that iron and steel artifacts were more difficult to make than bronze and copper artifacts because they required high temperatures to manufacture. Likewise, bronze artifacts were more difficult to produce than were materials made from stone, which could be picked up off the ground. This method became known as the **three-age approach** and became the foundation on which archaeologists were to classify materials across time and space for nearly a century. In fact, the core ideas of this system are found in chronologies throughout the world. In parts of North America, for example, archaeologists divided the past into the Paleoindian, Archaic, and Woodland

three-age approach The method pioneered by C. J. Thomsen that linked stone, bronze, and iron material culture together in three successive periods. The basic concept of this method was adopted throughout much of the world.

periods. In Central America, archaeologists discussed Preclassic, Classic, and Postclassic periods.

In the developing scientific world of the nineteenth century, not everyone was willing to accept Thomsen's scheme as absolute. Questions arose about the validity of this system—for example, did the three periods in fact exist, or were they the result of some accident in ordering the Danish museum's collections? One of Thomsen's assistants, Jens Jacob Asmussen Woorsae, who had helped him develop the three-age approach, took on the task of testing the scheme he had helped devise. In 1843, at the age of twenty-two, Woorsae published *The Primeval Antiquities of Denmark,* which was translated into English in 1849. In this volume Woorsae documented the position of material culture in barrows (long burial mounds) and other prehistoric places in Denmark. He demonstrated conclusively that iron and steel materials tended to be recovered in layers above bronze and copper artifacts and that these, in turn, tended to occur above strata containing solely stone materials. Although there was a small overlap between each of the periods, there could be no doubt that there were three discrete eras in the region. What may prove equally important, though, was that the conclusions of Thomsen and Woorsae had to be tested; they could not simply be accepted as fact until they had been carefully scrutinized. This method of testing is at the heart of the sciences, including social sciences such as archaeology.

In France, and elsewhere on the European continent, similar finds were being made, though scholars noted differences in the distribution and appearance of the materials from places such as Denmark, France, and Switzerland. Especially to those working with Stone Age materials, it became evident that there were at least two periods within the Stone Age. In 1865 Sir John Lubbock, later to become Lord Avebury, published his work entitled *Prehistoric Times.* In it he proposed dividing the Stone Age into two categories, the **Paleolithic,** or Old Stone Age, and the **Neolithic,** or New Stone Age. This division was based on the shape of the tools, with Paleolithic tools tending to be sharp and designed for cutting, skinning, and scraping, whereas Neolithic tools tended to be large and useful for grinding grasses and grains. It seemed logical that, because the Paleolithic materials always came from strata below Neolithic materials, the Paleolithic forms must be earlier. It was further suggested that these tools represented a time before humans learned to farm, a suggestion that proved essentially correct.

Further research noted even more divisions in material, time, and space. The Paleolithic was eventually broken into three substages (Table 2.2), Upper, Middle, and Lower. The Upper Paleolithic finds were associated with the cave paintings and rockshelters of western Europe and were the closest of the three substages in time to the Neolithic. Subsequently the term **Mesolithic** was introduced to describe the time period between the end of the Upper Paleolithic and the beginning of the Neolithic. In effect, archaeologists had divided the Stone Age into three ages and then divided one part of this, the Paleolithic, into its own three ages as well.

Paleolithic A term popular in the Old World defining the "Old Stone Age," the period prior to the last glacial epoch.

Neolithic A term popular in the Old World applied to the era beginning roughly ten thousand years ago when humans began to domesticate plants and animals. The hallmark of this era is ground stone tools designed for plant processing.

Mesolithic An Old World term for the period of time that represents regional diversification in human adaptations following the abandonment of big-game hunting but prior to the development of domestication and horticulture.

TABLE 2.2	Substages of the Paleolithic		
Age	**Stage**	**Substage**	**Dates**
Iron	—	—	800 B.C.–Historic Records
Bronze	—	—	4000–800 B.C.
Stone	Neolithic	—	8000–4000 B.C. (*Earlier in Near East)
	Mesolithic	—	10,000–7,000 B.C.
	Paleolithic	Upper	35,000–10,000 B.C.
		Middle	100,000–35,000 B.C.
		Lower	2,000,000–100,000 B.C.
		Basal	More than 2,000,000 B.C.

Systems of Nomenclature

After more than a century of research, archaeologists have identified even more differences in material culture across space and through time. Developments such as the culture area concept and the regional approach have allowed researchers to find and define subtle but meaningful differences in the archaeological record. And, perhaps as much as in any discipline, archaeologists have provided names to each unique cluster of material culture in space and time. This has been done to make discussion of the specific groupings easier, but sometimes it seems to be more confusing than it ought to be. After all, it is easier to refer to a Solutrean period than it is to use a description something like "the period when people in western Europe made finely crafted, leaf-shaped spear tips, about eighteen thousand to twenty-two thousand years ago." Everyone who works in the region simply needs to use the period name, Solutrean, and they will be understood by anyone else working in the region who is familiar with the nomenclature for the different periods and what the different names mean.

The process of naming archaeological materials and time-space groupings differs greatly around the world. One of the few consistent elements in the nomenclature systems, though, is a tendency to seek to impose a meaningful order on the archaeological record. This means that naming systems often reflect divisions of the archaeological record according to the three primary variables, time, space, and material culture. Moreover, these divisions help archaeologists study the past in two different but complementary ways, diachronically (or across time) and synchronically (within time). For example, archaeologists interested in the development of human lifestyles in a particular region from humans' first arrival there through the present would employ a diachronic approach. They would compare different material cultures from a single region through time, probably in increments defined by the nomenclature we are about to discuss. On the other hand, archaeologists interested in the activities of people in one or more places at the same time would em-

TABLE 2.3
Pecos Classification

Pueblo V	1550–1900
Pueblo IV	1300–1550
Pueblo III	1150–1300
Pueblo II	900–1150
Pueblo I	700–900
Basketmaker III	450–700
Basketmaker II	0–450

ploy synchronic methods, perhaps examining the specific ways people made their livings in the region or regions under study.

This all brings us back to the question of what sort of naming approaches archaeologists use. Among the earliest sequences of this sort built in the New World were the **Pecos Classification** (Table 2.3), designed by Alfred Vincent Kidder, and the **Midwest Taxonomic System,** developed by William C. McKern. Kidder, whose work focused on the Pecos Pueblo and surrounding regions in the American Southwest, developed his system by employing what we now call the **direct historical approach.** Kidder worked under the assumption that he could analyze the form and shape of Puebloan pottery and work backward from the modern era (the turn of the twentieth century for Kidder), thus creating a classificatory sequence that divided the archaeological record of the American Southwest into meaningful temporal units. His system, modified by later researchers, is still useful today. Note that there is no Basketmaker I classification. Kidder, anticipating that others might be able to build upon his sequence, deliberately left room at the most distant end of his scale in order to allow additional classifications to be made.

McKern, who worked primarily in the American Midwest, approached his taxonomic system differently. He thought that there was little chance of firmly connecting the material culture of modern or historically known Native Americans with the archaeological record. Instead, he devised a system that treated each archaeological component as if it were a species of plant or animal. It was assumed likely to have other components that were essentially similar and that therefore could be grouped together. Each group of components could then, in turn, be grouped together as one might group species into genera. This next level of organization could then be grouped into an even greater grouping and so forth, until a broad picture of human activities comparable to a culture area was defined. McKern's original scheme (Table 2.4) is the basis for the nomenclature system used in much of the New World today.

Today, most archaeologists organize the archaeological record into a series of hierarchical levels. Beginning with the smallest level of organization, we usually discuss components as reflections of human activity in one place within a very short span of time, perhaps a few days through a number of years. Note that we don't often use sites in this way because each site may contain multiple components and therefore reflect many different uses of a place across long spans of time. If a number of components are found in a definable geographic region, say a river valley or other geophysical setting (such as old beaches or a set of hills), and these components are similar in both material culture and age, then archaeologists tend to group these components into what are sometimes called **phases.** Whenever possible, phases are tightly defined so that they refer only to a specific range of material culture in a small geographic area across a limited span of time, ideally no more than a few hundred years at most.

Should archaeologists find that generally similar phases exist across a wider region and longer spans of time, they sometimes define what are known as

TABLE 2.4   McKern's Original Scheme

Pattern
Tradition
Phase
Focus
Component
Broadest ⟶ Most specific

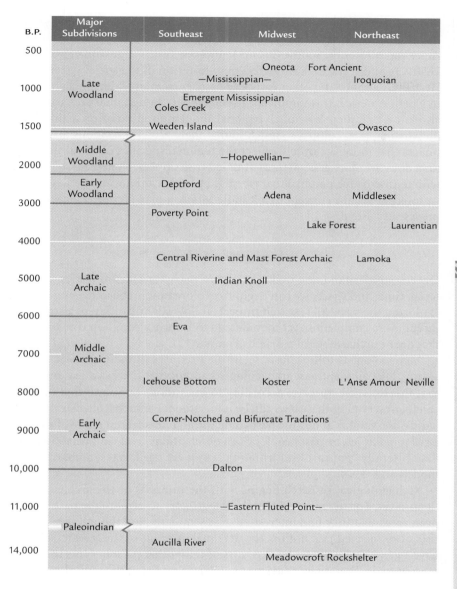

B.P.	Major Subdivisions	Southeast	Midwest	Northeast
500				
1000	Late Woodland	—Mississippian—	Oneota Fort Ancient	Iroquoian
		Emergent Mississippian Coles Creek		
1500		Weeden Island		Owasco
2000	Middle Woodland	—Hopewellian—		
3000	Early Woodland	Deptford	Adena	Middlesex
		Poverty Point		
4000			Lake Forest	Laurentian
5000	Late Archaic	Central Riverine and Mast Forest Archaic		Lamoka
		Indian Knoll		
6000				
7000	Middle Archaic	Eva		
8000		Icehouse Bottom	Koster	L'Anse Amour Neville
9000	Early Archaic	Corner-Notched and Bifurcate Traditions		
10,000		Dalton		
11,000		—Eastern Fluted Point—		
	Paleoindian			
14,000		Aucilla River	Meadowcroft Rockshelter	

FIGURE 2.11

Major chronological and regional divisions in eastern North America.

Pecos Classification An archaeological sequence for the American Southwest proposed by A. V. Kidder based on his work at the Pecos Pueblo using the direct historical approach.

Midwest Taxonomic System A classificatory system developed by W. C. McKern based on foci, phases, and traditions.

direct historical approach The tracing of material culture backward in time from known historical points using changes in typologies as guides.

phases Tightly defined categories of time and space that refer only to a specific range of material culture in a small geographic area across a limited span of time, ideally no more than a few hundred years at most.

archaeological cultures The definition of generally similar phases across a wide geographic region and long spans of time.

archaeological cultures. These are different from living cultures, which are generally thought of as societies of people who can be spoken to or otherwise defined socially. Rather, archaeological cultures reflect only groups of phases that document the persistence of similar material culture, and presumably some measure of human behaviors as well, across broad spans of time, perhaps one thousand years or more, and which occur in neighboring geographic regions. In this sense archaeological cultures do not reflect a single social group or society but an unknown number of social groups that share similar technologies and materials (Figure 2.11). For example, the Middle Mississip-

pian archaeological culture is defined by the building of flat-topped pyrami-
dal mounds and the use of generally similar ceramics. It spans much of the
American Midsouth, Southeast, and Midwest between approximately 900 and
1650 A.D. and is the archaeological manifestation of the social systems that
Hernando DeSoto and other early explorers encountered during their travels
in North America. It is important to remember, though, that archaeologists
also know that there was much regional and temporal variation within Middle Mississippian culture, so much so that there are a tremendous number of
phases that more accurately reflect the regional specifics of life at this time
than does the more general term Middle Mississippian. Nonetheless, when we
wish to discuss the patterns that we might perceive among and between these
various phases, the concept of a Middle Mississippian archaeological culture
proves very useful.

HOW WE APPROACH THE PAST

Once we understand that we have three primary variables to work with, material, time, and space, we can begin to explore how archaeologists go about
exploring the past. All research projects follow slightly different paths from
inception to completion, yet they all tend to involve a common core of events
that define archaeological research (Figure 2.12).

Archaeologists follow basic scientific premises in their approach to research. Like all scientists, archaeologists accept that there is a real universe,
that this universe operates according to immutable laws, and that through
careful observation these laws can be understood. For archaeologists the most
basic observations about the past come through the careful study of the material remains left by past peoples. Such observations create information called
data (literally "points of information") that are used to test archaeological
models and assumptions.

Archaeological research begins with the interests of the archaeologists
themselves. For the most part, archaeologists try to explore the past in ways
or in areas that they find interesting. Consequently, and though some scientists once rejected this notion, the personal interests of the researcher often
have a great deal to do with what sorts of things that person wants to do and
sets out to do. Eventually, restrictions will develop out of theoretical and practical concerns, but the initial impetus toward doing science, including archaeology, derives from an individual's own likes and dislikes.

These interests spur archaeologists to read about and participate in research that is defined geographically (where the work is done), mechanically
(how the work is done), and theoretically (how the results are interpreted).
When an archaeologist sets out to participate in research, a series of **research
questions** is defined. These questions are specific queries that define what the
archaeologist wants to know about a certain place. These questions can develop from an interest in culture history (the sequence of past events and societal developments) or from an interest in testing the applications of a new

research questions The
specific questions that archaeologists ask when preparing a
research program and seek to
answer when executing that
program.

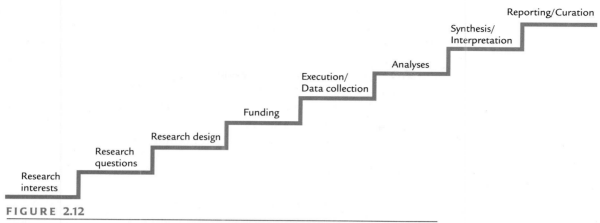

Reporting/Curation

Synthesis/
Interpretation

Analyses

Execution/
Data collection

Funding

Research design

Research
questions

Research
interests

FIGURE 2.12

The generalized sequence of steps in archaeological research.

technique or theory. Examples of research questions might be as broad as, How did the people living in the Upper Mississippi River valley prior to the historic era utilize natural resources? or as specific as, How did the artisans at a particular Maya workshop during the Terminal Classic acquire, produce, and distribute obsidian blades? Moreover, research questions can be nested together so that related questions lead the researcher from one topic to the next in a logical fashion.

Once research questions have been defined, archaeologists usually establish a series of hypotheses, or statements, about the archaeological record that they will systematically investigate. Hypotheses are tentative assumptions about how things worked in the past. Each hypothesis is accompanied by a series of statements defining the things that the archaeologist should recover if the hypothesis is valid. The same effect can be accomplished without stating formal hypotheses by making statements of expectations, that is, statements about what should be recovered but without tying these to specific hypothetical assumptions. The difference in the two approaches is largely philosophical and often revolves around the issue of whether or not the assumed statement can actually be tested archaeologically. Sometimes the best archaeologists can do is to recover data that is only indirectly related to the sorts of things that we want to know about. Ideally, though, statements and hypotheses should be as closely related to the specific research questions asked by the archaeologist as possible; they should inform the archaeologist about these questions.

Once statements or hypotheses are in place, archaeologists then design a research plan for acquiring the data needed to evaluate these statements. Researchers carefully plan what sort of tests they need to undertake, the equipment and personnel they will need, and the cost of supporting these people and equipment. Plans for acquiring permits, funds, and other necessities are also generated. Further, long-range plans are made for curating the material that is recovered, because it would be unethical and usually illegal to simply leave it to rot once excavated. These plans are collectively known as a **research design.**

Following the development of the research design, funding and permits can be sought. This step in the development of a project is essential because archaeologists must adhere to the laws of the places in which they excavate and they must take care of their crew. Funding can come from a variety of sources. In cultural resource management, funding is usually provided by the agency undertaking the construction that prompted the archaeological survey work. In more traditional academic spheres, funding must be solicited on a competitive basis from government and private sources, such as the National Science Foundation (federal) or the Leakey Fund (private).

Finally, when all of these steps have been accomplished, the archaeologists can proceed to conduct the field and analytical portions of the project. This is often the most enjoyable aspect of research, and it can take people to exotic and romantic locations. It can also be exceptionally problematic. In addition to supervising the overall research, the archaeologist in charge, usually called the principal investigator, or P.I., must maintain the budget, arrange for permits to be renewed, deal with potential logistical and personal problems, and still keep an eye on the progress of the project as a whole. Reports must also be sent to funding agencies, and unexpected situations of all sorts, ranging from mechanical breakdowns to political instability in the country where research is going on, must be addressed. There is an axiom in archaeology that fieldwork is never boring (Box 2.4).

The last phases in any project involve arranging for the long-term curation of all material culture recovered, the preservation of the site or sites explored for future research, and the publication of the results of the excavations and analyses. These are major issues that must be dealt with because these things make archaeology a positive activity for the world rather than an elaborate method for destroying records of past human activities.

SUMMARY

Archaeologists work with three primary variables, material culture, time, and space. The exploration of each of these variables first individually and then together as an integrated unit allows archaeologists to begin to understand how past humans were distributed across the landscape through time. Researchers can also develop a sense of technological, social, and sometimes ideological changes in space and time. Unfortunately, the integration of the three variables also results in a sometimes complex system of jargon that can be region specific. Nonetheless, it is essential for archaeologists to master terminologies and concepts in order to facilitate communication and further study.

Likewise, it is important to understand that archaeological research is not haphazard. Scholars follow specific steps to formulate research questions and hypotheses or statements about the past and then prepare research designs to

research design The plan for answering a series of research questions through the application of archaeological techniques and strategies.

digital elevation model (D.E.M.) A three-dimensional representation of the landscape within a defined area.

viewshed The area that can be seen from a given point on the landscape.

BOX 2.4

SEEING IS BELIEVING ON THE SALISBURY PLAIN

The Salisbury Plain lies in western England and is home to many impressive Neolithic monuments. The most famous of these is Stonehenge, though a second impressive henge encloses the heart of the entire town of Avebury, just slightly to the north. Also situated on the plain are long megalithic tombs, called barrows. These tombs were used at the same time as the Stonehenge and Avebury monuments, and the term *megalithic*, applied to both the barrows and the henges, refers to a common tradition of using massive stones in constructing symbolic and sacred places (*mega* meaning large, *lithic* meaning stone). In the case of the barrows, stone-lined passages led to stone-lined chambers, called cysts, in which the honored dead were buried.

David Wheatley from the University of Southampton wanted to know if the distribution of these barrows was random or whether there was a plan to their loca-tion. If there was a plan, Wheatley wanted to know what it was. His first step was to collect data on the physical position of all of the megalithic monuments in the Avebury and Stonehenge areas. Data on elevation, surrounding hills, and all associated geographic features were entered into a GIS program, in this case IDRISI, and used to prepare a **digital elevation model,** or **D.E.M.,** of the area. He then calculated **viewsheds** for each megalithic monument in these areas.

Wheatley then tested a simple hypothesis:

- H_0—that the sites are distributed irrespective of the number of other sites that are visible, and

- H_1—that the sites are not distributed irrespective of the number of other sites that are visible (e.g., that people built monuments in places from which they could see many other such monuments).

(continued)

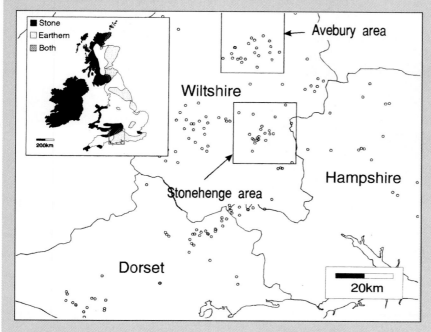

The distribution of long barrows and megalithic chambered tombs in the British Isles and especially on the Avebury and Salisbury Plains, western England.

BOX 2.4 (continued)

An example of viewshed analysis from a single long barrow on the Salisbury Plain.

The test involved simply overlaying all of the viewsheds he had already created in something called a cumulative viewshed. Each time a viewshed overlapped with another at the location of a megalithic structure, the computer recorded that event. When the computer had processed all of the data, the number of times viewsheds intersected at each monument was displayed. The total of these events was then statistically evaluated and found to be significant at the .05 level for the Stonehenge group but not significant for the Avebury group. This means that there is a 5% chance that the distribution of the various megalithic monuments around Stonehenge is random, though it is possible (but not definitive) that the distribution around Avebury is the result of chance. In other words, there is a strong possibility that the builders of the megalithic structures around Stonehenge used the positions of other monuments to determine the location of the structures to be built. At Avebury this might not be the case, though it

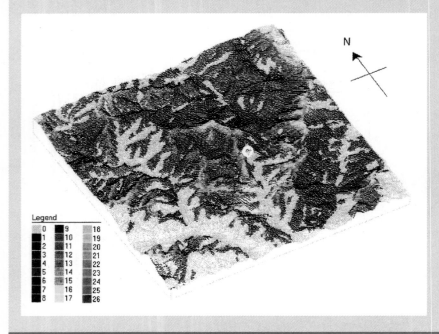

An example of a cumulative viewshed analysis for a 20-km-square area from the Salisbury Plain.

Legend

0	9	18
1	10	19
2	11	20
3	12	21
4	13	22
5	14	23
6	15	24
7	16	25
8	17	26

N

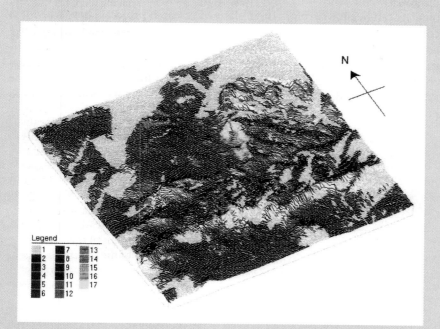

An example of a cumulative viewshed analysis for a 20-km-square area from the Avebury Plain.

still could be true for at least part of the time that monuments were built there. Further testing is required to assess that possibility.

The results of this sort of research can be used to infer the presence of other behaviors among the people who built the monuments around Stonehenge. Particularly important is the desire to make the burial places of the dead highly visible, especially from other burial places. Similarly, these burial places were highly visible to visitors going to Stonehenge itself, which is perceived to be the focal point for ritual and perhaps political activity in the region. Because many of the long barrows contain individual tombs, as opposed to tombs containing large numbers of individuals, it

seems likely that the position of the long barrows was selected in order to portray the importance of the people buried within. A person could not move about the Salisbury Plain without seeing these monuments. To place this in the context of a modern analogy, visiting the Salisbury Plain would be like visiting Washington, D.C. Even if you did not go to the city to see the Capitol or the White House, it is difficult to move through the city without encountering monuments to past presidents and important figures in American history. In this case, the political history and agendas of the current government are reinforced by the placement of monuments and tombs dedicated to past leaders whom our history tends to glorify.

evaluate these hypotheses and statements. Prior to undertaking the field and analytical components of the research, though, archaeologists must ensure that they have the required permits and funds to support their research and their workers. Finally, only after these things have all been addressed, archaeologists can begin to explore their planned research project. Then, when it is completed, they must assure the curation of the materials they have recovered, address the ultimate disposition of the sites they have excavated, and ensure that the work they have undertaken is published. The publication of archaeological research should ideally occur on multiple levels and be made available to as wide a segment of the scientific and popular communities as possible.

FOR FURTHER INFORMATION

Adams, R. E. W. 1998. Stratigraphy. In *Field methods in archaeology*, 7th ed., edited by T. R. Hester, R. F. Heizer, K. Feder, and J. A. Graham, 147–62. Mountain View, CA: Mayfield.

Adams, W. Y. 1988. Archaeological classification: Theory versus practice. *Antiquity* 62: 40–56.

Bamforth, D. B., and A. C. Spaulding. 1982. Human behavior, explanation, archaeology, history, and science. *Journal of Anthropological Archaeology* 1: 170–95.

———. 1962. Archaeology as anthropology. *American Antiquity* 28: 217–25.

Deagan, K. 1982. Avenues of inquiry in historical archaeology. In *Advances in archaeological method and theory*, vol. 5, edited by M. B. Schiffer, 151–77. New York: Academic Press.

Dethlefsen, E., and J. Deetz. 1966. Death's heads, cherubs, and willow trees: Experimental archaeology in colonial cemeteries. *American Antiquity* 31: 502–10.

Flannery, K. V. 1973. Archaeology with a capital S. In *Research and theory in current archaeology*, edited by C. L. Redman, 47–53. New York: Wiley-Interscience.

Harris, E. C. 1989. *Principles of archaeological stratigraphy*, 2nd ed. London: Academic Press.

Thomas, D. H. 1989. *Principles of archaeological stratigraphy*, 2nd ed. London: Academic Press.

3

INTERPRETING THE PAST

When you have eliminated the impossible, whatever remains, however improbable, must be the truth.

—Sherlock Holmes

All academic endeavors, including those in the natural sciences, are subject to the paradigms held by the people who undertake research. **Paradigms** are philosophical and scientific points of view that help structure the nature of thought and research. For all intents and purposes, paradigms are lenses through which a researcher sees information and constructs data. These lenses can focus, distort, or even blind a researcher's work and interpretations because they define what the researcher and, presumably, his peers accept as appropriate thought (Figure 3.1).

You have already encountered two of these paradigms in the form of processual archaeology and the direct historical approach. Although these ways of exploring the past are important, there are many more theoretical perspectives at work in modern archaeology. In order to understand how archaeologists interpret the past, it is important to understand the paradigms that structure archaeological thought and research. This chapter explores some of the more common and significant perspectives used in the discipline today.

-ISMS AND -ISTS

We will begin our exploration of archaeological interpretation with a discussion of the two most powerful, and sometimes conflicting, philosophical trends in modern archaeology. Processualism developed in the middle of the twentieth century; it emphasized scientific approaches to studying the past and espoused the notion that archaeology was a neutral endeavor. Postprocessualism came to the fore in the last decades of the century as a challenge to both the limits and the assumptions of these perspec-

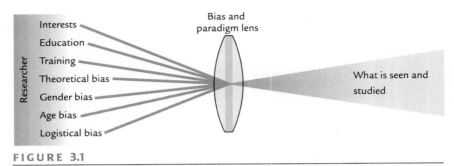

FIGURE 3.1

The overall relationship between a researcher and the material to be studied.

tives. Although there has been a great deal of cross-pollination between the paradigms and although very few archaeologists adhere to extreme positions of one or the other paradigm, the initial encounters between strong adherents of the two positions were electrifying, even being described at times as gladiatorial. Who says that theory must be boring?

Processual Archaeology

What is now called *processual archaeology* was originally called the "new" archaeology. It emerged as a related set of approaches designed to study the past using scientific methods during the late 1950s and early 1960s, though some of its tenets were espoused by Irving Rouse and Walter Taylor in the 1930s and 1940s. Rather than a single, cohesive approach, processual archaeology is best described as a philosophical position composed of many different specific techniques and approaches that share in the acceptance of something called **logical positivism.** According to this view, there is a knowable past that can be understood and interpreted from an essentially neutral perspective through the application of rigid, scientific-based archaeological techniques. In effect, adherents of this perspective argue that if we do archaeology correctly we will be able to discover and describe what happened in the past accurately.

The term *processualism* is applied to this branch of archaeology because researchers using this approach concentrate on the processes of past human behavior. As is discussed in the chapter on stone tools (Chapter 6), for example, archaeologists can study how stone tools were used by replicating them and then using the replicas. This use creates a series of patterns of utilization that can be directly compared with the archaeological material. When patterns match, archaeologists can state with a high degree of confidence that the material they excavated was used in a fashion similar to the manner in which the replica was utilized.

This connection between the archaeological material and its interpretation is called **middle range theory.** Processualists use such theory, originally de-

paradigm Philosophical and scientific points of view that help structure the nature of thought and research. For all intents and purposes, paradigms are lenses through which a researcher sees information and constructs data.

logical positivism The philosophical position that there is an objectively knowable past that can be discovered through rigid adherence to scientific methods.

middle range theory Bridging theory that enables archaeologists to link excavated data with their interpretations about past human lifeways.

TABLE 3.1 Examples of Some Middle Range Research		
Archaeological Material	**Middle Range Research**	**Interpretation**
Scatter of stone flakes	Ethnographic analogy or ethnoarchaeology	Position and activity of people on the site in the past
Wear and breakage pattern on stone tools	Experimental replication and testing to match wear patterns	The way people used the stone tools in the past
Gnawed and "scratched" bones	Controlled study and comparison of damage done to bone by natural agents (animals, weather) and human agents (butchering, breaking) to match damage observed on bones	The ways in which the bones received the observed damage; possible human or animal bone utilization patterns
Distribution of structures in a settlement	Ethnoarchaeology	The way in which humans may have elected to organize their communities and locate certain sorts of activity areas

fined by Lewis R. Binford, in the form of replicative studies and ethnoarchaeology (see Chapter 6) to create a concrete link between their interpretations and their data. This is in accordance with the scientific method, which dictates that research should involve observable, testable, and repeatable components. Middle range theory became a common demonstration of the scientific approach in archaeology and remains a valuable position in archaeology today (Table 3.1).

In addition to middle range theory, processualists tend to emphasize a research approach called the *hypothetico-deductive model*. In this approach archaeologists follow a set sequence of research stages that adherents argue helps ensure objectivity in research. These stages are

Observe phenomena.

Induce hypotheses that define what archaeological results can be expected if the hypotheses are accurate.

Test these hypotheses following scientific procedures, usually emphasizing falsification (the attempt to disprove rather than prove a hypothesis, thus encouraging objectivity).

Deduce, based on the results of testing, which hypotheses are viable and which are not.

Return to the observation stage and revise the research until such work is no longer possible. What remains is therefore provisionally accepted, and research continues.

The processual approach has clearly been one of the most influential models for archaeological research in the modern era. It provides a structure and series of rules in which archaeologists can work, though they are still free to innovate and expand upon existing ideas as needed.

Postprocessualism and Critiques
of the New Archaeology

Criticisms of the approach have been present since its inception. Beginning in the late 1970s, however, these criticisms became increasingly loud and sufficiently cohesive so that archaeologists began to explore them. At the heart of the criticisms is a series of philosophical issues coupled with a number of important research interests that processualism does not satisfactorily address. Although the strongest impetus for criticism emerged from the United Kingdom, archaeologists throughout the world began to reassess the strengths and limitations of processual archaeology. Some of these researchers argued for the abandonment of processualism altogether in favor of one of any number of alternative positions. Together these positions became known as the *postprocessual* movement, or postprocessualism.

The primary philosophical debates between the postprocessualists and the processualists center on the validity of logical positivism. Whereas processualists accept the notion that the past can be explored through archaeology in an essentially neutral way, their critics reject this premise. They argue that the mere act of interpreting the past, that is, explaining how a past society functioned in one or more areas of life, brings the unstated biases of the archaeologist to the forefront. For example, to describe past economies in terms of capitalist values or notions of possessions assumes that the past peoples using these systems shared these values. Demonstrably, this is not always the case.

As a consequence, postprocessualists have suggested that any well-codified paradigm for explaining the past is as valid as any other. In terms of economics, for example, Marxist perspectives on the tension between those who control resources and those who need to utilize them may be just as viable, perhaps even more so, than capitalist notions of such relations. More subtly, researchers such as Michael Shanks and Christopher Tilley argue that the life history and personal experiences of every archaeologist affect the ways in which that researcher views and describes the past. Everything from romantic notions of lost civilizations to deeply held views about the relationships between men and women can be subconsciously included in a researcher's description of the past. Moreover, in a politicized modern world, archaeological interpretations can sometimes be seen as extensions of political and social philosophies. Sometimes such extensions are clearly evident, but sometimes they are deeply concealed beneath seemingly sound scientific statements.

Based on these arguments, Shanks, Tilley, and others have argued that the processual method is not the only way to undertake archaeological research; it is simply one that is equal in value to all others. The danger in this position is that some people might assume that such relaxation of philosophical approaches allows for a relaxation in methodological standards and careful, genuine attempts to explore the past. This is clearly not so, and many postprocessual archaeologists conduct technically superb excavations. In this arena, both processualists and their critics tend to agree that there is no substitute for good research; they simply disagree on what constitutes a good philosophical paradigm from which to interpret that work (Box 3.1).

Another branch of the postprocessual critique deals less with a debate over logical positivism and more with a concern over what can actually be explored using processual approaches. For example, although processual methodology allows exceptional insights into functional categories of material culture— that is, in studying how things were used—and can be useful in exploring how past behaviors were organized on a technological level, this methodology strongly limits explorations of social and ideological behaviors.

For example, modern Americans tend to organize their calenders in a linear fashion, they tend to build rectangular or square structures, and they typically communicate with one another in very direct ways. If an anthropologist were to ask why, she would receive many different responses from Americans. Some would center on the functionality of square and rectangular structures, as well as the relative ease of building these shapes. Likewise, some people would explain that Americans communicate directly because it is the easiest way to pass meaning from one person to another. Careful research, though, would also detect undertones of family structure, kinship, concepts of how to use the natural environment, and a strong adherence to work ideals brought over by English immigrants to New England.

An archaeologist studying a past society is faced with precisely the same sorts of dilemmas. There is more to understanding how people behave than can be deduced from the study of processes and functions. Such research requires a different set of approaches that do not necessarily adhere to processual viewpoints. Such research must inevitably find its explanatory theory in more anthropological models of humankind. Indeed, many archaeologists argue that anthropological models developed to describe living peoples can be used as windows through which we can begin to explore peoples of the past. Some of this research follows the same methods laid out by the processualists, emphasizing the hypothetico-deductive process. Ultimately, however, they are different in that the answers archaeologists develop to their research questions are inferred; there is no test that directly reveals the symbolic aspects of past human societies. The best we can do is to explore these areas of human behavior and to explain as clearly as possible our interpretations and our reasons for making them. For some processualists, though, this is not acceptably precise.

MAKING IT WORK IN THE REAL WORLD

When the debates over philosophies and meanings end, archaeologists are still left with the task of making sense out of the material evidence of the human past. Yet the debates over what "-isms" and which "-ists" are most productive and most appropriate leave us with a range of practical approaches to addressing ranges of research interests and research questions. These approaches can be seen as more or less allied with processualism or postproces-

BOX 3.1

ONE PEOPLE, ONE POT:
GUSTAF KOSSINNA AND POLITICS OF NATIONALISM

Archaeology does not exist in a social vacuum. Just as the ideas of archaeologists are influenced by the prevalent philosophies of the times in which they lived, so, too, can the ideas of archaeologists be adopted and co-opted by the social and political movements of those times. Perhaps nowhere can we find a stronger or more colorful example of such connections as in the writings and ideas of Gustaf Kossinna (1858–1931). Kossinna was born into a wealthy family and was sent to the best German schools, where he proved to be an outstanding student. By the age of twenty-three, in 1881, he defended his thesis for a degree comparable to that of a modern doctorate. His work was largely on historical linguistics and the question of Indo-German origins, a question that would occupy his entire career.

Archaeologically speaking, Kossinna was first influenced by the ideas of Rudolf Virchow, who argued that laws of culture were similar to laws of biology. For Kossinna this meant that the materials produced by people were direct reflections of their racial and ethnic background. This idea seemed to be supported by the slightly later work of the Swedish archaeologist Oscar Montelius, who argued convincingly for a continuous Scandinavian ethnic presence in Denmark, Norway, and Sweden dating back to the Bronze Age. Kossinna therefore reasoned that, if Scandinavians dominated the northlands, Germans must have dominated northern Europe. Moreover, he also reasoned that these proto-Germans, or Indo-Germans as he called them, must have migrated outward from their ancient homeland, bringing civilization to the rest of Europe.

To prove this, Kossinna extracted bits of information from archaeology. Though he was a talented and provocative lecturer, he himself seldom excavated, nor was he a talented excavator. Nonetheless, as an armchair theorist, he took parts of works from other scholars and sought to prove that Germans were the original culture bearers in Europe and that all other people, from Slavs to Celts, were unenlightened peoples of lesser racial and ethnic groups. He proposed a view called "residence archaeology," meaning that the identity of past peoples could be established and traced throughout the places they had lived through the artifacts they made. This, in and of itself, is a reasonable idea akin to the direct historic approach of A. V. Kidder. Unfortu-

---

sualism, but, ultimately, they reflect any number of intermediary approaches and commonsense views.

Perhaps at the heart of these intermediary approaches is the notion that all archaeological interpretation is really dependent on the research questions being asked by the people who undertake research. Moreover, all research programs are affected by the research interests and methodological preferences of the archaeologists participating in the project. It is necessary for each archaeologist to synthesize the relevant positions and to apply them as best suits the work at hand. Although philosophical positions are not easily changed, specific field approaches and types of research can be adjusted to meet both philosophical and methodological needs. This section summarizes some theoretical approaches to studying a number of sorts of research questions. As you might gather, there will be exceptions, additions, and modifications to these approaches made by each archaeologist. Nonetheless, the general trends should remain evident.

nately, unlike Kidder's painstaking work, Kossinna's arguments were filled with simplistic comparisons that sought to equate one type of artifact with one ethnic group—hence the phrase, "one people, one pot," meaning one style of pot or other artifact. More significantly, he also argued that the original inhabitants of a territory had the right to reclaim that land regardless of who now lived on it. This sat well with the politics of pre–World War I unification and expansion. It would also sit well with later, World War II–era German politics of racial superiority. It had little to do with practical reality or archaeological data.

Kossinna's contemporaries, such as Carl Schuchhardt, objected to his uncritical use of the material record. Kossinna peppered his published retorts to such comments with venomous rhetoric about his critics' patrimony, intellects, and nationalities. Although it was clear that nationalism had become the dominant paradigm for Kossinna's explanations of the past, this, by itself, was not considered a great problem. Many of his contemporaries, especially in the area of East Prussia, were also strong nationalists. Even his critics, such as Schuchhardt, were nationalists in one form or another. Rather, it was Kossinna's poor archaeology and his mean-spirited, often self-serving, rhetoric that alienated him from many of his contemporaries. By most accounts,

Kossinna won most of his arguments not by force of reason or by weight of evidence but by direct ad hominem attacks. Thus, in the end, criticizing Kossinna's work did little for scholars save to provide fodder for another scathing response.

In summarizing Kossinna's career, Leo Klejn observes that despite all of his shortcomings, Kossinna's ideas proved influential for several generations of scholars. Indeed, he also raised important issues about the possibility of connecting social identities with archaeological remains, an issue that many archaeologists still wrestle with today. Yet the way in which Kossinna chose to impose his own political and racial beliefs on archaeology has condemned his legacy to one of mistrust and infamy. He has not been the last to bend scholarship to the will of politics. As Klejn (1999:246) concludes, "Unfortunately, the passions that provoked Kossinna's archaeology are again abroad in the world. There is renewed pressure to correlate cultures with ethnic groups. A serious analysis of Kossinna's [theoretical] heritage is necessary not only to solve the problems he raised, but also to avoid repeating his dangerous blunders."

Culture History

Much of the early work done in archaeology has been described as classificatory and/or historical in nature. Such work emphasized constructing chronologies and identifying regions or sites in which certain material cultural developments took place. These developments were then tied to general narratives of the emergence, rise, and fall of different societies. The culture area concept, the direct historical approach, the Midwest Taxonomic System, and the Pecos Classification all exemplify this sort of approach.

Though some archaeologists would like to claim that this approach has been replaced by more philosophically robust thoughts about exploring the past, this is far from the truth. Culture histories are an integral part of the way archaeologists convey their assessments about past human activities to each other and to the public. Without the continued definition and refinement of chronological sequences, it would be difficult to place modern archaeological discoveries in a meaningful human context. Indeed, many of the most successful archaeological authors take great pains to link their discussions of research results and interpretations to data derived from culture historical work.

The shortcoming of culture history is that it is essentially atheoretical. Although archaeologists can describe something and create a sequence of events based on their work, this does not get at questions about why things happened in the past. Indeed, culture history alone was never envisioned to deal with such complex questions. Yet, as a supplement to other modes of exploring the past, research on essentially culture historical issues is still a useful part of modern archaeology.

Behavioral Archaeology

Behavioral archaeology is the study of the relationships between human behavior and material culture in order to understand the nature of human behavior across time and space. Adherents of this approach, such as William Rathje and Michael Schiffer, both of the University of Arizona, argue that the most efficient way to understand trends and universals in human behavior is to highlight the ways in which artifacts illustrate human behaviors. They also hold that it matters little precisely where you engage in this sort of work because the goals of the work emphasize universal human behaviors, not culture-specific behaviors.

Behavioral archaeologists use a four-part classification scheme in their study of material culture. Regardless of the origin of any piece of material culture, that material can be measured according to its physical properties (weight, size, color), frequency of occurrence, association with other material remains, and provenience. Through the analysis of material culture in this fashion, behavioral archaeologists argue that the life history of the material can be identified. This history conveys information about where the material was first produced, used, and then, often, reused. The development of such sorts of histories led to the development of the concepts of C-transformations and N-transformations (see Chapter 5) by Schiffer and Rathje's innovative Garbage Project (Box 3.2). Likewise, behavioral archaeologists in general have adopted Binford's scheme of artifact function, that is, that material culture can operate on technological, sociological, and ideological levels.

Ultimately, the goal of behavioral archaeologists is to develop what they term correlates of human behavior. These correlates are essentially laws of human behavior that work in much the same way as natural laws function. They transcend the temporal and spatial boundaries of specific societies and inform modern scholars about the nature of human actions. Thus behavioral archaeologists seek to work from the level of specific material cultural remains upward, identifying patterns and trends, until they eventually identify universal laws of human behavior.

Critics of this approach question whether or not such laws actually exist. They point out that each culture is unique and that people in all places and all

BOX 3.2

ARCHAEOLOGISTS: WE DIG OTHER PEOPLE'S GARBAGE

Sometimes archaeological assignments in the classroom seem to get out of hand. In 1971, students of William Rathje at the University of Arizona were being trained in the philosophies and techniques of archaeological fieldwork. Students assumed responsibility for unique projects that were designed to illustrate how archaeological method and theory operated. Two of these students, Frank Ariza and Kelly Allen, elected to sample garbage thrown out at four locations, two in affluent suburbs and two in economically depressed neighborhoods. The expectation was that the people at each house site would show distinctive patterns of material disposal in their garbage, perhaps with the two sites in the affluent neighborhood and the two in the poor neighborhood showing some similarities because of common economic backgrounds. The results were surprising. All of the households consumed approximately the same amounts of steak and meat, but the households in the poor neighborhood revealed greater monetary expenditures on educational toys and household cleansers. The sample was too small to infer any real patterns, but the results were so different from the expectations that eyebrows were raised.

By 1973 these surprising results had given rise to the Garbage Project. William Rathje found the patterns and the potential for studying material culture from modern society so intriguing that he designed a long-term research project to study how Americans dispose of their garbage and to identify connections between these material patterns and behavior. It is also important to note that Rathje has been among those at the forefront of behavioral archaeology since its inception.

Today, the Garbage Project has expanded its research from the study of a few households to systematic sampling across major American landfills. Rathje's results are at once amusing, important, and troubling. First, garbage disposal is usually an impersonal act. This results in little concern being given to precisely what is thrown out and in what condition, because the people discarding the items feel that few, if any, people will know what they have thrown out. In effect, to most Americans, garbage is not a reflection of personal be-

havior, even though garbage contains the direct evidence for the materials being used by individuals. Our collection and deposition of garbage, however, tends to mix the remains of all households together in a mass that reflects the use of materials by a society as a whole but by no person or household as an individual.

Second, excavation at major landfills, such as at Fresh Kills Landfill on Staten Island in New York City, has revealed that our landfills are not operating as most of us envision them doing. Soft material, such as paper and even hot dogs from thirty to forty years ago, remains intact just as more durable materials from much earlier are also still present. It seems that our systems have created stable environments at the core of many of our major landfills, environments that tend to preserve material rather than encourage or assist in its decomposition. This lack of rapid, or even complete, decay is troubling to waste management officials and environmentalists alike, especially given the incredible rates of garbage disposal in most American communities (see table).

A final observation, and perhaps validation, of this sort of research deals with archaeological methods. Rathje's teams have identified a number of useful ways to identify and date certain types of artifacts that may otherwise have gone undiscovered. Significantly, some of these methods may be among the only effective ways to sort and date our own material remains, even though we tend to think that we keep written records of nearly everything that we do. For example, Rathje's research has revealed that old pull tabs from cans (the kind that detached completely from the can) could be used to help estimate rates of recycling, to date artifact deposits, and to identify specific products. When pull tabs were popular, most people, when recycling, discarded the tabs separately from the cans, placing them in the garbage, whereas the cans were put into recycling bins. By counting the number of tabs separated from cans and then comparing that number with the number of cans with tabs, Rathje could begin to estimate recycling rates. The tabs also vary in color and shape by product, making the identification of specific

(continued)

BOX 3.2 (continued)

	Roper (%)	Actual volume in landfills (%)
Disposable diapers	41	<2
Plastic bottles	29	<1
Large appliances	24	<2
Newspapers	11	~13
All paper	6	>40
Food and yard waste	3	~7
Construction debris	0	~12

beverage forms, and even brands, possible. Likewise, the dates for the use of these products is known, so that the presence of certain forms of pull tabs can be used as horizon markers in much the same way that certain forms of ancient pottery can be used to do the same. Perhaps it is true that the more things change, the more they stay the same.

Source: Rubbish! The Archaeology of Garbage, p. 103, by William Rathje and Cullen Murphy, 1992. By permission of HarperCollins Publishers (now Pearson).

times develop a baffling array of behaviors that archaeologists have trouble identifying, let alone synthesizing into universal correlates of human behavior. Thus, even if such behavioral laws exist, is it possible to work through artifacts in a meaningful way to identify these laws? Much of the debate, however, functions on the philosophical level, and behavioral archaeology, especially as it is applied by many researchers to study specific occurrences of human behavior, often affords researchers valuable insights into their own projects and how these results can be compared with the results from other projects.

Archaeology as Human Ecology

Significant portions of this text discuss issues related to reconstructing and understanding past environments. Deciphering the complex interactions between humans and these environments is a profitable and important aspect of modern archaeology. In many respects such research parallels the field of cultural ecology, which typically studies the interrelationships between the societies of living peoples and their environments.

One of the most influential researchers in the area of applying human ecological principles to the past is Karl Butzer. He is widely considered one of the most prominent innovators in this area and has been described variously as a cultural geographer, geoarchaeologist, and cultural ecologist. Butzer brings to his research projects an interdisciplinary approach that enables him to analyze archaeological, geological, and ecological data in the contexts of time and space. This enables him to compare human behaviors as they pertain to the environment through time and space. At the same time, his approach also enables him to identify environmental shifts in the past and the concomitant human reactions to these.

One of the many interesting areas of research that has developed in these lines is the field of **archaeoparasitology,** or the study of parasites in archaeological, and consequently human, contexts. Parasites exist in and around all human societies. Indeed, all people play host to some sort of furtive fauna, as one biologist has described parasites. These organisms range from lice to a host of parasitic worms that live in human and animal digestive tracts.

By identifying the presence and distribution of parasites across archaeological sites, researchers can determine a great deal about human interrelations with the environment. Because certain organisms only exist in certain environments or are originally specific to certain animal species, their presence on archaeological sites ties the people at these sites to those environments and animals that originally hosted the parasites.

For example, Karl Reinhard of the University of Nebraska has studied human-parasite ecology in the American Southwest. He has discovered a variety of different behaviors that influence the distribution of parasites in humans and, as a consequence, the health of the humans themselves. Reinhard has been able to show that hunters and gatherers tend to suffer less from parasitic infestations than do horticulturalists. A substantial portion of this dichotomy results from the ways in which humans dispose of their excrement and the length of time they spend in close contact with animals and animal waste. The greater the exposure to animal excrement of all sorts, the stronger the chance that parasitic infestation will become endemic and spread throughout a population (Box 3.3).

Exchange Systems and Archaeological Theory

This range of research interests centers on explorations of past networks of communication, including economic interchange. Far from being a coherent set of approaches, the study of exchange systems is best described as a vast series of approaches focusing on a somewhat common series of issues. More or less at the center of these issues is the notion of intergroup communication and interaction, though the mechanisms for such communication vary according to the research interests of the archaeologist. For example, V. Gordon Childe discussed migrations and the diffusion of technology across Europe in the millennia B.C. Both migration and diffusion represent different aspects of intergroup communication and interrelationships. Moreover, both migration and diffusion can occur in a number of ways, ranging from gradual movements and shifts in technologies to rapid, perhaps even violent, shifts in population composition and material culture. Questions can also be raised about the meaning of types and styles in archaeology and whether they reflect changes in past social groups or differences in organization among modern archaeolo-

archaeoparasitology The study of parasites in archaeological, and consequently human, contexts.

BOX 3.3

ARCHAEOPARASITOLOGY AND HUMAN ECOLOGY

As you might imagine, the American Southwest provides depositional environments well suited to the preservation of relatively delicate remains. Sometimes among these remains are the eggs or other remains of parasites, such as worms, found in animal, including human, digestive tracts. Sometimes these remains are found in preserved animal feces, which are called **coprolites,** and sometimes they are recovered in other materials preserved in the areas in which animals excreted such waste. Although the thought of excavating such remains may be repulsive to some and may lead to the production of amusing but vulgar sayings on the part of others, the data that can be obtained from such remains are extremely valuable.

Karl Reinhard has studied parasites in the American Southwest in the context of human ecology and made comparisons between societies who exploited their local environments in significantly different ways. Salmon Ruin, in northern New Mexico, and Antelope House, located in Arizona, on the Colorado Plateau, are two roughly comparable Anasazi settlements. They date to the time period around and just after the Anasazi florescence in the Chaco Canyon region during the twelfth and thirteenth centuries A.D. Salmon Ruin, however, is constructed on a broad, open floodplain, whereas Antelope House is a classic cliff dwelling and was constructed in a large cave.

The different choice of residential locations led to significant differences in human activities and, as a consequence, human-environment interactions. The residents of Salmon Ruin tended to raise a few crops and to forage for food in the dry desert plains. This environment was not conducive to the survival of most species of parasites while in the egg form, and people working in this environment tended to contract few internal parasites. Likewise, fecal material was widely dispersed in Salmon Ruin, and this dispersed the parasite eggs that could thrive in such areas of animal excrement. This, too, tended to limit the occurrence of internal parasites among the people living at this site.

Antelope House, however, is much different. Located in the shade of the cave and cliff walls, where water can stand without rapidly evaporating, parasite eggs thrived. Little direct wind passed through the site, and thus eggs that became airborne tended to stay in the air in the community for extended periods of time. The disposal of fecal material was problematic because of the rocky terrain. Most excrement was deposited haphazardly, often finding its way to the back of the caves where it accumulated. Moreover, the position of the community in a valley setting tended to limit the movement of the inhabitants of the site. They tended to grow most of their food in the valley, though they did make occasional forays farther afield to acquire other resources. The net effect was to reinforce extensive parasitic infestations among the site's inhabitants.

This sort of comparison illustrates the potential for using archaeoparasitology to help study human behavior in the past. Not only can the results of this work yield information on the health and physical condition of past humans, but also the sort of parasites and their frequency can be used to predict the presence of a range of subsistence and hygienic habits.

gists. The issues of defining the nature of the intergroup exchange and the data to be used to study it become essential in furthering any research of this sort.

Adding to the complexity of studies are the economic dimensions of exchange. Western scholars often adopt an implicitly capitalistic notion of how groups moved about in societies, whereas scholars in the former Soviet Union, unsurprisingly, often adopted a Marxist, even Leninist, view of exchange. Still others have argued that kinship groups should be viewed as the heart of all

coprolite Any formed fecal mass, including fossilized, frozen, or mummified forms.

exchange systems, and these scholars have therefore emphasized the notion of family production of goods.

Modern approaches to the study of intergroup exchange and communications have diverged markedly. Most scholars have abandoned the notion of diffusion, which is laden with monolithic and unscientific connotations, for the notion of trade. Scholars pursuing this line of research, however, usually include a variety of economic exchanges, not simply the transfer of one commodity in favor of another between partners. Concepts of reciprocity, ritual exchange, redistribution, and market exchange all must be addressed under the general discussion of trade. Moreover, studies of trade are still rife with questions about exactly what was traded and in what forms between different individuals and societies. In order to address these questions, some scholars have taken up studies of style and how it can best be defined (Box 3.4).

Cultural Evolution

Another strong approach to exploring the past is cultural evolution. Evolution is the notion that populations of organisms change at the genetic level across time and space as a result of natural selection and a series of genetic factors. The notion that a culture might be viewed as an organism in an evolutionary scheme was postulated shortly after Charles Darwin published *On the Origin of Species* in 1859. Indeed, the three-age approach, initially introduced by C. J. Thomsen and refined by Sir John Lubbock, is essentially evolutionary in perspective, though it is not tied directly to ideas of natural selection. As we discussed in Chapter 2, these early schemes tended to be unilinear—that is, they postulated that all societies developed through the same stages, becoming increasingly more complex and civilized over time. Such schemes tended to reinforce imperial notions of national and racial superiority and ignored the fact that evolution is a process that has no single direction.

Although unilineal evolution had been largely discredited by the early decades of the twentieth century, scholars in the middle of the century revisited and revised the idea that human societies could be viewed in evolutionary terms. Chief among these people was Leslie White of the University of Michigan. White argued that archaeology had consistently demonstrated that human society did follow predictable trajectories of growth and decline. He pointed out, however, that there was no single set of stages that a society needed to pass through and that cultural evolution could be described as multilineal. Multilineal evolution, or neoevolutionism, has come to describe approaches adhering to this general position.

White and his followers argued that there were certain universal patterns in human societies. These patterns revolved around the expenditure and capture of energy within societies as population levels changed (Figure 3.2). Simply put, all people need to get essential resources out of the natural environment in quantities that at least equal the energy they put into acquiring those

BOX 3.4

YOU'VE GOT STYLE!

There are few topics in archaeology that can be as controversial as the definition and application of style. For most readers, style simply refers to the way something looks, its representation as material culture. Few archaeologists would disagree with the basic premise of such a definition, though many would begin to disagree (usually with one another) about how to study style and how to interpret the results of such studies. Styles and their distributions through space and time have been argued to reflect everything from social identities to evidence for the migrations of entire populations. Sometimes such arguments appear to be valid; at other times they appear spurious at best. How, then, are we to approach this subject?

The best way may be to think about what style does. Few people would disagree with the notion that style conveys social information, either directly or indirectly and either intentionally or as a by-product of the production process. Nonetheless, information is conveyed from the person creating something in a certain style (or a person using some material made in a certain style, or a person using some material made in a certain style in a stylized way) to somebody who sees the item and recognizes the style. H. Martin Wobst describes this process best. The person activating a style by making it or using it transmits social information outward, probably directed at a group of people who live in the same society as the sender but who are not intimately familiar with the sender. Those who are very familiar with the person using the style already know who this person is, as well as his or her ideas and social position. Those who are too distant socially to interpret the style being employed by that person will not understand it, but such people are probably outside of the social world of the sender. The remaining category includes people who fall in the group between the immediate family and friends of the sender and the people who do not interact with the sender. The people in this category make up large segments of the social group in which the sender operates; these people are provided with an opportunity to infer something about the sender based on the style being displayed (see the figure).

If this sounds complex, then you are beginning to understand the problems with the use of style. Nonetheless, we all do the kinds of things Wobst describes. For example, we dress in certain fashions depending on the social environment we find ourselves in. If we are visiting close friends or family, we might not worry about dressing formally or even well. We will probably wear something that we like and are comfortable with. Such clothing, perhaps unintentionally, conveys to oth-

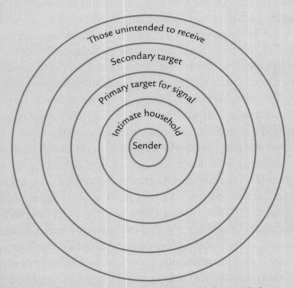

The relationship between an individual and the people he or she directly and indirectly interacts with.

ers ideas about us. Now, if we are appearing in a courtroom, especially as a participant in legal proceedings, we typically dress better. We do this because we want to convey an air of respectability and perhaps responsibility to the court officials, especially the judge and the jury. In effect, the style of our clothing transmits social information. We hope that it conveys specific meanings, or at least positive general meanings, to specific people who are not intimately familiar with us.

Now we can enter the world of exactly how style is transmitted and perceived. In general, style can be actively used (**active style**), as in the case of the courtroom example, or passively used, as in the case of visiting friends. In the courtroom we are actively trying to portray a certain social role; we are transmitting a message. In the latter case, we are not actively seeking to make a statement to our close friends and family; they know us. We are merely wearing things we like. This behavior unintentionally, or passively, transmits stylistic signals to others (**passive style**). In both cases, though, we might elect to wear clothing that has readily visible logos on it, such as Jordache, Pierre Cardin, or something similar. This, too, is a form of stylistic display because we are associating ourselves with the company whose label we display. People viewing that label tend to associate it with the image that company has sought to produce in the public sphere. We can use such "emblemic" displays of style to convey that we approve of or are in some way associated with that corporate image (**emblematic style**). If this were not the case, then many companies would find that their clothing or other items failed to sell well because other companies provide similar products for lower costs.

Having entered the world of style, imagine trying to apply this to the past. How do we identify the social contexts in which stylistic meanings were transmitted? As significantly, what did these stylistic displays mean, if anything? At one level, we can almost ignore these questions. If we can discern, or discover, patterns of stylistic representations in the past, then these patterns can be analyzed in terms of their spatial and temporal distribution. Studies focusing on exchange systems, then, can identify and map the movement of material from one social group to another without directly concerning themselves with what ideologies might be moving along with the materials.

If we want to understand the ideas expressed in styles, we must try to find a context in which to interpret those styles. Contextual archaeologists have developed a number of ways in which this might be accomplished. Perhaps the most meaningful way is to connect the styles with ethnographically or ethnohistorically recorded people. In this way we can either read about or ask someone what the styles mean. If there is no direct analog to the archaeological pattern, then we can turn to ethnographic analogy—that is, we can use evidence from a society that we think is similar to the one represented archaeologically as analogous information through which we can interpret the archaeological symbol. We might even study one or more such societies ourselves for archaeological clues to behaviors, thus performing ethnoarchaeology. Alternatively, we could construct or borrow an interpretive model with the assistance of cultural anthropologists. Based on known patterns of behavior among living groups, we can create a composite analog and use it to help interpret the archaeological data. Such research is akin to middle range research and, indeed, might even be defined as middle range research in some cases. Ultimately, however, we need to account for the temporal, spatial, and social distance between the people who made and used the styles and those of us who seek to understand them. In this sense, we are like the people at the edge of Wobst's communication system, too distant to directly interpret the meaning of what we see.

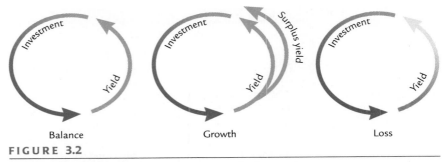

Balance   Growth   Loss

FIGURE 3.2

Leslie White's basic idea of energy capture and reinvestment.

resources. As long as people extract enough material from the natural environment to offset their expenditure of energy to acquire those resources, life continues. People, however, tend to be opportunistic and have complex cultures that enable them to extract resources far in excess of the energy they invest to acquire them. This surplus of resources can then be either spent or reinvested in the form of supporting larger, healthier families. As these families thrive and follow behaviors that yield surpluses, populations continue to rise. At some points, energy in excess of that needed to obtain resources can be spent on producing desirable but nonessential goods and services. As systems continue to increase their surplus energy and resources, increasingly complex sequences of energy investment develop, leading to craft specialization and class distinctions within the population (Figure 3.3). Ultimately, this system will continue to thrive or at least to exist as long as energy yields continue to be equal to or greater than energy expenditures. When this consistently fails to happen, the society retreats, cutting some investments and becoming less diverse and complex.

Cultural evolutionary theory leads to complex models for human behaviors. As archaeologists trace the ebb and flow of energy and resources within a society, they tend to discover the complex web of interactions common to all human populations. In past societies with large populations, as in present societies with large populations, these interconnections can be extraordinarily complex. Consequently, archaeologists often model behavioral systems—that is, general sets of human interactions such as food procurement, storage, craft specialization, management of civic infrastructures, and a host of other behaviors. Known as systems theory and championed by archaeologists (such as Colin Renfrew) who are renowned for their work on complex past civilizations, this approach is common in regions of the world in which humans built towns and cities. Besides its complexity, systems theory has limitations in that it cannot address the experience of the average person of the past nor can it escape the economic biases of those who employ it, whether Marxist or capitalist in orientation. Nonetheless, in the study of the rise and fall of the world's largest civilizations, there is little alternative other than to employ approaches common to systems theory (Box 3.5).

active style Expressions of meaning that are deliberately created and transmitted by an individual or group

passive style Expressions of meaning through stylistic displays that are the unintentional result of everyday activities

emblemic style Expressions of meaning through associations with a socially known emblem

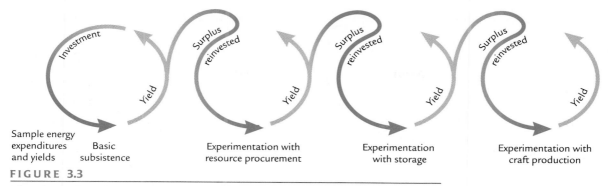

FIGURE 3.3

The relationship of excess energy yield to the elaboration of material culture according to Leslie White and his followers.

Archaeology as Natural Selection

A related perspective on archaeology and natural selection took shape over the last fifteen years of the twentieth century. A small number of archaeologists began to explore human behavior, in particular behavior as reflected by and deduced from material culture, in light of strict models of natural selection. This view holds that human societies are essentially complex organisms made up of individual cells. The behavior of the cells as a group and individually as they affect the group ultimately have ramifications in terms of the success of members of the group in surviving and reproducing their way of living. This logic filters down to the effectiveness, and hence survivorship, of individual artifact forms because these forms are used as part of behavior and are subject to success or failure.

Because archaeologists work from the material record of the past, though, evolutionary archaeology begins with the analysis of individual artifact forms and then continues to expand outward into other human behaviors. For example, if a specific shape, weight, and preparation of a projectile point make that tool more effective for hunting than other shapes, weights, and preparations, then the successful form will tend to dominate in the archaeological record. The assumption is that people adopted the form that worked best. However, factored into this notion of "best" must be the cost of producing the tool itself, as well as its longevity. Even highly efficient tools may be abandoned if they cause more disadvantages than they provide advantages.

It is difficult to assess the effectiveness of evolutionary archaeology and its limitations. Researchers are only now beginning to explore the ramifications of this approach and to explore its specific strengths and weaknesses. There appears to be a great deal to recommend this approach in terms of discovering past peoples' views of their own world. In many respects this approach is akin to Albert Spaulding's view of types, that they reflect real categories for past peoples that can be identified and explored through careful research. On

BOX 3.5

COLIN RENFREW AND CYCLADIC SYSTEMS THEORY

One of the best illustrations of systems theory at work is provided by Baron Sir Andrew Colin Renfrew, better known to archaeologists simply as Colin Renfrew. During the 1960s and 1970s, Renfrew published a series of influential pieces on the rise of civilization, the most famous of which is *Emergence of Civilization*. In it he combines a detailed understanding of the archaeology of the Cycladic Islands in the southern Aegean Sea, including data from his own work on Saliagos, with the comprehensive organizing schemes of systems theory.

The result was a model for the emergence of complex societies and civilization based on interconnected behaviors, especially maritime trade. This trade, along with the development of increasing craft specializa-

tion, religious movements, and the centralization of authority on a regional basis, combined to provide a sequence of communication that led to growth in all areas of the system. As trade expanded, specialists found increasingly larger markets for their goods. Rare and valuable commodities flowed into the trading centers of the Cyclades, allowing artisans, merchants, and would-be elite members of society to prosper. Likewise, food was abundant and easily transported by water, allowing people at all levels of the social scale not only to survive but also to thrive. Increasing prosperity in any one part of the system led to benefits in other parts of the system, although trade and the ability to move goods quickly and inexpensively by boat was at the heart of the system.

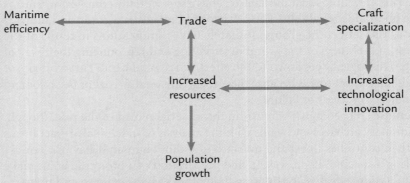

A simplified illustration of the relationships between maritime efficiency (the ability to move over open water), trade, and the emergence of civilization in the Cycladic Islands.

the other hand, cultural anthropology has consistently demonstrated that human culture is very flexible and adaptive. It also serves to insulate humans from natural selection by inventing and refining behaviors and technologies that benefit those who employ them. In seeking to identify such elements of culture, evolutionary archaeology shows promise. However, in seeking to apply natural selection to human culture, which in many ways insulates humans from the sorts of selective pressures common to other creatures, evolutionary archeology has yet to demonstrate conclusively that it has strong applicability and validity in archaeological research.

Contextual Archaeology

One of the approaches to understanding the past that owes its origins directly to postprocessual philosophies is contextual archaeology. This approach employs the notion that there is a recursive relationship between mental and physical aspects of human culture—that is, that these two elements of human culture are integrated into a continuous feedback loop. Nothing that is thought of lacks a physical expression in material culture, and nothing that is constructed in material culture lacks some measure of complementary thought and symbolism. For example, warfare is primarily a male occupation and, in the ancient world, tended to involve weapons such as the spear. Hence, social references to spears could also be references to warfare and/or to masculinity. This is precisely the sort of connection that we see between spears and many modern tribal populations throughout the world. The spear is a symbol of manhood and cannot be handled by women or children, regardless of the latter's sex. Only a man may carry a spear and only a man may engage in warfare, at least ideally.

The point here is that archaeologists excavate material culture and can attempt to put items in their symbolic contexts, hence the label *contextual archaeology.* In order to accomplish this, contextual archaeologists must have a framework or model for social behaviors into which to fit their interpretations of the connection between material culture and symbols. This model can be taken from ethnoarchaeological research, as Ian Hodder has sought to do in his research in Africa, or from anthropological models of behavior, as Christopher Miller, Hodder, and others have sought to do in their work on the Neolithic and Bronze Ages in northern Europe. Indeed, it is essentially this approach that Hodder is now employing in his extensive excavations at the Anatolian town of Çatalhöyük (Box 3.6).

The limitations of contextual archaeology center around the validity of the behavioral frameworks chosen to interpret the archaeological data. Processualists in particular have been quick to point out that there is not always a clear relationship between the frameworks chosen by contextual archaeologists and the societies that produced the material being excavated. Indeed, many have observed that there may be no connection at all between the model for contextualizing the archaeological data and the past as it actually was. Contextual archaeologists have typically acknowledged that this is true but then pointed out that archaeology, as they see it, is about discovering the different ways that people may have lived. Moreover, the contextualists argue, they take great pains to justify their selection of frameworks and in the process of explaining these models do more to justify their position than do many archaeologists who do not explicitly state their biases.

BOX 3.6

THEN AND NOW:
ÇATALHÖYÜK IN THE POSTPROCESSUAL ERA

Nestled in the highlands of Anatolia, just south of the midpoint between the Black and Mediterranean Seas, lies a substantial mound called Çatalhöyük (Catal meaning mound or hill, Hüyük being the place name). The mound that defines the site is no less than 15 meters tall, 500 meters long, and 150 meters wide, or 50 feet by 1550 feet by 500 feet. Between approximately 7000 and 5000 B.C. this was home to between five and ten thousand people who crowded into mud-brick homes similar in design to American pueblos, each standing two to three stories tall. Each home had a flat roof that allowed people to work atop their homes, as well as in courtyards outside their main entrances. The site has been called by some the first city in the world, though its size and population are dwarfed by the true cities that developed at about 3500 B.C. in Mesopotamia. Nonetheless, five to ten thousand people living in close proximity is rare at this early date; perhaps only a few substantial settlements in the Near East show similar numbers.

The site was originally explored by James Mellaart in the late 1950s and early 1960s. Mellaart and his Turkish-born wife Arlette spent four hurried and busy seasons at the site supervising a crew of more than fifty workers. At the time this work was conducted, most archaeologists were still working with cultural historical approaches and techniques that appear primitive by today's standards. At the time, though, they were standard practice. Mellaart had his workers explore as much of the site as they could using picks and shovels and typically did not screen any of the excavated **matrix.** Artifacts and ecofacts were picked directly out of the soil, many being missed. Amazingly, Mellaart and his team managed to recover a wide variety of materials, including evidence for wheat, barley, lentils, and peas. Obsidian tools dominated the lithic assemblage, leading the Mellaarts to speculate that the site's wealth was achieved through the long-distance trade of this material.

Most amazing of all, though, were the finds of substantial shrines. In approximately 20% of the two hundred or more buildings excavated, researchers came across brightly painted shrines featuring bull's horns, female breasts, and leopards. Each home was roughly the same size, about 300 square feet per level, based on a central chamber flanked by smaller storage rooms. The regularity of the houses and the appearance of shrines led to the interpretation that some central au-

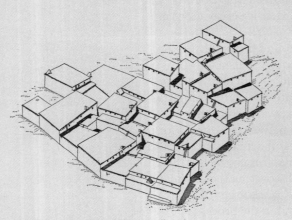

Level VII of Çatalhöyük from Mellaart's excavations.

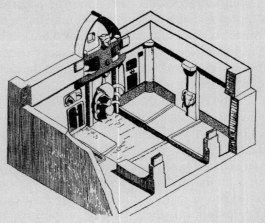

An artist's interpretation of a shrine from level VIB of Çatalhöyük.

thority existed at the site. This was bolstered by the discovery that deceased ancestors were buried under the floors of the houses, so that their powers and social achievements were never far away. Clearly, Mellaart thought, this was proof of a central authority and of a complex religion based on fertility, one that may have been the precursor of later Greek and Anatolian fertility cults based on the notion of a primordial goddess. In fact, Mellaart's interpretations have been adopted by many modern goddess cults, who view Çatalhöyük as a sort of Mecca for the worship of female deities. Yet, before Mellaart could further explore his thoughts, a series of events transpired that placed him in disfavor with the Turkish government. He was not permitted to continue his work at the site.

The early 1990s found Çatalhöyük at the forefront of a new major excavation effort. Ian Hodder of Cambridge University, who as a student had heard Mellaart lecture about the site, now heads a major interdisciplinary exploration of the site slated to last for nearly twenty-five years. Unlike Mellaart, though, Hodder has the advantage of thirty-five years of technological and methodological advances designed to tease out every possible bit of information from the site. Perhaps more significantly, Hodder is also a pioneer and strong advocate of postprocessual archaeology, especially in the form of contextual archaeology. For Hodder there is little in the way of a single past. Rather, there are multiple pasts that are connected to the present through the eyes and minds of those who study the past. Therefore, in order to understand the site as thoroughly as possible, Hodder is seeking to understand as many interpretations of the site as possible. Specialists in a host of approaches patrol the site, collecting carefully prepared samples of everything from soil, most of which is processed through flotation (see Chapter 4), to paleoethnobotanical remains. Hodder's team is proceeding with exemplary concern for interdisciplinary research and careful excavation methods. His team works slowly and meticulously. In six seasons they have uncovered three complete houses. Mellaart's team excavated 200 houses in four seasons. The difference in time and approach is largely due to modern understandings of the amazing amount of data that can be recovered if we have the resources to recover them. Needless to say, Hodder has extensive private backing for his project and nearly unlimited resources.

Yet Hodder's work is controversial in many respects. He has challenged Mellaart's interpretation of the

(continued)

Aerial view of the Çatalhöyük site.

BOX 3.6 (continued)

brightly colored paintings and relief work in many of the homes as shrines. Instead, Hodder sees them as elaborate expressions of personal ideas that are present in all of the homes. Hence, he argues, these remains do not indicate the presence of an organized religion or a religious hierarchy, merely of a common belief system that individual people expressed in different ways. Likewise, the presence of the dead beneath house floors is seen by Hodder as a representation of spirituality and respect among extended families and not as a statement of social power or family prestige. The organization of the town, too, Hodder sees as indicative of community and family interaction rather than something that could only be produced as a result of a governing agency.

Needless to say, Mellaart, now seventy-four years old, disagrees sharply with the new interpretations, and he is not alone. Though few people have questioned Hodder and his team's excavation work, his interpretations have been sharply questioned by some. Much of the debate centers around Hodder's perspective that there are multiple valid views of the past. Others focus on his use of personal experience and extreme postprocessual positions to contextualize his data. Hence, his interpretations, just like Mellaart's, are open to debate. Hodder, though, welcomes such debate. He notes that such a wide range of views adds to our overall knowledge about the site. Whether this broad range of perspectives is valid, however, remains a point at the heart of heated debate.

Cognitive Archaeology

Paralleling contextual archaeology in many respects is the field of cognitive archaeology, now championed by Sir Colin Renfrew, one of the most influential archaeologists of the twentieth century. Renfrew defines cognitive archaeology as the study of past ways of thinking and thought as inferred from the archaeological record. Though some theorists have seen this as essentially a postprocessual approach, Renfrew rejects this notion, arguing that this sort of research transcends the boundaries of the processual-postprocessual debate. In fact, for Renfrew, cognitive archaeology represents a synthesis of both viewpoints that seeks to apply the strengths of both philosophical traditions to interpreting past human behavior.

In order to do this, Renfrew has argued that cognitive archaeology must study the ways in which cognitive processes functioned in different social and environmental contexts. Ultimately, this will enable archaeologists to explore the connections between cognition, or how people thought about their world, and the natural and social environments that promoted the development of these thoughts. These may sound like lofty goals, but they are essentially the same as those laid out at the opening of this text, though they emphasize cognitive processes over other ways of exploring the past. For the most part, though, Renfrew and adherents to cognitive archaeology are asking questions about what life was like for past peoples and exploring different ways of discovering this. This is precisely the sort of approach employed by Robert Salzer at the Gottschall site (see the Original Essay, page 83).

matrix A general term applied to the sediments and other material, such as boulders, gravel, or stone, in which archaeological materials are found.

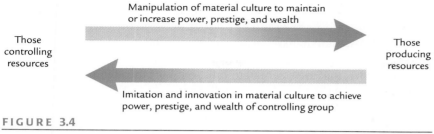

Manipulation of material culture to maintain
or increase power, prestige, and wealth

Those
controlling
resources

Those
producing
resources

Imitation and innovation in material culture to achieve
power, prestige, and wealth of controlling group

FIGURE 3.4

A simplified diagram of the fundamental assumption of Marxist archaeology.

Marxist Archaeology

Regardless of an individual's political opinions, there is little doubt that the writings of Karl Marx and Frederick Engels, especially *Das Kapital,* were among the most influential compositions of the nineteenth and, arguably, the twentieth centuries. The focal point for Marxist ideology is the tension between those people who produce economic capital, the proletariat, and those who control this production and profit most from it, the bourgeoisie. This tension can be described with the classic euphemisms "haves," "have nots," and "the struggle for economic control." In essence, those who work to produce capital always seek to attain greater amounts of their products or more rewards for their products, whereas those who control these resources seek to retain this material for their own use. This is a never-ending struggle, as those who produce material typically overthrow those who control wealth only to establish themselves as the new controllers. This is Marx's and Engel's point of departure for arguing for a communist state.

Archaeologists often make use of the dichotomous relationship between the producers and controllers as a model for explaining past social and economic dynamics. As Marx himself did, Marxist archaeologists argue that this is human nature and that all people in all times tend to adhere to this dialectical relationship. As a consequence, it is possible to explore the organization of past societies by tracing the distribution of material culture throughout a society. Rare material items, or those materials that tended to reinforce social status, are particularly good items to trace through a society because these items are likely to have been used to establish class and social boundaries (Figure 3.4).

The limitations of this approach center on the assumptions made about the nature of human interrelations. Marxist archaeologists assume that people have, in fact, always tended to acquire control of important resources. Moreover, these people then always tended to manipulate these resources to maintain or increase their own social and economic positions. Such assumptions do seem to operate in some instances but not in others. Marxist theory is particularly weak in working with small groups of humans in ecologically rich environments. In such circumstances there seems little chance of any individual or group gaining control of enough essential resources to establish significant differences in wealth or prestige between themselves and others. Some Marxists, though, have recognized this problem and have been exploring the control of perceived essential resources, such as access to spirit beliefs and group lore, that are essential to most humans throughout history. Such efforts have met with mixed results thus far.

Feminist and Gender Archaeology

Another approach often linked to postprocessualism is feminist archaeology. This branch of archaeology seeks to explore the past as it relates to and was experienced by women. Archaeology developed in an age dominated by men who thought principally about the role of men in the past. This is unfortunate because it clearly fails to address the contributions and experiences of approximately half of the people who ever lived. More than being an afterthought or an apologist movement, feminist archaeology is a dynamic approach that is making real contributions to our understanding of the past world. It is also a movement that has usefully pointed out and, hopefully, deflated some unfortunate representations of past human life.

For example, Allison Wylie, among others, has studied the ways in which women are portrayed in archaeological reports and textbooks. In more than 95% of the illustrations that actually depicted women (most depicted only men), they were shown performing domestic tasks such as cooking and feeding children. Moreover, in many of these illustrations women are shown performing hard physical labor alone or only in the company of their children, something that is not at all accurate. Most living societies, for example, organize themselves so that women work together, sharing stories and assisting each other. Likewise, numerous illustrations showed women working on their hands and knees in front of men or in other positions that our culture considers subservient. Significantly, many of the tasks that women are shown performing on their hands and knees were rarely, if ever, performed in such positions. Hide scraping, for example, was typically done by women in Plains Indian cultures, but it was done with the hide firmly attached to a wooden rack, thus keeping the hide clear of the ground and making the entire surface accessible. The point to all of this is that women are often underrepresented and misrepresented in the archaeological literature, which has the effect of notably distorting any claim to objectivity in exploring or discussing the past.

Archaeology has also progressed in terms of accomplishing field and research projects utilizing, at least in part, a feminist perspective. This began with the research interests of modern archaeologists, a significant number of whom are now interested in understanding how women lived in the past. These interests are being translated into specific research questions and thus are being incorporated in research designs. Yet there are problems in implementing such approaches. First, artifacts are typically gender neutral, and there are few clear ways to distinguish between materials used and made by men and those used and made by women. Moreover, even in cases in which archaeologists are able to deduce likely connections, the distribution of such materials rarely provides any clearly discernible patterns related to the activities of either males or females. As a consequence, distinguishing male activities from female activities in the archaeological record, except in the cases in which skeletal remains are present, is problematic. This difficulty has served to limit the field applications of feminist and gender-based archaeology, though, as with all problems, clever innovations yet to be developed may obviate this shortcoming.

SUMMARY

Archaeology is the study of the material remains of the human past. It, like all pursuits of knowledge, must be viewed in the context of the people and societies that undertake such studies. As a consequence, it is doubtful if archaeologists in any time or any place will make interpretations about past human behaviors that are completely free of their own biases. The degree to which this is true sets the stage for strong philosophical debates between those who believe that a great measure of objectivity can be achieved and those who believe that significantly less objectivity can be achieved. In many respects this debate is at the heart of the processual-postprocessual debate.

Regardless of the philosophical positions that archaeologists adopt, all such scholars agree that it is important to undertake methodologically sound explorations of the past and to explain as fully as possible what we believe past peoples were doing and why we think that this is so. The specific research interests of individual archaeologists, however, will ultimately factor into what specific sorts of theoretical approaches and paradigms will be adopted on any given project. Indeed, even within the same project, different archaeologists might interpret the same data in different lights. Rather than a weakness, this diversity should be incorporated as a strength. The interdisciplinary and intertheoretical insights that can be gained through such diversity can help archaeologists develop a more complete perspective on past human activities than can otherwise be achieved through a single theoretical approach.

Conflict will nonetheless continue to occur as adherents of one theoretical approach to the study of the past debate their positions with adherents of other approaches. Likewise, disagreement will continue to exist on the specific interpretations archaeologists make about the past and about human activities. So long as they are confined within the structure of academic discourse, such disagreements are healthy examples of a vibrant and developing field. It is only when they become personal, or ad hominem, that academic discourse breaks down and personal, political, and even career agendas begin to dominate a field. Thus far, much of the debate between adherents of the various theoretical positions discussed here, and countless other positions, has been of a healthy variety. Consequently, diversity should be seen not as chaos but as strength and growth.

FOR FURTHER INFORMATION

Binford, L. R. 1967. Smudge pits and hide smoking: The use of analogy in archaeological reasoning. *American Antiquity* 32: 1–12.

———. 1981. Behavioral archaeology and the "Pompeii premise." *Journal of Anthropological Research* 37: 195–208.

———. 1983. *Working at archaeology.* New York: Academic Press.

———. 1989. *Debating archaeology.* San Diego: Academic Press.

———, ed. 1977. *For theory building in archaeology.* New York: Academic Press.

Beaudry, M. C., ed. 1989. *Documentary archaeology in the New World.* Cambridge: Cambridge University Press.

Butzer, K. W. 1982. *Archaeology as human ecology: Method and theory for a contextual approach.* New York: Cambridge University Press.

Claasen, C. P. 1991. Gender, shellfishing, and the Shell Mound archaic. In *Engendering archaeology: Women and prehistory,* edited by J. M. Gero and M. W. Conkey, 276–300. Oxford: Basil Blackwell.

Clarke, D. L. 1968. *Analytical archaeology.* London: Methuen.

Gero, J. M., and M. W. Conkey, eds. 1991. *Engendering archaeology: Women and prehistory.* Oxford: Basil Blackwell.

Early, T. K., and R. W. Preucel. 1987. Processual archaeology and the radical critique. *Current Anthropology* 28: 501–38.

Hodder, I., ed. 1989. *The meaning of things: Material cultural and symbolic expression.* London: Unwin Hyman.

Preucel, R. W., ed. 1991. *Processual and postprocessual archaeologies: Multiple ways of knowing the past.* Occasional Paper 16. Carbondale: Southern Illinois University, Center for Archaeological Investigations.

Schiffer, M. B. 1976. *Behavioral archaeology.* New York: Academic Press.

Shanks, M., and C. Tilley. 1992. *Re-constructing archaeology,* 2d ed. London: Routledge.

Walker, W. 2000. Behavioral archaeology. In *Archaeological method and theory: An encyclopedia,* edited by L. Ellis, 69–73. New York: Garland.

ORIGINAL ESSAY

THE GOTTSCHALL SITE

Robert J. Salzer

Robert J. Salzer (Ph.D., Southern Illinois University) is Professor of Anthropology at Beloit College. He has dedicated his career to understanding Wisconsin archaeology.

The Gottschall Site (47 Ia 80) is a small sandstone cave that is hidden in the upper reaches of a small creek in rural southwestern Wisconsin. In 1974, a local farm boy discovered more than 40 paintings, or *pictographs,* on the wall of the cave. Although ravaged by erosion, faded by the passage of time, and obscured by growths of lichen, the artwork depicts a variety of animal and human figures.

When I learned about the find, my mind was filled with questions about who the artists were and when the artwork was done, so I began developing a strategy to try to find answers to these and many other questions. My very first priority, however, was to preserve the paintings by recording them photographically. We first used color film, but the images were so faded that we could not figure out details in the renderings. With the help of colleagues, we next tried to enhance the images by using color infrared film (Figure 1). Professor James Scherz (University of Wisconsin, Department of Civil and Environmental Engineering) had an idea that we might get better enhancement if we illuminated the wall with ultraviolet light to make the minerals fluoresce and recorded the result on color infrared film. The results were impressive, and, based on these enhancements, it was possible to make black-and-white tracings (Figure 2). As we shall presently see, the effort to preserve the paintings was certainly worthwhile.

Other paintings were similarly enhanced (Figure 3). When recorded on color infrared film, the "Bison Panel" became much clearer, and accurate tracings were made (Figure 4). Another group of images was particularly interesting, and, for reasons that will soon become clear, we called these figures the "Red Horn Panel." Close inspection of this panel revealed that the surface of the cave wall had been sanded down before the delicate fine-lined fig-

FIGURE 1

Color infrared image of the "Pipesmoker." (Photo by James Scherz and James Valiga)

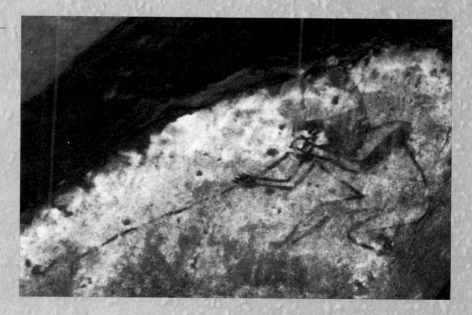

FIGURE 2

The "Pipesmoker" figure. (Tracing by
Mary Steinhauer)

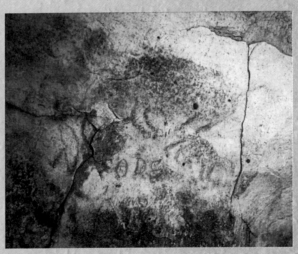

FIGURE 3

The "Bison Panel" in natural color. (Photo by Brian Molyneaux)

FIGURE 4

The "Bison Panel." (Tracing by Mary Steinhauer)

ures were painted. This is interpreted to mean that the
animals and humans in this group were done at the same
time, so they are parts of a composition (Figure 5).

Who did the artwork? What do the images mean?
When and why were they done? These anthropological
questions remained to be answered. They are part of our
efforts to understand human behavior. In this case, the
apparent antiquity of the paintings suggested that arch-

aeology, with all its growing sophistication, would provide ways to answer these issues. As it turned out, however, it would be archaeology, working with ethnographic
information, that would seemingly provide some of our
answers.

Around 1900, anthropologist Paul Radin helped elders
of the Native American people we now call the Ho-Chunk
(formerly called the *Winnebago* by anthropologists and

FIGURE 5

The "Red Horn Panel."
(Tracing by Mary Steinhauer)

others; but, in their language, they call themselves the *Hochungara*) record large volumes of information about their traditions. The elders feared that their old ways would be lost as their culture changed rapidly under the influence of acculturation to the white man's world. Among these oral traditions were many legends of events that happened in former times, and among these was one story that attracted our attention: the "Legend of Red Horn." Actually, another colleague, Professor Robert L. Hall, urged that we carefully read this legend because he thought that the figures described in the legend were the same as those depicted in the "Red Horn Composition."

The legend about Red Horn is a saga of heroic proportions, and it is lengthy. Important excerpts describe the hero, whose name was "*He-who-has-deer-lungs-thrown-at-him.*" He was the youngest of ten brothers, and he won a foot race when he was very young. At that point, he announced that, henceforth, people should call him "Red Horn." He also made the point that the spirits would know that he was also "*He-who-wears-human-heads-as-earrings.*" This is the name of one of the primordial deities who was created by Earthmaker when he caused the world to come into being.

Red Horn became an important leader of his people. One day, people from a nearby village came to Red Horn and told him that they had been attacked by a mysterious race of giants who killed many people and sacked their village. Through an intermediary, Red Horn contacted the giants and arranged to play a game of lacrosse to resolve their differences, and the giants agreed. The stakes were to be high; the losers would be killed. On the day of the game, Red Horn was accompanied by his friends, including Turtle and Storms-as-he-walks. The latter was actually a Thunderbird who had come down from the Upperworld to live on earth as a mortal. The opposing team was led by a giant chieftainess who had red hair. She caught the ball in her racquet and ran into the woods, followed by Red Horn. They immediately fell in love and she betrayed her people so that Red Horn's team won the game and all of the giants were killed (except the woman, who became Red Horn's wife).

The legend goes on to describe subsequent events in Red Horn's life, but we have enough information to recognize what Hall was so excited about. The two human figures on the left in the Red Horn composition (see Figure 5) are larger than the one on the right. They would be the giants, and the human on the right would be Red Horn, whose image is rendered in greater detail than the rest. We cannot see if Red Horn is wearing human heads as earrings because that area of his head has been overpainted. Close examination of one of the giants reveals that it has a swirl of red paint behind its head, suggesting that this might be the red-haired giantess. Above the giants is a figure that certainly looks like a turtle. Between the giants and Red Horn is a falcon-like bird that has a crest. It is said that Thunderbirds can be distinguished from

FIGURE 6

An excavated profile of the stratified deposits in the cave. The scale is 30 cm long, and the horizontal dimensions of the exposure are nearly 2 m. The upper ("gray") sediments are deposits that have washed down into the cave from erosion of the farmer's field on the blufftop above. (Photo by the author)

FIGURE 7

Collecting Kubiena samples in stainless steel boxes. (Photo by the author)

falcons because they always tie cedar boughs to their heads, which means that this figure could be Storms-as-he-walks. It certainly seems that Hall's interpretations deserve our attention.

The ethnographic data cannot be used uncritically, but, in this case, the match between the characters and the plot of the legend with the figures painted on the wall of the cave are surely compelling, if not totally convincing. What can archaeology do to help solve this matter?

Excavations at the cave began in 1984 and are still continuing. In our initial test excavations we discovered that the floor deposits in the cave are deep, clearly stratified (Figure 6), and contain abundant and well-preserved artifactual remains. These ideal conditions might permit us to find out when the paintings were done and, based on the artifacts associated, might inform us about who the artists were.

Because there was good reason to believe that the various layers were laid down by water that had flooded the cave, I sought the help of another colleague, a geoarchaeologist and one of my former students, William Gartner, who analyzed the sediments for his master's thesis in the Department of Geography at the University of Wisconsin at Madison. Gartner was to tell us what he could learn about how the sediments were laid down. He would also use those data to help us understand what the local and regional environment was like when people were in the cave. To do this, he would collect bags of the stuff, as well as *Kubiena* samples—blocks of dirt—that could be processed to become hard "bricks" that can be cut in thin slices to be analyzed microscopically (Figure 7). Neither he nor I was prepared for his discovery that a substantial portion of the sediments in the cave was actually made by humans; like many discoveries, this one was made by accident. Standard procedures for analyzing samples of sediments involve testing for carbonate content by introducing a known amount of hydrochloric acid to a given amount of the dirt sample and measuring the amount of carbon dioxide generated. When he first tested the man-made dirts, the reaction of the acid and the dirt was, literally, explosive—the entire testing apparatus blew up.

The violent reaction occurred because these unusual sediments were made with a high proportion of calcium carbonate. Microscopic study of the Kubiena samples indicated that the ingredients used were mostly ashes from burning coniferous trees and grasses. Another important ingredient was "cooked" and powdered limestone. Smaller proportions of unburned crushed and ground clamshell and bone were also mixed in. The nearest outcrop of limestone is 2 miles from the sandstone cave; the source of the clams is the Wisconsin River, 8 miles away. Proof that these fabricated sediments were made in the cave came from the discovery in our excavations of a

FIGURE 8

A section through the earthen oven (Feature 85), showing the limestone slabs. (Photo by the author)

FIGURE 9

View of the excavations. The paintings are on the wall in the background. (Photo by the author)

large earthen oven that still had slabs of "cooked" limestone in its bottom (Figure 8). There is no report of such man-made dirts, so we are calling these special kinds of artifacts *anthroseds*. Why anyone would make a dirt is problematic, but they seem likely to have served some ritual purpose. Support for this interpretation comes from the observation that some fireplaces, some piles of bone, some postholes, some unusual piles of dirt, and even the earth oven itself were capped by anthroseds, whereas others were not.

Excavations of both the anthroseds and the natural sediments inside the cave are made easier by the fact that both sediments are perpetually moist. Procedures used at this site involve removing each of the many layers of sediments in 2-cm levels (or until a new layer is encountered), leaving all objects encountered in place (Figure 9). After exposing these items, the unit is photographed in color and black and white and mapped, with each item assigned a field catalog number and put into its own individual specimen bag. This procedure, called *proveniencing* or *piece plotting*, allows for analysis of spatial relationships between items, as well as the quantitative and qualitative analyses of the objects themselves.

This is slow, tedious work, but this care and precision has been rewarded many times. Excavations underneath the Red Horn composition involved removal of sediments that began washing into the cave after the field above it was plowed in 1870. Beneath this cap is a relatively thin series of prehistoric natural sediments. The lowest of these contained a series of irregularly shaped small burnings that we called "Feature 29." The light from these fires would have illuminated the Red Horn composition (it is dark in the cave), and they are interpreted as reflecting multiple episodes of viewing the paintings. A few centimeters below, in the uppermost portion of the anthrosed layers, we found a thin layer of sanding debris (from the wall sanded prior to painting the Red Horn group) and a paint spill that matches the blue-gray color of the paintings. The paint spill is about the size of a half-dollar and is a mere 1.5 cm thick. With minor reservations, I take this to mean that we have found the residues of the Red Horn paintings and that they are associated with the anthroseds. Charcoal from Feature 29 was submitted for radiocarbon dating using the accelerator mass spectrometry technique. Without being calibrated, the assay yielded a date of A.D. 860±75. Another fireplace, Feature 1, was found in the layer immediately above, and it produced two "standard" assays of A.D. 880±70 and 980±70. These assays are, of course, of the same date, because they all overlap at one standard deviation. A good estimate, then, for the fires that were used to view the Red Horn composition is about A.D. 900–950. The more deeply buried sanding debris and paint spill should be earlier, albeit not much earlier. This is, of course, the proper sequence of events: first the sanding and the painting, then the viewing. Further, at least the activities associated with doing the artwork are associated with the (end of) ritual behavior in the cave, because the evidence for them was found in anthroseds.

If all of these hard data and interpretations are correct, the implications are worth exploring. They imply that at least some of the ideological ancestors of the modern Ho-Chunk people were in the cave, painting the images of the Red Horn legend, more than 1,000 years ago. The data also lend support to the idea that at least some oral traditions can be handed down by word of mouth for at least that long a period of time. Further, the data clearly indicate that much can be learned about the past in North America if we combine ethnographic and archaeological information.

Lying near the paint spill and the sanding debris were fragments of a pottery vessel of the type (Madison Cord Impressed) that archaeologists in the Wisconsin area usually regard as the ceramics used by the people who built low mounds in the form of animal and even human effigies. These have been dated to the range of approximately A.D. 750–1250, and, based on such cross-dating, the assays from the cave and the pottery associated with the anthroseds and the paintings are in agreement, lending further support to the credibility of the dates for the Red Horn composition. All of this lends strong support to the claim that the Ho-Chunk have made repeatedly over the past 100 years: that the spirits made their ancestors build the effigy mounds. Archaeologists have been unable to confirm their claim because the building of the effigies (and the associated distinctive type of pottery) did not continue into modern times, even though the Ho-Chunk surely did. Resolving these (and other) examples of discrepancies between the ethnographic and archaeological data is a major problem that anthropologists will have to address thoughtfully in the years to come.

Further, and particularly spectacular, support for a Ho-Chunk presence was found in our excavations. While removing the uppermost natural sediments near the back wall of the cave, we recovered a carved and painted human head sculpted out of the local sandstone. It is about 26 cm high and was painted with vertical blue-gray lines, with a dotted circle painted on the chin. The inside of the mouth was painted with orange-red pigment. The colors, the style of painting, and the elongated nature of the head and the torsos on the figures on the wall are rather similar (Figure 10). Early last century the elders told Radin that the Ho-Chunk sometimes paint the mouths of the deceased with red color to show their ancestors in the after-

FIGURE 10

The carved and painted sandstone head from the cave. The head on the right is that of the author, included for scale. (Photo by Chuck Savage)

world how happy they are to join them. A modern Ho-Chunk visitor to the cave commented that the Bear clan still paints a circle on the chin of the dead person prior to burial. Further, the head was found in association with a pile of debris that includes animal bones and fragments of a broken pottery vessel. The pot is quite similar to those made by the builders of the effigy mounds, that is, the ancestors of the modern Ho-Chunk. These data imply not only that the head is related to these people's ancestors but also that the head is in some way related to mortuary behavior, perhaps a portrait of a revered person who had recently died. We have radiocarbon assays from the stratum immediately above (A.D. 1060±70) and in (A.D. 1010±70) the stratum in which the head and the associated debris were found, indicating a date for the head of about A.D. 1000–1050.

Although the analyses of the animal bones from the cave are still in progress, thanks to Professor James Theler, we have information on the bone found with the head. It consists of the remains of five or six young deer and one dog. Based on the eruption of the molars of the deer, they were killed in the late fall or early winter (November–December). Further, the particular bones represented are the marrow-rich bones—the best and most nutritious

FIGURE 11

The "rolls" found in the bottom of a small pit at Gottschall. (Photo by the author)

cuts. According to Radin, the most important ceremony of the Ho-Chunk was the Winter Feast, for which a number of deer were killed to provide the food. A dog that had been raised for this specific purpose was ritually strangled for the feast. In the ceremony, individual people represented the major deities. In one version of the ritual, only the person representing the deity "Disease-giver" was allowed to eat the dog, and this person was also given the best cuts of the deer. Although most Native Americans celebrated their important rituals in the winter and although many rituals involved eating a dog, these data do no damage to the idea that the ideological ancestors of the modern Ho-Chunk were present in the cave.

During the 1998 field season, we excavated a small pit (Feature 162) that we assumed had been used to bury garbage. There was, however, very little that could be called refuse. In the bottom—reflecting perhaps why the pit was dug—we found a series of tightly rolled objects. They were originally made of some sort of fabric, such as animal hide, that had been covered on one side by a layer of lime that appeared white or light gray. These rolls had been carefully placed in the pit (Figure 11). In the Ho-Chunk Winter Feast, the hides of the deer killed were given to postmenarcheal women to be processed and made to be as white as possible. The host of the feast painted sym-

bols on each hide that represented the deity it would be offered to. After the feast the hides, having served their purpose, were disposed of. The rolls at the Gottschall site were removed from the ground intact and remain unexcavated. We hope that future technology will be suited to the task of viewing any symbols that might once have been painted on them.

The Gottschall site data illustrate just one of the many special insights rock art can have on our understanding of the events of the past that we archaeologists study. I also want to emphasize that archaeological research is a cooperative and collaborative enterprise—no one scientist can be an expert in all the fields that are brought to bear on gaining understanding of the past. The kind of archaeology that I do is firmly built on the theoretical foundations of the field of anthropology; not all archaeologists are anthropologists. It is a kind of research that attempts to integrate both archaeological and ethnographic information.

Most important, I want to use the data and interpretations resulting from our research to bring attention to an obvious fact—one that is, unfortunately, sometimes forgotten. The archaeological record that we dig up represents the by-products of the trials, tribulations, beliefs, fears, creativity, and ideas of those sometimes forgotten

FIGURE 12

The damage done to the figure of Red Horn. (Photo taken by the author)

but real people who left a record of their having lived on this planet. Ancient peoples throughout the world have given this modern world their descendants—their progeny, who are proud of the heritage that was left for them. For all our sakes, we must protect and learn from the legacy of our ancestors. It is a primary responsibility of archaeologists to conserve and preserve the treasures that lie buried in the ground.

There is a postscript to this essay that serves to emphasize what I mean in a most distasteful way. In April 1993, one or two people visited the Gottschall cave and, using a masonry saw, tried to remove the painted figure of Red Horn from the wall. They did not succeed (Figure 12). At the beginning of this essay, I indicated how fortunate it was that we worked so hard to protect the fabulous paintings in the cave by recording them photographically as our very first order of business. The damage that was done to the paintings mars their beauty, but the paintings and the information they contain survive. It is a profoundly important fact that the future of the past lies with all of us, here in the present.

The work in the cave goes on, regardless of the damage, but it continues with a heightened sense of responsibility to care for the past. Who knows what we will find next summer?

4

FINDING THE PAST

One of the most common questions asked of archaeologists is how we know where to find sites. To many it appears as though archaeologists have some mysterious ability to spot places on the landscape at which past peoples left material remains. In fact, there is something to an archaeologist's ability to "read" the landscape, but this is hardly an arcane ability. Instead, it is a combination of hard work, experience, scholarship, and familiarity with basic human needs.

In this chapter we explore the different ways in which archaeologists combine these variables in order to find the past. This process of searching for sites is known by a variety of names throughout the world. The most common terms used to label this process are **reconnaissance** or **site survey.** In the world of cultural resource management (CRM), this is typically referred to as **phase I** research, meaning it is the first type of research that must be undertaken in the assessment of archaeological resources. As will be explained, though, archaeologists often begin their research in the library and with predictive models. They physically undertake a search for sites across the landscape only if it is called for by their research design and only when they have acquired a basic understanding of the geology and the ecology of the search area. Once the decision to begin a search is made, archaeologists have a myriad of tools and techniques at their disposal (Figure 4.1). In large part, the size of the search area and the

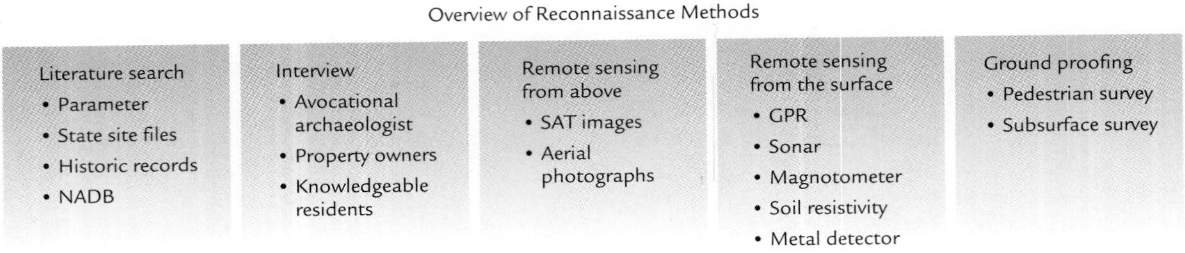

Overview of Reconnaissance Methods

Literature search	Interview	Remote sensing from above	Remote sensing from the surface	Ground proofing
• Parameter • State site files • Historic records • NADB	• Avocational archaeologist • Property owners • Knowledgeable residents	• SAT images • Aerial photographs	• GPR • Sonar • Magnotometer • Soil resistivity • Metal detector	• Pedestrian survey • Subsurface survey

FIGURE 4.1

Overview of reconnaissance methods.

likely placement of sites in the earth in that area will limit the range of approaches that can be applied.

RECONNAISSANCE PRECEDING FIELDWORK
Literature Search

reconnaissance (or site survey) The systematic search for archaeological sites and remains.

phase I The initial stage in cultural resource management research, assessing the likely presence of cultural resources within a defined area.

National Archaeological Database (NADB) Contains references to archaeological reports from across the country and is particularly useful when searching for cultural resource management reports.

documentary archaeology The use of documentary sources to generate or enhance perspectives on the past, even in the absence of known archaeological materials.

The first place an archaeologist tends to look when searching for sites is in the library or in a specialized database of site locations maintained by a state government or by a government agency such as the Army Corps of Engineers or the National Park Service. In Europe such records are often held by comparable government agencies and public trusts designed to protect archaeological resources. The best known and arguably the largest data set in the United States is the **National Archaeological Database (NADB),** which is accessible via the Internet. The NADB contains references to archaeological reports from across the country and is particularly useful when an archaeologist begins searching for extant research reports in any area that he or she is interested in. By accessing such a database, the archaeologist learns the titles and appropriate publication information for work germane to the project to be undertaken.

Other important written resources include firsthand accounts of cultural resources in a given area. In many cases in which literate explorers encountered other peoples or their material remains, a written record exists that provides direct information about what might be present and where such things might be found. Sometimes referred to as **documentary archaeology** by some, such information can be collated and examined in order to explore cultural resources through written records. Although this is not a substitute for fieldwork, this sort of research is an important extension of archaeological research. Having such firsthand accounts of the past helps to add depth and texture to the archaeological research.

For smaller projects, though, it is often more efficient to turn to the archaeological records kept by each state in the United States and by each province in Canada, as well as by comparable geopolitical units in other nations. In the United States such records are kept by the *state archaeologist* and by the **state historic preservation officer (SHPO)**. The records contain summaries of locations of known sites, what sorts of material culture are known to exist on these sites, and, usually, references to who first recorded the site, as well as to any additional research that has been done there. Such records are closely guarded by states, however, because potential looters are keenly interested in knowing where sites are. Likewise, it is the goal of all state archaeologists and their colleagues to protect the past, and this sometimes means limiting the number of people who know the locations of sites. The assumption is that the fewer people who know about the location of a site, the less likely it is that large numbers of people will visit the site. In turn, this will help ensure the site's preservation.

Yet another useful form of background research and survey is **oral history.** Although this is sometimes surprising to some students, archaeologists often learn about the presence and even the nature of archaeological sites by talking to people who regularly work on the land in the survey area. Farmers, for example, typically have an outstanding knowledge of archaeological resources on their properties, and many have been collecting small samples of the material from these sites over the generations. Such collection has recently been made illegal in some parts of the world, including Canada, in an effort to prevent the loss of cultural resources through such intermittent collecting. Such laws, however, are hard to enforce and have had the negative effect of making people such as farmers less willing to share information with archaeologists. Hence, though this sort of law is well intentioned, the benefits of the law must be carefully weighed against the harm it might do.

A range of other resources and strategies exist for identifying sites based on existing data. In many cases a thorough literature search will unveil a great deal of pertinent data. Such searches must include books, special publications of site reports (sometimes called site monographs), and, most especially, a thorough search of the technical **journals** specific to archaeology. Journals typically publish four or more issues per year and contain scholarly discussions of sites, research projects, methods, and theoretical issues related to the discipline of archaeology. Many students tend to overlook journals when undertaking research for classes at many colleges and universities, but most of their instructors can illuminate them on the advantages of using journal articles. First, journal articles are highly specific and therefore allow students to find precisely the sort of information that they need. Second, journal articles are typically more timely than are books, which often take years to prepare and publish. Third, it is often easier and more efficient for students to read a 40-page journal article than it is to identify a comparable number of useful pages in a 400-page book. Fourth, journals serve to introduce students to current issues, presentation styles, and researchers according to the topical categories covered by the journal (Table 4.1).

state historic preservation officer (SHPO) The person charged with reviewing archaeological reports and helping to mitigate potential damage to archaeological sites as a result of approved development.

oral history Traditions and tales passed from generation to generation by word of mouth.

journal A serialized scholarly publication, such as *Antiquity, American Antiquity,* and the *Journal of Field Archaeology.*

TABLE 4.1   Archaeological Journals

Journal	Coverage	Web Address
American Anthropologist	Multidisciplinary flagship journal of the American Anthropological Association	http://www.ameranthassn.org/
American Antiquity	Flagship journal of the Society for American Archaeology; coverage specializes in North America	http://www.saa.org/Publications/
Ancient Mesoamerica	Coverage includes topics related to Maya, Aztec, Olmec, and other Mesoamerican archaeological cultures	http://uk.cambridge.org/journals/atm/
Antiquity	Premier journal of European archaeology; publishes articles from throughout the world	http://intarch.ac.uk/antiquity/
Archaeology Magazine	Popular magazine covering archaeology from throughout the world in a readable, colorful way	http://www.archaeological.org/
Current Archaeology	England's premier popular archaeology magazine, focuses on U.K.-related archaeology.	http://www.archaeology.co.uk/cahome.htm
Current Anthropology	A professional multidisciplinary journal that publishes archaeological discussions	http://www.journals.uchicago.edu/CA/
Discovering Archaeology	A relatively new popular magazine covering archaeology from across the world	http://www.discoveringarchaeology.com/
Environmental Archaeology	A professional journal	http://www.shef.ac.uk/uni/academic/A_C/ap/envarch/
European Journal of Archaeology	A relatively new electronic journal with professional articles from Europe	http://library.usask.ca/ejournals/14/6/1461_9571.html
Heritage Archaeology Journal	A publication dedicated to the Pacific Rim	http://www.heritagearchaeology.com.au/
Historical Archaeology	The flagship journal of the Society for Historical Archaeology	http://www.sha.org/
Journal of Field Archaeology	A professional journal dedicated to discussing field methods and issues	http://jfa_www.bu.edu/
KMT: Journal of Ancient Egypt	An accessible journal dealing with ancient Egypt	http://www.egyptology.com/kmt/
Latin American Antiquity	Coverage includes all archaeological issues pertaining to Mesoamerica	http://www.saa.org/Publications/

Remote Sensing

In addition to written resources, archaeologists have the ability to use high technology to find archaeological sites. Satellite images, aerial photographs, sonar, and data from airborne radar units can all provide archaeologists with valuable data about where sites might be found, in addition to providing images of the sites themselves. Other forms of technological probes are specifically designed to be used in the field. Ground penetrating radar, magnetometers, metal detectors, and a variety of similar devices provide small-scale data based on their use on archaeological sites. Such field testing is discussed subsequently, but I introduce the basic group of tools here because all of these things are examples of **remote sensing.** This is a technology-driven branch of **archaeological reconnaissance** that seeks to identify and display physical anomalies that may reflect the remains of past human activity. Hence, remote sensing does not directly detect artifacts or features; it detects differences in a range of physical traits in or on the earth that have the potential to be related to human activity. Examples of such things include anomalies in the local readings of the earth's magnetic field brought about by the presence of stone that contains metals, such as a wall, or changes in the density and reflectivity of soils that might suggest pits, burials, or buried structures.

All of these resources require archaeologists to acquire specialized information, something that has been difficult in the past. Recent advances in electronic communication and electronic commerce, though, have enabled most archaeologists to find and often acquire regional survey information from their own desktop computers. For example, the **United States Geologic Survey (USGS)** has digitized maps of most of the United States. Along with the spatial and geophysical data presented in such maps, basic architectural information is also presented about the presence or absence of buildings. Thus archaeologists can identify standing structures in their research areas, an important piece of information for researchers working with historic-era sites. Similarly, earthen structures dating to earlier time periods, such as mounds, as well as known historic monuments, are also recorded on these maps. Maps, however, are limited in the sense that they contain only information that is already known. Thus archaeologists are unlikely to find new sites by examining any sort of map, though they may be able to identify areas that are likely to contain unknown sites.

Satellite images and aerial photographs, on the other hand, are accurate representations of things that are present on the earth. Both photographic and satellite data can be used to visually survey large areas of land for evidence of archaeological remains (Figure 4.2). Large remains, such as buildings, mounds, or substantial surface scatters of material culture, can be accurately identified and mapped, though buried deposits and smaller objects remain essentially invisible to such visual surveys (Figure 4.3).

Additional techniques have been developed that can help to enhance what archaeologists can identify through such mechanisms. For aerial photographs, one of the most useful methods of enhancing data is to use shadows and naturally occurring phenomena to better locate archaeological deposits. In the former case, photographs of the same area are taken at dawn, noon, and dusk. The highest elevation photos, those taken at noon, reveal the greatest number of directly visible features in the frame, though these features are difficult to interpret because this sort of photograph provides the least sense of depth and texture. If archaeologists first examine this range of photos and then either compare or overlay images from the early morning and evening photographs, when the sun strikes the survey area at the most radical angles, then

remote sensing The application of technology to identify cultural resources without having to ground proof or otherwise excavate.

archaeological reconnaissance The process of searching for archaeological sites.

United States Geologic Survey (USGS) The government agency charged with the recording and dissemination of information related to the geology of the United States and its holdings.

FIGURE 4.2a

At Rio Azule, Guatemala, excavators check for potentially fragile remains with a fiber-optic video system before beginning to excavate. This allows the archaeologists to select excavation methods designed to protect the fragile remains.

FIGURE 4.2b

Infrared satellite image of the Poverty Point site on the Bayou Macon, Louisiana. The site dates to approximately 1600 B.C. and features a central plaza surrounded by 150-foot-wide embankments of earth, which appear red on the image because of their different heat properties.

FIGURE 4.3

The Great Bear effigy mound group at Effigy Mounds National Monument, Iowa, represents a series of related features (the mounds) that form a prehistoric composition, shown in this aerial photograph outlined in white.

shadows become visible. These **shadow marks** provide a sense of depth and texture that reveal otherwise invisible cultural features. This method is particularly good for identifying old agricultural fields in which furrows still exist, as well as earthen depressions or piles of earth associated with past construction activities.

A variant of this approach is used to examine areas of land that are planted with crops such as wheat. This technique seeks to identify **crop marks,** which are really patterns of differential growth within cultivated fields (Figures 4.4, 4.5). The technique is based on the recognition of the fact that plants growing over buried stone features, such as walls or dense rock scatters, typically do not prosper as well as do plants growing adjacent to such buried features. If someone takes an aerial photograph of a cultivated field in which buried stone features exist, especially if the photo is taken from an oblique angle to maximize the effect of natural shadowing, the pattern of the stone features becomes visible in the differential growth of the plants. Those plants over the stone features tend to be shorter, whereas those adjacent tend to be larger (Figure 4.6). In some cases the stone features are shallow enough that they dramatically limit the growth of plants over them, and in such cases the disturbance they cause is easily seen. In situations in which the features are more deeply buried and the plants suffer less retardation as a result of the presence of the stones, it is necessary to rely on the natural shadows cast by the larger and healthier plants. In both cases, though, the crop marks provide direct evidence of past human activity that would otherwise be invisible. **Soil marks** are the range of color changes visible in the earth's sediments and soils that can indicate the presence of buried cultural resources.

Satellite images have many of the same properties that aerial photographs possess, but they are also composed of digital information. What this means is that each dot in a satellite composition also has data assigned to it. So, whereas an archaeologist might use a satellite image in the same way as a photo, he or she also has the option of examining and analyzing the data ascribed to each point within the image. Such data might commonly include temperature and elevation information, but any type of data that can be generated by modern satellite technology could conceivably also be included. This has the practical advantage of making such information easily manipulated by computer software packages. We might, for example, tell the computer software to display in red all points with an elevation more than 2 meters lower than the average of all terrain represented in the image. Hence, without worrying about shadows and angles being overlaid, the software will display all low points in the image frame. If such low points display some form of pattern, such as lines or clusters, then the archaeologist can infer that some sort of meaningful feature is present. Dry river beds, old roads and trails, and even ancient house depressions can all be observed in this way. In many respects the satellite imagery simply works like a photograph to which a computer database is attached. In this respect, such work is representative of one of the features of a geographic information system (GIS).

shadow marks Comparable to crop marks, shadow marks are the distribution of shadows created by cultural resources on an archaeological site that are identified through aerial photography.

crop marks Differences in the health and distribution of crops that reflect buried archaeological materials; usually used in conjunction with forms of remote sensing.

soil marks Comparable to crop marks and shadow marks, soil marks are the distribution of differential sediments on an archaeological site that can indicate the presence of buried cultural resources.

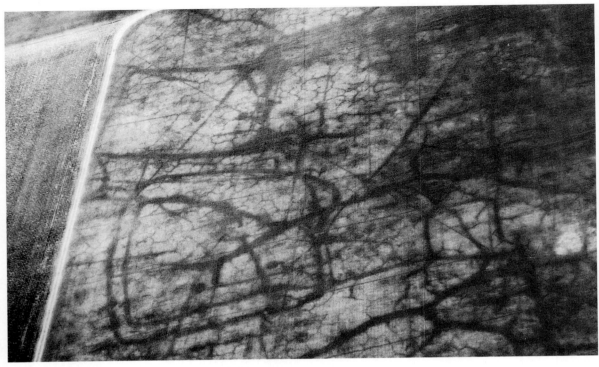

FIGURE 4.4a

An aerial photograph of crop marks southwest of Orton Longeville, Cambridgeshire, United Kingdom. The field is crossed with areas of differential crop growth resulting from subsurface disturbances.

FIGURE 4.4b

A schematic of the archaeo-logical walls (linear seg-ments) and wells (dark spots) of the Roman farm-stead near Orton Longeville superimposed on an aerial photo of the area.

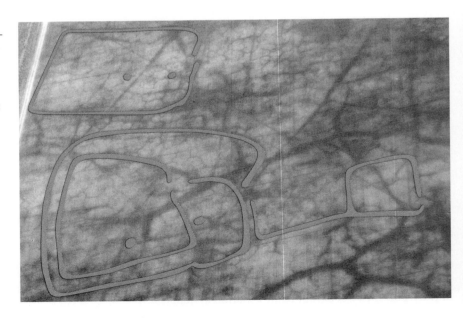

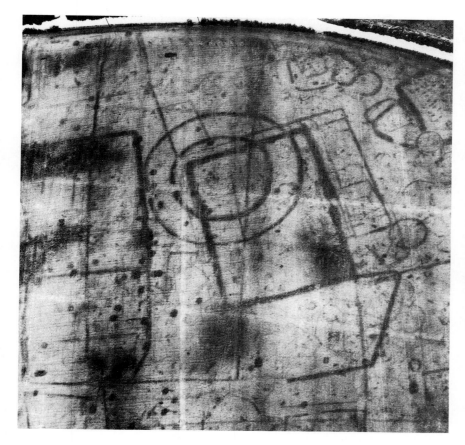

FIGURE 4.5

An aerial photograph of the Mucking site, Essex, United Kingdom. This is the largest site in the United Kingdom to be identified through aerial photography and then to be subsequently excavated based on the results of the aerial photographs. The center features overlapping walls of a Roman villa, whereas the circular areas represent the remains of slightly earlier Iron Age (Celtic) round houses. At the edges of this photograph are the rectangular marks typical of the later Anglo-Saxon settlement of the site.

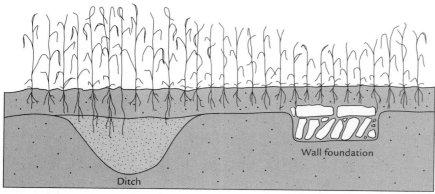

FIGURE 4.6

Two types of crop marks resulting from the enhancement (a) or limiting (b) of root growth in an agricultural field. The subsequent differential height of the plants affected by the enhancement or limiting of root growth is what is highly visible in aerial photographs.

An idealized view of how SLAR can be used to find archaeological sites in heavy ground cover. The energy from the radar passes through the foliage and is reflected off the denser structure of the buildings.

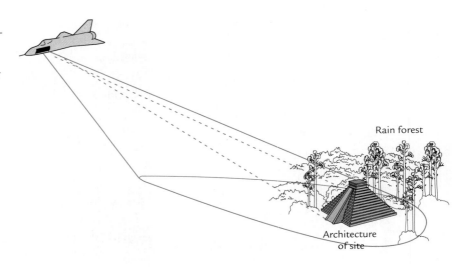

Rain forest

Architecture of site

sideways-looking-airborne-radar (SLAR) Projects electromagnetic (radar) pulses from an aircraft. These pulses are differentially reflected by various soil, sediment, and stone types and can be used to identify cultural resources.

ground penetrating radar A form of remote sensing that emits radar signals into the earth and then registers their return, thus plotting patterns of buried materials and sediments.

sonar A form of remote sensing in which a data collecting unit sends an electromagnetic signal outward, usually into water. The signal penetrates through the water at a known rate; when it encounters something that it cannot penetrate, it is reflected back to the data collector. The time it takes the ping to return and the pattern of the return is collected by the sonar unit and is subsequently displayed in a readout.

Sideways-looking-airborne-radar (SLAR) is another form of remote sensing that is particularly useful in exploring large areas of terrain. SLAR is based on the ability of electromagnetic (radar) pulses to differentially reflect various soil, sediment, and stone types. These reflections are patterned because they represent the distribution of different materials across the landscape. Linear bands or other shapes of naturally occurring stone appear as corresponding shapes on the readout, each differentiated from others by its density as recorded in the time it takes the radar signal to bounce off the stone and return to the measuring instrumentation. Square and rectangular features, such as stone buildings, also appear as distinct radar signatures and thus provide information on where past settlements existed. SLAR instrumentation is typically mounted on or in aircraft that fly over predefined geographic ranges on tightly defined pathways. Knowing these flight paths is what enables archaeologists to combine the radar data with more traditional geophysical maps and thus locate archaeological sites. SLAR also has the advantage of penetrating cloud cover and foliage, making it particularly useful in the tropics (Figure 4.7).

Although these techniques are good at identifying archaeological resources on a large scale, it is sometimes desirable or necessary to work on smaller scales. In such instances remote sensing provides archaeologists with a range of tools well designed to identify small-scale material remains. These tools include magnetometers, electromagnetic resistivity, ground penetrating radar, sonar, and metal detectors.

Ground penetrating radar (GPR) and **sonar** work in essentially the same manner. A data collecting unit sends an electromagnetic signal outward, into the ground in the case of GPR and into water in the case of most applications of sonar. The signal, or ping, penetrates through the soil or water at a known rate; when it encounters something that it cannot penetrate, it is reflected

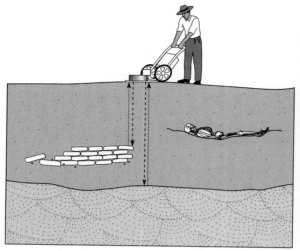

FIGURE 4.8a

An overview of how ground penetrating radar (GPR) functions. A signal is emitted from the radar machine and is subsequently reflected by the material it encounters in the earth. Different materials result in different reflections, which are then recorded by the machine. The result is a sort of map of what is beneath the ground surface.

FIGURE 4.8b

A technician pushes a GPR unit mounted on a low cart. The apparatus at the front of the cart emits the signal and the machinery mounted at the rear reads and records the reflections of that signal.

back to the data collector (Figure 4.8). The time it takes the ping to return and the pattern of the return is collected by the GPR or sonar unit and is subsequently displayed in a readout. This readout can be interpreted by trained specialists and can serve to identify such things as differential soil density, perhaps suggesting the presence of pits, burials, or similar features or walls or other phenomena that block the signal. If sufficient time is taken and the equipment is sensitive enough, then a general outline or shape can be identified based on such signals. This is particularly valuable in working on nautical sites when the vessels being examined contain iron as an essential component.

Magnetometers, on the other hand, are often highly mobile units designed to measure changes in magnetic fields and/or gravitational fields. Although such units can be easily upset by the presence of strong electrical fields, such as power lines, they can provide good, basic data about what is beneath the surface of the earth. In general, such units read the magnetic field of the earth at a specific location and record the data. They can be mounted on a pole and used to collect data on a predetermined grid, or they can be mounted on sleds or sledges and used to provide continuous reports. When the data are interpreted, the archaeologist is essentially looking at a graph of either the magnetic field or the gravitational field across the landscape. In both cases, though, anomalies in the pattern are interpreted as potential indicators of human disturbances. A skilled operator with advance knowledge of what is

magnetometer Usually a highly mobile unit designed to measure changes in magnetic fields and/or gravitational fields.

being searched for, such as an old building foundation, can often make insightful inferences about what the readouts mean, thus helping to define likely places to continue the search for the material in question. In the event that the archaeologist is not sure about what may be present, the general pattern of anomalies themselves must be used as an indicator of areas likely to provide evidence of past human activity.

Metal detectors are simple tools that emit a cycling magnetic field and receive electrical signals resulting from distortions of these fields. When a detector passes over a metal object, including buried ones, the cycling field that they emit is distorted. This distortion produces an electrical signal, which triggers the beeper in the detector. Although metals are particularly strong sources for disruption, other things—such as strong discrepencies in soil density that might be produced by a filled ditch, pit, or burial—also trigger detectors. Such tools are very useful in helping archaeologists to identify metal artifacts and modern intrusions onto sites, such as power lines or buried cables. Unfortunately, metal detectors have acquired a bad reputation in archaeology because many amateur enthusiasts use such devices precisely as archaeologists do. In some cases this has led to the looting of archaeological resources. Over the past several decades, however, and especially in Europe, metal detecting enthusiasts have embraced archaeology and have contributed to both the discovery and preservation of cultural resources. Nevertheless, some archaeologists still shun metal detectors because of this reputation. As always, though, it is not the technology that is at fault but people who make decisions about what to do with the data that are collected. This is why education is essential from the standpoint of preserving cultural resources.

Each of these forms of remote sensing requires ground proofing of some sort. Although the data they provide are very useful in identifying where to look, the data are not usually specific enough to distinguish between archaeological and naturally occurring geological features. Similarly, these techniques do not always provide good detail about the precise nature and range of archaeological resources that might be present. Even metal detectors can only identify variations in the magnetic field they produce. They cannot distinguish between a modern bottle cap and a three-hundred-year-old spoon or other artifact. At this point, then, we need to look at ground-proofing strategies that are capable of identifying specific cultural resources.

metal detector A simple tool that emits a cycling magnetic field and receives electrical signals resulting from distortions of these fields. When a detector passes over a metal object, including buried ones, the cycling field that it emits is distorted. This distortion produces an electrical signal, which triggers the beeper in the detector.

GROUND-PROOFING METHODS

Pedestrian Survey

The most common form of archaeological reconnaissance has traditionally been pedestrian survey. This method of survey simply involves taking fieldworkers to a place at which there may be archaeological materials and then having these people systematically walk over the area searching for evidence of those remains (Box 4.1). The key word here is *systematically*. It is impor-

BOX 4.1

SO THIS IS ARCHAEOLOGY:
A FIRSTHAND EXPERIENCE IN SURVEY

It was about 7:00 A.M. and 30°F when we began work. A cold gray December morning in New Jersey promised to rapidly turn into a cold gray December day. In front of me lay about thirty-five acres of field, mostly tilled, along a low series of terraces above a permanent stream. Around me stood about fifteen people, thirteen of whom were crew members like me. One was the crew chief, and the last was the principal investigator (P.I.). We were all working for a major cultural resource management firm that had been contracted to identify any significant cultural resources along a corridor through which the New Jersey Department of Transportation had proposed to build a road. The background research and what was known of Native American settlement behavior in the area indicated that this was a likely place to encounter prehistoric cultural remains. There was also an outside chance that some of the soldiers who had participated in the Battle of Princeton had visited or camped on the site. It was difficult to assess this possibility through the historic documents because the battle and the movements of troops leading to it were poorly documented. Historians, in fact, had commented that it was more of a series of low-intensity skirmishes across the landscape than a major set-piece battle. So here we were, fifteen very cold, bleary-eyed people, looking for the past to help determine if the road could come through.

The P.I. already had permission for us to conduct our work on the land, which was still privately owned. We began by flagging transect lines that the P.I. and crew chief had already mapped onto a USGS topographic quadrangle map. Ten of us formed a line at 5-meter intervals, each of us carrying a bundle of wire pin flags. Whenever we encountered an artifact, we were to insert a flag into the ground next to it. The crew chief and two other crew members were assigned to measure the distance along the transects and begin a rough map of the find spots. The remaining crew members were assigned to prepare equipment for subsurface testing. Because the field had been plowed and because the sediments were partially eroded from years of farming, we thought there was little chance that we would need to undertake this sort of testing in most of the area. There was a small stand of trees in one corner of the property where soil was not eroded and no plowing had taken place for some time. Some subsurface testing needed to be done there, and the remaining crew members were the ones assigned to do it.

We walked over that field for the rest of the day, scanning the paths of our transects for any sign of human material culture. The morning passed slowly; we found and flagged only recent historical materials, especially fragments of modern beer bottles. By lunch our morale was ebbing away, it had gotten colder, and it became clear to many of us that the site was more badly eroded than we had previously thought. While sitting in our cars, heaters running, dining on bologna and cheese sandwiches and enjoying tea or coffee from thermoses, many of us mused over the value of continuing the work that day. The soil exposed by the plowing was of the type that usually sat at the bottom of intact soil profiles, usually dating to eras long before humans could feasibly have entered the New World. As we finished lunch, some folks looked longingly at the P.I., hoping for a sign that their apparent torment in the cold, seemingly sterile sediments would be cut short. Luck was not with them, though; we pressed on.

To be fair, some of the crew took all of this in stride. They had been on surveys before that had found little or nothing. The veterans pointed out that, in a way, finding nothing was good, because it would allow the entire team to move on to other areas in need of survey. Somehow, though, the newer crew members took little solace in this viewpoint. They were just cold, and it was difficult for some of them to keep from bunching together on their transects. What was worse to them was that the subsurface testing crew fared no better in the wooded corner of the survey area. It seemed that the trees were not very old and rested in previously plowed sediments.

We finished work at about 4:30 that afternoon. A light snow was beginning to fall, and we had found a

(continued)

grand total of three pieces of historic earthenware, dating to no earlier than the middle of the nineteenth century, and about seventy pieces of broken glass, most with the characteristic embossing and mold lines of modern bottles. Everyone was a bit disappointed; every archaeologist wants to find things when they look to the earth. Yet what we did that day was not in any sense a failure. We kept to our research plan and explored an area that had the potential to yield significant archaeological material. The fact that we failed to find anything significant despite our best efforts might have been personally disappointing, but it was good archaeology. It was time to go home and, in the morning, move on to another survey location.

tant that archaeologists examine regions for sites along specified pathways and at fixed intervals. Ideally we would like to examine every inch of every possible site, but this simply is not feasible in terms of available time and available funds. Consequently, we have adopted sampling methodologies based on statistical models, which are discussed a bit later in this chapter. For now, though, it is important to understand that there are good reasons for preparing rigid controls for surveys.

The first step in preparing a systematic coverage of the area to be surveyed is to select intervals at which to place crew members. Such intervals are in large part dictated by the research design of the archaeologists in charge, though the local terrain sometimes limits these things as well. In North America the typical intervals range from 5 to 15 meters between each crew member. This range corresponds to legal mandates of most state and federal agencies about what distances are acceptable. The general rule of thumb is that the tighter the interval between crew members, the greater the likelihood that the crew will find evidence of material culture if such evidence exists. The 15-meter interval represents the interval at which most archaeologists feel there is a reasonable probability of finding any archaeological materials. Computer simulations and controlled field trials have indicated that this is indeed usually the case.

Once an interval has been selected, the crew carefully sets out walking across the survey area, each member walking a **transect** (a predetermined, usually straight path) that can be defined on a map (Figure 4.9). Each crew member scans the ground searching for artifacts or ecofacts. If such remains are found, they might either be collected and their position recorded on a map or flagged, depending on the protocols established by the archaeologists in their research design. The flagging method allows the archaeologists to view the distribution of the material culture on the landscape immediately, whereas the method of collecting materials requires archaeologists to create a master map before seeing such clustering. Both systems eventually require that maps be made, so it is really a matter of whether the archaeologists need to see the artifact patterning immediately and whether they intend to collect and analyze artifacts from the site.

transect A predetermined, usually straight path used in archaeological reconnaissance.

FIGURE 4.9

The basic distribution of crew members performing pedestrian survey. Note that crew members will walk a straight line, maintaining the predetermined distance between themselves and coworkers.

Pedestrian survey is limited to areas of good visibility. It is particularly useful in areas in which there is little deposition of sediments, such as in arid or semiarid regions, and in places in which the ground has been cleared for tilling. The latter has the additional advantage of moving buried artifacts to the surface where they can be spotted. In areas of dense foliage, such as in forests, or in which it is likely that substantial sediments have been deposited over archaeological remains, such as on the floodplains of rivers, then surface survey techniques are unlikely to be of much use.

Subsurface Survey

In such cases archaeologists can turn to **subsurface testing** techniques. These work essentially the same way as do pedestrian surveys, but the intervals also control the precise points at which archaeologists will locate tests. For example, if crew members are working in 5-meter intervals, then each crew member or team of crew members will again line up at the appropriate interval. Each member will then walk 5 meters along this transect and do a subsurface test at this point. Once this test is completed, they will walk another 5 meters along the same transect and then excavate another test. This method will be repeated until the entire survey area is dotted with tests that form a grid.

There are several different ways to excavate a subsurface test. In each case, however, the goal is to identify whether or not cultural resources are present and in what sedimentilogical contexts. These tests typically must be relatively rapid to complete and limited in how much of the site they disturb. A balance

subsurface testing The process of excavating small, controlled tests in search of buried cultural resources.

FIGURE 4.10

Fieldworkers backfilling a completed 2 m × 2 m excavation unit at the Samuel site, Oswego, Illinois. In this case it was important to fill in the excavation unit and pack it exceptionally well because the field was going to be turned over to agriculture in the coming years.

must be struck between cost, potential information gained, and time constraints. Consequently, most archaeologists adopt a policy of excavating a small test, often less than 1 meter in width, as deeply as possible.

In North America the most common example of this policy is the shovel test. Here a shovel is used to excavate a test of approximately 50 cm × 50 cm downward as far as possible. Such excavations rarely penetrate to a depth of much more than 1 meter simply because it becomes impossible to remove any more matrix through the small horizontal opening with a shovel. As these tests are excavated, the archaeologists working on them typically pass the matrix they remove through a screen in order to find any cultural material. A record is kept of each change in matrix texture, color, and material content. Once the test is excavated to its maximum possible depth, or to a depth that correlates with sediments that predate any possible human use of the area, the test is *backfilled* (the excavated material is placed back into the hole) and the excavators move on (Figure 4.10).

In some cases in which archaeologists need to dig deeper, soil augers, power augers, and other specialized tools can be used to extend the test downward. In other places, rather than shovels and augers, archaeologists have experimented with posthole diggers to extend and regulate their tests (Figure 4.11). Regardless of the tools employed, the key elements in subsurface testing are (1) to regulate the size of the excavation unit so that archaeologists can compare the contents of one test with those of another and (2) to carefully record not only what is found but also where it is found. Although this type of test-

FIGURE 4.11

Sometimes archaeologists employ auger-coring, as shown here, for subsurface testing.

ing is designed to identify the sorts of materials that might be present in the survey area, test units are still archaeological excavations, and, as you know, it is the context in which materials are found that is most important to archaeological research (Box 4.2).

PUTTING IT TOGETHER

An important element of archaeological reconnaissance is that it is interpreted in light of human behaviors. What this means is that archaeologists do more with the data they generate than write them down. As the third general goal of archaeology, archaeologists seek to identify past human lifeways. Part of this goal means that archaeologists will develop as thorough an understanding as possible of where past peoples chose to live and why they chose to live in such locations: Sometimes resources help determine where people choose to live; other times access to defense or community labor play important parts in the decision-making process. The sum of these processes, however, is recorded by the careful survey of a region.

This patterning in the archaeological record allows archaeologists to produce models of past behaviors. Once archaeologists identify what factors played significant roles in the placement of archaeological sites, we can generate predictive models. Such models serve to indicate where sites are likely to be found in a well-defined geographic region. Archaeologists then undertake the testing of this model; that is, they ground proof their predictions. Over

BOX 4.2

PERSISTENCE PAYS OFF:
MARY LEAKEY AND THE STORY OF ZINJ

It was the last day of the field season in 1959. Louis Leakey was confined to camp by a nagging illness. He was also in a dark humor about a generally unproductive season of fossil hunting in Olduvai Gorge. He and his wife, Mary, along with their pack of dogs, walked large areas of their survey region every year, sometimes multiple times each year. The geography of Olduvai Gorge is such that the annual rains erode sediments and expose fossil material that had lain buried the previous year. Thus every year the Leakeys and other fossil hunters combed through their research areas in search of new evidence about hominid origins.

On this particular day, Mary had decided to make one last survey in the area around a known fossil-producing area, FLK. FLK was short for Freda Leakey Korongo; Freda was Louis's first wife and a korongo was a small valley. Mary and the dogs, which helped locate and warn the Leakeys of the presence of potentially dangerous snakes, spent the morning poring over the area. Nothing new seemed to be present, but Mary persisted in her meticulous search. It was her last chance to search the area for quite awhile, so she decided to make the best of her opportunity. This was, after all, part of their overall search strategy, and the work had to be done.

Just before giving up and returning to camp, she spotted something intriguing protruding from the sediments. She looked more closely, and there it was. What she had found was a fragment of the skull of an early hominid, one that would capture the fascination of anthropologists for nearly a year before another find at the same site would upstage it. The fossil came to be known as *Zinjanthropus boisei*, a name selected by Louis Leakey that translated to "nutcracker man." The fossil, which became known simply as Zinj, had a small cranium with a sagittal crest (a longitudinal ridge running from the front to the back of the skull), a massive jaw, and broad flat teeth. To the Leakeys this suggested that the creature had specialized in processing heavy seeds and nuts, an inference that still seems correct today. Science has since renamed the fossil *Australopithecus boisei* to denote its likely tangential position to the main line of human evolution leading to modern humans. Despite this position, though, members of this genus and species thrived in the grasslands along the edges of the forests that once dominated what is now the African Rift Valley, surviving from approximately 2 million years ago to as late as nearly 1 million years ago. It is interesting to note that the entire story of identifying and exploring this creature's place in the world began with diligent archaeological survey. It seems that one person can make a great deal of difference in exploring the past.

time a variety of models have been developed throughout the world, and, in some cases, these have served to structure the type and sort of research that has been undertaken in these regions. In effect, once you learn what to look for and where it is probably going to be found, you have a good idea of where to undertake a search for archaeological sites.

Although predictive models are useful and can be powerful tools in helping to structure research, it is vital that archaeologists remember that they are just predictions, not proven fact. If we rely on our models before we thoroughly test them, then we run the risk of missing significant portions of the past. If, for example, our model predicted that no sites higher than 1,000 meters above sea level existed and if we never checked to determine whether this was accurate, then we might miss any sites that actually existed there. Because

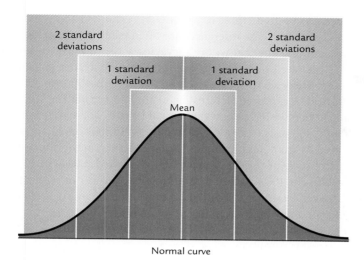

Normal curve

FIGURE 4.12

The standard distribution, or normal curve, of statistics. Note that approximately 66% of all points will fall under the curve within a single standard distribution of the mean (average) of all measured points.

models are usually based on existing data, we may know or might be tempted to assume that someone had already checked for sites at or above 1,000 meters. But it would be premature to assume that no sites existed there. To be sure, we would have to assess how well the work that our model is based on was performed and how representative it is likely to be of the real situation. To do this, we need to understand more about how sampling works.

SAMPLING BASICS

Everything about site survey that we have discussed so far is based on something called the **normal curve.** You may be more familiar with the normal curve as the *bell curve* or the *standard distribution.* This is a statistical construction that predicts how points would be distributed on an idealized mathematical curve. According to this curve, approximately two-thirds, or 66%, of all the points fall under the center of the curve within 1 standard deviation from the *mean.* The mean is nothing more than the average value of all the points, and the *standard deviation* is a measure of how far away from this value all of the points on average tend to fall. A total of approximately 95% of all points are predicted to fall within 2 standard deviations of the mean. Continuing outward, 98% of all points are expected to fall within 3 standard deviations of the mean. A good statistics book will explain how and why it is that, the farther away from the mean we go, the percentage of all points thought to fall within the curve increases, yet never quite reaches 100% (Figure 4.12).

What this means to archaeologists is that we never have the entire picture of the past unless we excavate an entire site and recover every artifact. We seldom if ever do this because of the need to preserve some of the past in place for future generations; therefore, all of our interpretations are based on infer-

normal curve The standard bell-shaped distribution of statistics in which approximately two-thirds of all points under the curve fall within 1 standard deviation of the mean value.

ences. **Inferences** are predictions based on what is known about a certain situation. In archaeology, these inferences are often based on the bell curve.

For a moment imagine that we are surveying a 100 m × 100 m square parcel of land (a total of 10,000 square meters). If we excavate a subsurface test every 5 meters, then we will have excavated a total of 400 tests (20 tests on each of 20 lines). Assuming each test is 50 cm × 50 cm at the surface (0.25 square meter), then we have excavated a total of 100 square meters of surface area (0.25 m × 400 tests). If we divide the total number of square meters we have excavated by the total number of square meters on the site, we can calculate the percentage of the site that we have excavated, a total of 1% (100 m/ 10,000 m = 0.01, or 1%). As you might imagine, this is not a very high percentage. However, based on the normal curve and probability theory, there is a 66% chance that any piece of material we excavated is representative of the site as a whole. On the other hand, it also means that there is a 34% chance that our material is somehow atypical, representing behaviors that occurred in only a small segment of society. In order to increase our chances of better understanding an archaeological site, it is important that we excavate a representative sample of the site, that is, enough of the site that we can be reasonably confident that our sample includes the majority of behaviors recorded in the archaeological record.

SUMMARY

Archaeological reconnaissance represents a large portion of the research being done today in archaeology. It is closely allied with geography in many respects, and the application of GIS software has enabled scholars to learn more about the spatial and temporal distribution of material culture than ever before. Such research has also allowed archaeologists to generate powerful predictive models that help to narrow their search for answers to specific research questions. Such models, however, must be tested, for they are simply modern constructions based on our assumptions and inferences about past human activity. As such, they are not necessarily good representations of the past and should be subject to the same standards of research and testing that all archaeological models are held to.

In addition to modeling, archaeological reconnaissance has a sizeable component dedicated to sampling strategy and methodological issues. The use of satellites, aerial photography, and computer imaging has enabled researchers to identify material traces of the past that were previously invisible. Similarly, other remote sensing technologies, such as ground penetrating radar, magnetometers, and sonar, also contribute to finding remains of the past. In almost all cases, though, the application of such techniques must be followed up by standardized archaeological testing, such as pedestrian survey and subsurface testing.

inference A determination arrived at by reasoning.

Without a doubt, the world of archaeology is enriched and enabled by reconnaissance techniques. Likewise, it is here that most archaeologists spend most of their time, especially in the world of cultural resource management.

FOR FURTHER INFORMATION

Ammerman, A. J. 1981. Surveys and archaeological research. *Annual Review of Anthropology* 10: 63–88.

Davis, J., and A. P. Sullivan. 2000. Surveys, Multistage and Large-Scale. In *Archaeological method and theory: An encyclopedia,* edited by L. Ellis, 610–12. New York: Garland Publishing.

Ebert, J. I. 1984. Remote sensing applications in archaeology. In *Advances in archaeological method and theory.* Vol. 7, edited by M. B. Schiffer, 293–362. Orlando, Fla.: Academic Press.

Hole, B. 1980. Sampling in archaeology: A critique. *Annual Review of Anthropology* 9: 217–34.

Krakker, J. J., M. J. Shott, and P. D. Welch. 1983. Design and evaluation of shovel-test sampling in regional archaeological survey. *Journal of Field Archaeology* 10: 469–80.

Lightfoot, K. 1986. Regional surveys in the eastern United States: The strengths and weaknesses of implementing subsurface testing programs. *American Antiquity* 51: 484–504.

———. 1989. A defense of shovel-test-sampling: A reply to Shott. *American Antiquity* 54: 413–16.

Madry, S. L. H., and C. L. Crumley. 1990. An application of remote sensing and GIS in a regional archaeological settlement pattern analysis: The Arroux River valley, Burgundy, France. In *Interpreting space: GIS and archaeology,* edited by K. M. S. Allen, S. W. Green, and E. B. W. Zubrow, 364–80. Bristol, Penn.: Taylor & Francis.

Mueller, J. W. 1974. *The uses of sampling in archaeological survey.* Memoir no. 28. Washington, D.C.: Society for American Archaeology.

———, ed. 1975. *Sampling in archaeology.* Tucson: University of Arizona Press.

Nance, J. D. 1979. Regional subsampling and statistical inference in forested habitats. *American Antiquity* 44: 172–76.

———. 1981. Statistical fact and archaeological faith: Two models in small site sampling. *Journal of Field Archaeology* 8: 151–65.

———. 1983. Regional sampling in archaeological survey: The statistical perspective. In *Advances in archaeological method and theory.* Vol. 6, edited by M. B. Schiffer, 289–356. New York: Academic Press.

Nance, J. D., and B. F. Ball. 1986. No surprises? The reliability and validity of test pit sampling. *American Antiquity* 51: 457–83.

———. 1989. A shot in the dark: Shott's comments on Nance and Ball. *American Antiquity* 54: 405–12.

Plog, S. 1978. Sampling in archaeological surveys: A critique. *American Antiquity* 43: 280–85.

Redman, C. L. 1982. Archaeological survey and the study of Mesopotamian urban systems. *Journal of Field Archaeology* 9: 375–82.

———. 1987. Surface collection, sampling, and research design: A retrospective. *American Antiquity* 52: 249–65.

Shapiro, G. 1984. A soil resistivity survey of 15th-century Puerto Real, Haiti. *Journal of Field Archaeology* 11: 101–10.

Shott, M. 1985. Shovel-test sampling as a site discovery technique: A case study from Michigan. *Journal of Field Archaeology* 12: 457–68.

———.1989. Shovel-test sampling in archaeological survey: Comments on Nance and Ball, and Lightfoot. *American Antiquity* 54: 396–404.

Weymouth, J. M. 1986. Geophysical methods of archaeological site surveying. In *Advances in archaeological method and theory*. Vol. 9, edited by M. B. Schiffer, 311–95. Orlando, Fla.: Academic Press.

5

EXCAVATING THE PAST

An ill-considered excavation is liable to develop into chaos.

—*Sir Mortimer Wheeler*

Inevitably an introduction to archaeology must address when, why, and how archaeologists excavate the past. Not every archaeologist excavates, and not everything that we know about the past has come through digging. Nonetheless, excavations are at the heart of archaeological explorations of past human behaviors, and they conjure in the mind perhaps the most romantic visions of the discipline. Thoughts of Howard Carter discovering Tut's tomb and entering a world sealed nearly four thousand years earlier, or even the dashing but fictional Indiana Jones sprinting through a distant jungle, drive home to many of us exciting fantasies of discovering lost societies in exotic locations. Yet, aside from the fantastic and entertaining world of Indiana Jones, there are real protocols and methods that help us to tease from the earth information about past lives and behaviors. It is careful adherence to these methods and the inventive but reliable expansion of their workings that enable us to undertake archaeological research. This chapter describes the basic concepts of fieldwork and provides us with vivid examples of how archaeology works on, and in, the earth (Box 5.1).

THE DECISION TO EXCAVATE

Once archaeologists have decided on a research project, defined their research questions, and determined that excavation is the best way to answer these questions, then they can begin planning to undertake such work. The importance of the relationship between research questions and fieldwork should be reemphasized, because the latter is specifically designed and undertaken to answer the former. Consequently, there is no single, correct way to excavate any archaeological site or groups of sites. Rather, regionally specific standards exist that all excavations within the area must meet in order to be considered acceptable and professional. Beyond these standards a nearly infinite

BOX 5.1

GRIDLOCK: LAYING OUT AN EXCAVATION AREA

Two of the most fundamental techniques used in modern archaeology are establishing a site datum and laying out a grid system on a site. A **site datum** acts as a control point from which all measurements on an archaeological site are ultimately made. All other datum points, such as unit datum points, ultimately reference the site datum. Tradition holds that it is desirable to place this point in the southwestern corner of the site so that all horizontal measurements will be to the north and east, thus eliminating possible confusions between southeastern and southwestern quadrants or comparable issues. In part this tradition is related to surveying methodology in which measurements are taken in northings and eastings, that is, measurements to the north and east. Archaeologists simply made use of the existing survey technology and codified it.

Sometimes, though, it is neither desirable nor possible to place the site datum in the southwestern corner of the site. First, archaeological sites have a way of changing shapes as archaeologists explore them more intensively. Second, the conditions of some sites make it problematic to take all measurements from a single point, let alone one that is in an extreme corner of the site. The larger the site, the more likely it is that archaeologists may prefer to use multiple site data or to place a single, master site datum near the center of the site.

Actually placing a site datum is very simple. An archaeologist places the point and then measures the horizontal bearing, distance, and vertical angle from this point to a known geological point, preferably one that serves as a benchmark for geologists. This known point helps archaeologists to fix their datum in place on the face of the planet. New technologies, such as global positioning systems (GPS), allow archaeologists to fix a datum in new ways. A GPS unit reads signals from satellites and then calculates its position on the planet in relation to these satellites. A careful triangulation between multiple GPS units, or the assistance of one very powerful unit, allows archaeologists to place a datum point in relation to this satellite positioning system. This is the same system used today by most militaries to ensure that people are in the right places at the right time to accomplish their assigned tasks.

Once the site datum is in place, archaeologists are free to establish any number of subsequent data. In many cases each excavation unit has a unit datum placed in the southwestern corner. All measurements in that unit are calculated from the unit datum, which is, in turn, measured to the site datum. In this fashion every location, indeed every artifact and feature, can be placed precisely on the site and on the face of the planet by tracing its provenience through the site datum.

A site grid is in many ways a complementary tool to the use of a site datum. Archaeologists overlay a grid on a site map by positioning the grid in relation to the position of the site datum. The grid serves to demarcate equal areas of the site, ranging from 1-meter squares to 1-kilometer squares, according to the research design,

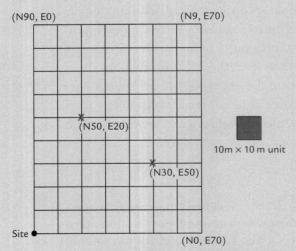

(N90, E0)   (N9, E70)

(N50, E20)

(N30, E50)

10m × 10 m unit

Site •

(N0, E70)

A basic grid layout at a hypothetical archaeological site. Note that the site datum is placed in the southwest corner of the site at North 0, East 0 and that "X" marks have been placed at the North 50, East 20 and North 30, East 50 points.

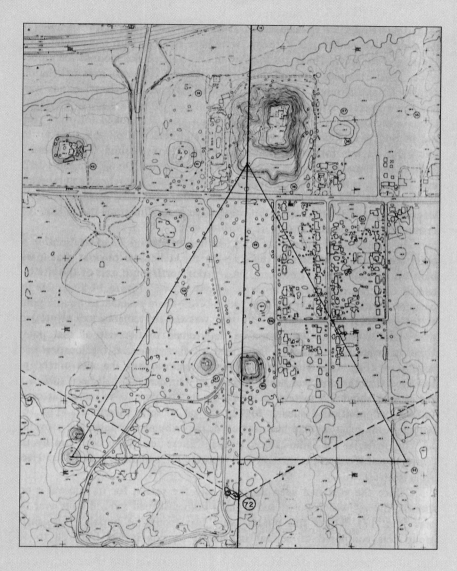

An overview of Cahokia, showing the locations of major mounds and known features. Such a large site often requires archaeologists to use multiple grids and to integrate these into a single, master plan.

although the latter typically are not useful to guide excavations (they work well with survey approaches, however).

By stating the coordinates of a point on a site, such as the location of a unit datum, archaeologists can guide fieldworkers directly to that point. For example, be-

cause the site datum is the control point for the site, it usually receives the coordinates North 0, East 0 (N0, E0). If a researcher wanted a person to place a unit datum, she might instruct the crew member to go to North 60, East 60 (N60, E60) and place the point there. The crew
(continued)

BOX 5.1 (continued)

member would then use one of a number of measuring devices to find a spot that is 60 meters north of the datum, and then 60 meters east of that point. In other words, the worker would walk 60 meters north from the datum, turn right, walk another 60 meters, and place the point.

To facilitate moving about a site without having to measure every point directly back to the site datum, archaeologists usually elect to establish a replica of the site grid on the ground. They begin this process by mapping in a straight line directly north from the site datum. (Sometimes other angles can be used, depending on the field conditions and research design.) This is usually accomplished with the aid of a transit, a theodolite, a siting compass, or another instrument that allows a person to map a straight line over significant

distances. Points are then measured along this line and marked, usually with wooden stakes. For example, on many of my sites I place a stake every 10 meters along this line, called the north **baseline.** The process is then repeated at a 90-degree angle to the east, thus establishing an east baseline. If desired, south and west baselines may also be established.

The presence of these baselines allows any crew member to get her bearings on the site so long as she can see points on the baseline. If a site is so large that points cannot be seen, intermediate points can be measured across the site. The presence of such points is often helpful, as they assist in rapidly and accurately locating positions across the site. These points also assist archaeologists in translating data recovered in the field to the master maps they keep of all excavations.

site datum The master control point on an archaeological site into which all measurements are eventually tied.

baseline A line placed on a site at a 90-degree angle from at least one other such line. These lines together allow archaeologists to identify their position on a site quickly and easily. Such baselines are invaluable tools when mapping a site.

number of variations on fieldwork exist, each designed to generate the specific sorts of data that can answer the questions asked by the archaeologists.

Some of the more common standards of excavation in modern archaeology center on recovering accurate, representative data and adequately preserving the sites that are excavated. As I discussed previously, archaeologists understand the need to preserve significant portions of the sites on which they work for future generations of archaeologists and for the world community as a whole. We know that our best efforts today will be bested by future technologies and innovations. Likewise, we also understand that there will be new questions posed in the future, as well as reevaluations of current questions. Combined, these will further what we know about the past, as well as how that past is integrated with the present and perhaps the future. In undertaking fieldwork, archaeologists must carefully balance the information they are likely to acquire through their work against the loss of resources for future generations that this work will cause. This important test is a key standard that all archaeologists should ideally hold themselves and their community to. Archaeologists police themselves through constant evaluation of the state of current research and field undertakings, making sure they do the best that they can with what they have.

Statistical Sampling

In the field this standard is expressed in the methods by which an archaeologist selects the places to dig and the areas to preserve. The selection is usually

"We'll put a unit here; there seems to be a depression from an old house."

FIGURE 5.1

Nonrandom sampling of sites is based on the preferences and biases of the excavators. At times, especially in the case of experienced excavators, the ability to observe and interpret the landscape can help archaeologists find material remains they might otherwise have missed

done through a sampling procedure that parallels the sampling discussion presented for archaeological reconnaissance. Given the overall size of the site to excavate, an archaeologist can carefully calculate what percentage of the site will be excavated. This method also has the pragmatic effect of helping to address questions of cost and of the manner in which limited resources, usually in the form of time and labor, will be assigned.

Once an archaeologist develops an understanding of how much of a site can be excavated, the next step is to determine where, precisely, to place **excavation units.** There are three basic approaches to this: intuitive sampling, **random sampling,** and stratified random sampling. **Intuitive sampling** is nothing more than placing excavation units wherever the archaeologist elects to put them (Figure 5.1). This provides the researchers with the ability to investigate visible features on the site and to pursue excavations according to a system that meets the logistical needs and preferences of the team. On the other hand, this method has the disadvantage of locating excavation units according to a system that might not be sensitive or well designed to uncover what is really present at the site. In short, this system is subject to the exclusive biases of the archaeologists in charge and is not designed to statistically analyze the site.

Intuitive sampling was the hallmark of many early archaeological surveys, and it is easy to understand why. Imagine the expectations and interests of the early excavators of the Egyptian pyramids or of the early Maya archaeologists at the sites of Copán and Tikal. The impressive monuments at these sites drew both the imagination and curiosity of these researchers. In these large structures, it was thought, were the mightiest achievements of past peoples, and therefore these were the most important things to be investigated. There is no arguing with the importance of such structures to past peoples, but there is also no question that such things represented only the worlds and lifeways of the elite, those few people who dominated these past societies.

excavation unit A defined horizontal area that will be systematically excavated; a unit defines the horizontal location of a sampling location on an archaeological site.

random sampling The use of random number methods in selecting locations for archaeological testing and exploration.

intuitive sampling The use of personal preferences in locating archaeological tests and excavation units.

For a time, until the past thirty-five years or so, many of our interpretations of Egyptian and Maya culture focused on their ceremonial worlds. For many archaeologists, including the brilliant researcher Sir Eric Thompson, the Maya were seen as peaceful people who were obsessed with astronomy and the passage of time. These were the interests that seemed to be represented in the elite dwellings, and this conclusion seemed to be further supported by the absence of large populations at such sites. If there were no cities, Thompson and others reasoned, there may have been little or no real warfare, because there were no political and social centers to initiate such conflicts.

During the 1960s, though, the work of a younger generation of archaeologists began to identify troubling trends with this view of the Maya. It seems no one had actually tested the assumptions of earlier archaeologists that all, or at least most, of Maya society was represented by what was known of the elites and their compounds. One study that sought to test for the lifeways of the nonelite was undertaken by Wendy Ashmore at the Maya site of Quirigua, Guatemala. Quirigua is dominated by a plaza area containing numerous stelae (sculpted stone monuments) that in many respects conforms to what is known about many other Maya centers. Here, though, Ashmore was able to follow modern irrigation ditches along their lengths and, in the profiles (side walls) of these ditches, found a great number of small Maya homes. Rather than being a vacant ceremonial center occupied only by priestly astronomers, Quirigua was an urban center with a much higher population than initially imagined. Subsequent work near other Maya sites, including Copán, has revealed that some Maya centers were at the heart of large political groups with populations in the tens of thousands. Likewise, warfare is now seen as endemic, something more typical of what we might expect from other societies. Rather than representing the societies of the Maya, intuitive sampling of elite monuments served to focus archaeological interpretations on only a limited segment of those societies. Only as archaeological theory grew and developed did researchers think to look for the rest of Maya society and, through that search, begin to understand the cultural systems of these people more completely.

On the opposite end of the spectrum from intuitive sampling is **strict random sampling.** This method of determining where to locate units requires that the archaeologist establish a grid system atop a map of the site (Figure 5.2). Each cell in the grid is then given a sequential number. Once this is completed, the archaeologist then turns to a table of random numbers, such as is found in most statistics books. A sequence of numbers is selected at random from this table and then compared with the site grid. Each number from the table is marked on the grid, defining where excavation units will be located.

This method has the advantage of placing units across a site without relying on any excavator biases, whether conscious or unconscious. Hence, the excavators could not be accused of subconsciously avoiding unpleasant excavation conditions, such as patches of poison ivy, nor of consciously trying to place units in areas of the sites that might be perceived to have more elaborate material remains than other portions. Moreover, if sufficient units are exca-

strict random sampling The use of random number methods in the selection of locations for archaeological testing and exploration to the exclusion of all other methods.

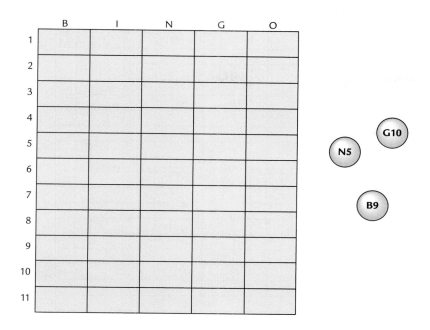

FIGURE 5.2

Random sampling relies on notions of statistical probability to help archaeologists explore a site. The random selection of test units can, for example, help archaeologists find material remains in places they would ordinarily not think, or prefer, to dig, such as in the middle of a patch of poison ivy.

vated, then random sampling correlates with the standard distribution. In this manner the archaeologist can predict that each unit has about a 66% probability of containing material that is representative of the activities that once took place on the site.

The method has some disadvantages, however. Most obvious is that some areas of a given site may compel archaeologists to explore them based on the project's research design. However, these areas might not be randomly selected for exploration, and thus the archaeologist might be left with a bit of a conundrum. If we return to our example of a Maya site, then it is easy to imagine a situation in which a random sampling method might not locate any excavation units near any of the known structures or other architectural features. Although such features might not reflect the most common activities at a site, they are nonetheless important elements of the site. The archaeologist cannot completely ignore these structures in most cases, especially if the project is one designed to explore the total range of behaviors at the site.

Fortunately for archaeologists, there are sampling methods that mitigate the problems inherent in both intuitive and random sampling procedures. A **stratified random sample** requires an archaeologist to divide the site into zones or sections. A fixed number of excavation units are then assigned to be placed at random in each zone (Figure 5.3). Thus, by defining a section of the site that is obviously important to the archaeologist, such as a cluster of buildings or a courtyard, as a zone and then deciding how many units to assign to that area, the archaeologist makes certain that at least some excavation will take

stratified random sampling A method of sampling by which an archaeological site is first divided into zones or sections and a fixed number of excavation units are assigned to be placed at random in each zone. Thus, by defining a section of the site that is obviously important to the archaeologist, such as a cluster of buildings or a courtyard, as a zone and then deciding how many units to assign to that area, the archaeologist makes certain that at least some excavation will take place in that area.

FIGURE 5.3

A stratified random sample allows archaeologists some flexibility in exploring a site. By allocating specific numbers of units to be excavated in each zone or by the placement of some units according to the preference of the excavators, this method attempts to accentuate the best aspects of both nonrandom and random sampling methods.

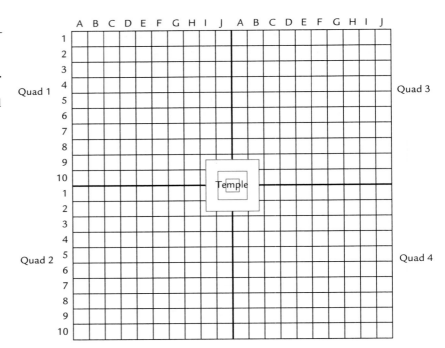

place in that area. This allows a level of random sampling across the site while also ensuring that essential investigation takes place.

A fourth method, *hierarchical random sampling,* combines intuitive sampling with random sampling in a slightly different way. A variation on a stratified random sample, this method allows an archaeologist to place a percentage of the total possible excavation units on the site through random sampling. The remaining units are then assigned intuitively by the archaeologist. This method is used extensively by cultural resource management archaeologists in some regions, because it allows them to hold a certain number of excavation units in reserve. Should the initial testing of the site identify areas of significant interest, then additional units from the reserve pool can be located in these places. This method allows archaeologists to stay within their fixed budgets and time frames while providing them with some flexibility in sampling sites. In the event that no areas of special concern are identified, then the excavation units in the reserve pool can be assigned randomly, essentially expanding the initial range of randomly selected units.

Methodological Standards

Other standards address accurately recovering meaningful and useful data from the site. In general this means that the archaeologists involved in a project are required to adopt specific methods of data recovery that are designed to work with the physical environment and the theoretical issues prevalent in the region where they work. In dry, sandy regions, such as are common in parts of the American Southwest, archaeologists are often faced with a lack of natural stratigraphy on their sites. Sediments deposited on such sites tend to accumulate slowly in many areas. This means that very old artifacts can sometimes be found adjacent to artifacts of very recent origin. Alternatively, artifacts may appear to be distributed vertically through one continuous layer of sediments. Noting this fact early in this century, Nels Nelson devised a method of dividing such seemingly homogenous earthen layers into arbitrary zones of 1 foot or less. This allowed Nelson to artificially segregate the artifacts and, in this manner, to identify consistent vertical patterns of artifact distribution. By doing this on a variety of sites, Nelson was able to identify the sequence of artifact types and begin to develop an understanding of the chronology of material culture.

Such methods are not used in other parts of North America in which there is clear and well-defined stratigraphy. For example, at the Gottschall site in southwestern Wisconsin, Robert Salzer has been excavating a rockshelter (a shallow overhang in a rock face) in natural stratigraphic levels. The site is located at the top of a small valley, and water regularly flows into the rockshelter, bringing with it local sediments that are deposited across the site. This happened so regularly in the past that very few of Salzer's levels are more than a few centimeters thick. Consequently, it is easier for the archaeologists to carefully remove each naturally deposited layer of sediments in each excavation unit as a single provenience.

A similar situation exists on some historic sites at which areas of the site have been filled or in some way covered over with large deposits. Such deposits represent a single event, and in most such situations it makes little sense to artificially segregate zones of this fill (*fill* is the term applied to the sediments moved onto the site in this single, human-produced episode). At the Octagon House, a late nineteenth–early twentieth century site in Decorah, Iowa, for example, archaeologists from nearby Luther College were able to explore the backyard of the house in advance of the construction of a new garage. Initial testing revealed that approximately the top 2½ feet of the soils were mixed and seemed to represent a single filling episode (Figure 5.4). Subsequent interviews with some longtime residents of the town revealed that the backyard of that house and several adjacent homes were filled and leveled between 1910 and 1912. This period corresponds to expansion of the nearby county courthouse, an event that allowed local residents to acquire large amounts of sediments and stone (for retaining walls and landscaping). Subsequent work at the house treated this fill zone as a single depositional unit, and no attempt was made to impose artificial levels on this zone. Because the material was carted to the site and scattered about in a landscaping process, the actual contents of this zone tell us little, if anything, about human behaviors at the site. Rather, the presence of the fill zone itself is more significant, because it tells us that the owners of the house had the resources and interest to undertake a major landscaping project.

FIGURE 5.4

A photograph of strata at a historic site in Iowa. Note the layer near the top followed by the two thicker strata beneath (lower right, then lower left).

More specific standards are usually associated with sampling issues, including the method of recovering material culture from the site. Some sort of standardized excavation unit is typically expected in terms of size and the manner in which matrix is excavated. Such standard units might conform to an arbitrarily defined size (such as 1 m × 1 m, 2 m × 2 m, etc.) and use the **arbitrary unit size** method, or to an observable physical feature, such as exemplified by the **architectural unit method** (Figures 5.5, 5.6). In this method observable architectural zones of predefined structures are excavated as a single horizontal provenience. Thus a room within a palace or any other sort of structure would be treated as its own excavation area. The idea is to try to correlate archaeological units with the divisions of space constructed by past peoples.

In cases in which no observable structures exist to define areas of excavation or in which the archaeologist has devised research questions that require consistently sized units of spatial control, it is necessary to work with arbitrarily sized units. Remember, although the word *arbitrary* is associated with these units, this term means only that the researchers pick the size of the unit they will use most commonly across the site. This means that once the researchers select a unit size, they will use that size consistently. Only in special cases, such as those in which there is insufficient space to locate the standard size of excavation area chosen, will other sizes be used.

Unlike the architectural unit method, the arbitrary unit size method is more closely allied with statistical sampling. Because each unit is of the same size, it is possible to directly compare the number and types of artifacts recovered in each unit. In theory at least this allows archaeologists to more objec-

arbitrary unit size The selection of a standard size for an excavation unit based on personal preferences.

architectural unit method In this method observable architectural zones of predefined structures are excavated as a single horizontal provenience. Thus a room within a palace or other sort of structure would be treated as its own excavation area. The idea is to try to correlate archaeological units with the divisions of space constructed by past peoples.

A pair of 1 m × 1 m squares under excavation at Rmiz, Czech Republic. The choice of this size unit was based on the excavator's preference for a metric site grid and his sampling design rather than on any condition specific to the site, such as the size of a structure or observable feature.

FIGURE 5.6

Sir Arthur Evans's excavations at the Palace of Knossos (Minoan Greece) employed architectural unit methods. Here, entire rooms of buildings were excavated as a single provenience.

tively explore the archaeological site and to test hypotheses. If the excavation units were of different sizes, then archaeologists would have to account for the differences in order to determine if they were finding the same sorts and amounts of material from each unit. This is not so easily done because the results are based more on predictions than on directly observable data.

Similarly, the arbitrary unit size method requires archaeologists to make no assumptions about the nature of the deposits being excavated. An excavation unit is treated as a probe into an unknown universe, at least for purposes of sampling. With the architectural unit method of excavation, however, there is a stronger temptation to make assumptions about the purpose and nature of the space being excavated. Sometimes this has advantages, especially in situations in which there are historic or ethnographic records that help to define structures on a site. This can also be the case in situations in which large amounts of archaeology have been conducted on similar structures so that the researchers have a good idea of what they are likely to find in similar settings on their own sites. In these cases archaeologists are forearmed with knowledge of the conditions and materials they can expect to find.

The danger lies in situations in which there is no such good data on which to make assumptions about the nature of a structure or the past use of space within it. In these instances archaeologists must be sure not to project their own biases about how space and buildings are used onto the archaeological record. Most Americans, for example, are familiar with households in which there are relatively few people living under the same roof and sharing common spaces. Much of the rest of the world, including most other industrialized nations, are familiar with households in which there is less space available and therefore more sharing of rooms. Consequently, if American archaeologists were to interpret the use of rooms based on their view of the use of space, then it might be that such interpretations would frequently be wrong. For example, when dealing with domestic structures, cross-cultural studies consistently demonstrate that most of the world's societies use less space for more people. One need only travel outside of the United States to see vivid examples of this trend. As always, though, students of archaeology are reminded that no one method is always better than any other method, only that some methods answer some research questions better than do others. Consistency in approach, though, is at the heart of archaeological excavations and therefore defines one of the basic standards against which all research projects are evaluated (Box 5.2).

At this point it is important to discuss why archaeologists tend to excavate using squares and rectangles rather than other shapes. The answer, as you might anticipate, has to do with recovering usable data in a consistent manner. Archaeologists could excavate circular units, if they chose to, by defining the size of a unit based on the radius of the circle. Practically, however, it is difficult to consistently excavate a circle with hand tools when there is no structure to follow. The straight edges of squares and rectangles are much

BOX 5.2

AUGUSTUS PITT RIVERS AND
THE STANDARDIZATION OF FIELD METHODS

During the latter half of the nineteenth century, archaeology was only just beginning to develop an identity separate from antiquarianism. Although Thomas Jefferson had long before conducted systematic excavations on his property in Virginia to demonstrate that Native Americans had, in fact, built the mounds there, many archaeologists still utilized divergent and idiosyncratic methods to recover and record their data. Indeed, because Jefferson was not primarily a historian or an archaeologist, his work was little known in many scientific circles. For the most part, archaeological research in this era can best be characterized as chaotic and piecemeal, though with an overall direction formed by the expansion of Darwinian notions of evolution and, later, by social Darwinism.

Against this background of seeming chaos emerged Augustus Henry Lane Fox Pitt Rivers, a remarkable figure who typifies the notion of a gentleman adventurer and scholar. Pitt Rivers began life in 1827 as A. H. Lane Fox, the second son of an English gentleman and a Scottish noblewoman. Through a series of chance inheritances and good fortune, he inherited the estate of his second cousin and took the surnames Pitt Rivers (his cousin was baron of Rivers). He also became an officer in the English Army, in which he served in Crimea and Canada, as well as in London and Windsor. As a dashing young officer he married Alice Stanley, an English noblewoman, and through her family made the acquaintance of such philosophical luminaries as Sir John Lubbock, Thomas Huxley (Darwin's so-called bulldog), and Herbert Spencer. Perhaps unsurprisingly, Pitt Rivers became an ardent advocate of Darwinism and was at the forefront of its application in interpreting the history of societies. It was this thinker, soldier, and gentleman who eventually made the acquaintance of many early archaeologists, including the premier English Egyptologist of the day, Sir William Flinders-Petrie.

Pitt Rivers came to archaeology late in life, after his retirement from the service as a general and his inheri-

tance in 1880. During these last twenty years of his life, though, he conducted a remarkable sequence of excavations at Cranborne Chase in the United Kingdom, which happened to be on his own property. With the assistance of draftsmen, younger assistants, and laborers from his estate, Pitt Rivers encountered and systematically explored everything from Neolithic barrows to Iron Age hillforts and Romano-British settlements. The remarkably rich area in which he worked produced such copious amounts of data that most archaeologists could have spent their entire lives working on just one or a few of these sites. Instead, Pitt Rivers systematically explored as many as possible, with the exception of a single Roman building, and published the results of his work at each site.

This in itself was remarkable for his day and was due in substantial part to Pitt Rivers's abilities as an organizer. Though a stern taskmaster and, at times, cantankerous, Pitt Rivers insisted that all excavations be conducted according to a fixed plan. Each "spit" (a measured excavation unit of a fixed size and regular shape), as he called his excavation units, was to be sharply defined and excavated in the same manner as every other spit. Profiles of the walls were to be made and detailed notes taken about everything encountered in excavating the spit. These notes and drawings, many supposedly made by Pitt Rivers himself, were then collated and used as the basis of his publications. Hence, Pitt Rivers is often viewed as a driving force in the standardization of archaeological techniques. This standardization allowed comparison between different specific field techniques and the growth of archaeological methodology in general.

Recent scholars have taken exception to some of Pitt Rivers's work and question how much he himself accomplished and how much was actually done by his assistants. Likewise, they challenge the notion that Pitt Rivers was particularly good at interpreting the things he did find and point to occasional inconsistencies in

(continued)

BOX 5.2 (continued)

the work he directly undertook. In some respects these criticisms are justified, though primarily in light of more recent investigative techniques and not in light of the methods commonly employed during the late nineteenth century. However, the real strength of Pitt Rivers's contributions to archaeology is not his personal work but his sometimes acidic insistence on rigid controls, defined approaches, and publication. These things provided a framework in which other archaeologists, even some contemporaries of Pitt Rivers himself, could innovate more dynamic and successful excavation techniques.

easier to establish and follow, making them more efficient shapes for controlling excavations. Similarly, the flat walls that excavation of such shapes produces allow archaeologists to better see and map the levels of sediment that have been excavated.

The final elements of methodological standards in archaeology center around the analysis and preservation of the data from the site. Because archaeological excavations remove material remains from their contexts, it is essential that careful and thorough records be kept of all fieldwork. There are few, if any, places in the world in which modern archaeologists do not insist upon recording every bit of data generated through their research. Similarly, these records and the material remains they represent must be curated for future generations. To do otherwise is to lose portions of the past forever, and this is simply unacceptable.

DIGGING INTO THE PAST

Now that we have an idea of what sorts of standards are common to archaeological investigation, we need to turn to an examination of the various methods that have been devised to recover the past. As always, it is important to realize that the specific methods of excavation are designed to answer specific research questions. Each set of techniques that an archaeologist adopts is selected to do certain things, and different archaeologists, asking different questions, may prefer different methods of recovering data. There is no single correct way to excavate, but as we discussed previously, there are always standards that must be adhered to.

Vertical Approaches

One of the basic decisions made on all sites is whether, at a given time and in a given place, archaeologists need to get a great deal of information about how a site was deposited (a diachronic perspective), or whether they are principally interested in what happened at a site within set periods of time (a synchronic approach). Archaeologists primarily interested in a diachronic ap-

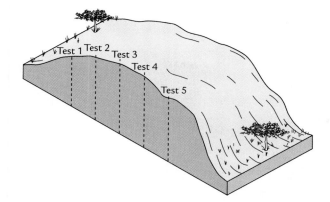

FIGURE 5.7

A vertical approach emphasizes the collection of information in a way that limits the horizontal excavations on a site but provides a great deal of information about the development of the site across time.

proach might first opt to excavate using a **vertical approach** (Figure 5.7). In this vein the researchers might choose to excavate in a small number of locations but to carry their excavations downward, as deeply as safely possible, in short order. This provides a series of views into what is present at the site, level by level, through time. Based on these vertical exposures the excavators can then determine if the site can answer all of their research questions, how to go about recovering the data if they are present, and where best to concentrate their resources. The vertical exposures also give the researchers the opportunity to collect data that can help to date the different levels of the site, thus enhancing the archaeologists' abilities to focus their resources.

There are many different forms of vertical approaches. Perhaps the most common is known as **test pitting.** In this method excavators place units of predetermined size across the site using intuitive, random, or stratified random sampling strategies. These units are then excavated downward until the crew reaches bedrock, sediments that clearly predate any form of hominid (humans and their closest, upright ancestors) presence, or until the unit is too deep to safely work in. Records are made of what was found, and at what depth, and drawings are made of the natural and cultural strata revealed by the work. In many cases this sort of work is the hallmark of what is sometimes called **phase II** research in cultural resource management, meaning the systematic evaluation of a known site's cultural material and its context.

A variant of test pitting is the use of **test trenches.** Rather than relying on relatively small windows into the past, such as are produced in test pitting, some researchers find that their questions are better answered either by digging a series of test pits immediately adjacent to one another, thus forming a line or trench, or by excavating a rectangular test unit with a long horizontal axis. The end product in both cases is a long, usually relatively narrow trench that enables the researchers to record a great deal of information about the cultural and natural stratigraphy on a site. Sometimes, as is the case with mounds of earth covering structures or other, similar features, trenches represent the only practical way to excavate into or through the feature while still

vertical approach The excavation of deep but relatively narrow units, usually employed to identify the type of natural and cultural deposits present on an archaeological site.

test pitting The placement of single or small groups of excavation units across a site in order to acquire as much localized data as possible from the site being explored. Such data helps archaeologists define both the vertical and horizontal distribution of archaeological materials on the site.

phase II In cultural resource management, refers to the testing and assessment of cultural resources on an already-discovered archaeological site.

test trenches Isolated or small groups of trenches excavated to preliminarily determine the natural and cultural distribution of materials across the site.

FIGURE 5.8

Although once thought to be poor technique, the careful use of heavy equipment on some sorts of archaeological sites has become accepted practice. Especially in urban situations, heavy machinery such as backhoes and bulldozers may prove the only efficient method of excavating through rubble-packed areas.

sondage A term popular in Europe, a sondage is an area of intensive testing, often in the form of trenches or contiguous archaeological units.

maintaining good stratigraphic controls. In parts of Europe such test trenches are referred to as **sondages.**

In certain situations it may be desirable to excavate test trenches with power machinery, including bulldozers and backhoes. Once considered unthinkable in archaeology, the use of such equipment has gained increasing acceptance because of the cost and time benefits that these machines offer. They are frequently employed on sites at which substantial layers of fill or noncultural material has been deposited atop or within archaeological deposits. For example, modern sediments resulting from flooding need not be carefully excavated by hand because they contain little, if any, information useful to archaeologists. Alternatively, power machinery has also proven useful on industrial sites and on sites at which there is quite a bit of rubble or other heavy material that must be removed in order to interpret the site. At the Lakehurst Railroad Roundhouse, an early twentieth-century railroad facility near the southern New Jersey shore, a bulldozer was used to clear substantial amounts of rubble that had been deposited when the roundhouse (literally the place where trains were turned around to go in the other direction) was demolished. Without the aid of such machines it would have been difficult, or perhaps impossible, to excavate the rooms and facilities that lay buried beneath the rubble (Figure 5.8).

Less frequently, power machinery has been used in place of smaller hand tools to remove matrix from undisturbed areas of sites. In such cases the ar-

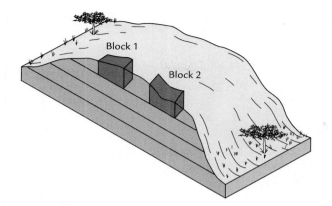
Block 1
Block 2

FIGURE 5.9

A horizontal approach emphasizes the collection of data specific to individual periods in the past from across the site rather than the collection of information about all occupations at the site in small horizontal areas.

chaeologists are trading resolution, the ability to see the fine details of what is going on at a site, for increased coverage. Power machinery simply can move a great deal more matrix than can a human crew, though it is not very forgiving when it encounters fragile objects or materials representing features. One such use involved the excavation of a city block in downtown New Brunswick, New Jersey. The city had committed to revitalizing an economically depressed section of the downtown district and needed to mitigate the damage that this work would do to the historic occupation of the area. As is too often the case, time and money were limited, and the area of investigation was quite large (portions of two city blocks). In this case the archaeologists in charge of the project opted to use a backhoe to systematically trench across the site in an effort to reveal long segments of the natural and cultural deposits. Once these trenches were in place, more traditional archaeological units were excavated based on the data provided from the trenching. In some cases the trenches enabled archaeologists to excavate features that were partially exposed by the backhoe, thus giving the excavators a unique and beneficial side view of the deposits as they were removed. Some of this benefit was offset, however, by the loss of some information that was simply obliterated by the backhoe. Nonetheless, given the limitations of the excavations and the requirement to sample a large area, the backhoe work was generally considered successful in this case.

Horizontal Approaches

Archaeologists who already have an idea of the layout of a site or where best to get at the data that they anticipate will answer their questions might elect to adopt a **horizontal approach** (Figure 5.9). In this approach archaeologists excavate large, contiguous areas of the site in order to obtain a good sense of what is present within a narrow range of time. Unlike the vertical approach, the horizontal approach emphasizes breadth of excavation rather than depth. If, for example, we were on a project focusing on the third century A.D. Roman occupation of a site in eastern Spain, then there would be no need to excavate

horizontal approach
A strategy of excavation designed to open large areas of a component to facilitate better understanding of that particular area.

FIGURE 5.10

An example of block exca-
vation underway at Colonial
Williamsburg. The ability to
see large, contiguous areas
of the site at the same time
helps archaeologists interpret what happened at the
site and provides clues
helpful in determining
where best to utilize future
resources.

block excavation method
The excavation of an area of a
site without leaving intervening walls or pillars in the area.
This method allows archaeologists to expose contiguous
areas of floors better than
does a baulk method.

downward beneath the level containing this information. Depending on the
nature of the research questions, the team might simply stop their work at the
appropriate stratum (level of earth) and concentrate on expanding their excavation units laterally to uncover as much of this Roman component as
possible.

Just as was the case with vertical approaches, an archaeologist might adopt
many different sorts of horizontal approaches. At the heart of these different
approaches is the difference between a block system and a baulk system. A
block excavation method involves the systematic removal of all of the matrix
within the area of excavation down to and including the site component being
explored (Figure 5.10). No divisions will be visible between the excavation
units once they have been excavated save for any stakes, flags, or pins the crew
elects to place. This method has the advantage of producing an area that is
easily viewed and simple to *planview* (to map the horizontal distribution of

FIGURE 5.11

Baulk excavations in the Near East. The baulks allow archaeologists to compare the different strata between excavation units and provide an important record of this layering that can be recorded at a later date.

material remains at a given depth). This method also allows the researchers to trace the paths of walls or other features across the site without intervening pedestals or zones of matrix. The only major detriment to the approach is that the profile walls, so important to archaeologists' understanding of the soil layers at the site, are moved away from the center of the block as excavations proceed. It can sometimes be difficult to trace strata across a block excavation, especially in situations in which there are complex relationships between the different strata on the site (dipping, intermixing, and filling, for example).

A **baulk excavation method** is one in which pillars or walls of matrix are left intact between adjacent excavated areas (Figure 5.11). These baulks allow investigators to view vertical profile walls in close proximity to their areas of excavation and can be useful as a means of crossing a site without having to walk in areas under excavation. The downside to the baulk method is that these walls of soil, even if only half a meter thick, make it difficult to trace patterns of features and artifacts horizontally across a site. The matrix left in place sometimes masks changes in direction in a line of posts; at other times such baulks might even conceal important data. Again, depending on the specific questions and conditions particular to each excavation, it is impossible to state that one method is superior to the other. At best an archaeologist can

baulk excavation method
The excavation of an area of a site leaving vertical pillars or walls in place, thus enabling archaeologists to better correlate excavations with already defined strata.

understand the benefits and limitations of each approach and select the one that best meets the needs of the project at hand.

LEVELS, LAYERS, AND PRESERVING CONTEXT

The preceding discussions focused on the distribution of excavation units on a site, that is, their placement across the landscape. Once a unit has been located, however, we must move on to a discussion of how the sediments within the boundaries of that unit can be removed. There are many ways that this can be done, though most of these are dictated first by research questions and second by the depositional environment of the site.

A **depositional environment** is nothing more than the physical setting in a given location and includes such things as the types of sediments (clay, silt, or sand), the soil pH, the amount of water in the ground, and comparable factors. Each of these things affects the preservation of material remains, as well as how those remains are positioned. Of primary concern is whether or not the material remains are **in situ,** meaning in their original place of deposition into the archaeological record. Many people are surprised to learn that the archaeological record is not static, that things happen to material culture even after the people who made and used it dropped or otherwise left it on the ground. When an artifact is found in a place to which it was moved after having been originally deposited, it is said to be in a **secondary context.**

Michael Schiffer has studied the way in which material culture is moved about once it is deposited, and he has identified two categories of disturbance. Those caused by natural factors are called **N-transforms** (natural transformations), whereas those caused by human activities are called **C-transforms** (cultural transformations). For example, burrowing animals such as moles might move artifacts around in the course of their normal lives. This would be an example of **bioturbation,** or the churning of sediments and material culture by animals or even insects. Sediments subject to repeated freezing and thawing events might also be mixed; thus material culture within the sediments might also be subject to movement as the matrix expands and contracts with freezing and thawing. Both of these examples illustrate N-transforms (Figure 5.12).

Unsurprisingly, C-transforms come in a wide variety, because human activities tend to be complex and to occur across long spans of time. Imagine for a moment that someone in the American Southwest accidently breaks a ceramic vessel by dropping it on the floor of the room in which a family often slept. The initial deposition of the pot, the one which reflects most closely the place the pot was used and eventually broken, is in this room. The person who dropped the vessel, however, may have found it inconvenient and perhaps physically uncomfortable to walk across the broken pot each day and therefore may have cleaned up the pieces and thrown them out. Consequently, the remains of the ceramic vessel found their way into the archaeological record

---

depositional environment The physical setting in which material culture is found. Depositional environments include such things as sediment types, soil pH, the amount of water in the sediment, and similar physical factors.

in situ In place.

secondary context The position in which material culture is found after it has undergone either or both C-transforms and N-transforms.

N-transforms The movement and reposition of cultural material on an archaeological site by natural agencies, such as animals or freeze-thaw action.

C-transforms The movement and redistribution of material culture by human agencies.

bioturbation Disturbance of sediments related to the archaeological record by animals such as moles and gophers.

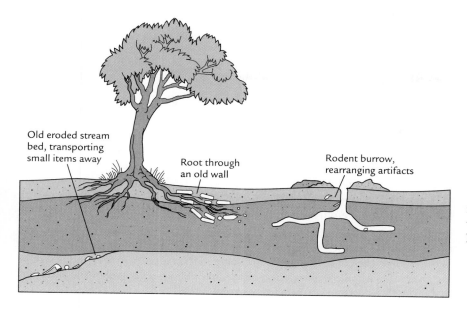

Old eroded stream bed, transporting small items away

Root through an old wall

Rodent burrow, rearranging artifacts

FIGURE 5.12

Natural transformations involve the movement or reworking of material culture by natural agents, such as erosion, rodent burrowing, and plant growth. In this drawing, material has been brought onto the site from elsewhere by an old stream, and the actions of a rodent and a tree root have repositioned material culture both vertically and horizontally on the site.

in a small pile within a midden (a pile of material discarded by humans). This is an example of a C-transform in the past (Figure 5.13).

Now imagine that the site in which this material was deposited has been reused by modern people, perhaps because many places that were good to live in before are still good places to live in today. Modern development may have cut through the ancient midden and pushed the fragments of the vessel around, perhaps even out of the midden. Finally, let us assume that it is here that an archaeologist first observed and recorded the material. The vessel fragments would be said to be in secondary context (meaning other than in situ) and would have undergone two C-transforms separated by one thousand years.

A common question asked at this point is whether archaeologists think that material in secondary contexts is helpful in interpreting past behaviors. Certainly the mere presence of archaeological material is useful to researchers, but, as you know, it is the provenience and context in which the material is found that is most important to scholars. Nonetheless, materials in some secondary contexts are helpful to us. Material culture found in secondary contexts that came about through the actions of the people who used the material, as in the example of the broken pot being placed in a midden, tell us something about past human behaviors. In this case we know that the site was large enough so that people had defined areas for garbage disposal. Likewise, we know that the pot was broken elsewhere and deliberately placed in the midden. Excavation of the midden might also reveal what other material was in use at the same time and provide archaeologists with an idea of what sorts of things were considered expendable and what sorts of things were too important or too expensive to discard very often.

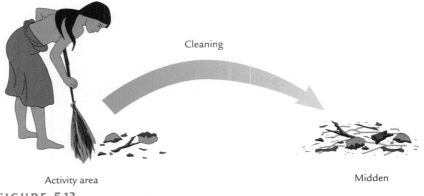

Cleaning

Activity area

Midden

FIGURE 5.13

Cultural transformations involve the redistribution or reworking of material culture by human activities, such as by cleaning or the deliberate reuse of an old item found in the ground. The example of a person cleaning a room or activity area and depositing gathered material elsewhere is a good example of how items used in one place can find themselves deposited in completely separate areas.

Other materials in secondary contexts are less useful. The material deposited as fill at the Octagon House (discussed earlier in this chapter) is so far removed from its original context that it tells us very little about the past. In fact, at the Octagon House the excavators noted many stone flakes (by-products of producing stone tools) that probably dated to the era before the arrival of Euroamericans in the region. This material was likely unknowingly dug from its original context near the county courthouse and simply moved along with the sediments to be deposited in the backyard of the Octagon House. Such material provided little information to the researchers save that there may have been an archaeological site near the courthouse that was destroyed during the expansion of that facility.

As you may imagine, it is only through careful excavation that archaeologists can determine the context in which material remains are found. In order to maintain control of their work, archaeologists dig in predefined levels. Such levels might be defined by naturally occurring strata, as at the Gottschall site, or they may be defined arbitrarily much in the way that Nels Nelson defined them early in the twentieth century. In both cases careful attention is paid to how matrix is removed and processed.

In most parts of the world nonfill matrix is removed in thin strips by hand tools such as masons' trowels, flat-bladed shovels, or comparable tools. The excavators remove the material while being careful to search for material culture. If the research is designed to explore the precise distribution of this material, the archaeologists typically try to record each piece in the spot in which it is found by recording its location in relation to the excavation unit's datum point. A **unit datum point** is the place from which all measurements are taken

unit datum point The control point from which all measurements in a specific excavation unit are made.

FIGURE 5.14

Student archaeologists screen sediments from the Samuel site, Oswego, Illinois. All sediments at the site were passed through ¼″ sieves in order to sample the range of small finds, such as pottery fragments and bone, present at the site.

in the excavation unit and is traditionally located in the southwest corner. The process of recording the precise coordinates of the material culture is called **point proveniencing** or **piece plotting.** Assuming the unit datum is in the southwest corner of the unit, then measurements are taken to the north and to the east, and then the depth of the material is recorded. These three coordinates allow archaeologists to precisely position each artifact on a site map and make it possible for scholars to execute very fine-grained forms of research.

On large sites with great quantities of material culture, point proveniencing is often considered to be too slow and too expensive to be efficient. On large historic and classical sites, for example, archaeologists might recover thousands of pieces of pottery every day. Likewise, such sites tend to cover large areas and represent complex behaviors. In most such cases archaeologists must try to recover the data they need to answer their research questions in a timely fashion. To do this, they remove matrix from units and process it through sieves. Often a ¼-inch or smaller mesh is used and buckets or other containers of matrix are poured into the screen for processing. The sediments are forced through by shaking, hand pressure, or water, leaving behind larger objects, including artifacts. Such recovery methods allow archaeologists to place material culture on a map of a site according to the location of the excavation unit and the level of the sediment being removed at the time. In most cases this is sufficient to allow archaeologists to determine the activities undertaken at the site by past peoples in a timely and efficient manner (Figure 5.14).

In still other circumstances researchers elect to screen only a sample of the matrix excavated, perhaps one of every ten buckets (a 10% sample), or to do away with screening altogether. On large sites in parts of the Old World it

point proveniencing/piece plotting The precise three-dimensional measurement of a single piece of material culture in relation to an archaeological site.

would be virtually impossible to recover every fragment of material culture, especially common sorts of material culture such as pottery at a Roman villa or medieval castle. Moreover, because much of the material is already well known from previous excavations and historic records, archaeologists stand to learn little by examining each and every piece. Hence, only a sample of the site's sediments are screened, though a conscientious attempt is made to identify and record significant finds in the locations at which they are first encountered (Box 5.3).

SPECIAL RECOVERY TECHNIQUES

There are several different sorts of specialized recovery techniques in archaeology. Among the most common of these are water screening, flotation, and soil sampling. Each of these techniques is designed to recover special, often hard-to-get at, data. They are adopted by excavators in the same manner as other excavation techniques but tend to be viewed as specialized attempts to collect very specific things. Because of this they represent an option more than a standard feature in archaeological research.

Water screening comes in many forms (Box 5.4). The principle common to all variants of this approach is forcing matrix through screens or filters by water pressure. In the most basic form, water screening involves using standard screen sizes (that is, the same used in the more conventional dry screening process) and water pressure, often from a hose or pump. The pressure of the water forces the matrix through the screening rapidly and in a controlled manner (the velocity and amount of water pumped through the screen can be controlled). More commonly, a finer mesh screen is chosen for this process because the water is so efficient at forcing the matrix through the sieving. The advantages of this system include the ability to more easily screen clayey soils, which are difficult to force through screening by hand, as well as the ability to monitor and control the water pressure. Such methods have the disadvantage of possibly breaking delicate material remains or grinding them into mesh, thus damaging the remains. These things happen because the screeners, those operating the water pressure and searching for artifacts, often cannot assess what is in the mesh until after the water has done its work. By this time any damage that is likely to occur has already been completed.

Flotation takes two primary forms, one based on air pressure or water movement and the other based on chemicals. The basic idea is to pour matrix into a small container of water, such as a bucket, drum, or metal pan, into which a series of increasingly fine screens have been placed. The water is agitated by stirring it, by relying on natural currents in streams and rivers, or by forcing air into the container. Light objects tend to float to the surface. Chemicals can also be used to change the specific gravity of the water so that a similar effect is created. The material on the surface is then scooped off with a small straining device and collected in its own plastic bag or foil packet. This is called the **light fraction.** The material that sinks in the container is sorted through in-

water screening The application of water under pressure to force sediments through screens.

flotation The use of water or air pressure and sometimes chemicals to cause light materials such as seeds and charcoal to rise to the surface in a container of water, where they can be collected.

light fraction The portion of the material that rises to the surface in a flotation tank.

BOX 5.3

THE TOOLS OF THE TRADE

It has been said that a craftsperson is no better than his tools. To some great measure this is a truism that archaeologists also live by. Just as research questions lead to hypotheses and methodology, so too do they lead to acquiring the right tools to get the job done. This box presents a simple overview of the sorts of tools a typical archaeologist might work with on any given site. Although some sites, such as those under water, require specialized equipment not mentioned here, most archaeologists would find that the gear listed below would be sufficient to do almost everything they needed to do on a regular basis and perhaps some extra sorts of things as well. (Please note, however, that a whip, fedora, and handgun are strictly optional accessories.)

- bundle of twine (for creating unit boundaries)

- large nails, chaining pins, or wooden stakes (for marking corners of excavation units)

- trowel (#4 or #5 Marshalltown are the preferred styles in much of North America; for excavating sediments by hand)

- shovel (usually sharpened flat shovel; for carefully removing sediments in thicker layers)

- picks, mauls, and related tools, if required (for breaking through rubble)

- wooden or bamboo skewers (for detail work)

- paint brushes, ranging from "0" modeling brush through ½-inch painter's brush (for detail work)

- whisk broom (for cleaning stones or architecture)

- plumb bob (for identifying a vertical plane; for measuring depth and shaping walls)

- line level (for identifying horizontal planes, measuring depths, and creating flat floors)

- pruning shears (for clearing small roots)

- two measuring tapes or engineers' folding rulers (for measuring within the excavation unit)

- dust pan or scoop (for collecting sediments)

- durable buckets (for transporting sediments to sieves for processing)

- sieve or screening unit (for processing excavated sediments)

- permanent marker (for recording on artifact bags, tags, or marking flags)

- tags or recording forms for artifact bags (to ensure excavated materials are not lost)

- artifact bags (preferably *not* paper, which disintegrates when wet; coin bags and durable plastic bags [4 mil] often work well)

- record-keeping forms or notebook, including graph paper for measured sketches (depending on the methodology adopted by the project leader)

- mechanical pencil and extra lead or pencil and sharpener (for note taking)

- ruler (for drawing diagrams in notes)

Access to:

- cameras (for recording material in situ photographically)

- measuring scales (to provide a measured scale of reference for photographs)

- axe, saw, machete, pruning hook, and similar brush-clearing tools (for clearing overgrowth)

creasingly finer layers of mesh and then is collected. This is called the **heavy fraction.** The advantages of flotation are that it is typically gentle and that it enables archaeologists to recover very small and frequently delicate remains, such as fragments of charred seeds, pollen, and tiny fragments of plant remains. The only detriment to the system is that is slow and therefore expensive. As

heavy fraction The portion of material that sinks in a flotation tank.

BOX 5.4

EL JUYO AND THE SEARCH FOR DETAIL

El Juyo is a cave located near Santandar on the Cantabrian coast, in northwestern Spain. It contains a series of important deposits from the Magdalenian period (ca. 15,000–10,000 B.C.), the period of time at the end of the Upper Paleolithic that saw the creation of the extensive cave paintings at the Spanish site of Altamira.

Les Freeman, a seasoned archaeologist from the University of Chicago, has been excavating at El Juyo for over a decade and has undertaken one of the most ambitious soil processing and data collection procedures ever attempted in archaeology. In order to obtain the maximum amount of data from the site, Freeman and his workers excavate using precise controls and point proveniencing. More significantly, however, every grain of matrix excavated from the site is processed through a series of increasingly finer meshes. An excavated matrix is placed in a series of flumes in which water transports the material downhill. The material first passes through a series of standard mesh screens, each one finer than the preceding. The finest of these screens is somewhat smaller than window screen, and it collects what most archaeologists would consider the most minute material remains. Freeman then has the water and remaining matrix pass through a set of ceramic filters. These filters are so fine that they collect microscopic specimens of everything ranging from pollen to species of snail thought to have been extinct in the Cantabrian region by the Magdalenian period. The net result of this processing is that archaeologists now have as complete a sample of all material encountered at this site as they are ever likely to get. With the assistance of paleontologists, paleobotanists, and a host of other specialists, the tiny amounts of data are beginning to yield information that will help Freeman's team describe in minute detail both the ecological conditions at and around the site and the changes that take place in all depositional environments through time.

Les Freeman collects data in El Juyo.

always, archaeologists must weigh the advantages of the method against its cost (Figure 5.15).

Unlike the two previous methods, soil sampling is merely the process of collecting controlled amounts of sediments from precisely defined proveniences. The collected sediments may be used for any number of purposes or may be curated for future research. It is also usually the process through which samples for flotation and sometimes water screening are collected. The standard collection technique is to wait until an excavation unit has been com-

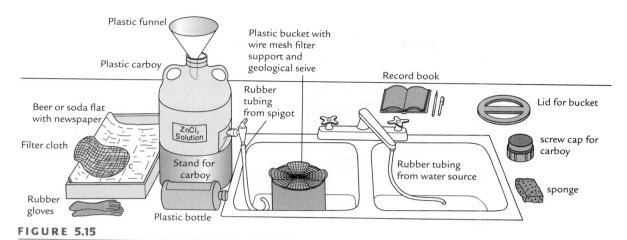

FIGURE 5.15

A basic chemical flotation system can be established in most laboratories. This system relies on changing the specific gravity of the liquid into which sediments are poured. By increasing the specific gravity, items that would normally sink in water float and can be easily recovered.

pleted and then to remove a designated amount of matrix from the side wall of the unit. First, the top layer of matrix is scraped away from the wall to reveal fresh soil; this soil is then removed and placed into a waterproof bag. By removing soils that are only now exposed, excavators minimize the chance that modern material, such as pollen from local trees, is introduced into the sample. This is important given the time and expense of processing a soil sample, through flotation or in a chemistry laboratory, to test for such things as pH levels.

ARCHAEOLOGICAL DATING

There are numerous methods for establishing the age of archaeological remains. Some of these methods have been extensively explored and are considered reliable, whereas others are new or innovative approaches that are still being evaluated. All dating methods, however, need to be considered in light of precisely what sort of information they provide to archaeologists and how that information is then used by archaeologists to apply dates to components, sites, phases, and cultures.

The first set of variables to be addressed concerns what is actually dated on an archaeological site. Most dating methods work on only a small range of raw materials, meaning that the same technique cannot be used to date all material from a site. Still, if we date one item, and we know that other material remains are associated with it, we can usually safely extend the date from the one object to all of the associated objects. This is called **indirect dating,** meaning that we are dating objects based on their association with another item that has been directly dated. By **direct dating** archaeologists mean that

indirect dating The application of a date obtained for one item, through one or more of the methods discussed here, to a second object thought to be associated with the dated material. For example, the application of a date obtained on the charcoal in a fireplace to the rocks in that same fireplace, or any tools mixed into the fireplace, would be indirect dating.

direct dating The use of a dating technique directly on the object being discussed, such as the charcoal from a fireplace or a piece of obsidian.

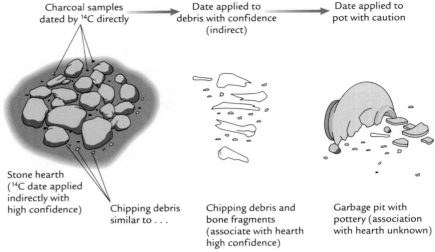

Charcoal samples
dated by ¹⁴C directly $\longrightarrow$ Date applied to
debris with confidence
(indirect) $\longrightarrow$ Date applied to
pot with caution

Stone hearth
(¹⁴C date applied
indirectly with
high confidence)

Chipping debris
similar to . . .

Chipping debris and
bone fragments
(associate with hearth
high confidence)

Garbage pit with
pottery (association
with hearth unknown)

FIGURE 5.16

Direct and indirect dating. In this example a direct date is obtained on the charcoal from a stone hearth (fireplace) via radiocarbon dating. That date is applied directly to the charcoal. It is then applied to material believed to be associated with the charcoal, such as the rocks that make up the hearth. These stones are said to be indirectly dated because the age ascribed to them is based on the strength of the association between the stone and the directly dated charcoal. Eventually, that same date might also be extended to other material, such as the chipping debris, also believed to be associated with the hearth. The further the material is removed from the directly dated material, though, the more likely it is that an indirect date may be erroneous.

they have used one of the many available techniques to assign a date to a single object. Archaeologists can, of course, directly date any number of objects, but the dates apply first and foremost to these objects. All extensions of those dates to associated materials rely on the archaeologists' ability to convincingly establish meaningful relationships between the directly dated items and the materials they wish to indirectly date (Figure 5.16).

The second set of variables in dating deals with the type of date that can be established for any material remains. There are two broad categories of dates—relative and chronometric, sometimes also referred to as *absolute* dating. Relative dating techniques do not provide an age in terms of calendar years. Rather, they provide information on whether or not a given material remain is older or younger than any other given remain. In effect, relative dating provides statements such as "X is older than Y but younger than Z." This information, although not detailed, is nonetheless valuable. Moreover, these techniques are sometimes the only way to acquire dates from archaeological sites. This is especially true in cases in which the sites have been disturbed or in which archaeologists are working with previously excavated collections. Relative dating techniques include such fundamental archaeological processes as stratigraphy and seriation, as well as methods borrowed from the natural sciences, including the measurement of chemicals in archaeological material (the so-called F-U-N sequence, see the following section) and the use of paleontological data.

Chronometric, that is "time measured," dating techniques generate an age for material remains in approximate calendar years. Some dating techniques, such as dendrochronology (tree-ring dating), can provide very precise dates in terms of years whereas others, such as radiocarbon dating, provide average dates with a standard deviation. Such dating techniques are typically based on statistical evaluations of data and therefore usually include a range of dates that bracket the likely real age of the material dated. Nonetheless, chronometric dates provide good estimations of the finite age of archaeological materials.

Using the sets together allows archaeologists to describe dates in one of four manners. A date can be relative and direct, relative and indirect, chronometric and direct, or chronometric and indirect. Try to envision how these labels might be employed as you read about the specific sorts of dating techniques archaeologists use.

Relative Dating

Relative dating techniques are those that provide information about the age of an item in relation to another item. This means that these methods do not provide calendar dates but merely statements about the relative age of one item or set of items in relation to other items. These techniques can be subdivided into the different ways in which these comparisons are made. Three approaches exist—archaeological, geological, and chemical.

You are already familiar with the standard forms of archaeological and geological dating. Archaeological methods involve ordering material culture through stylistic changes, much like modern people order the shapes of automobiles or the styles of clothing. The establishment of a chronology based on seriation, however, also allows archaeologists to compare the styles of material culture between sites, a process known as **cross dating.** If, for example, pottery is analyzed on one site and placed in a sequence based on seriation, then the sequence in which the pottery occurs can be applied to ceramics found on other sites. The major deficit in the technique is that, if one end or the other of the seriation cannot be anchored as early or late in time, then archaeologists cannot be sure which way the styles changed.

Stratigraphy, the study of layers of sediments, is the common geological method applied to archaeological dating. This process is based on the Law of Superposition, usually attributed to the eighteenth-century English geologist Charles Lyell. This law states that sediments at the bottom of a geological sequence are usually older than those on top. If there are dips, strikes, erosion, or other geologic anomalies that invert sequences, these are usually visible to trained researchers. The fact that this process is to some degree visible in

cross dating The process of assigning a date from a dated archaeological sequence to an undated sequence based on similarities in material culture between the sequences.

nearly all excavation conditions makes stratigraphy a common first step in dating all excavated material remains (Figure 5.17).

Significantly, stratigraphy and seriation can often be combined. Artifacts from across the different layers of a site can be organized first by stratigraphic position and then by stylistic changes. This allows researchers to anchor the ends of the sequence generated through seriation to stratigraphic levels. This means that archaeologists can determine in what ways styles changed from early to late.

Another approach to relative dating is derived from paleontology. This branch of geology involves the study of the remains of ancient animals, their relationships, and their distribution. Occasionally, cultural materials are found in association with ancient animals. The sequence in which these animals appeared, spread, and sometimes went extinct allows archaeologists and paleontologists to collaborate and provide relative sequences to both the geological and archaeological material.

Chemical approaches are the most varied of the three branches of relative dating. All, however, are based on the rates of observable chemical reactions. Perhaps the most famous of these techniques is known as the F-U-N series, which uses the presence of fluorine, uranium, and nitrogen in material such as bone to determine relative length of deposition. These materials accumulate in bone through such processes as absorption or leaching of the elements by the movement of groundwater through and around the bone. Bones deposited at about the same time tend to have equivalent amounts of the F-U-N elements in them. Bones that have substantially less or more of the elements must be either older or younger than the other remains.

Some dating techniques can function as both relative and chronometric methods. Sometimes this has to do with the history of the development of specific techniques, some of which were first envisioned as relative methods but have been refined to become chronometric and some of which are controversial and are accepted as relative but not as chronometric approaches. **Obsidian hydration** is a technique that conforms closely to the former, whereas amino acid racemization is an example of the latter.

Obsidian hydration measures a thin layer of water that begins to adhere to the surface of **obsidian** when it is first exposed to air (Figure 5.18). Whenever a new segment of an obsidian fragment is broken open, the fresh surface begins to absorb microscopic amounts of water. The process, first noticed by geochemists Irving Friedman and Robert Smith in the late 1950s, allows scientists to measure the average thickness of the hydration layer and apply to the measurement a mathematical formula that accounts for the average rate at which this process takes place. Simply put, researchers calculate the average length of time it should take for a hydration level as thick as the one found on the sample under analysis to accumulate. In theory this can produce a chronometric date. There is great variation in the rates at which different obsidians absorb water, however, because each type of obsidian has a unique chemical

obsidian hydration A dating technique that can be both relative and absolute. Fractures on the edge of obsidian pieces are examined under a microscope to identify the thickness of the hydration (bonded hydrogen atoms) layer that has accumulated. The thicker the level, the longer that fracture has been exposed to the atmosphere.

obsidian Sometimes referred to as volcanic glass, this is a form of stone that has no internal blocky structure. Consequently, it can be made to have an exceptionally sharp edge, though it is typically brittle.

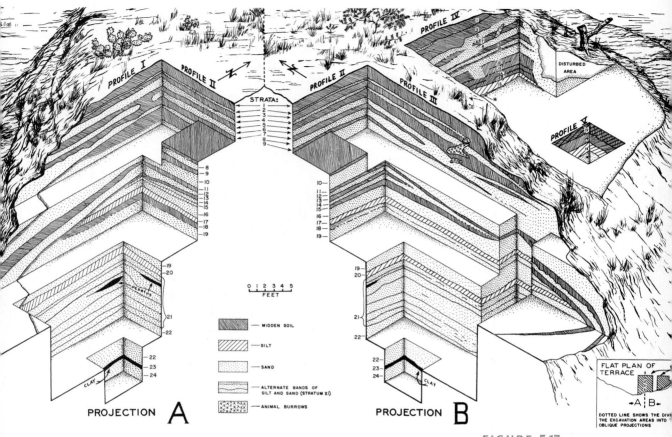

FIGURE 5.17

A drawn stratigraphic profile from the Devil's Mouth site, Texas. It is important to note the way the different strata at the site are illustrated and correlated for archaeological purposes.

composition. Only if this composition is accounted for can obsidian hydration yield an absolute date.

Other problems also exist, including the resharpening and reuse of obsidian by ancient peoples. Each reworking of an edge resets the hydration level to zero, and the process of absorption begins again. Thus, obsidian first used two thousand years ago but resharpened by an enterprising individual five hundred years later will yield only the younger date. This can be problematic in cases in which styles and functions of artifact use have changed in the meantime.

Fortunately, even without specific data on the origin of the obsidian and despite the problem of resharpening, obsidian hydration can be used as an outstanding relative dating technique. In situations in which obsidian is the preferred raw material for stone industries, as is the case in much of the American West, Mesoamerica, and along the Pacific Rim, substantial piles of obsidian fragments can be unearthed in waste areas and workshops. Such deposits can sometimes reflect the accumulation of centuries of flaking debris and

FIGURE 5.18

Obsidian hydration analysis. The worked edge of an obsidian tool is magnified and the hydration layer on it measured. By comparing this measurement with a predetermined constant representing the rate at which hydrogen atoms bond to fresh obsidian, a specialist can estimate the age of the tool.

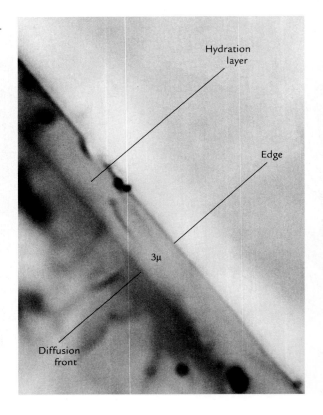

broken implements. By measuring the hydration layers on the broken pieces, however, archaeologists can sort the debris into temporal categories. Although no specific dates may be achieved, the use of the relative technique allows researchers to measure the rate at which obsidian debris was deposited at the site during different occupations. Such information is crucial when studying the development or decline of craft industries, for example.

Amino acid racemization measures the rate of conversion of amino acid to its mirror image form. In theory, this process will occur at a known rate that can be accounted for so that measurements of the ratio of amino acid to its mirror image form can be used to calculate a chronometric date. Such calculations are dependent on the presence of amino acid in bone, teeth, or shell and on the ability to calculate the rate at which proteins decay into amino acids, their building blocks.

The protein in bone, for example, is collagen. Unfortunately, the enzyme called collagenase, which promotes the decay of collagen, is present in differing densities in different sediment systems. The presence of fecal matter also increases the rate of decay. Consequently, if the presence of such conditions is not properly assessed and accounted for, amino acid racemization tests typically yield ages far in advance of the actual age of the bone. Teeth seem less

FIGURE 5.19

Dendrochronology. This cross section from an ancient tree allows archaeologists to measure and plot the thickness of each annual growth ring on the tree. Comparing the pattern of archaeological samples to known samples allows scientists to provide accurate dates for past events.

susceptible to this problem and have been the focus of a great deal of research since the early 1980s. Nonetheless, amino acid racemization may not yet be sufficiently developed for many researchers to accept as a chronometric technique, though its applications as a relative technique are comparable to those of obsidian hydration and the F-U-N series.

Chronometric Dating

Chronometric dating techniques are those that return an actual age estimate for the item under study. There are a host of such techniques, and, based on their approaches to analysis, these can be grouped into four categories: enumerative, radiometric, dosimetric, and chemical.

Enumerative methods are the most accurate of the dating techniques. Such approaches are based on counting the evidence of a known event having taken place, such as the growth of tree rings on annual cycles. The two best known methods are dendrochronology and varve analysis. **Dendrochronology** is based on the counting, measurement, and patterning of annual growth rings in trees (Figure 5.19). Each species of tree undergoes an annual growth cycle

enumerative methods Dating techniques based on the observation and counting of measurable events, such as the growth of tree-rings or deposition of sediments.

dendrochronology The analysis of growth rings in trees in order to determine the age of the wood being studied.

FIGURE 5.20

Dendrochronological samples can be spliced together in order to extend the range of a dating sequence. This process allows researchers to extend the effective range of dendrochronology beyond the life span of any single tree.

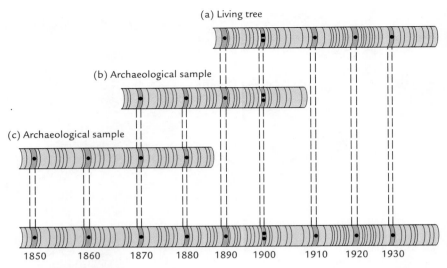

(a) Living tree

(b) Archaeological sample

(c) Archaeological sample

1850   1860   1870   1880   1890   1900   1910   1920   1930

Reconstructed master sequence

in which it deposits new cellular material atop existing material. These growth rings vary in thickness based on the local climate and how this climate reflects the ideal conditions in which a particular species of trees lives. If local conditions are ideal, growth rings tend to be thick and dense. Poor conditions yield narrow, less dense rings.

To calculate an age based on dendrochronology, we must have a sample of archaeological wood with the growth rings intact. Likewise, a master comparative sequence of growth data must be available for the region in which the sample originated. By plotting the thickness of rings of the archaeological sample in sequential order and then comparing this pattern to the control sample, specific patterns of years are identified based on common growth patterns. Because the control sample is linked to a known master chronology, the years in which the identified pattern of growth occurred can be located and a date assigned to the archaeological sample (Figure 5.20).

Varve analysis works in much the same ways as does dendrochronology. Varves are discernible patterns of sediments deposited each spring through fall in lakes adjacent to glaciers. Because little if any sediment is deposited during the winter, clear annual patterns of sedimentation are identifiable. These are, in turn, tied into known warm and cold periods that have known temporal distributions. By matching the pattern of varve deposition with the known climatic patterns, accurate dates can be obtained.

Enumerative techniques are limited by the availability and distribution of the material analyzed. Clearly, not all sites have preserved material of sufficient size and structure to allow for dendrochronology. Likewise, relatively few areas yield long sequences of comparative data that can be used for generat-

varve analysis The study of the patterned, seasonal deposition of sediments in lakes adjacent to glaciers.

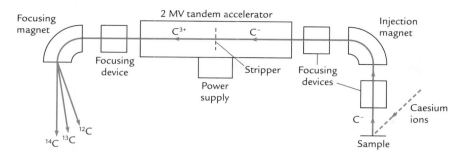

FIGURE 5.21

A schematic for the process-ing of carbon 14 through tandem electrostatic accel-erators specifically designed to detect the carbon 14 atoms.

ing dates. Varve analysis is likewise limited in where it can be employed. The requirements of both climatic data and the presence of the varves limit its ap-plication to areas such as Scandinavia, where it has been used to good effect.

Radiometric dating techniques are among the most widely employed chronometric approaches to archaeological dating. These techniques are based on the decay of radioactive isotopes that have half-lives that are known and measurable. In most of these techniques the amount of a given radioactive isotope remaining in a sample is measured and compared with the amount that should be present in a modern sample. The difference, expressed as a percentage, is compared with the half-life of the isotope, and a chronometric age is calculated (Figure 5.21).

Importantly, the measurement of the remaining amounts of isotope must be repeated thousands of times to ensure an accurate result. Because the age that is calculated for the sample represents only the mean age of all of the cal-culations, a standard deviation is also calculated. The mean and deviation are based on the idealized standard distribution, also called the bell curve, and represent the likely range of dates in which the real date of the sample falls. One standard deviation from the mean indicates that there is an approxi-mately 66% chance that the real date of the sample is within the presented date range. Doubling the standard deviation increases the probability that the actual date falls within the defined range to approximately 95%. The exten-sion of the range to include 3 standard deviations increases the probability of bracketing the real date to approximately 98%. In effect, archaeologists can trade temporal resolution for increasing assurances that they probably have the real date of the sample within the boundaries of their standard deviations (Figure 5.22).

For example, a standard radiocarbon date might read 500 years before pres-ent (the mean), plus or minus 25 years (the standard deviation). This means that there is about a 66% chance that the actual date falls between 525 and 475 years before present, the range defined by the mean plus or minus the standard deviation. In this case the range totals 50 years. The standard devia-tion could be doubled to raise the probability of bracketing the actual date to 95%, but this means that the range of possible years increases from 50 to 100

radiometric dating tech-niques A range of dating techniques based on princi-ples of radioactive decay and change among specific mate-rials, such as bone, wood, and certain forms of stone.

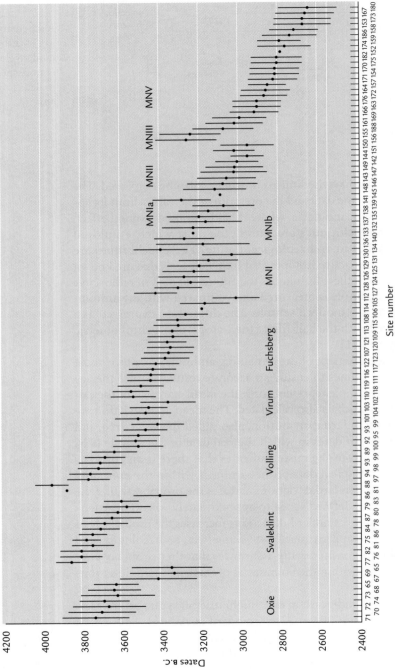

FIGURE 5.22

The distribution of radiocarbon dates for Funnel Beaker (TRB) sites in Denmark. The mean of each date is marked with a small tick, and the longer lines represent the standard deviations. Note that many of the dates overlap. It is important for researchers to get as many dates as possible.

years. Archaeologists would state that they are reasonably certain that the age of the dated sample is between 450 and 550 years before present.

The remaining two approaches to chronometric dating are dosimetric and chemical. Because the common chemical dating methods, amino acid racemization and obsidian hydration, have already been discussed in connection with relative dating techniques, this information will not be repeated here. Dosimetric approaches are based on the exposure of certain materials to radiation. Such techniques include optically stimulated luminescence, thermoluminescence, electron spin resonance, and fission track dating.

Both **optically stimulated luminescence (OSL)** and **thermoluminescence (TL)** techniques measure light emitted from materials such as baked clays, heated or burnt stone, and waterborne and windblown sediments. OSL works primarily on sediments, whereas TL works primarily on heated clays and stones. The common principle uniting the approaches is that exposure to radiation causes electrons to separate from atoms. Some of these electrons are caught in what are called traps, or defects in the material being heated. This process continues until the traps are full, a state called saturation.

By exposing the sample to radiation (energy) in the laboratory, the traps can be opened and the energy that is emitted in the form of light can be accurately measured. This radiation dose, as it is called, can be combined with an estimate of the annual dose that the sample received prior to testing. The susceptibility of the sample to radiation must also be known. In theory, though, knowing these variables allows the precise age of the sample to be calculated by determining the total amount of radiation received by the sample.

The problems with luminescence techniques are notable: The annual dose of radiation received by the sample must be accurately estimated. This estimation is based on both the chemical composition of the sample and the depositional environment from which it was recovered. Both of these factors can change over time, meaning the annual dose of radiation received by the sample can also change over time. The moisture history of the sample is also crucial, because water attenuates radiation effects. Finally, the process of measuring the emitted radiation from the sample destroys the sample, making it impossible to retest it. Any one or any combination of these potential problems can lead researchers to question the validity of this sort of dating, and this is precisely what has happened. Although some researchers accept the validity of OSL and TL dates, many researchers prefer to avoid using them because of the potential problems. Some few researchers have even gone so far as to reject all dates based on these techniques because of concerns over the likelihood of sample contamination or concerns over the problems discussed previously.

Electron spin resonance (ESR) is a technique that has been rapidly developing since the early 1970s. The method works best on tooth enamel, shells, and burnt stone and has an effective range between a few thousand to ap-

optically stimulated luminescence (OSL) and thermoluminescence (TL) Related dating techniques which attempt to measure the amount of energy trapped in sediments (in the case of OSL) or heated clays and stones (in the case of TL) by reheating the material and then measuring the amount of energy released in the process.

electron spin resonance (ESR) A technique best suited for the analysis of tooth enamel, shells, and burnt stone, it uses a spectrometer to measure the amount of energy released from an object when bombarded with microwaves.

proximately five hundred thousand years ago. The method uses microwaves to bombard the sample with radiation and then uses an ESR spectrometer to measure the trapped electrons. This measurement (the ESR reading) is then compared with the total dose of radiation the sample was exposed to in the laboratory. The result is used to create a dose response curve that yields an estimation of the total dose of radiation the sample has been exposed to. Finally, this accumulated dose is divided by the dose rate to yield an age in years before present. Because the electrons are not actually freed in this process, ESR dating is repeatable.

In theory, ESR dating has an unlimited range. Practically, however, exposure to more than trace elements of uranium, which is common in groundwater, imposes an upper limit to the technique. The last interglacial epoch, approximately one hundred sixteen thousand to one hundred thirty thousand years ago, was marked by increased amounts of groundwater from melting glaciers. This had the effect of exposing most, though not all, potential archaeological samples to increased levels of uranium. Nonetheless, ESL has the potential to make further significant contributions to paleoanthropology.

Fission track dating functions differently from the three previously discussed approaches. When atoms of ^{238}U (uranium 238) fission, they do so at a constant rate (half-life of 8.2×10^{15} years). In the process of fissioning, the nucleus bursts apart into two parts that are violently repelled from one another. These atomic bodies create fission tracks in crystalline materials and obsidian. By counting the frequency of fission tracks and comparing this to the known rate for fissioning, the age of the sample can be calculated. The range of errors in estimating an age based on fission tracks is between 5% and 10%. Because of this error range, fission track dating works best on samples older than one hundred thousand years.

SUMMARY

The decision to excavate a site is not made lightly. Once an archaeologist has committed to undertake such work, that person has accepted the obligation to meet the methodological and theoretical standards common in the region. Moreover, the researcher is obligated to see the work through to its completion, including the preparation and publication of the results of the work.

The specific methods of excavating a site are directly related to the questions that first provoked the research. Each action on a site, including decisions about how to define space on the site, to sample the area, to size the excavation units, and to remove and process matrix, are all dictated by a combination of what the researchers want to know and the local depositional environments. There is no one best way to excavate any archaeological site, nor is there any single best way to execute any operation or methodology on that

fission track dating A dating technique based on the observation and measurement of fission tracks in crystalline material created by the fissioning of ^{238}U atoms.

site. Rather, there are a variety of solutions to the problems at hand, and it is the role of the archaeologist to determine which of these solutions works best. In this sense archaeology is a creative activity, an art form of sorts. In the end, however, it is the professional and ethical responsibility of the archaeologist in charge of a project to make responsible decisions and to do the best work possible given all of the circumstances that prevail on the project.

FOR FURTHER INFORMATION

Aitken, M. J. 2000a. Luminescence dating. In *Archaeological method and theory: An encyclopedia,* edited by L. Ellis, 222. New York: Garland.

———. 2000b. Optical dating. In *Archaeological method and theory: An encyclopedia,* edited by L. Ellis, 414–15. New York: Garland.

———. 2000c. Radiocarbon dating. In *Archaeological method and theory: An encyclopedia,* edited by L. Ellis, 505–508. New York: Garland.

———. 2000d. Thermoluminescence dating. In *Archaeological method and theory: An encyclopedia,* edited by L. Ellis, 630–34. New York: Garland.

Alexander, J. 1970. *The directing of archaeological excavations.* London: Baker.

Allman, J. C. 1968. The Incinerator Village site. *Ohio Archaeologist* 18: 50–55.

Alva, W. 1988. Into the tomb of a Moche lord. *National Geographic* 174 (4): 516–49.

———. 1990. New tomb of royal splendor. *National Geographic* 177 (6): 2–15.

Arnold, J. R., and W. F. Libby. 1949. Age determinations by radiocarbon content: Checks with samples of known age. *Science* 110: 678–80.

Baillie, M. G. L. 1982. *Tree-ring dating and archaeology.* Chicago: University of Chicago Press.

———. 2000. Dendrochronology. In *Archaeological method and theory: An encyclopedia,* edited by L. Ellis, 150–54. New York: Garland.

Bowman, S. 1990. *Radiocarbon dating.* Berkeley and Los Angeles: University of California Press.

Coote, G. 2000. Fluorine-uranium-nitrogen dating. In *Archaeological method and theory: An encyclopedia,* edited by L. Ellis, 218–26. New York: Garland.

Eighmy, J. L., and R. S. Sternberg, eds. 1990. *Archaeomagnetic dating.* Tucson: University of Arizona Press.

Friedman, I., and F. W. Trembour. 2000. Obsidian hydration dating. In *Archaeological method and theory: An encyclopedia,* edited by L. Ellis, 409–13. New York: Garland.

Gillard, R. 2000. Amino acid racemization/epimerization dating. In *Archaeological method and theory: An encyclopedia,* edited by L. Ellis, 13–17. New York: Garland.

MacNeish, R. S., M. L. Fowler, A. G. Cook, F. A. Peterson, A. Nelken-Terner, and J. A. Neely. 1972. *Excavations and reconnaissance: The prehistory of the Tehuacán valley.* Vol. 5. Austin: University of Texas Press.

Rule, M., 1994. *The Mary Rose: The excavation and raising of Henry VIII's flagship*. London: Conway Maritime.

Shaw, J. 2000. Archaeomagnetic dating. In *Archaeological method and theory: An encyclopedia*, edited by L. Ellis, 44–47. New York: Garland.

Woolley, C. L. 1934. *Ur excavations. Vol. II: The royal cemetery*. Oxford and Philadelphia: British Museum and University Museum, University of Pennsylvania.

———. 1961. *Digging up the past*. Baltimore: Penguin Books.

THE SINDH ARCHAEOLOGICAL PROJECT: FIELDWORK AT THE EDGE

Louis Flam

Louis Flam (Ph.D., University of Pennsylvania) is Associate Professor of Anthropology at Lehman College and The Graduate School of The City University of New York. He has conducted archaeological field research in the American Southwest, Thailand, Kuwait, Afghanistan, and, for the past twenty-five years, in Pakistan. He is the director of the Sindh Archaeological Project and the excavations at Ghazi Shah.

Three geographic regions of the Old World provide evidence for the rise of the world's earliest civilizations: Mesopotamia, the Nile River valley, and the Indus River valley. The last-named region, oftentimes referred to as the Greater Indus Valley, lies predominantly in present-day Pakistan. The Indus civilization (2600–1900 B.C.) was first discovered in the early 1920s at two sites, Mohen jo Daro on the floodplain of the Indus River in Sindh Province (southern Indus Valley) and Harappa in Punjab Province (northern Indus Valley).

The Sindh Archaeological Project has been conducting archaeological and geomorphological research in the Lower Indus Valley. The research design of the project has included three major objectives: (1) to study the geomorphology and landscape evolution of three subregions of the Lower Indus Valley (the Indus River plain, the Kirthar Mountains, and Sindh Kohistan); (2) to explore the Sindh Kohistan and Kirthar Mountains subregions for prehistoric sites; and (3) to select one prehistoric site in the mountains for intensive excavation. To accomplish the research goals of the project a twofold research strategy was envisioned. First, it was necessary to adopt a regional approach. The three subregions of the Lower Indus Valley possessed different resources and environmental limitations relevant to human settlement in the prehistoric past, and the precise role of these factors through time needed to be defined and explained. Second, it would be critically important to conduct new explorations in all three subregions and to intensively study their diverse geomorphic and archaeological evidence. That would be easier said than done.

The floodplain of the Indus River was easily accessible through good roads and widely inhabited villages. But the Kohistan and particularly the Kirthar subregions were extremely dangerous. Leopards, poisonous snakes (vipers, cobras), scorpions, and a landscape cut up by tectonics and erosion, with no roads, were some of the natural dangers inhibiting access to the latter two subregions. Desert conditions prevailed, which meant almost no water and food resources were available. Very few people live in the Kohistan and Kirthar subregions. The only places inhabitable by settled groups were locations in which natural springs produced a small yet steady flow of surface water. Other groups living in the subregions were nomadic, tending their herds of sheep, goats, and camels. Indeed, the weather, the landscape, and the lack of water and food sources were very real and immediate problems that had to be solved before any attempt to carry out research in the subregions. But another problem was potentially even more dangerous. With the former Soviet Union's invasion of Afghanistan in 1979 came a huge influx of assault rifles into Pakistan, and Sindh was not excluded. Armed with the AK-47 (Kalashnikov rifle), *dacoits* (bandits) used the mountains as a base and refuge from which to carry out their exploits of kidnapping, murder, and terrorism. There would be only one way to overcome all the obstacles and difficulties of doing research in the Lower Indus Valley—friends.

From the very beginning of my interest in the Indus civilization, I intended that Pakistan be more than just a laboratory in which to base a career in archaeology. Pakistani friends in graduate school inspired me to learn about the people and culture of their country, and so when I began doing fieldwork I possessed not only a dedication to doing archaeological fieldwork in Pakistan but also a love of and commitment to the country. Because of the research goals I mentioned, I established myself in Karachi.

FIGURE 1

Louis Flam (left) and Shabir Ahmed Khan Chandio at a newly discovered prehistoric site.

Living there, I became friends with two people who were to have a tremendous influence on my personal and professional growth. One was Shabir Ahmed Khan Chandio, chief of the Chandio tribe, which had more than 3.5 million tribesmen spread throughout Pakistan, the majority of whom were concentrated in the Kirthar Mountains subregion of western Sindh (Figure 1). The other individual was Dr. Mohammad Hasan Rizvi, an internationally known ophthalmologist of Pakistan who had an interest in the archaeology of Sindh Kohistan. Without their help and friendship, none of the work I have been able to accomplish in Pakistan would have been possible. I was also fortunate to have the support and encouragement of the government of Pakistan and its Department of Archaeology and Museums, a highly professional and dedicated group whose headquarters are in Karachi.

My first expedition and the beginning of the Sindh Archaeological Project was in the Indus River floodplain subregion. Support came from a Fulbright Fellowship, which allowed me to live in Pakistan for one and one-half years. During this time I studied the Indus River and the changes in its course during the Holocene epoch (from 8000 B.C. to the present day). To confirm evidence derived from aerial photo composites and landsat imagery, a three-month expedition was carried out into the interior

FIGURE 2

Nomads camp in the Kirthar Mountains.

154

FIGURE 3

One of our "kitchens" in the Kirthar Mountains.

FIGURE 4

Stuck in the Kirthar Mountains.

of Sindh to study the river and its ancient course remnants, as well as to revisit previously discovered archaeological sites. For three months I traveled alone on a motorcycle, carrying only a change of clothes, notebooks, drawing supplies, and photographic equipment. Throughout Sindh, people in the towns and villages opened their hearts and homes to me, watched over and took care of me—a total stranger! When I explained what I was doing, people helped in every way they could and gave whatever they could in generous hospitality.

Five years later I returned to Pakistan to specifically carry out other aspects of my proposed research objectives. Research grants from the American Institute of Pakistan Studies, the Smithsonian Institution, the National Science Foundation, and two more Fulbright Fellowships permitted me to establish a residency in Karachi and live in Pakistan for six continuous years from 1982 to 1988. During that time arrangements were also made to excavate at the site of Ghazi Shah.

Throughout the Kirthar subregion, my friend Shabir and I either camped out in the open, lived with nomads, (Figure 2), or were welcomed into the small hamlets of Shabir's tribal people. We drank and bathed in spring water that was gently flowing in the river courses and ate berries and vegetables growing wild in the desert. We brought with us dry lentils, wheat, and rice and ate local vegetables generously given to us by Shabir's people. We hunted gazelle (Figure 3), wild goats (Ibex), and wild sheep

(Urial) that live in the piedmont plains and mountains, and we also fished in pond water in the stream beds. Traveling in the Kirthar was not easy. In the piedmont area we traveled in four-wheel-drive vehicles. But the vehicles could only go so far before becoming bogged down in mud or sand (Figure 4) or stopped by rough terrain. When this occurred, Shabir arranged for camels to be brought to us (Figure 5); when it became too dangerous for the camels to walk and climb through the narrow river channels and rapidly rising elevations, we climbed for days and weeks at a time to reach the upstream areas of the mountains.

Our explorations in the Kirthar Mountains and piedmont subregion recorded twenty new prehistoric sites, and we know from talking with Chandio tribesmen in the mountains that there are many more sites waiting to be discovered. Most of the newly discovered sites are located on elevated terraces long ago abandoned by the rivers as they eroded their courses through the mountains. As living settlements in the past, the growth of the

FIGURE 5

Camels brought for
transportation.

sites through time was horizontal rather than vertical on the landscape (unlike the famous "mound" sites of the Near East and South Asia at which growth was vertical—new buildings constructed over old—oftentimes creating high mounds with buried structures and other cultural evidence; see the following description of Ghazi Shah). The arid environment preserved the archaeological sites well, although sometimes violent rainstorms and winds in the subregion were factors in the erosion of the sites after their abandonment. Thus, without any excavation foundation, walls of buildings and their plans are articulated on the surface of the old river terraces. Pottery sherds and other artifacts are spread all over the sites, and this helps to approximately date them to the ends of the fourth and third millennia B.C. In addition to the building foundations on the surface of the sites, the old terraces also present clear evidence of an irrigation system used in prehistoric times to bring water from the then-active rivers to the settlements' agricultural fields. The irrigation structures were created with local stones, and the former agricultural fields are clearly outlined with stone markers. Archaeologists working in Baluchistan had previously found prehistoric sites with clearly demarcated buildings and fields but thought the stone field markers were remnants of house walls. Our new research in the Kirthar

Mountains clearly proves them to be irrigation systems and agricultural fields more than five thousand years old. In addition, very large stone dams (known locally as *gabarbands*) such as we found in Sindh Kohistan are also found in the Kirthar subregion—again, directly associated with prehistoric sites of the fourth and third millennia B.C. (Figure 6).

The third research goal of the Sindh Archaeological Project was to select a site in the Kohistan or Kirthar subregion to excavate. Excavation would answer some of the chronological questions raised by the surface finds from newly discovered sites and would provide a window into prehistoric lifeways not available through exploration finds. The site of Ghazi Shah was selected for excavation. Financial support for the excavations was provided by the Smithsonian Institution and The Research Foundation of The City University of New York. Ghazi Shah is located in the northernmost portion of Sindh Kohistan at the foot of the Bhit Range, very close to the southernmost area of the Kirthar Mountains subregion. The archaeological site is located approximately 1.5 kilometers east of Pir Ghazi Shah village. The village is well known throughout South Asia for the shrine of Pir Ghazi Shah, a Muslim saint who lived in the village during the Mughal period (A.D. 1605–1764). Hundreds of thousands

FIGURE 6

A *gabarband* in the Kirthar Mountains.

of people make an annual pilgrimage to Pir Ghazi Shah's shrine, where *jinns* are exorcised from possessed individuals and worshippers pray for good health and male children. In the present-day village, it is chronicled that Pir Ghazi Shah lived on top of the archaeological mound, and we have found archaeological evidence at the site to substantiate this. The primary source of water for Pir Ghazi Shah is a perennial spring located approximately 4 kilometers to the west of the village in the Bhit Range of Sindh Kohistan. There is abundant geological evidence to indicate that the spring was flowing in prehistoric times.

It takes eight hours of driving to reach Ghazi Shah from Karachi, the last two hours of which require four-wheel-drive vehicles. The village and site are in a remote tribal area of Sindh Kohistan, and there are no paved roads to Ghazi Shah, only intermittent camel and donkey paths. The archaeological team lives in a two-room mud-brick house in the village, which is rented from a local land-owner, Zawar Amir Bux Jamali, who has provided a tremendous amount of support and friendship for the project and its team members. There is neither electricity, gas, nor plumbing in the village, and for the most part food and excavation supplies for the team have to be brought from the nearest towns, which are about a two-hour drive away. The spring water from the Bhit Range flows through the village in an open channel and is used for drinking and washing. Drinking water is boiled for twenty minutes and then filtered, but despite these precautions team members have at times suffered from typhoid and a host of other illnesses, including dysentery and malaria. The team works at the site seven days a week. A typical day begins at 5:30 A.M., with a walk outside the compound wall of the house to "find a tree." (There are no toilet facilities at Pir Ghazi Shah.) It is still dark and bitter cold outside. When we return to the house a hot cup of tea is served around the "kitchen" fire (Figure 7). Plans for the day are discussed and a lot of joking and storytelling take place. As the first light begins to creep over the horizon, equipment is loaded into the vehicle, breakfast is served, and as quickly as possible the 1.5-km drive is made to the site. Workmen are hired from local villages to assist with the excavation work. Work proceeds until 10:00 A.M., when hot tea and biscuits are served to everyone. Digging continues until 1:00 P.M., when a lunch break is taken for thirty minutes. After lunch, work continues until 4:40 P.M. Back at the house everyone bathes, using a plastic bucket and cup with water heated over the kitchen's wood fire. Once everyone has bathed, tea is served, and if there are no guests who have come for tea, daily notes are checked and the day's work and future days' work are dis-

FIGURE 7

The "kitchen" in our house at
Ghazi Shah.

FIGURE 8

The mound/site of Ghazi Shah.

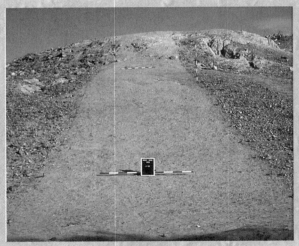

FIGURE 9

Area of Ghazi Shah chosen, with its surface cleaned for
excavation.

cussed. The sun sets around 6:00 P.M., dinner is served at 7:00 P.M., and the day ends at 8:30. For the team's safety, we are guarded both at the site and at the house twenty-four hours a day by an armed team (with AK-47s) from the Sindh police; remembering the murder of archaeologist Nani Gopal Majumdar in 1938 by bandits, we are very grateful for their care and consideration.

The archaeological site of Ghazi Shah is a single mound presently 2 hectares in area, with a maximum height of 11 meters above its surrounding plain (Figure 8). The site was originally discovered by Majumdar, who test excavated the site with two large trenches and several small "pits." His excavations revealed an Islamic occupation of the Mughal period on the flat topmost portion of the mound and occupations of the Indus civilization (2600–1900 B.C.) and Amri culture (3500–2600 B.C.) below. The recent excavations at the site have begun on the flat top part of the mound in the northwest area of the site. A series of 5 m × 5 m squares continue down the slope of the mound (Figure 9). It is generally thought that the upper excavation squares will reveal more recent archaeological data and the lower squares older materials. Thus far, the lowest and earliest strata of occupation have not yet been reached at Ghazi Shah, so it is unknown just how early the site was first occupied. But the excavations have pro-vided a complete and continuous sequence of cultural developments correlated with radiocarbon dates for western Sindh from 3500 to 2000 B.C. Every season of field research uncovers new data that will alter our present ideas about the Indus civilization and the cultural processes that brought about its emergence. Ghazi Shah is also yielding important data about the cultures that developed prior to the rise of the Indus civilization.

The architectural remains, the artifacts, and the ecofacts discovered during the course of excavations at Ghazi Shah have been important and in some cases spectacular (Figure 10). Mud-brick walls and rooms appeared right below the site surface, with no overburden of postoccupational debris. Some of the rooms had niches with artifacts left in situ. Cattle bones, sheep and goat bones, and fish bones were found on the floors of rooms and in strata. Experiments are now being conducted at Lehman College to extract DNA from the fish bones with PCR amplification for DNA sequencing and thus allow identification of specific fish species. All excavated soil was sifted through 1 mm mesh, catching the tiniest bone (e.g., fish vertebrae), botanical remains (e.g., seeds), and artifacts.

One of the most interesting finds was the great number of beads retrieved (Figure 11), as well as evidence of a "tool kit" used for bead manufacturing (Figure 12).

FIGURE 10

Same area of Ghazi Shah after excavation; note the walls and rooms of houses.

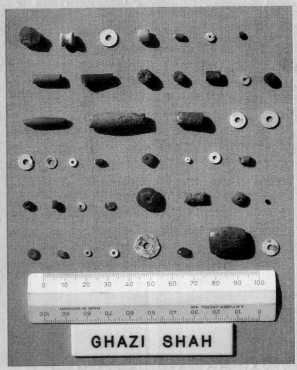

FIGURE 12

Bead manufacturing "kit" from Ghazi Shah, showing raw materials, bead drills, beads, and polishing stone.

FIGURE 11

Some of the beads unearthed at Ghazi Shah.

Beads of copper, shell, clay, steatite, agate, carnelian, and lapis lazuli have been recovered. Also found were unworked chunks of agate and lapis lazuli, along with micro flakes formed by working the stones into beads. Barrel-shaped agate beads were recovered in various stages of production. In addition, numerous whole and broken micro bead-drills were discovered. The majority of the drills were made of an olive green cryptocrystalline variety of silica known as prase or chrysoprase. Also found were pieces of unworked prase, micro flakes 1–4mm in size, from shaping the stone into drills and partially finished drills in different stages of production. These drills are similar to those previously reported from other sites in Sindh, in Baluchistan, and in Iranian Seistan. The source of the unique material for manufacturing the bead drills was also located. Another critically important find came from strata of the Indus civilization.

A pottery sherd stylistically datable between 2500 and 2000 B.C. and confirmed to that date by proximate radio-carbon sample exhibited a cursive inscription between the horizontal lines of decoration on the shoulder of a jar. The writing of the Indus civilization is invariably represented in block form, and the characters are very distinct in style. A search of the archaeological literature found no parallels between known potters' marks and the cursive inscription from Ghazi Shah. This is the first discovery of a cursive script in the Greater Indus Valley, but to which script of the ancient world is it possibly related, or is it an entirely new script? The inscription has no similarities at all to any known Indus script nor to the writing systems of Mesopotamia, Egypt, the Iranian Plateau, or Central Asia that I have been able to find. Further research is required to understand if this is one example belonging to the Indus civilization of many that have yet to be unearthed or if it is an import from another culture. Since the discovery of the Indus civilization in the 1920s, archaeologists have questioned whether there might have been writing not only on the seals we have in abundance but also on some perishable material. The inscription from Ghazi Shah revives the possibility of the existence of texts, written on fragile materials, which are yet to be discovered, possibly at Ghazi Shah.

6

STONE IN THE ARCHAEOLOGICAL RECORD

Civilizations come and civilizations go, but stone tools are forever.

—Archaeological bumper sticker

Stone tools are among the most common forms of artifacts consistently found in the archaeological record. Once a person makes a stone tool, it is difficult if not impossible to erase the evidence of the presence of the tool. The chips that are removed to shape the tool, the tool itself, and the stone left over from the production process all bear landmarks that an archaeologist should be able to identify. Such marks are predominantly human and do not occur in nature with great frequency. Consequently, they are direct reflections of human behaviors. More significant, most forms of stone do not disappear from the archaeological record. Some forms of stone may weather, so that their edges become rounded and they lose some of the detail of their attributes, but few stones disappear completely. We have stone tools, for example, that are 2.5 million years old and represent the productive efforts of the earliest members of the genus *Homo,* the genus to which you and I belong. For these reasons, then, stone tools are often viewed by archaeologists as the starting point for learning the specifics of material culture and for interpreting the development of the human lineage.

In discussing stone artifacts we need to define precisely what sorts of things we are covering. Stone tools and the by-products of their production are referred to as **lithics,** a term used in archaeology to refer to the full range of stone material culture resulting from human activities. **Flintknapping,** or knapping, is the term often applied to the production of **chipped stone tools** (Figure 6.1). These tools are those produced by the removal and shaping of stone primarily by percussive methods, that is, by hitting a stone with something hard in order to break the stone into a desired shape. Chipped

FIGURE 6.1

Some of the attributes of a North American Clovis Point (ca. 11,500 B.C.). Notice the delicate flaking and careful notch, or flute, on this point. Clovis Points represent the earliest widespread evidence for human specialization in big-game hunting in North America.

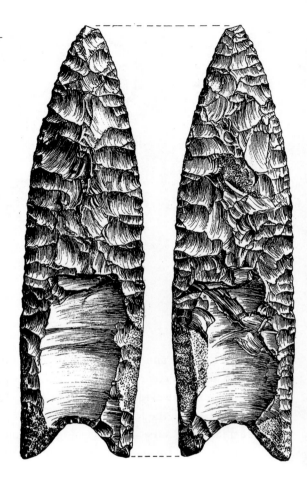

lithics The full range of stone material related to or resulting from human activity.

flintknapping The process of chipping stone into shapes usable as tools or for expressive purposes.

chipped stone tools Tools that have been produced through direct or indirect percussion, or a combination of these, or through pressure flaking.

ground stone tools Tools that are produced by pecking and grinding stones into desired shapes.

replication An example of middle range theory based on the production and use of modern stone tools to identify patterns of wear and breakage directly comparable to those found on archaeologically observed material culture.

stone tools are primarily, but not exclusively, associated with hunting and gathering societies. A second group of tools, **ground stone tools,** are produced by the grinding of stone using water, sand, and other coarse material to produce a finished tool (Figure 6.2). Ground stone tools are primarily, but not exclusively, associated with societies that produce their own food in the form of grains and cereals or that intensively collect some naturally occurring plant.

As we discuss how archaeologists study and interpret stone tools, we will address issues of replication studies. **Replication** is the process of producing stone tools in the present that look like stone tools from archaeological sites and then using the new tools in a variety of ways. The effectiveness of the new tools is gauged, and the way in which they wear and break is compared with wear and breakage patterns observed on archaeologically recovered tools. When matches are found, then archaeologists believe they have identified the ways in which the archaeological tools were likely to have been made and utilized.

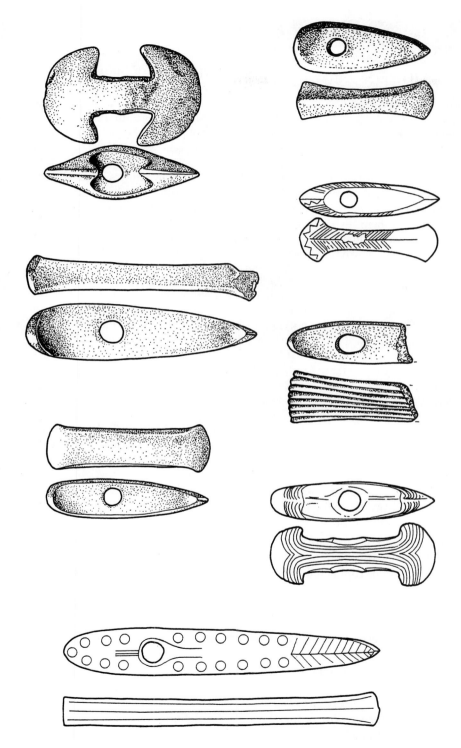

FIGURE 6.2

A variety of ground stone implements from the Neolithic Funnel Beaker Culture (TRB) in Europe, ca. 3500 B.C.

BOX 6.1

ODE TO AN OLDOWAN TOOL

Oldowan tools represent the oldest known type of stone tools. They date to at least 2.5 million years ago and represent humankind's first durable record of its technological capabilities. The first members of the genus, known as *Homo habilis,* literally the handy man, used these tools as a way to supplement their own abilities to process a vital resource, meat. Although we once thought of these early hominids as hunters, we now tend to think of them as creative generalists that would flinch neither at killing an unwary small animal nor at scavenging usable flesh from animal kills.

When the famous **paleoanthropologist** Mary Leakey first sat down to work with the earliest known stone tools, she described the material as being a collection of simple unifaces (worked on only one side) produced by direct percussion. Other, later forms, now called Developed Oldowan, were known to be bifacial (worked on both faces), but these were clearly more recent than the set of tools Leakey had set out to study and were therefore left for later consideration. As Mary Leakey worked through the tools, she sought to apply standardized rules for creating typologies to the tools before her. She succeeded in distinguishing a series of tool types that successfully labeled the range of variation in the tools.

It was not until nearly twenty years later that a new generation of archaeologists began to seriously question the effectiveness of some of the tool types Leakey described. This younger generation had the advantage of being trained in a more scientifically derived, critical tradition that sought to test hypotheses systematically, something neither Leakey nor many of her generation typically undertook. Researchers such as Nicholas Toth of the University of Indiana replicated Oldowan tools and then tried to complete a variety of tasks with them, such as cutting meat and scraping hides. The tools proved poor implements for most of these tasks, and this finding left Toth and others wondering if there might not be another explanation as to how the tools were created. As an alternative explanation, Toth began testing the effectiveness of the flakes that were struck from his replicated tools at completing the same tasks that he had attempted with what were assumed to be the finished tool. The flakes, as it turned out, were much more efficient at these tasks. Toth went on to suggest that it was the flakes and not the objects originally identified as tools that were the intended products of *Homo habilis's* stone tool making. Toth and others began to argue that what Leakey had identified as tools were simply cores, not the intended finished products of tool manufactures.

---

paleoanthropologist A person who specializes in the study of hominid evolution and related disciplines, including archaeology, anatomy, and ecology.

mineral Naturally formed chemical elements or compounds, each possessing a specific chemical composition and usually appearing in crystal form.

Such work is an example of middle range theory, which is designed to link explanatory theory to archaeologically observed data (see Chapter 3). The production of replicated tools and their experimental use is perceived as a bridge, or middle range, that connects the two known points, the present and the past. Such work is a major component in processual archaeology, and middle range theory is closely associated with one of the most vocal advocates of processual theory, Lewis Binford (Box 6.1).

THE PROCESSES OF FLINTKNAPPING

What Stone Is

Perhaps to the surprise of many people, the definition of what stone is can be complex. Although most people accept a commonsense definition of stone as

The challenge to Mary Leakey's work was received differently by different segments of the archaeological community. Some hailed the revised ideas as novel and a great leap forward, whereas others challenged the replication studies as inconclusive. Subsequent studies were undertaken, and, over the years, the pendulum of scholarly interpretation has settled more or less in between Leakey's original interpretation and Toth's revised arguments. Without doubt some of the flakes that were considered to be by-products of tool manufacture seem to have been used as tools, and perhaps these were deliberately struck from cores as finished tools. Some of Leakey's original tool categories, however, also seemed to perform a useful variety of tasks. So, in the end, it seems that *Homo habilis* was both more creative and more opportunistic than anyone gave it credit for, being able to both produce tools at need and to utilize available raw materials in creative and efficient manners.

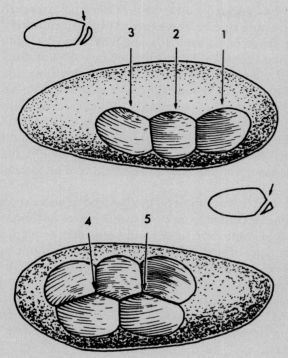

Sketches of two of the various types of Lower Paleolithic Oldowan tools. It was these sorts of tools that Mary Leakey set about organizing into typological categories and that were later reproduced and tested by Nicholas Toth.

something that is hard, granular, and found in nature and that can be used to break other things, there is a more technical way to define stones. The things we commonly refer to as stone are more properly defined as minerals and rocks. **Minerals** are naturally formed chemical elements or compounds, each possessing a specific chemical composition and usually appearing in crystal form. Quartz is an example of a common mineral. **Rocks,** on the other hand, are aggregates of one or more minerals and can be defined by both their physical properties and mineral content. Rocks can be subdivided into *igneous* forms, those that have cooled from a molten state, such as obsidian; *sedimentary* forms, which have formed through the accumulation of sediments, such as sandstone; and *metamorphic* forms, which formed in a solid state from preexisting rocks due to conditions such as heat, pressure, and chemical changes. Chert is an example of a metamorphic rock.

rock An aggregate of one or more minerals that can be defined by both physical properties and mineral content. The three forms are igneous, rock that has cooled from a molten state; sedimentary, rock that has formed through the accretion of sediments; and metamorphic, rock formed from preexisting rocks subjected to extreme heat, pressure, or chemical change.

All forms of rocks and minerals can be used by humans, and archaeologists encounter a wide variety of such items in their research. For the most part, humans have tended to prefer certain sorts of stone for accomplishing tasks that require a sharp edge while preferring other sorts of stone for tasks such as grinding. For tasks that require an edge, rocks such as obsidian and **chert,** sometimes also called flint, are among the finest raw materials available. Both possess the attribute of having a glasslike or very small-grained physical structure. Like glass, the individual grains composing obsidian are invisible, and the material usually feels smooth to the touch and reflects much as does a mirror. Chert has a slightly larger grain size, referred to as microcrystalline, and can be found in a wide range of qualities. The finest-grained cherts tend to be considered the best for working into edged tools, though even the most coarse varieties can be used effectively. Stones such as basalt, rhyolite, and quartzite, which possess larger grain sizes, can also be fashioned into useful cutting implements.

Although obsidian and chert in some form or another tend to be the most effective materials for producing cutting tools, such materials were not always easily available to past peoples. Moreover, some groups of people developed preferences for using other types of stone for some tools for a variety of reasons, ranging from the ease of acquiring the material to the symbolic importance of the color of the raw material. Chalcedony, which is a fibrous form of quartz, many other forms of quartz, petrified wood, and even shale have been used by some people to produce cutting tools. One of the interesting aspects of stone tool research in archaeology is determining why people selected certain raw materials over others.

The Anatomy of a Flake

The elements that define a stone tool are sometimes easy to distinguish. In cases in which a tool looks like something we are familiar with in our own culture, such as an arrow tip, we tend to recognize the stone version of that tool quickly. Sometimes, though, we need to look beyond easily identifiable artifacts at the full range of materials produced by the human working of stone.

The place to begin is with the production process. When stone is flint-knapped, three distinct types of elements can be produced: the tool, assuming one is being fashioned; the **flakes,** the pieces of stone struck off a rock in the manufacturing process; and the **core,** which is the piece of rock being shaped into the tool. In many, but not all cases, all three components will be present. As archaeologists learned through trial and error, sometimes nothing more sophisticated than the flakes themselves were intended to be the tool. Flakes have sharp edges, and large ones are ideally suited for cutting and scraping. In general we call such flakes **utilized flakes,** meaning that the flake was struck from the core and then used, or *flake tools,* which to some archaeologists means that the flake was then modified in some way to produce a slightly more sophisticated finished tool, perhaps by making a notch in one end that could be

chert A microcrystalline metamorphic stone commonly used as a stone tool. Sometimes used as a synonym for flint.

flakes The pieces of stone struck off a rock in the reduction sequence, each usually having a striking platform, bulb of percussion, and similar identifying features.

core The parent stone from which flakes are struck.

utilized flakes Flakes that have been used as tools without further modification, such as sharpening or grinding.

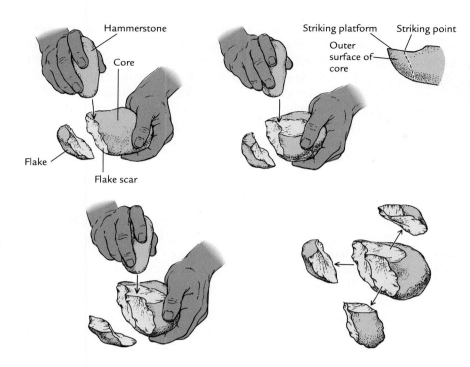

FIGURE 6.3

The anatomy of a flake. The major landmarks on a flake are essential in identifying the presence of human-made artifacts. Although chance events might produce a stone that looks like a flake, the consistent presence of these landmarks on stone from throughout an assemblage indicate the presence of human activity.

used for engraving. In both cases, though, archaeologists tend to classify flakes used in these ways as **expedient tools,** meaning tools that were made to meet a specific, perhaps even one-time, need and then were usually discarded.

Regardless of their intended use, all flakes share a common morphology. Flakes tend to be relatively longer than they are wide, though this is affected by the manner in which the flake is struck off (see later in this chapter). Each flake has a *ventral side,* the side that was attached to the core, and a *dorsal side,* the back side that was exposed prior to the flake being struck from the core (Figure 6.3 and Figure 6.4). We call the end of the flake that was actually struck when the flake was removed the *proximal end,* and the end opposite it is called the *distal end.* If you were to hold one of these flakes in your hand, you might orient it by placing the dorsal side down with the proximal end nearest to your wrist. As you look at the flake in your hand, you will be looking at the ventral face.

The ventral face is important to archaeologists because it shows attributes that help distinguish a human-made flake from fragments of stone that might have occurred naturally, perhaps by having fallen out of a cliff face or tumbled down a vigorously flowing mountain stream. On the proximal end along the ventral face archaeologists can usually identify a specific point at which the object used to strike the flake from the core actually hit. This is called the *striking platform,* and it usually shows some degree of crushing as a result of the force that drove the flake from the core.

expedient tools Tools that are formed quickly and for immediate use. Such tools often do not conform to typological standards and are often made using a flake.

On the ventral face just beneath the striking platform there is almost always a raised, fairly smooth area. This region of the flake feels like a ball or portion of a sphere, and under scrutiny it can be seen to resemble a small hill on the face of the flake. This is called the *bulb of percussion,* and it is a by-product of the force that created the flake beginning to be transmitted down the length of the flake. The bulb of percussion is unique on each flake from the core, because it receives the full range of forces applied to the flake, those that separate it moving along the length of the flake, and those that are dissipated into the knapper's hand or into space by the lateral force imparted by the blow.

A flintknapper must strike the core with a hammer (the object used to deliver force to the core) at an angle. The reason for this is that force is transmitted in a cone. Physicists call this a *Hertzian cone,* and it has an angle at its apex of approximately 90 degrees. Anyone who has ever had a window broken by an errant stone or had the misfortune of shooting a pellet or BB into a pane of glass has seen the outline of the cone in the depression on the side opposite to that struck by the projectile (i.e., the inside of the window).

In practical terms this means that if you strike a stone in a straight downward motion and transmit the entire cone of force to the core, then the stone is likely to shatter as the force races through it. In order to control the force and strike off only a flake, a flinknapper must swing the hammer in an arch and strike the core with an oblique blow. A portion of the force is sent along the edge of the Hertzian cone, and the rest of the force travels off into space. It is the force traveling downward parallel to the edge of the core that drives off the flake.

Sometimes an astute observer can spot a small, usually angular scar near the base of the bulb of percussion. This is called the *bulbar scar,* and it represents a point at which the bulb of percussion essentially ends. In effect, it marks the point at which the force transmitted to the flake now travels only downward, all lateral force having left the flake or been dissipated in the production of the bulb of percussion.

Beneath this point, and depending in part on the quality of stone being used to produce a flake, careful observation may also reveal *conchoidal ripples* passing through the flake, as well as roughly *vertical stress lines.* The ripples mirror the angles of the bulb of percussion and resemble water rippling away from the place where a stone entered a pond. In reality the forces are essentially identical, and the analogy of these ripples to water is quite strong. The vertical stress lines also flow away from the bulb of percussion at angles that are perpendicular to the edge of the bulb. These lines mark the passage of force through the flake (Figure 6.4).

The dorsal side of a flake struck from the exterior of the core may show a large amount of **cortex,** the weathered outer surface of the stone. This is a **primary flake,** one that was detached from the core in the beginning of the reduction sequence. The **reduction sequence** describes the order in which flakes were struck from a core. The presence of some cortex on the dorsal side

cortex Sometimes also called *rind,* the weathered exterior of a stone.

primary flake A flake that has substantial amounts of cortex on it and that was one of the first flakes removed from the core when the stone was initially broken open.

reduction sequence The various stages that a stone tool goes through from the point at which it is first struck to the point at which it is worked for the last time.

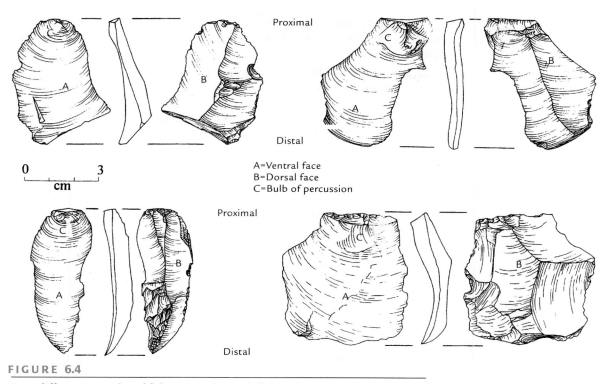

Proximal

Distal

0   3
cm

A=Ventral face
B=Dorsal face
C=Bulb of percussion

Proximal

Distal

FIGURE 6.4

Four different examples of flakes. Note that each flake is typically parallel sided and as long as, if not longer than, it is wide.

that does not cover the entire face indicates a **secondary flake,** one that was removed after the flintknapper had broken through and begun to remove the cortex.

On secondary and **tertiary flakes,** tertiary being those that show no evidence of cortex, additional landmarks may be present. All of the landmarks that were visible on the ventral surface may be visible as negative images on the dorsal surface of the next flake to be struck from the core in that place. Think of the core as an onion. As you peel one layer away from the onion, you reveal another layer immediately beneath it. If there were marks on the inside of the layer of onion just peeled off, these marks would have made impressions in the outside of the next layer. In terms of a flake, then, a *negative bulb of percussion* (a divot rather than a raised spot) and a *negative bulbar scar* (a small projection rather than a divot) might be visible on the dorsal surface.

If the new flake is not perfectly aligned with the preceding flakes that were removed—and they rarely are—then the dorsal side of the new flake may also have long ridges running from the proximal to the distal edge of the flake. Such ridges are good landmarks for orienting the flake because they occur only on the dorsal face and are often very visible.

secondary flake   A flake that may have some cortex on its surface (usually less than 20%) and that was struck during the rough shaping of a stone tool.

tertiary flake   A flake that has no or very little cortex on it and that was struck during the final shaping of a stone tool.

All of these landmarks are important and potentially useful attributes for analysis. These landmarks do not occur in the natural world with any appreciable frequency. To believe they did, we would have to postulate that gravity somehow causes rocks to consistently strike other rocks using principles of the Hertzian cone, and this seems patently ridiculous. It seems unlikely that rock falling from a cliff face or tumbling down a stream would frequently strike at precisely the correct angles with sufficient force to produce flakes. Rather, humans and their ancestors, with the cognitive and motor skills to understand the angles required, seem to be the primary agents for the production of flakes.

Because of this, some archaeologists find that collecting all of the flakes, cores, and tools from a given area and attempting to rebuild the actual cobbles of rock that were worked provides insight. This work, called **refitting,** is similar to working a complex three-dimensional jigsaw puzzle and is not for the impatient. Yet, by undertaking this process, archaeologists can understand a number of important things. They can identify the precise methods through which stone tools were produced, including the way the raw stone was prepared and reduced. This, in turn, provides archaeologists with information about how valuable a commodity the stone was. If the stone was rare, then we see a great deal of use of even small cobbles; if it was easily gotten, then there tend to be larger amounts of waste. Likewise, refitting cores helps researchers to map the distribution of stone materials across a site. We can make inferences as to whether stone tools were being produced by specialists in the community, whether they were given as gifts, or whether they were sold in markets.

Another branch of lithic analysis involves identifying the chemical signature of specific sorts of stone. Fragments of the stone to be studied are typically exposed to high energy lasers, melted, and then vaporized. During the process, the gases released from the stone are sampled by specialized sensors and identified. The percentages of the different elements present in the sample are then calculated and placed on a graph. This graph represents a distinctive chemical signature. Researchers use this technique on both archaeologically recovered materials and samples taken from known stone quarries. By identifying the sources from which stone was quarried, archaeologists can trace the distribution of stone across the landscape, thus learning something about human movements and trade patterns.

Hammering Away

Having discussed what a flake is and how it can be used, we now turn to the other end of manufacturing technology—the tools used to produce flakes. There are a number of ways to strikes flakes from a core. The earliest and most common method was through **direct percussion,** in which an object is brought down with force on top of a core along the edge of an imagined Hertzian cone. If the object used to strike the flake is as hard as or harder than the core stone, we call this method a **hard hammer technique** and the stone

---

refitting The reconstruction of a core by fitting all of the flakes struck from that core back together.

direct percussion Striking a core directly with a hammer or billet in order to drive off a flake or the use of an anvil on which a core is directly struck to drive off a flake.

hard hammer technique The use of a percussive instrument that is as hard as or harder than the core to strike a flake from that core.

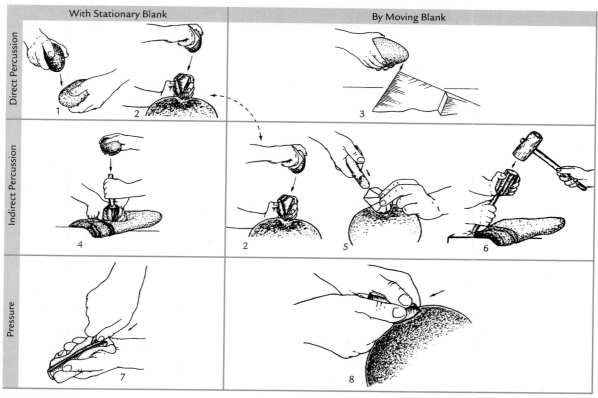

	With Stationary Blank	By Moving Blank
Direct Percussion	1 2	3
Indirect Percussion	4	2 5 6
Pressure	7	8

FIGURE 6.5

Three basic methods of detaching flakes from cores. Note the difference between the two percussion methods and the pressure flaking method.

that was used to strike the core a **hammerstone.** Flakes produced by this method tend to be long and often are thick. If an object that is softer than the stone of the core, say an antler fragment or a hard wood, is used to strike off a flake, then we call this a **soft hammer technique** or a **cylindrical hammer technique** (*cylinder* originally referred to the shape of an antler in cross section). The actual object used for striking in this method is usually referred to as a **billet.** Flakes struck in this manner tend to be broader and shorter than those struck by a hammerstone, and they are also often thinner. This difference is related to the bending and contortion that a billet undergoes when it strikes a core: In good condition, both antler and hard wood are sufficiently rigid to drive a flake from a core, but in the process they distort and thus do not transmit as much force to the flake as does a hammerstone (Figure 6.5).

In **pressure flaking,** a small antler tine or other tough, small implement is placed on the edge of a tool or core. The flintknapper exerts force on the antler tine while supporting the edge opposite to where the tine is applied. As the

hammerstone The stone used to strike a core in order to detach flakes.

soft hammer technique or **cylindrical hammer technique** The use of a percussive instrument that is softer than the core to strike a flake from that core.

billet An antler, bone, or wooden implement used to strike flakes from a core.

pressure flaking The controlled application of increasing pressure to a core in order to strike off a flake.

knapper increases the force applied, a small, broad, thin flake is pushed off the supported edge. This method is particularly good for detail work, such as the final finishing of a tool or the resharpening of a tool's edge. Tiny flakes driven off in this manner are called *retouch flakes*.

A more unusual method of direct percussion can also be used. In this method an anvil stone is positioned firmly on the ground. This anvil needs to be relatively heavy and durable because the flintknapper strikes the core directly against the anvil. By controlling the angle at which the core is held, the knapper can produce predictable flakes. Sometimes the shape of these flakes can be further determined by preparing a specifically shaped stone core that will help channel the force of the blow along predictable pathways through the core. This technique is the hallmark of **Levallois,** or *tortoise core,* **technology,** the stone tool technology usually associated with archaic forms of *Homo sapiens.* This method employs a core that in cross section resembles the shell of a turtle—hence the name tortoise core—and typically produces long, relatively flat, and relatively thin flakes.

Punching Away

Another way to produce flakes is called **indirect percussion.** In this method a punch (a more-or-less straight shaft) is positioned on the core and then it, rather than the core, is struck. Because the force of the blow travels along the axis of the punch, the angle of the punch determines the way in which the Hertzian cone is applied to the core. This allows a flintknapper to carefully position the punch and then apply force more indiscriminately to the top of the punch with some form of hammer.

Because of the mechanics of using a punch, and because it allows control, indirect percussion is often associated with the production of **prismatic blades.** These blades originally appear in the archaeological record during the Upper Paleolithic, some thirty thousand years before present, and are a hallmark of modern humans. The technique continues in use today in the production of gunflints for black-powder firearms. In its basic form, a prismatic blade is a flake that is at least twice as long as it is wide, has steep, parallel sides, and is trapezoidal, usually prismatic, in cross section. The blades can be easily broken to form a variety of other tool forms, and the sharp regular edges of the blades make them ideal cutting tools (Box 6.2). Such tools are produced by first preparing a special form of a core, called a **polyhedral** (many-sided) **core.** Although the production of the core itself takes time and skill, once it is prepared a skilled knapper can punch a great number of regularly sized prismatic blades very quickly (Figure 6.6). Thus the time saved in punching the precise form of blades desired compensates for the time it takes to prepare a core (Box 6.3).

There are a variety of different ways to position a punch on top of a core. Perhaps the most simple method is to place the core between two wooden slats,

Levallois technology A Paleolithic technique common to archaic forms of the genus *Homo* in which a tortoise-shaped core is struck against an anvil in order to produce a long, broad flake.

indirect percussion The use of an intermediary punch to focus the power of a blow on a specific point of a core.

prismatic blade A flake struck from a polyhedral core, at least twice as long as it is wide, with steep, parallel sides, and trapezoidal (prismatic) in cross section.

polyhedral core A specially prepared many-sided core from which prismatic blades may be struck.

BOX 6.2

STONE-AGE EYE SURGERY

Donald Crabtree was an exceptionally talented flintknapper. In fact, he may have been one of the best stone workers of this or many other centuries. As he aged, however, he began to have trouble with his eyesight due to cataracts, growths on the eye that impair and blur vision. They typically require surgery to remove. In this day and age this surgery is often performed with lasers; in the 1960s, though, Crabtree's only available option seemed to be surgical steel scalpels.

Being somewhat of a renegade, and knowing stone tools better than nearly anyone in the world, Crabtree approached his physician with an intriguing alternative—to use stone tools to perform the surgery. Although no photograph exists of the surgeon's face at the time this was suggested, I have mixed images of horror and amusement crossing the man's face. He declined Crabtree's invitation and suggested that the surgical steel would make cleaner cuts and thus facilitate more rapid healing. Crabtree, who had envisioned using freshly made obsidian blades as scalpels, countered that his stone tools were sharper. Eventually, Crabtree arranged for a scanning electron microscope to take high magnification, high resolution images of the operating edges of both the surgeon's scalpels and his own obsidian flakes. Much to the surgeon's surprise, the obsidian was demonstrably sharper. Sometime later, after Crabtree's cataracts had been successfully removed, other physicians began experimenting with the use of obsidian blades for delicate surgical procedures. These stone tools, from a modern stone age, remained in use until they were replaced by light amplified stimulated emissions of radiation, or lasers.

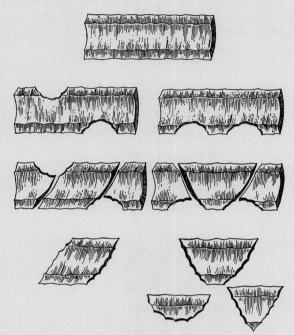

A variety of tools made on and from prismatic blades. At the top is a prismatic blade which in and of itself is a useful cutting implement. The addition of notches or the selected breaking of the blade to form smaller pieces produces edges well suited for everything from carving bone to making projectile points and gunflints.

tying the ends of the slats together to lock the core in place. This produces a vise that can then be held in place by other stones or by the flintknapper's feet. Once arranged in the vise, the knapper holds the punch with one hand and strikes it with a hammer held in the other hand. Alternatively, the flintknapper could place the punch in the base of a crutch that is positioned in front of the artisan's chest. Holding the core in his hands, the artisan pushes down

FIGURE 6.6

The use of a punch to detach a prismatic blade from a polyhedral core. Here an antler tine is being used to channel the force from a hammerstone directly to a preselected point of the prepared core's top. Such precision allows the flintknapper to repeatedly strike predictable flakes from the core.

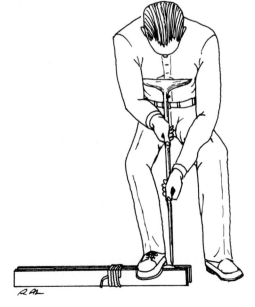

FIGURE 6.7

The use of a chest crutch to detach a prismatic blade. As in Figure 6.6, a punch is used to channel force to a precisely selected point in the core's top. In this case, however, the energy to detach the flake comes from the flintknapper's torso rather than a blow from a hammerstone or billet.

firmly with chest and abdominal muscles, driving off a blade. This *chest punch method* was still in use in parts of the world at the turn of the twentieth century (Figure 6.7). If the flintknapper has an assistant, one person can hold the core in place with both hands while a second person manipulates the punch and hammer.

BOX 6.3

THE UPPER PALEOLITHIC:
ART, ARCHAEOLOGY, AND SOCIETY

The Upper Paleolithic period is defined as the period during which modern humans arrived in Europe and began to produce their characteristic prismatic blade and polyhedral core technologies. Some of the earliest sites are in places such as Bacho Kiro in the Balkan Mountains of Bulgaria and date to approximately 40,000 years ago. Other, better known examples are from western Europe and include the impressive cave art sites of Lascaux, France (dating to between 17,000 and 16,000 years ago) and Altamira, Spain (dating to between 22,000 and 13,500 years ago).

In general, archaeologists recognize five principal cultural periods within the Upper Paleolithic. The rise and fall of these periods seem to correlate with temperature fluctuations and probably with the shift in plant and animal resources that accompanied such shifts. The range of cultural expressions demonstrates that, rather than being a time defined by homogeneity, the Upper Paleolithic is an era defined by a startling and wonderful array of diverse material forms. Of particular interest to us are the prismatic blades and such items as burins, *batons de commandement,* Venus figurines, and even a lunar calendar; the extensive and truly beautiful cave paintings are a hallmark of the Upper Paleolithic.

All of these things seem to be dramatic expressions of human creativity and the expansion of human ideas into both portable and nonportable media. Burins were extensively used to incise wood and bone, often to produce decorative patterns. Such tools are not present before the Upper Paleolithic, and there is no consistent evidence for artistic or ideological expression on bone or wood. Certainly some utilitarian work was done with burins as well, but it is their use in producing portable art that is most interesting.

(continued)

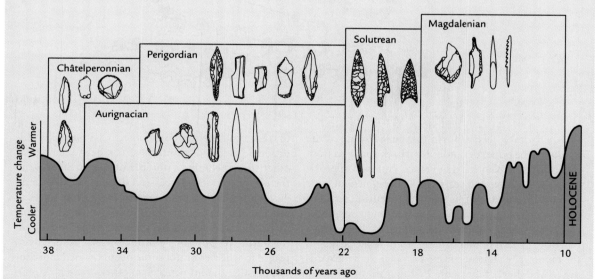

A timeline for Upper Paleolithic technology displayed against changes in the northern European environment. Note the range of tool forms present in the Upper Paleolithic as compared with any previous era of the human past.

BOX 6.3 *(continued)*

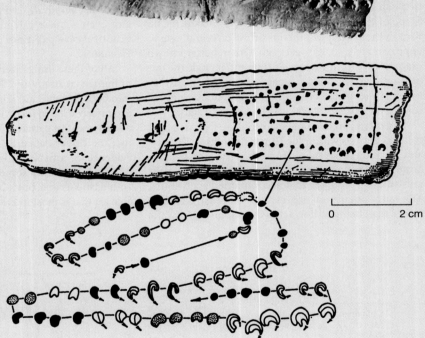

Carved bone plaque from Abri Blanchard, France. The sequence of carvings on its face, redrawn at the bottom, led Alexander Marshack to suggest that this represents a lunar calendar or date log.

It may have been a burin that made some of the marks on the bone Alexander Marshack analyzed from the site of Abri Blanchard in France, dating to approximately thirty thousand years ago. The fragment of bone of most interest contains a long, serpentine series of sixty-nine notches, which, Marshack suggests, indicates that people counted the passage of time using a repetitive system of marks designed to reflect stages of the moon. The sequence from Abri Blanchard, according to Marshack, represents 2¼ lunar months. Using this system, Marshack argues that Upper Paleolithic people were able to track the movement of animals through seasons and to predict when certain resources would become available. They may also have been able to track time for ceremonial and social purposes. Additional inscribed counts have also been recorded at other sites, including a number of sites in Siberia and the eleven-thousand-year-old deposits at Grotte du Tai, France. Here a more lengthy serpentine series of notches in bone seems to record a full 3½ years of time.

Another use of bone has also raised questions about the nature of Upper Paleolithic society, especially in regard to whether or not some people gained more social prestige and influence than others. *Batons de commandement*, literally batons of commanders, are made from antler usually obtained from reindeer. They are carved with decorative patterns and often have a hole drilled through them near the location at which antler tines join the main shaft of the antler. Such items do not seem to exhibit much, if any, use wear and have been variously argued to represent material for signaling social power (hence the name), as magical wands or devices, and as utilitarian tools for the straightening of spear shafts. We cannot be sure of the precise nature of these tools, but the fact that they are decorated and do not occur in great numbers reinforces the notion that they may operate on sociotechnic or ideotechnic levels.

Venus figurines represent another class of material culture unique to the Upper Paleolithic. The items are some of the world's earliest representations of the human form, in this case a woman with ample characteristics. These figurines have been most recently interpreted as magical charms representing fertility, suggesting that the women portrayed by the images were pregnant, and as ideological representations of a goddess figure, again referencing female associations with reproduction. More peripherally, a small number of scholars have suggested that the figurines symbolize expressions of human sexuality and male desires. It is doubtful that we will ever be sure which, if any, of these interpretations is most appropriate or even if the figurines might have had multiple interpretations among past peoples. What is clear, however, is that Venus figurines were not, strictly speaking, tools for everyday use in society.

The most famous Upper Paleolithic artistic expressions are those in caves such as Lascaux in France and Altamira in Spain. Lascaux was first brought to the attention of modern scholars in 1942 when a young boy, playing with a flashlight, observed the paintings on the walls and roofs of chambers in the cave. Eventually, primarily after World War II, scholars were persuaded to examine the paintings, though some expressed reluctance because they believed that such amazing stories of cave paintings were either fabricated or described a modern hoax. Much to their surprise, and to the chagrin of some, the paintings proved to be authentic.

What scholars encountered was a cave with three long passages and two "galleries," or wide areas. In these were twelve separate compositions of paintings, including depictions of aurochs (a form of wild cattle), bison, ibex, bears, a rhinoceros, a reindeer, and human images (in part or full). Other engravings and signs,

The famous Venus of Willendorf, Austria. Such figures may have had many different purposes, but they clearly represent the ability of modern humans to transfer abstract thoughts to the material world.

including handprints showing missing fingers, were found throughout the cave system. Dating of the organic components of the pigments indicated that the majority of the paintings date to between seventeen thousand and sixteen thousand years ago, during the Magdalenian period. Reindeer bones were also recovered in great abundance from the floor of the cave, suggesting that some sort of feasting, offerings, or other ritualized events took place here.

(continued)

BOX 6.3 (continued)

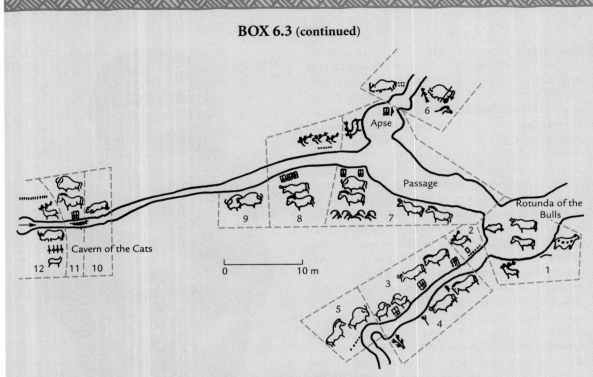

The overall layout of Lascaux Cave, France. Note the different galleries, or areas where images are depicted.

Without doubt, Lascaux and caves like it were special places, locations to which individuals or small groups of people could go to undertake some sort of ceremony or rite. What these rites may have been, however, we are at a loss to explain for certain. Although we can interpret much of the art in various ways, such as incantations to ensure successful hunts or the fertility of important game animals, we cannot know the specific ideas and beliefs that the people who utilized the cave brought with them. Fortunately, the careful research of archaeologists, artists, and art historians continues to add to our knowledge of such places and the range of activities associated with them. As this catalog of activities is expanded and made deeper, it may be that we will gain additional insights into the beliefs and social systems responsible for these magnificent creations.

Against this backdrop of expressive culture, many people have asked simple but meaningful questions, including, Why did all of this happen during this period, and why did it all happen seemingly at once? The

burin An Upper Paleolithic stone tool with a sharpened corner or projection specifically designed to engrave wood or bone. This tool is closely associated with the production of decorative art.

Ground Stone Tool Technology

Unlike chipped stone tools, most ground stone tools tend to be technologically more similar to each other. In large part this stems from the relatively more narrow range of purposes such stone tools have. Whereas chipped stone tools served as everything from projectile points to awls or even to **burins,** ground stone tools are often more closely associated with processing plant material or fibers, though ground stone can also be used for cutting or

A detail of a horse painted over some form of cattle or oxen. Note also the other shapes painted onto (pictographs) and pecked into (petroglyphs) the rock wall around the central forms.

second of these questions is easily answered because it is based on semantics rather than on archaeological data. Simply put, not all of these materials and behaviors did occur at the same time and in the same place. The Upper Paleolithic spans nearly forty thousand years, and we draw data from all over the Old World, especially from western Asia to northern Africa and across Europe. Given this much time and this much space, we might expect a great deal of cultural variation and a variety of cultural adaptations, and this is precisely what we see.

The first question, however, poses a more subtle problem. Although we have a wide geographic area and a lengthy span of time, so did earlier periods, such as the Lower and Middle Paleolithic. Yet there is nothing comparable to the range of expressive material culture that we see during the Upper Paleolithic. The traditional answer, and one which we have yet to overturn, centers on the arrival and florescence of anatomically modern humans in those regions during the time period defined by the Upper Paleolithic. In essence we are saying that all of this variation occurred because we modern humans are fundamentally different from our predecessors in what we can conceive of and display. This does not mean that our predecessors were ill-mannered brutes, though by our social standards we might perceive them as such. Rather, the differences in the variety of material culture simply reflect the differences between modern humans and our predecessors, the archaic humans.

scraping purposes. Throughout the world it is with the processing of plant material that these tools are often most closely associated, though, and it is their presence that helped to spur the definition of the Neolithic period (Box 6.4).

Most ground stone tools are made from coarse stone such as rhyolite or limestone. The abrasive nature of such stones aids in the grinding and pulverizing of such things as rice, wheat, and corn, the three major cereal crops of

BOX 6.4

V. GORDON CHILDE AND THE NEOLITHIC REVOLUTION

Interesting things tend to happen when scholarship is mixed with deeply held personal convictions. Vere Gordon Childe was born in Australia and developed a deeply felt attraction toward issues he considered matters of social justice and welfare, eventually also adopting Marxist notions of conflict and change. He was also committed to the notion of **cultural evolution,** that societies tend to evolve from simple to complex as time passes and as population rises.

He meshed these ideas together in a series of influential books that sought to present a synthesized view of European prehistory. In two of his classic works, *The Dawn of European Civilization* (1925) and *The Danube in Prehistory* (1926), Childe not only described the material culture found across broad regions but also sought to explain how this material was produced and distributed. In this respect he became one of the first archaeologists to systematically ask and attempt to answer questions about how and why things happened on such large scales.

Perhaps the zenith of Childe's distinguished career came with the publication of *Man Makes Himself* in 1936. Childe's strong Marxist tendencies were in clear evidence as he discussed what he thought were the two great leaps in humankind's social development, the origins of food production and the origins of urbanization. The former he dubbed the *Neolithic Revolution* and the latter the *Urban Revolution,* and for Childe both were inextricably linked with the growth of human civilizations. Humans, he argued, developed food production at about 10,000 B.C. in an effort to meet high population levels and shrinking amounts of land suitable for hunting and gathering wild plants and animals. The hallmarks of this revolution were a rapid switch to domestication of plants and animals, making pottery for storing foodstuffs, making ground stone tools for processing grains, and sedentism (living in permanent, nonmobile communities). Each of these four traits, Childe argued correctly, reflected human adaptations to environmental and population pressures.

The impetus for these revolutions was increasing temperatures and aridity in the Near East after the last Ice Age. Archaeologists had long observed that this area of the world seemed to have some of the earliest civilizations, and, in fact, Egypt and Mesopotamia were believed by many scholars to be the cradles of all later civilizations. Accordingly, Childe postulated what came to be known as *oasis theory,* the notion that as the climate became more harsh people were forced to retreat to the few remaining pockets of good land, in places such as river valleys and along coastlines. In these areas, faced with the needs of survival, people innovated rapidly and generated the four characteristics of the Neolithic Revolution. As time passed, the population in these oases grew rapidly, forcing people to again adapt rapidly. Craft specialists and government officials appeared, and along with them came urbanization and civilization. Such, Childe argued, was the manner in which human civilization was born.

However, these theories were not borne out by future research. Although the four characteristics of the Neolithic Revolution are all human responses to perceived needs and stress, they do not always happen together, nor do they tend to develop very quickly in many cases. For instance, at the end of the last Ice Age people lived along a part of the Jordan River system, at a site now known as 'Ain Mallaha. Jean Perrot and a team of French archaeologists carefully excavated the site and

cultural evolution The theory that all cultures tend to move from simple to complex as they grow in size.

the modern world. Basalt, slate, and sandstone are also used in manufacturing ground stone implements and are best known for their use in producing decorative or symbolically meaningful items, such as the basalt portrait heads of the Olmec or the atl-atl weights of the North American woodlands (Box 6.5). In order to produce a ground stone tool, an individual needs to quarry or in

V. Gordon Childe (center, back row) posing with workmen.

identified permanent buildings and ground stone but no good evidence for domestication of either plants or animals and certainly no pottery. Two of the four characteristics were present but not the others. Similar situations prevailed at Jericho, Jarmo, Ali Kosh, and other sites throughout the Near East. Rather than being a Neolithic Revolution, the process seemed to be gradual Neolithic evolution. As often proved the case with Childe, his insights were incredible, but his sense of timing proved to be incorrect. Still, for a researcher who spent his career working out insights and sequences prior to the development of modern dating techniques (see Chapter 5), Childe's accomplishments seem all that much more remarkable.

some way acquire a large block of the desired abrasive stone. This stone is then broken into its rough shape through a process called **pecking and grinding,** a combination of direct percussion, or pecking, and abrasion, with sand, rough stones, and water being used like sandpaper. Pecking alone might be used to produce some ground stone tools, whereas grinding typically is used in com-

pecking and grinding A combination of direct percussion and abrasion used to produce ground stone items.

BOX 6.5

TOOLS, TASKS, AND TECHNOLOGIES

Archaeological material culture has many aspects. For the most part it has been traditional for archaeologists to discuss the effectiveness of this tool or that tool in accomplishing a given task. Indeed, archaeologists developed significant portions of middle range theory simply to try to interpret how good a tool might be at accomplishing one or more tasks. Yet in the early 1960s Lewis Binford, an early proponent of such studies and the person responsible for the term middle range theory, also realized that some forms of material culture functioned in ways other than technologically. Others had observed the same thing much earlier, and archaeologists such as Irving Rouse and Walter W. Taylor had published work on the need to view human behavior as a complete system, not just as a series of mechanical responses designed to accomplish work.

Binford, however, discussed the matter systematically and suggested a series of terms that accounted for what he thought was the possible range of uses for any item of material culture. Material that accomplished mechanical tasks such as cutting or piercing was known as **technomic,** meaning that it served a technological purpose. It is at the technomic level that much of archaeology has traditionally been done.

Some material culture, however, seems to display some sort of social communication or social statement of identity. For example, if we look at the way people dress in our own culture, we can see that people dress differently for different occasions. If clothing were purely technomic, this would not be necessary, because a well-designed set of clothing might meet the needs of shelter, cover, and protection for a wide range of circumstances. Why would a person need an expensive suit?

---

technomic A category of material culture inferred to have served principally technological ends, such as cutting or piercing.

grinding platform, or **metate** Usually a substantial slab of abrasive stone on which grains and other plant materials are pulverized.

grinding stone, or **mano** Usually a hand-sized block or cylinder of abrasive stone designed to pulverize grains or other plant materials on a grinding platform.

bination with pecking or some other shaping method. Once the object has been roughed into shape, nearly all of the remaining work will be done with abrasives and hard grinding. Some additional chipping may be done in order to refine the shape or to produce some form of decoration, but in general grinding is the primary finishing method. In some societies a final layer of pigment is added to parts of the tool as a decoration.

The two most common forms of ground stone tools are grinding platforms and grinding stones. Such tools can take a variety of forms, but a **grinding platform,** or **metate,** is typically a thick slab of abrasive stone that is sometimes supported by three or more luglike legs. A **grinding stone,** or **mano,** is made of comparable material but is designed to fit into a person's hands so that he or she can slide it or roll it over the surface of the platform. Manos may be oblong blocks or rounded tubes, resembling modern rolling pins. Grinding platforms and stones are used together: Some plant material, usually dried, is set on the platform and pulverized by the grinding stone. The resulting powder is scraped from the platform and either mixed with water and cooked or stored as flour.

Other types of ground stone tools include such things as spindle whorls and loom weights, net sinkers, and similar objects. A spindle whorl, for example, is a round weight, in this case made from stone, through which fibers are passed. The weight is then held in front of the operator and spun, thus spin-

Why do judges wear robes? The answer is that there is a social element to dress. Modern people alter their dress in order to fit into the social environments they find themselves in. This is likewise true of other forms of material culture, from homes to automobiles, even to pens. In general an inexpensive $2 ballpoint pen writes as well as a $100 ballpoint pen, but the display and ownership of the more expensive pen conveys a social message, one of wealth and affluence, to others. This type of behavior is an example of conspicuous consumption, and it is sometimes related to items that are considered **sociotechnic,** those that function more on the social than the technological level.

Binford further argued that other items of material culture operated primarily on the ideological level. For example, the possession of a good luck charm, such as a four-leaf clover or rabbit's foot in Western culture, does little either technologically or socially. However, the presence of such items works on the level of the possessor's belief in good fortune and therefore reflects ideology. Displays of religious medallions or similar items often operate in the same way. Material culture that functions in this manner is known as **ideotechnic** in Binford's scheme.

Not everyone has accepted Binford's arguments and categories as useful. Some postprocessualists have challenged the notion that any piece of material culture must function at any level. They have pointed out that some people possess certain items simply because they happen to like those items. This critique can be especially powerful at the level of sociotechnic and ideotechnic interpretation. There is usually less doubt about whether an object could or did physically perform some mechanical task, but there is a great deal of debate over how to interpret more esoteric forms of material culture.

ning and extending the fibers held on one end by the operator and on the other end by the spindle whorl. Loom weights are used to weigh down and stabilize strands of fibers as a loom operator weaves them together.

Ground stone implements were also used to process wood. During the Neolithic period in Europe and the Archaic period in North America people produced heavy, grooved axes designed to cut and process wood. These axes were inefficient compared with modern hard metal axes, but they did adequately meet the needs of people by providing heavy, durable tools that channeled the force of a blow to a relatively narrow striking edge. The grooves served as a means to mount the stone in a wooden handle, thus allowing a worker to increase the amount of force of a blow. Other woodworking implements included adzes, celts, hoes, and gouges.

More rarely, ground stone is used as a medium to produce art or other forms of display. Such stone may come in a variety of forms and may range from small figurines through life-sized or larger statuary. Among the most famous large figures are the large basalt heads associated with Olmec culture on the Gulf Coast of Mexico. Here, some thirty-five hundred years ago, people shaped basalt into portrait heads of important people, likely chiefs or other influential leaders. The scale of the heads, however, is what captivates many people's attention. Some of these heads stand fully 6 feet tall and nearly as wide. Archaeologists are left to speculate why such monuments were produced, but

sociotechnic A category of material culture in which items are inferred to have served social roles, such as identity marking.

ideotechnic A category of material culture inferred to have served to display or communicate ideological statements, such as connections to spirits or religious tenets.

FIGURE 6.8

One of the world's largest class of ground stone works are represented by these Olmec portrait heads. These heads can rise to nearly 2 meters in height and were likely used to emphasize the importance of specific leaders in Olmec society.

FIGURE 6.9

A carved and polished *platform pipe,* 16 cm long, made in the form of a panther. This pipe is associated with the Hopewell Interaction Sphere of the eastern United States, ca. 500 B.C. to A.D. 300.

most researchers accept that they have something to do with statements of power, prestige, and authority (Figure 6.8).

More-portable ground stone art is common to the Hopewell Interaction Sphere, a large territory of loosely allied trading partners and their societies that stretches from Ohio to Missouri and from the Great Lakes to northern Florida. Some Hopewell artisans became very skilled and specialized, at least for part of their time, in producing beautifully carved and ground platform pipes. Many of these pipes are in the form of beavers, birds, and a variety of other animals (Figure 6.9). That such pipes were prized possessions is demonstrated in their limited numbers and the distance over which some of them seemed to have been traded. Like the Olmec portrait heads, some archaeologists have suggested that these pipes reflect the affluence of those who possessed them, a form of **conspicuous consumption** in which the ownership and display of prestigious goods lends social prestige to the person making the display. Others have suggested that the pipes have a ritual significance, whereas still others have suggested that the societies that used them simply found them attractive. Of particular interest to many archaeologists, though, is the fact that none of these uses is exclusive.

SUMMARY

Stone tools represent the oldest known evidence of human technology. Although it is likely that wood or bone tools were used before stone tools were developed, such ephemeral materials are not preserved through the ages. Consequently, it is through the study of stone tools that researchers begin the search for our earliest ancestors. From these beginnings archaeologists have been able to trace and document a stunning variety of forms and uses for stone tools that continue into the present. The core mechanisms of producing stone tools, chipping and grinding, are common to most if not all of the forms of this amazing variety, and for this reason archaeologists often begin to teach the study of the past through the study of stone tools. Without a doubt, stone tools have the longest presence in the archaeological record and served all of the purposes of processing that today are served by dozens of specific tools.

FOR FURTHER INFORMATION

Adams, J. L. 1988. Use-wear analysis on manos and hide process stones. *Journal of Field Archaeology* 15: 307–15.

Bordaz, J. 1970. *Tools of the Old and New Stone Age.* Garden City, NY: Natural History Press.

Bordes, F. 1968. *The Old Stone Age.* New York: McGraw-Hill.

Cahan, D., L. H. Keeley, and F. L. Van Noten. 1979. Stone tools, toolkits and human behavior in prehistory. *Current Anthropology* 20: 661–83.

Crabtree, D. E. 1972. *An introduction to flintworking. Part I, An introduction to the technology of stone tools.* Occasional Paper no. 28. Pocatello: Idaho State University.

Keeley, L. H. 1974. Technique and methodology in microwear studies: A critical review. *World Archaeology* 5: 323–36.

———. 1977. The functions of Paleolithic stone tools. *Scientific American* 237 (5): 108–26.

———. 1980. *Experimental determination of stone tool uses: A microwear analysis.* Chicago: University of Chicago Press.

Keeley, L. H., and M. H. Newcomer. 1977. Microwear analysis of experimental flint tools: A test case. *Journal of Archaeological Science* 4: 29–62.

conspicuous consumption
The use or display of excessive resources for a given task in order to display affluence, prestige, power, and/or identity.

Newcomer, M. H., and L. H. Keeley. 1979. Testing a method of microwear analysis with experimental flint tools. In *Lithic use-wear analysis,* edited by B. Hayden, 195–205. New York: Academic Press.

Odell, G. H. 1994. Prehistoric hafting and mobility in the North American midcontinent: Examples from Illinois. *Journal of Anthropological Archaeology* 13: 51–73.

———. 2000. Use-wear analysis. In *Archaeological method and theory: An encyclopedia,* edited by L. Ellis, 651–55. New York: Garland.

Potts, R., and P. Shipman. 1981. Cutmarks made by stone tools on bones from Olduvai Gorge, Tanzania. *Nature* 291: 577–80.

Sackett, J. R. 1966. Quantitative analysis of Upper Paleolithic stone tools. In *Recent studies in paleoanthropology,* edited by J. D. Clark and F. C. Howell, *American Anthropologist* special issue; 68 (2, pt. 2): 356–94.

Toth, N. 1985. The Oldowan reassessed: A close look at early stone artifacts. *Journal of Archaeological Science* 12: 101–20.

Whittaker, J. 1994. *Flintknapping: Making and understanding stone tools.* Austin: University of Texas.

Wright, R. V. S., ed. 1977. *Stone tools as cultural markers.* Canberra: Australian Institute of Aboriginal Studies.

7

POTTERY IN THE ARCHAEOLOGICAL RECORD

Pottery is formed and informed: pottery making is an additive process in which the successive steps are recorded in the final product. The shape, decoration, composition, and manufacturing methods of pottery thus reveal insights— lowly and lofty, sacred and profane—into human behavior and the history of civilization.

—Prudence Rice, 1987, p. 25

Certain kinds of artifacts have a mystique about them. These items sometimes draw disproportionate measures of attention from the public and, occasionally, from archaeologists. Whereas many of the earliest archaeologists and their public were often enamored of royal tombs and golden burial furniture, many more recent archaeologists have focused their attentions on pottery. Whole pots and mosaic floors are grand finds, often having a romantic flavor in terms of popular appeal, but the thousands on thousands of broken fragments of ceramic products from sites throughout the world have also drawn great amounts of attention. In this chapter we will explore what pottery is, how we study it, and, perhaps most important, examine why some archaeologists seem so obsessed with this material.

WHY ARCHAEOLOGISTS STUDY CERAMICS

In her outstanding summary work on ceramics *Pottery Analysis: A Sourcebook,* Prudence Rice discusses many of the reasons why archaeologists study ceramics. Her discussion can be summarized in five main points.

1.   Pottery occurs on archaeological sites with appreciable frequency. Archaeologists have no choice but to classify, analyze, and make interpretations of such materials simply because they represent such a large part of the archaeological record.

2.   Pottery is nearly indestructible. Although different forms of ceramics, such as cups, tiles, and pipes, may break, the fragments of these things remain intact in the archaeological record. Although some lightly fired **terra-cotta** or unfired clay pieces may disintegrate, most ceramic sherds (fragments of larger ceramic pieces) are akin to stone; they simply do not degrade and disappear in most depositional environments.

3.   Because pottery breaks and enters the archaeological record in fragmentary form, most casual artifact collectors are not interested in obtaining the broken pieces. Although whole vessels are highly prized by collectors, sherds are usually left in place. This means that archaeologists are more likely to obtain a more complete perspective on a ceramic assemblage than on a lithic assemblage from which collectors may have removed all visible complete projectile points.

4.   Pottery in its various forms tends to have been present in all social strata of those past societies that made pottery. Consequently, unlike precious metals or other rare goods, ceramics reflect the day-to-day lives of a cross section of past society. This allows archaeologists to ask research questions related to a broader range of past populations than some other materials.

5.   Pottery breaks with appreciable frequency. As a result, ceramics are constantly being replaced with new ceramic items. Over time, as styles and technologies change, ceramic assemblages change. Archaeologists can observe these changes and use them to answer questions about changing social and technological relations within a society. Because pottery is frequently decorated, modern researchers can observe changes in decorative motifs through time, ideally identifying and accounting for the distribution of patterns in terms of changing cultural dynamics within a society. This is frequently difficult and subjective work, but it provides a tremendous opportunity to glean insights into the lives of past peoples.

MATERIALS AND MANUFACTURE

Pottery can be defined as all forms of human-made products constructed from clay (Figure 7.1). Most ceramics are fired, though clay shaped into forms and then allowed to bake in the sun and those items produced with the intent of firing but not actually fired (called greenware) also belong within the larger category of ceramics. Minimally, it contains three basic ingredients, clay, water, and some form of coarse **inclusion** usually referred to as **temper.** The use of the term *temper*, however, implies that the person who made the pottery deliberately added the material to the **paste,** or *fabric* as English archae-

terra-cotta Ceramics fired at under 900°C. Such wares tend to be porous and somewhat delicate.

pottery All forms of human-made products constructed from clay.

inclusion Any object other than clay or water present in the paste of a ceramic; items used specifically as temper are a special form of inclusion.

temper Coarse inclusions deliberately added to a paste for purposes of improving the firing characteristics of that paste.

paste The mixture of clay, water, and inclusions, including temper, used to create ceramics.

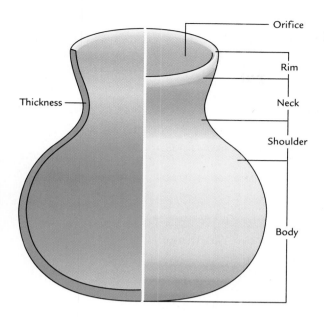

Orifice
Rim
Neck
Shoulder
Body
Thickness

FIGURE 7.1

The generalized anatomy of a pot.

ologists tend to call it, in order to enhance the stability or firing characteristics of items made from the paste. (Paste is the mixture of clay, water, and coarse materials that will be hardened and thus form some piece of ceramic.) Not all coarse materials in the paste, however, are deliberately added by the potter. Sometimes the clay itself contains larger fragments of quartz or other minerals that cannot be or are not completely removed before the clay is used to produce pottery. Likewise, sand, shell, grasses, and a host of other materials can conceivably find their way into a paste accidentally. Consequently, archaeologists tend to use the term *temper* to refer to materials likely to have been deliberately added to the paste, while using the term *inclusion* to refer to materials that may not have been deliberately added. It is not always easy to determine if something was intentionally added to a paste, though in cases in which the inclusions are nonlocal or in which they have been prepared through crushing, pulverizing, or other processing methods, archaeologists can usually safely infer that the materials represent deliberate actions and are therefore temper.

Pottery is not limited in its form or function to containers. Although most people tend to think first of pottery as bowls or similar items, other forms of ceramics include figurines, statuary, tiles, bricks, writing tablets, drainage pipes, smoking pipes, electrical insulators, and a wide variety of other items. Likewise, the paste that such items are manufactured from varies significantly. In fact, because humans have made and continue to make so many different ceramic items, any classification and analysis of such materials must be commensurately broad (Table 7.1).

TABLE 7.1 Chronological Sequence of Developments in Pottery and Ceramic Technology

Development	Europe	Near East	Far East	Western Hemisphere
Fired clay figurines	Dolní Věstonice, Czechoslovakia, 30,000 B.C.			
Pottery		Anatolia, 8500–8000 B.C.	Japan, 10,000 B.C.	Various, 3000–2500 B.C.
Kiln	[England, late 1st millennium B.C.]	Iran, 7th millennium B.C.	China, 4800–4200 B.C.	Mexico, A.D. 500
Wheel		3500 B.C.	China, 2600–1700 B.C.	[16th century A.D.]
Brick—adobe		Zagros, 7500–6300 B.C.		Coastal Peru, 1900 B.C.; Mexico, 900–800 B.C.
Brick—fired		Sumer, 1500 B.C.		Mexico, A.D. 600–900
Stoneware	Germany, 14th century		China, 1400–1200 B.C.	
Glazes				
Hard		16th century B.C.	China, 1028–927 B.C.	
Lead		100 B.C.	China, 206 B.C.–A.D. 221	
Celadon			China, 4th century	
Fritted			China, 8th century	
Tin	Southern Italy, 13th century; England, 17th century	Assyria, 900 B.C.		
Salt	Germany, 16th century			
Porcelain	Germany 1709; France 1768		China, 9th–10th century; Japan, 1616	
Bone china	England, late 18th century			
Gypsum plaster mold	Italy, 1500			
Jiggering	1700			
Slip casting	1740			
Pyrometric cones	1886			

Source: Rice 1987

Materials

Clay is an interesting sediment. It is the finest form of all sediments, meaning that the individual sizes of grains that compose clay are smaller than those that make up silt and sand. Because clay is composed of such fine grains, it tends to stay afloat in water longer than do other sediments, and it is this relationship between clay and water that is essential to forming the clay into an object. Wet clay seems sticky and slick because it is essentially in a solution of water; the more water in the solution, the runnier and more slippery the clay feels. The less water in the solution, the harder and more solid the clay feels. The right balance of water and clay allows the clay to be formed into complex shapes and to hold these shapes for long periods of time.

As a rule, purer clays, that is, those with lower percentages of silts, sands, and other coarse inclusions, are better for producing complex shapes, such as pots and figurines. Less pure clay can be used, but these tend to have weaker bonds because the larger sediments do not share the same property of staying in solution with clay. Such clays, however, are usually more than adequate for producing adobe (sun-baked clay) or fired bricks.

In nature clays can be obtained from either primary or secondary deposits. **Primary clays** are those that are formed in situ as certain sorts of sedimentary rock decay through chemical weathering processes. **Secondary clays** are sediments that have been moved from their original point of formation and redeposited, perhaps several times, by natural forces such as wind and water. Often secondary clays can be located adjacent to old streambeds and along oxbows (steep bends and side channels in streams). Such clays are by-products of clay that moved downstream in solution, along with silts and sands. As the water flow slows and the energy of the stream dissipates, the heavier particles begin to fall out of solution. Clays are the last particles to precipitate from the water, and this typically happens when the energy in a stream is quite low.

In the cases of both primary and secondary clays, people who regularly collect such materials develop a good idea of geological principles in action. Though it is doubtful that a potter collecting clay five thousand years ago would explain how clays are formed and deposited in the precise ways that geologists today do, such a person would doubtless have a practical knowledge of these phenomena, though that knowledge might be couched in the language of traditions, religion, or even simple good fortune.

Tempering agents can be obtained in any number of ways and may take any number of forms. At the technological level, temper allows spaces for clay to expand and realign itself during firing so that the walls of the object being fired do not crack or crumble. It is an aplastic material that adds stability to the vessel. Tempers such as grass and straw tend to burn away during firing, leaving gaps in the walls of the objects they were formed into. Such items are typically weaker than ceramics fired with more durable temper, such as grit and shell, that do not burn away under most firing conditions.

Interestingly, not all material deliberately added to a paste is technologically advantageous or even technologically functional. For example, some groups of Native Americans who participated in the Hopewell Interaction Sphere, a trading network that extended over much of the middle and eastern United States between approximately 200 B.C. and A.D. 450, added small

primary clays Clays formed in place by the chemical and physical weathering of rock.

secondary clays Clays deposited in secondary locations, usually by erosion and the flow of streams.

BOX 7.1

HOPEWELL: IDEAS, TRADE, AND ALLIANCE
IN THE FIRST MILLENNIUM A.D.

Between approximately 200 B.C. and A.D. 450, a comprehensive trading network thrived across much of the eastern half of North America. Ranging from Kansas City in the west to the shores of the Great Lakes in the north, east to Pennsylvania and south to northern Florida, a suite of material culture was traded between members of small-scale societies. Copper, obsidian, marine shells, mica, and a host of other items circulated throughout this trade network, sometimes with some areas of the trade network seeming to prefer specific sorts of items over others. Yet each region demonstrates that this trading network did not define an archaeological culture but instead a series of allied societies. This group has become known as the Hopewell Interaction Sphere, and it marks the power and pervasive nature of face-to-face contacts and trading relationships in prehistory.

The most famous, and perhaps most socially elaborate, of these societies existed in southern Ohio along the Scioto River and in central Illinois along the Illinois River. In Ohio, at sites such as Mound City and Seip, the people participating in the Hopewell Interaction Sphere built elaborate earthen mounds, often in geometric shapes. Once thought to be defensive in nature, archaeologists have argued over the past thirty years that the mounds, which sometimes form enclosures, are symbolic. Robert Hall of the University of Illinois at Chicago has suggested that some of these enclosures may represent places where the spirits of deceased relatives could be contacted but contained. More recently, archaeologist Brad Lepper of the Ohio Historical Society has suggested that some of the mounds are tied into a sacred roadway, that they, in fact, represent a physical manifestation of people's beliefs about how the world is organized. This mound group has been labeled the Great Hopewell Road and is argued to be parallel to Anasazi roads in the American Southwest and Maya sacbes (sacred roads) in Mesoamerica. Such symbolic interpretations are hard to test, yet we only have to look at our own cultures and societies to see equivalent examples. Many Christian churches are laid out in the form of a crucifix for symbolic reasons, and the city of Washington, D.C., was laid out in order to emphasize its role as the center of the federal government.

Although archaeologists cannot excavate the face-to-face communications of past eras, we are able to recover evidence of past social structures and trade. Evidence from many societies participating in Hopewell trade, but especially from the Illinois River valley, indicates the presence of strong lineage groups. These **corporate lineage groups,** groups of direct descendants and ancestors involved in trade on behalf of the whole line (or lineage), may have groups of allies in other societies. These allied lineages traded between each other and passed on their connections from generation to generation through a form of exchange known as *balanced reciprocity* (see Chapter 9). Accordingly, gifts and trade are presented from members of one lineage to members of another lineage. In return, on the next trading expedition, the lineage that received goods originally is obliged to make similar presentations to the lineage that originally provided the materials. This

amounts of mica to the paste used to form certain types of pots. It is difficult to speculate on precisely why this was done. Modern pottery experimentation makes it clear that mica has no special advantages in firing and that, in general, its platy (long, flat) structure makes it less efficient as a temper than inclusions with blockier structures. Yet the mica does have a reflective property, so that those fragments that are exposed on the surface of a pot would reflect

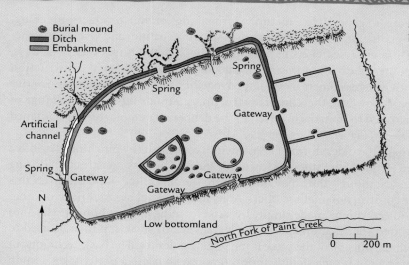

Burial mound
Ditch
Embankment

Spring
Spring

Artificial channel

Spring
Gateway

Gateway

N

Gateway
Gateway

Spring
Gateway

Low bottomland

North Fork of Paint Creek

0   200 m

A plan of the earthworks, showing burial mounds, at the Hopewell site.

sort of behavior has been identified in living societies by social anthropologists and represents a well-documented and viable sort of exchange between geographically separated societies.

One of the primary forms of evidence for the presence of corporate lineage groups, and one of a cluster of important behaviors that appear throughout many societies participating in the Hopewell Interaction Sphere, is the presence of similar forms of burial mounds. These mounds are built atop an ossuary, which is usually a log-lined crypt in which the remains of several people are deposited and which is sometimes covered by a wood or stone lid. Archaeological evidence suggests that a small hut may have been built over the tomb to protect it or mark its location. The pattern of remains in these ossuaries, though, is important. Usually there is a single individual or a small group lying in an extended position (on their backs, as if sleeping flat), but the remains of many other individuals are jumbled in the corners and along the walls. This seems to represent a behavior in which a deceased member of a lineage is laid out in state in the ossuary; perhaps he or she is visited by living members of the lineage in a form of ancestor veneration. Eventually, someone else of importance in the lineage dies, perhaps the heir of the person originally laid to rest. The decomposed bones of the original person are simply swept aside, and the new body is laid in an extended position. This pattern is repeated until the ossuary becomes too full or until the lineage moves to another location. When this happens the ossuary is covered, the hut burnt, and the whole system covered by a small conical mound. The fact that burials of this sort have been found at the far extremes of the Hopewell Interaction Sphere, as well as throughout the central portions of its area, suggests that burial symbolism focusing on a lineage was an important component of the sphere function.

any intense light, such as firelight. This in and of itself does not explain why some peoples used mica as an inclusion, but it is one possible explanation. Unless, or until, archaeologists devise a more effective way of determining what mica may have done on a technomic, sociotechnic, or ideotechnic level for those who used it, all explanations remain possibilities rather than either probabilities or certainties (Box 7.1).

corporate lineage group A group of direct descendants and ancestors who combine efforts and work to benefit the lineage as a whole, usually under the leadership of a senior kinsman or lineage chief.

Methods of Construction

There are, in general, five methods for making ceramic products: pinching, slab construction, coil construction, mold construction, and wheel construction. Different researchers have grouped these methods in a variety of ways, with some subdividing these five categories into additional construction methods, whereas others have lumped together some of the methods. For our purposes, however, these five construction methods represent the range of options open to humans involved in the deliberate manufacture of hardened clay objects (Figure 7.2).

Perhaps the oldest form of constructing ceramics is by **pinching** clay into a desired shape. Many students learn this form of pottery construction during art classes, though they may not explore the full range of possibilities this simple construction method offers. At its simplest level blocks, bricks, or other solid objects can be made simply by hand forming a moist lump of clay into the desired shape. Simple tools, such as a stick or shell, can then be used to smooth the outside of the piece if the potter so desires. The basic technique of pinching a pot is only slightly more complex. To begin a potter takes a lump of moist clay and forces openings into it with a hand or small tool. Clay is dislodged outward or simply removed from the original lump until the desired open area is created. The clay is then formed by hand into its rough exterior shape, with care being taken to preserve the desired opening. The pot is then finished by carefully shaping the vessel into its final shape, usually with simple hand tools such as wood, shell, and bone. If desired, additional elements of clay can be applied to the vessel to form handles, feet, decorative elements (such as effigies or faces), or a variety of other elements. This technique is called **applique** and simply involves smoothing the applied element onto the vessel under construction, essentially cementing the element to the vessel using the wet clay of each item (Box 7.2).

Another quite old technique is **slab construction.** In this method a potter selects a handful of clay and then smooths this material into a slab of desired height, length, and thickness. This slab is then joined to other slabs in order to form a finished ceramic piece. The slab method can be used to create a variety of basic shapes, the most common of which are square, rectangular, or cylindrical. As with pinch construction, slab construction may be carefully finished by hand, and applique is sometimes used to produce handles and other shapes. The oldest known pottery in the Middle Atlantic states (the Carolinas through coastal New York) was formed in this manner and is known as Marcey Creek. These flat-bottomed, heavy vessels are direct imitations of the carved steatite (soapstone) vessels that are known from before 2000 B.C. and that the Marcey Creek vessels seem to have replaced. Analysis of Marcey Creek pottery demonstrates that these vessels were typically built by forming and attaching slabs of locally quarried clay tempered with crushed steatite. The construction process was often carried out with the pot resting

pinching The creation of a ceramic item by hand forming a ball of paste without the use of a mold, wheel, slabs, or coils.

applique The addition of paste to an otherwise finished or nearly finished ceramic item in order to create a definable, discrete element, decorative or functional, to the piece.

slab construction The construction of ceramics by preparing flattened slabs of clay and then joining them together.

Pinch

Begin with
a depression

Remove clay in
interior by pinching

Smooth and
finish exterior

Slab

Roll a slab

Shape slab

Smooth join

Finish surface

Coil

Roll clay

Coil clay

Add coils
and smooth

Finish surface

Wheel

Add clay

Shape pot

Final vessel

FIGURE 7.2

Generalized methods of ceramic construction, pinching, slab, coil, and wheel forming.

BOX 7.2

A LOOK AT ANGLO-SAXON POTTERY

The Anglo-Saxons dominated large portions of England between the early fifth century A.D., when the Romans finally withdrew their troops from the area, to 1066, when William the Bastard, later known as William the Conqueror, defeated the Anglo-Saxon army at the Battle of Hastings. During their tenure several different kingdoms existed in England, and a variety of distinct and regional forms of ceramics arose.

Most Anglo-Saxon potters quarried their clays locally and sold their vessels in an area consisting of no more than several villages. They produced wares that served utilitarian functions, such as containers and plates, but also produced funerary urns, in which the cremated remains of the dead were sometimes buried. The most common wares were produced using a pinching technique in which the potter selected a ball of paste, removed the center, and then pressed the paste into form. Experienced potters often were able to produce relatively thin-walled vessels. Other potters rolled strands of clay and coil built their products. Both construction techniques were then modified and decorated in a number of ways. Many pots were embossed

by raising the clay of the vessel's shoulders from the inside. Less frequently paste was appliqued to the exterior to create bosses. Embossing of both sorts was frequently used to divide a pot into four panels, which were then stamped or incised, sometimes after firing.

Once completed, a pot was left to dry. In the damp English climate this often took several days, during which the vessel could lose nearly a third of its weight and be reduced dramatically in overall size. The dried vessels were then fired, usually in open-air firings known to some in the United Kingdom as garden bonfires. Only two Anglo-Saxon kilns have ever been recovered, and it seems as though kilns were restricted to a very few of the most productive, and perhaps wealthiest, potters. The fired ceramics from both kilns and open firings tended to be porous and to fall within the range of terra-cottas and earthenwares. Some vessels were subsequently burnished using an abrasive and wax. The resulting pots had a lustrous sheen and an increased resistance to sweating, which is the movement of liquids through the porous vessel walls.

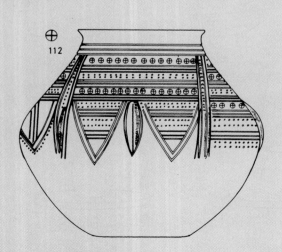

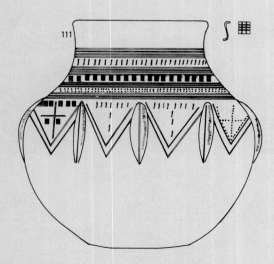

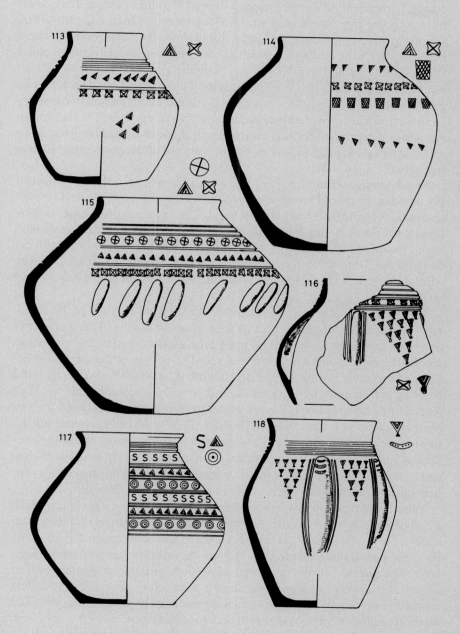

Anglo-Saxon stamped decorations. The vessels depicted here represent the extensive use of stamping made by Anglo-Saxon potters during the middle of the first millennium A.D. in the United Kingdom. Complex patterns of different stamps were applied to produce larger, intricate compositions.

on a woven mat, imprints of which are sometimes visible on the bottom of the finished vessel.

Another widespread construction method is called **coil construction,** or *coiling.* In this method a potter selects a desired amount of clay and then carefully rolls the clay into a long strand. This strand is then added to other strands by pinching them together. In this manner the potter builds an item in the desired form, perhaps occasionally stopping to allow parts of the object to dry slightly (to add stability) before changing angles or adding significant numbers of new courses of coiled strands. This method allows a potter to produce complex shapes in a controlled fashion, and it dominated pottery construction during the late prehistoric eras throughout much of the Americas. Once a ceramic item was constructed, it could be further treated by smoothing or scraping, as well as by any number of decorative and surface treatments (Figure 7.3).

Mold construction of pottery has two different expressions. First, simple wooden or carved stone squares into which wet clay is forced to produce bricks represent a basic sort of mold. Clay is forced into shape in these frames, the frame is then removed, and the resulting blocks are either allowed to dry in the sun or fired. This method of mold production is quite old, existing in the Near East from about ten thousand years ago. It is not, however, what most people think of when someone mentions mold construction of ceramics.

Instead, most people, archaeologists included, tend to think of the elaborate ceramic forms of people such as the Nazca and Moche of Peru, the latter of whom have been acclaimed by some art historians and archaeologists as among the finest potters to have ever lived. The potters of these cultures developed methods for producing precise, often naturalistic, molds by hand forming and shaping wood, ceramic, and, more rarely, stone. Clay was then forced into these molds. Different pieces from related molds could then be joined together to form a finished product. Mold production allowed potters to produce and reproduce elaborate shapes for ceramic items, including containers, quickly and efficiently. Potters invested a significant amount of time and energy to developing their molds, but once these were finished large numbers of elaborate finished pieces could be created quickly (Box 7.3).

Wheel construction involves the use of a rapidly turning wheel onto which a ball of wet clay is positioned. Wheel throwing a pot requires that the potter control the rate of rotation of the wheel, which was accomplished in antiquity by a foot pedal, while shaping the clay on the wheel by hand or with simple tools. This method allows the potter to produce gently curving, thin-walled ceramics relatively rapidly. This system is particularly useful for producing containers of various sorts, though solid pieces can be produced as well. The method requires a great deal of skill and good hand–eye, as well as foot–eye, coordination. This method tends to develop and persist only in societies in which **craft specialization** (people doing one sort of work to the exclusion of

coil construction The building of a ceramic piece by rolling strands of paste and then combining these to form a single piece of pottery.

mold construction Pressing paste into a prepared form, or mold, which imparts its shape to the paste.

wheel construction The construction a ceramic form through the use of a mechanical wheel that turns the developing form at varying speeds.

craft specialization The ability of part of a population to work at a single task to the exclusion or near exclusion of other forms of work.

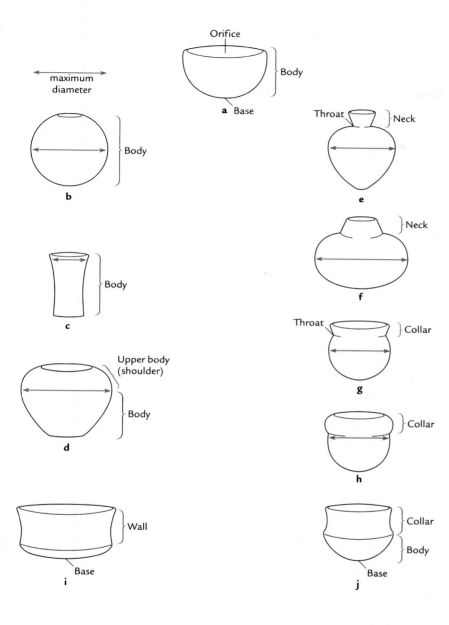

FIGURE 7.3

The anatomies of different vessel forms. Because clay is plastic, it can be formed into an almost unlimited number of shapes. Because of this, archaeologists need to be aware of the different parts of a wide variety of ceramic forms.

BOX 7.3

MOCHE: ARTISANS IN CLAY

Between about A.D. 100 and 700, a powerful and expansive empire flourished on the northern coast of Peru. The civilization is known today by the name Moche, which is the name of the valley, and of the river that flows through it, where this civilization originated. Its primary site is known today as Cerro Blanco and is dominated by the badly eroded but still magnificent ruins of two enormous structures, sometimes referred to as pyramids, Huaca del Sol and Huaca de la Luna. *Huaca* translates roughly to "sacred place." Both structures were massive complexes made from mud brick atop which the rulers and elite of Moche culture held court and administered their empire.

Michael Moseley, a specialist in the rise of civilizations on the western coast of South America, has argued that Huaca del Sol was the administrative center of the empire and that it contained both the imperial palace and a royal mausoleum. The original structure seems to have been built in four stages in the form of a stepped cross, with the broadest layer at the base and the narrowest layer, measuring approximately 1,115 feet by 525 feet, forming the apex. The bricks themselves are an important element to consider in a discussion of ceramics. Each segment of the Huaca del Sol appears to have been built by a different workforce, each fulfilling a special kind of tax called *mit'a*. Accordingly, different communities within the empire were charged with providing labor and materials for state projects. To fulfill this tax, the communities sent workers who impressed makers' marks into the formed adobe bricks they produced. The marks probably provided a method for the government to keep track of which communities had fulfilled their obligations.

Moche culture, however, is even better known for its spectacular ceramics. Moche artisans raised pottery production to new heights by creating thin-walled, well-fired polychrome (painted multiple color) vessels in a variety of forms. Among the better represented forms are stirrup-spouted vessels, many of which portray warriors going to battle or parading captives. Scholars citing the work of Christopher Donnan have linked these images to a motif called the Presentation Scene, in which warriors collect captives and pass them on to successively higher authorities until, at last, offerings are made to a king or, perhaps, a god. These vessels could be manufactured in a variety of methods, but mold construction dominates the pottery produced at the height of Moche civilization. Sometimes these stirrups were provided with double spouts and could be made to whistle as water entered one spout and forced air out of the other.

Despite the craftsmanship and beauty of these vessels, however, it is the effigy pots created by the Moche that most people hail as among the finest ever produced. Most of these, which were produced as containers, are also stirrup-spouted but, rather than having a flat bottom and globular body, the remainder of the vessel was molded into a finely crafted effigy. Portraits of human faces, complete with the careworn lines of age, as well as the forms of crawfish, peanuts, and a host of other plants and animals were also molded. One articular form features a bound, nude captive being held in the paws of a gaping jaguar. The work of Elizabeth Benson on Moche symbolism and lore has been used to suggest that such pots represent the sacrifice of prisoners to one of the primary deities of Moche society, a jaguar-formed god of the sky.

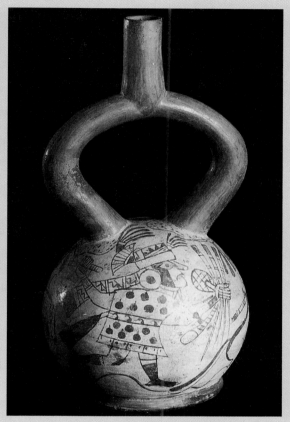

Moche effigy vessel. The Moche artisans who lived in northern Peru during the first centuries A.D. produced some of the finest mold-made ceramics in the world. The figures, many of which relate to Moche ideology and religion, have made them highly prized among collectors and unscrupulous art dealers alike.

A portion of a presentation scene. Some of the elaborate painted panels on Moche pots reflect variations on the theme of collecting war captives and presenting them for sacrifice to a powerful leader or divine being.

others), is established. The method first appeared in the Near East between about 4000 and 3500 B.C., the period during which the first cities appeared, and had spread to China by about 2500 B.C. The technique was brought to the New World in the sixteenth century A.D. with the arrival of European explorers, soldiers, and colonists.

It is important to consider that none of these methods for making pottery exists in isolation from other construction methods. It is therefore not uncommon to see two or more construction methods used in conjunction with one another to produce a final product. For example, slab-built handles and spouts are sometimes added to wheel-thrown vessels. Analysis of some coiled ceramics from both the American Southwest and south central Asia reveals that potters sometimes began coiling atop a shaped slab or simple mold-produced base. The essential reason for making pottery is to produce items that are either usable or desirable in the society that manufactures them (or one in which the manufacturers can trade). It is doubtful if ancient craftspeople limited themselves to one construction method or another except when circumstances dictated such.

Surface Treatments and Decorations

Any discussion of ceramics would be incomplete without a discussion of the things that can be done to alter the appearance of ceramics. There are two categories of things that can be done to ceramic—surface treatments, which are technological in nature, and decorations, which are sociotechnic or ideotechnic in nature.

Surface treatments come in a limited number of forms, each of which is designed to change the physical characteristics of a ceramic item for technological purposes. These treatments may have decorative effects as well, but the fact that they alter the performance characteristics of the pottery itself is used as the hallmark of surface treatments. One of the most common forms of surface treatment in the ancient world is cord impression. This is a technique in which a cord-wrapped paddle or similar device is used to impress at least one surface of a ceramic vessel, usually the outside. This paddling, which is supported on the opposite side of the pot by an anvil stone or another paddle, serves to compress the clay of the vessel while imparting a roughened texture to the surface. Experiments have shown that this roughening increases the overall surface area of the pot and assists in conveying heat evenly through the vessel during firing. The roughening also provides a textured surface for grasping and holding the vessel, something not to be overlooked in view of the fact that most terra-cottas and earthenwares sweat, that is, they can become wet and slippery.

Another common form of surface treatment is the application of a **slip.** A slip is a thin coating of fine, watery clay that resembles a paint. A piece of greenware can be dipped into a slip or the slip can be poured or brushed onto it. This slip will fire evenly because of its fine nature and will prove to be more

surface treatments Modifications made to the surface of pottery for either technological or functional purposes.

slip A thin coating of fine, watery clay that can sometimes be made to resemble paint.

moisture resistant than the primary paste of the item. In effect, the slip is used as a sealing agent to improve the ceramic's ability to resist permeation by liquids. Slips can be made in a number of different colors and therefore can be applied as decoration as well. In general, if a slip is applied over broad areas of a ceramic item, as opposed to in a small area, in decorative bands, or painted motifs, archaeologists are more likely to classify the slip as a surface treatment than a decoration.

Glazes represent another common form of surface treatment. Glazes are vitreous (glassy) coatings that are melted into the outer layers of a ceramic piece in order to make that piece watertight. Glazes are similar to slips but are combined with other elements and then applied to the surface of a ceramic form. Elements such as lead, alkaline, and tin are used as flux in the glaze— that is, they are added to the mixture to lower the temperature at which the glaze will vitrify. When a glaze-covered form is fired at a consistent, high temperature, the glaze bonds with the ceramic as it turns into a glasslike layer. Like slips, glazes can be decorative as well as functional, though, unlike slips, it is rare to see a glaze used solely as a form of decoration. Most people are familiar with a variety of glazes, such as those that we see on modern ceramic food bowls, floor tiles, and even on decorative flower pots. Among the oldest forms of glazes are tin, which produces an opaque white appearance, and lead, which produces a clear to slight yellowish-green appearance. Tin glazes first appeared on brick panels among the Assyrians about 900 B.C., and lead glazes seem to have developed in China about 200 B.C.

Decorations can be created by altering the form or shape of the ceramic or by adding colors, slips, or, more rarely, glazes. Decorations may, of course, communicate ideas about what people find attractive or relate ideas of group identity or history, or they may reflect ideological belief systems. Whatever level of meaning their purpose is ascribed to, as a general rule of thumb, the more socially complex a society is—that is, the more people who live in close proximity to one another—the more elaborate ceramics tend to become. This is due to both the increased volume of people who need such commodities and their increased ability to support craft specialists—individuals who work either part- or full-time at a specific craft and then trade their products for other items they need to survive. Hence, the most elaborately decorated ceramics tend to come from urban societies or societies that traded directly with urban populations.

Decorations that affect the shape of a ceramic include such things as punctations, stamps, incising, embossing, and applique. **Punctations** are depressions forced into wet clay by the potter, using a finger or small tool. These depressions can be aligned in rows or patterns to present more complex compositions but are typically organized in lines or columns. **Stamping** is impressing an object into the wet paste of a ceramic to form a repetitive pattern. Some stamps can be very simple, such as a two- or three-pronged piece of bone, whereas others can be elaborately carved stone seals, such as those used in Mesopotamia and later in the Indus River valley. These cylinder seals were

glaze A vitreous (glassy) coating that is melted into the outer layers of a ceramic piece in order to make that piece watertight.

decorations One or more of a series of modifications performed on pottery for purposes that were primarily nonfunctional.

punctation Pressing nodes or other shapes into the surface of pottery, usually one shape at a time.

stamping The use of a prepared, multitined or pictorial image on clay to impress a pattern into the surface of pottery.

designed to be rolled across a tablet or envelope of wet clay in order to sign or seal a document with the identity of the seal's owner. Consequently, each seal tends to be unique and complex both to deter forgery and to express the wealth and power of the seal's owner.

Embossing is sometimes thought of as punctation or stamping in reverse. Embossing is raising a pattern on the surface of a ceramic piece, usually by impressing the opposite side with a simple tool or stamp. This technique can be used to raise anything from simple dots to words, phrases, or complex symbols. Because of the thickness of most ceramics, however, embossed patterns tend to be simple more frequently than they are complex.

More complex patterns, such as nested or repetitive geometric designs, are often incised into ceramic. **Incision** is the process of carving lines into a ceramic piece before that piece has completely air dried. Some potters prefer to incise patterns when the clay is relatively wet; this produces deep, broad lines with ridges of displaced clay along the edges of the lines. Other potters prefer to wait until the piece is essentially dry before incising a pattern; this technique tends to produce shallow, delicate lines with little or no accumulation of clay along the edges of lines (Figure 7.4).

Applique, as you know, is the addition of clay elements to the basic ceramic form. Such elements can be functional, as described in the section on shaping pottery, or they can be strictly decorative. It is sometimes hard to determine what is a decorative element and what is a functional element. For example, handles can be added to a pot strictly for decorative purposes, as can feet, spouts, or other projections. Some additions, though, are complex forms of decorative art. Geometric patterns, animal or human effigies, or religious iconography have all been applied to pottery in a large number of the world's societies.

A different type of decoration alters the final appearance of the ceramic without changing its shape. Such decorations include painting, slipping (a decorative rather than a functional slip), glazing (a primarily decorative glaze, as is used on Assyrian tiles), burnishing, and, more recently, transfer printing. Paints made of various natural chemical compounds, as well as slips, are brushed on or applied to pottery with fingers in many societies. In most cases painting occurs after firing to ensure that the paint is not burnt away, although slip has been known to have been applied both before and after firing processes.

Burnishing typically occurs during the greenware state (see the following section). Once a piece of pottery has dried, a potter uses some form of mild abrasive to polish the surface, then fires it. This produces a ceramic with a glossy sheen without having to reach temperatures capable of vitrifying the paste or a slip. Archaeologists also argue that this process is technological, that the act of polishing the clay better aligns the particles of clay for even firing. Whether this is really a technological process has been debated, though, and opinions vary with researchers who study different cultures. Like a slip, this process may serve technological and decorative functions.

embossing The raising of portions of a ceramic piece to form decorative or functional patterns.

incision The carving of lines into ceramics.

burnishing Polishing a ceramic using a simple abrasive in order to harden or add sheen to the surface.

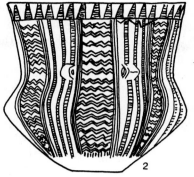

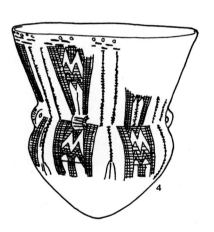

FIGURE 7.4

Highly incised funnel beaker style ceramics from the Neolithic era in northern Europe. The wide range of decorations available to ceramicists make this medium ideal for personal, as well as cultural, expression.

During the historic period potters developed techniques to apply prepared patterned decorations to ceramics. **Transfer printing,** developed in England during the middle of the eighteenth century, involves applying colored paper impressions derived from inked templates to the surface of unfired or partially fired pottery. A glaze is then added over the transfer print, and the item is fired completely. The result is that the item shows the colored transfer print but the soft print itself is sealed under the item's glaze. **Decals** are variants of this same idea developed in the middle of the nineteenth century. A prepared decal is applied directly onto the surface of an already fired ceramic piece. The result is a slightly embossed appearance and, in some cases, a propensity for the decal to chip or wear away over time.

transfer printing Colored paper impressions derived from inked templates applied to the surface of unfired or partially fired pottery.

decal A transferable decoration added to the surface of pottery beginning in the middle of the nineteenth century.

Firing

Once an item is shaped, it is allowed to sit in a dry environment so that the water will begin to evaporate from the piece, drying the clay to what we call the **greenware state.** In this state the formed item is stable but brittle; it is essentially nothing more than shaped sediments held together by small amounts of water and the bonds created by forming the item when the clay was wet. Blocks and items with massive shapes may be sufficiently stable at this point to use in construction, but more delicate items or items that will be handled regularly usually need further preparation.

Air-dried ceramics that are set aside for firing undergo an additional set of preparatory stages. In societies that use kilns, which are essentially open-topped, ventilated ovens capable of producing very high temperatures, the ceramics are carefully placed into the kiln along with fuel. Sometimes old or damaged pieces of already fired ceramics are used to subdivide the kiln. This is done so that, should a pot explode during firing (usually a product of heating too rapidly), the fragments of that pot will be contained and not ruin other pieces being fired. Kilns and **kiln firing** are unique in this aspect of mass firings (Figure 7.5). Because they produce very high temperatures, potters can create very hard pots, but the expense in fuel is high. Consequently, most potters only operate their kilns when they have enough dried pieces of pottery to fill it.

Once the kiln is filled and readied, the fuel is ignited. Typically, a slow-burning, relatively low-temperature fuel or arrangement of fuel is used at first in order to raise the temperature in the kiln gradually. This procedure allows the pieces within to continue to dry out and reduces the possibility of one or more pieces exploding. The potter might use slightly wet wood or fuels that can attain high temperatures but that the potter controls by spacing the fuel or adjusting the amount of oxygen in the kiln. The temperature is gradually increased to the desired firing level. For this step the potter may use more closely packed fuel, admit more oxygen to the kiln, or add hotter burning fuel. Once the firing temperature is reached, however, the potter need only monitor the flow of oxygen into the kiln and wait for the fuel to burn out. After this happens, the entire kiln and its contents are allowed to cool. Only when the ceramics within are cool enough to handle does the potter remove them and see the results of the firing.

Open-air firing is a different process. In this method a single pot or small group of pots is fired, often in a small depression in the earth. This pit is lined with any number of materials, possibly including damp leaves, twigs, and even moss. The vessels to be fired are placed in the pit and carefully covered with more of this material. Additional layers of fuel that are designed to burn at higher temperatures are then added on top of and around the ceramics (Figure 7.6). The entire pile is then usually covered by damp mats. The leaves and twigs are subsequently ignited and begin to heat the entire firing pit. This

greenware state The state of a ceramic after it has been formed and allowed to air dry but prior to it being fired.

kiln firing The use of a prepared structure for the process of hardening ceramics by creating high temperatures.

open-air firing The heating and hardening of ceramics in pits or simple, above-earth, temporary structures.

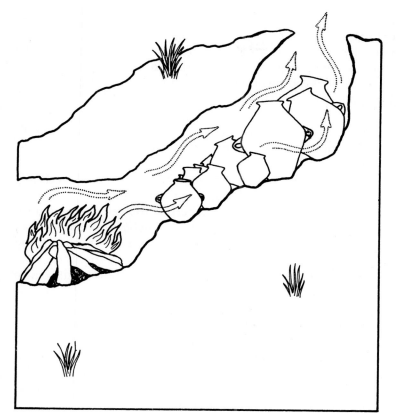

FIGURE 7.5

Kiln firing. This diagram shows the basic
components of kiln firing. Here, early
Chinese potters dug a kiln into the hillside along with a ventilation shaft. Fuel
was placed at the base of the kiln and
lit. The rising heat from the fires passed
over the ceramics and in the process
fired them.

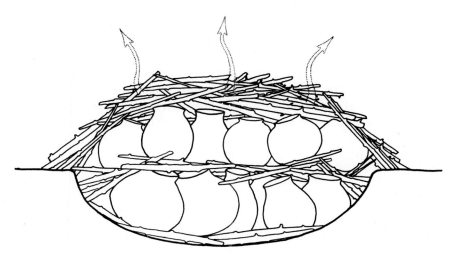

FIGURE 7.6

Open-air firing. Here a
potter has constructed a pit
into which the vessels to be
fired have been placed. As
the vessels are positioned,
fuel is carefully arranged
around and perhaps inside
of each piece in order to
ensure proper firing takes
place.

brings the temperature of the ceramics up before the main fuel in the pit ignites. Once this happens, the main stage of firing begins as the entire pit heats up. The potter controls the flow of air into the pit by opening or closing the slightly damp mats (the dampness prevents them from catching on fire). The potter can maintain this control or step back, remove the coverings, and allow the fuel in the pit to burn quickly and at a high temperature. The entire pit is allowed to smoke for a day or more, depending on the preferences of the potter and the ambient humidity. Once the fuel and any remaining coals are allowed to burn out, the potter can carefully sweep away the ashes and see the results of the firing.

The temperature at which ceramics are fired helps archaeologists classify pottery. In general, archaeologists recognize four levels of firing: terra-cottas, earthenwares, stonewares, and porcelains. Terra-cotta is the term applied to ceramics fired at under 900°C. Such wares tend to be porous and somewhat delicate. The earliest known fired pottery in the world is terra-cotta, and many societies regularly produced such wares for their day-to-day uses. Indeed, it is only in the last three to four thousand years that the technology to consistently fire ceramics at temperatures beyond 900° has been available (Box 7.4).

Earthenwares are also porous, often delicate, ceramics that tend to be fired at slightly higher temperatures, ranging from 800°C or 900°C up to 1200°C. The clays used in earthenwares tend to be heavier and often include particles of clay that are relatively large, nearing the small end of particle sizes assigned to silts. Earthenwares have been used to produce everything from tablewares (plates, cups, and the like) to fired bricks and tiles.

Stonewares are made from medium- to coarse-sized clay particles that are fired at approximately 1200°C to 1350°C. The combination of particle size and high heat results in a grey to brown paste after firing, as well as a partially vitrified body. This means that the paste has become densely packed and has begun to approach vitrification. This makes stonewares very hard and typically very durable. They also tend to be relatively heavier than comparably sized earthenwares or terra-cottas.

Porcelain is pottery fired at extremely high temperatures, usually somewhere between 1300°C and 1400°C. The paste is made from white kaolin clay that is mixed with quartz and ground feldspathic rock, which acts as a flux. When fired at sufficiently high temperatures the feldspathic rock melts and gives the finished product a great degree of hardness and a translucent luster (Table 7.2).

HOW ARCHAEOLOGISTS STUDY CERAMICS

Taken as a package, ceramics represent a valuable resource that enables archaeologists to ask and often answer complex questions. There are three broad and general categories that encompass the sorts of work commonly undertaken

earthenware Ceramic usually composed of relatively dense, heavy clays, sometimes with noticeable inclusions, and fired at temperatures between approximately 800 and 1200°C.

stoneware A ceramic made from medium- to coarse-sized clay particles, fired at approximately 1200° to 1350°C. The combination of particle size and high heat results in a grey to brown, partially vitrified body.

porcelain White kaolin clays fired at extremely high temperatures, usually somewhere between approximately 1300° and 1400°C.

TABLE 7.2   Ceramic Bodies and Their Characteristics

Body Type	Porosity	Firing Range	Typical Applications	Comment
Terra-cotta	High: 30% or more	Below 900°C	Flowerpots, roof tiles, bricks, artware; most prehistoric pottery	Unglazed, coarse, and porous; often red-firing
Earthenware	Usually 10%–25%	Wide: 800–1200°C	Coarse: drainpipes, filters, tiles, bricks Fine: wall and floor tiles, majolicas	Glazed or unglazed; body nonvitrified
Stoneware	0.5%–2.0%	1200–1350°C	Glazed drainpipes, roof tiles, tableware, artware	Glazed or unglazed; vitrified body
China	Low: usually less than 1%	1100–1200°C	Tableware	White, vitrified
Porcelain	Less than 1%; often nearly 0%	1300–1450°C	Fine tableware; artware; dental, electrical, and chemical equipment	Hard body; fine, white, translucent; "rings" when tapped

in relation to ceramics: technological studies, ethnoarchaeological studies, and stylistic studies.

Technological Studies

Of these three categories, technological studies are most closely related to the natural sciences. Such studies tend to emphasize the physical description and analysis of ceramics, including identifying and quantifying their physical properties, methods of construction, and elemental composition. Physical properties include such characteristics as the hardness of a ceramic, usually measured using Moh's scale of hardness from geology; its color, recorded using standard descriptions from a Munsell soil color book; and the nature and size of temper, usually identified through direct examination using a magnifying lens or microscope. Methods of construction are also typically observed in this fashion and noted. It is important to record these physical characteristics because they represent objective elements that can be tracked across time and space. These records allow archaeologists to compare and contrast ceramics diachronically and synchronically, evaluating overall patterns of ceramic development and distribution.

Studies designed to identify the elemental properties of ceramics can also contribute to their description, though such techniques are perhaps more valuable in providing insights into where past peoples obtained their raw materials for ceramic production. Such insights have the potential to identify previously unknown trade and economic networks, as well as identifying specific potters or groups of potters who distributed their products in the past.

BOX 7.4

THE SILENT ARMY IN XI'AN

Sometimes archaeology benefits from accidents. In 1974 workers digging a well about 65 kilometers east of the city of Xi'an in Shaanxi Province (central China) hit something hard. A brief exploration revealed the presence of very old material, and archaeologists were eventually summoned to explore what the workers had encountered. What they found was nothing short of spectacular. It was part of an underground complex that would turn out to be the palace and burial tomb of Qin Shi Huang, the first emperor of China, who lived between 259 and 210 B.C. The palace was allegedly constructed over thirty-six years by more than seven hundred thousand laborers. It was laid out as a miniature of the universe, complete with rivers formed by mercury and stars represented by precious stones.

Guarding the palace was an army of approximately eight thousand life-sized terra-cotta warriors. It was fragments of these clay soldiers that the workmen had encountered and that prompted archaeologists to open expansive horizontal excavations in the area 1200 meters east of what is believed to be the heart of the palace and the mausoleum. Four large pits have been identified, one of which (Pit 4) was empty but three of which, Pits 1, 2, and 3, contained individually crafted terra-cotta warriors, each originally equipped with its own weapons, life-sized horses with bronze harness, and two cast-bronze chariots.

Historians of the Qin Dynasty have suggested that the layout of the soldiers is significant and adheres to military doctrines of the age. Pit 1 contains six thousand terra-cotta foot soldiers, each realistically carved before the paste was allowed to air dry and then painstakingly finished after firing. The torsos of the warriors were individually formed and fired, then mounted atop separately produced solid clay legs. The forming process involved hand building the torso, carving various details such as hair, eyes, and clothing, and then applying a fine slip. The detail is so precise that warriors can be attributed to known historical groups from across the empire, each showing different hair styles, facial features, and expressions. Faint traces of paint adhere to some figures, and scholars have been able to identify the presence of different military units, each defined by different color tunics and symbols of rank. Of the figures in the three pits, those in Pit 1 may prove to be in the worst condition due to the collapse in antiquity (206 B.C.) of a roof that covered the figures.

Pit 2 contains the remains of approximately sixteen hundred figures, including cavalry, archers, infantry, and chariots. The figures were constructed as were the figures in Pit 1 but were arranged into four discrete units. Pit 3 is the smallest of the pits containing figures, about 15% the size of Pit 1, and contains the remains of what is thought to represent an elite command unit composed of an as yet undetermined number of figures.

Precisely what the figures represent is a matter for some discussion. Without doubt Qin Shi Huang was making a tremendous statement of power and wealth with the preparation of the tomb and the army. He may have also been reviving an age-old custom of kings being buried with soldiers and other retainers, though for unknown reasons this first emperor of China opted to be buried with terra-cotta soldiers instead. Historians tell us that the emperor was a fierce and pragmatic leader, so it may be that he wanted the opulence of being

petrological studies The study of the physical structure of the rocks and minerals in ceramics.

For the purposes of this introduction, the various avenues of research can be divided into petrological and compositional categories.

Petrological studies typically involve preparing a thin section of a ceramic by slicing a piece of the material to a thickness of approximately 0.03 mm. This slice is carefully mounted on a slide and exposed to polarized light. The entire slide is then rotated so that the researcher can observe the colors and

A ceramic soldier. Archaeologists excavate and record the details of a 2200-year-old ceramic soldier in China. Each of the approximately 6,000 figures was created by hand; no two are alike. This army accompanied China's first emperor into the afterlife as a sign of his power and importance.

accompanied into the afterlife by an army but recognized that it would be difficult to arrange for the sacrifice of so many people. Whatever the reasons, he left our world a truly magnificent window into his world.

Perhaps we will know more when the main portion of his mausoleum is excavated. For now, it sits as testimony to an era of fierce wars and astonishing social and political power.

patterns present in the raw materials of the ceramic. These characteristics allow a scientist to identify what materials are present and in what percentages. A record of these materials can be compared with existing geologic descriptions, and, if a close match is found, the researcher may infer that the material in the ceramic was quarried from the same place as was the known geologic sample. Such studies have been instrumental in identifying the pref-

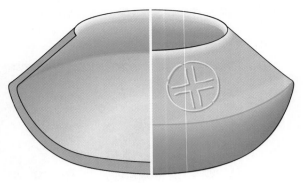

FIGURE 7.7

A Ramey Incised vessel. Such vessels were prestigious and symbolic items for the Mississippian-era residents of the American Bottom, Illinois. These sorts of vessels were decorated in ways that reflected religious and political symbolism and were given, perhaps containing sacred medicines, to only a small number of people.

erence of Anglo-Saxon potters to extract their raw materials from a limited range of resources, most of which tend to be near the location at which the pottery was made and used.

A comparable form of petrological analysis focuses on the percentages of minerals present in the ceramic paste rather than on identifying where components of the paste may have been obtained. The most common method of analysis is again to prepare a thin section. The researcher then measures the smallest and largest particle sizes present in the sample and records the data. By compiling a catalog of records, archaeologists can identify changing patterns in pottery technology through time and space. Alternatively, the archaeologist may elect to count the number of grains from each category of grain sizes present in the sample (a process sometimes called **point counting**). The archaeologist can then use these data to map changes in manufacturing over time or to compare pottery from different locations.

James Stoltman of the University of Wisconsin at Madison has used this method to analyze economically and ritually important vessels dating from the Late Woodland period around the confluence of the Wisconsin and Mississippi Rivers. These vessels, called Ramey Incised, are characteristic of the adjacent Mississippian culture at the site of Cahokia, several hundred miles south of the study area (Figure 7.7). Stoltman wanted to know if the material he recovered from southwestern Wisconsin represented local copies of the Ramey Incised wares or whether he could demonstrate direct interactions between the Late Woodland peoples of Wisconsin and Cahokia. Stoltman performed a series of point counts on ceramics from both regions and came to the conclusion that many of the Ramey Incised wares from southwestern Wisconsin came from Cahokia. More significant, Stoltman found that the range of variation in his sample of Wisconsin sherds was smaller than the range of

point counting Categorizing individual grains of sediment exposed by thin sectioning by size and sometimes by shape and then counting.

grain sizes present in vessels from Cahokia, suggesting that only a subset of the Cahokia population, perhaps a single workshop or potter, regularly traded vessels into Stoltman's Wisconsin study area.

Compositional studies tend to emphasize the elemental composition of ceramics. This sort of research is particularly useful in identifying the sources from which clays were obtained. The techniques used to accomplish this are highly technical and represent good examples of archaeometry. Four techniques are most often used to accomplish these ends: atomic absorption spectrophotometry (AAS), neutron activation analysis (NAA), optical emission spectroscopy (OES), and X-ray fluorescence (XRF). It is important to note that these techniques each function differently but share the property of identifying a significant number of elements (between about twenty-five and ninety) known to humankind. Use of these processes, which I emphasize here, results in a graph of the elements present in the sample. This graph can be compared with samples from other archaeological sites, as well as with geologic samples. This comparison allows archaeologists to unambiguously attribute the materials used in the production of a given ceramic piece to specific outcrops of that material, thus enabling them to better identify and envision previously unknown or poorly known exchange networks. Some materials for pottery were traded across surprisingly long distances and between apparently distinct cultures.

Ethnoarchaeological Studies

One of the most productive areas of ceramic research over the past several decades has been ethnoarchaeology. **Ethnoarchaeology** is the study of living or historically recorded societies and how people in these societies produce, distribute, use, and discard material culture. The ability to examine firsthand or through firsthand accounts how people work with their material allows archaeologists to identify and understand more of the complex factors involved in day-to-day living than they otherwise could.

For example, Colin Renfrew of Cambridge University has outlined a simple model that accounts for five primary ways in which material culture, including pottery, can be distributed within a society:

1. The consumer comes to the producer directly.
2. The producer travels directly to the consumer.
3. Both consumer and producer travel to an intermediate location, such as a market.
4. The producer provides products to a third party, who then distributes the material to consumers.
5. The producer provides goods to a central authority or agency that then redistributes these and all other goods throughout the society as needed.

compositional studies The study of the elemental composition of ceramics, usually through technologically sophisticated archaeometric techniques.

ethnoarchaeology The study of living or ethnohistorically known peoples for the purposes of generating archaeologically useful data.

Archaeologists, however, have to determine how each of these methods might actually work when put into practice. They ask questions such as, How would a given product, such as ceramics, be distributed in the archaeological record if a society used one of these five methods? The best way to answer such questions is to find a society that actually uses these methods and then examine the examples of a specific commodity that appear in that society. By tracing and documenting the construction, distribution, use, and discarding of the commodity, an archaeologist creates a known example of a given distribution pattern. Then patterns identified from archaeological sites can be compared with the known example in order to determine if the archaeological pattern matches any known patterns. If so, then archaeologists can make a compelling case for the presence of a range of very specific behaviors in the society responsible for the archaeological materials.

On another level, ethnoarchaeology allows archaeologists insights into the identity of potters and how they integrate into a given society. Some typical questions that may seem basic, but that are difficult for archaeologists to answer, may be profitably explored through ethnoarchaeology. Some of these questions are Do men, women, or both make pottery? Do potters work individually or in groups? If potters work in groups, how are the potters organized, and is there a commonality to their work? Dean Arnold has spent a great amount of time investigating these and other questions in both Peru and Guatemala, locations in which traditional potters still produce wares by hand. Arnold discovered that potters do tend to work in groups, sometimes organized by kinship and sometimes by proximity of residence, and that these potters tend to have similar solutions to common problems. Each potter must obtain raw material, usually locally, and these raw materials allow potters in the same region to produce similar qualities of ware. Potters producing materials in the same areas tend to make similar-appearing wares, sometimes because these are the sorts of things that tourists buy and sometimes because local preferences and traditions dictate the manufacture of certain sorts of ceramics.

Stylistic Studies

In many ways stylistic studies of ceramics form the most controversial branch of research undertaken by archaeologists. Through stylistic studies, archaeologists categorize ceramic products by form and decorative elements. Ideally, the distinctions made in establishing categories should be in some way meaningful: That is, the categories should reflect real differences in the material culture as it was perceived or used in the past. Unfortunately, without good contextual information on these categories obtained through ethnoarchaeology or ethnohistoric documents, it is nearly impossible to discern if the categories that modern archaeologists create have relevance to the past. Fortunately, experiments with stylistic studies have indicated that persistence and the willingness to explore multiple avenues of research can yield provocative and potentially significant results.

One of the most famous examples of this approach was undertaken by James Hill at Broken K Pueblo in Arizona. Hill's work, which eventually became known to many as *ceramic sociology,* focused on identifying the presence and distribution of social groups at Broken K Pueblo. Hill quantified and mapped the distribution of all ceramics across the site and eventually began to focus on a series of forms known as snowflake black on white (a description of the decorative pattern of these ceramics) (Figure 7.8). Hill reasoned that if women were the potters in Puebloan societies, as some ethnohistoric sources suggested, then it would be possible to identify potters or small groups of potters who learned their craft together. If similar stylistic expressions of ceramics clustered together over space and time, then Hill reasoned that the people living in the society probably practiced matrilocal residence: Women remain living with or near their mothers even after they marry; their husbands move to live with them. This also would mean that potters remained together for long periods of time, teaching their children and grandchildren styles and methods that would be distinguishable from other groups of potters living in the same community. Patrilocal residence, however, wherein women moved to the homes of their husbands after marriage, would result in a wholesale mixing of ceramic styles as unrelated women moved into new homes and produced ceramics alongside women who had learned to make pottery in different ways. At Broken K Pueblo the pottery did cluster in groups of rooms, leading Hill to suggest that potters remained working together for long periods of time and that this may indicate the presence of matrilocal residence.

There are problems with this sort of work, however. Although Hill had evidence to suggest that women were potters in some Pueblo communities, in other Pueblos it appeared that men were the potters. The question was raised whether the people at Broken K belonged to a society in which women or men made the ceramics. If the latter, then Hill's results would essentially be backward: It would have been the men who were staying in the homes in which they learned ceramic skills, and the society would have been practicing patrilocality.

On a more mechanical level, some researchers question whether we can identify specific potters or groups of potters. In effect, researchers are asking whether we have reliable methods for demonstrating observable and meaningful differences in the manner in which people make and decorate their ceramics. Ethnoarchaeological research has produced conflicting results; in some cases it is possible to distinguish between different groups of potters, whereas in other instances it is nearly impossible to do this even though the researchers can actually see the potters at work. Nonetheless, advocates of stylistic research argue that the fact that it is sometimes possible to get results makes this approach viable. Moreover, they argue, research involving computer-assisted mechanisms for measuring stylistic variation may make it both possible and economical to undertake this sort of work on broad scales.

A markedly different approach to stylistic studies centers around interpreting the meaning of the shape of and decorative motifs on ceramics. For

FIGURE 7.8

The Distribution of Select Ceramic Sequences from Broken K Pueblo. The distribution of so-called Snowflake Black-on-White wares, among a few others, suggested to the archaeologists that the people who made such ceramics tended to live with the same family of people all of their lives. Thus, if women were taught to make pottery by their mothers, the women must have stayed and worked with their families even after they married, indicating a matrilocal residence system. As some critics have observed, however, if men were the potters then the distribution could just as easily reflect a patrilocal residence system, that is men stayed living with their families even after they married.

example, in the Upper Midwest of the United States archaeologists have defined at least three separate archaeological cultures that existed side by side between approximately A.D. 1000 and 1300. The most socially complex of these was the Mississippian culture, which produced a variety of ceramic forms, including effigy vessels, slipped and painted wares, and burnished ceremonial vessels. For a variety of reasons, archaeologists have assumed that the second of these cultures, Oneota, was in some ways influenced by or in contact with Mississippian culture. These assumptions are based partly on the elaborate geometric patterns on Oneota ceramics, some of which have been ethnographically linked to expressions of a sacred thunderbird, something that is parallel to ideas known from Mississippian culture. The third culture, Late Woodland, was traditionally thought to be less affected by Mississippian ideas and to reflect a less complex system of social interactions. This belief was largely based on the apparent lack of elaborate decoration on Late Woodland ceramics, which tend to be cord impressed and do not exhibit painting, slipping, or complex geometric incising.

Recent work by archaeologists in the region, perhaps most notably by David Benn of Bear Creek Archaeology, Inc., has demonstrated that Late Woodland ceramics are not as simplistic as once thought. Smoothed images that appear to be side-by-side triangles connected at their apexes have been interpreted to represent thunderbirds. In fact, these images do seem to be directly comparable to the geometric designs on Oneota ceramics. Also, some of the cord marking present on the Late Woodland ceramics has been reinterpreted as fabric impression: Woven fabrics are pressed into wet clay to transfer the woven pattern to the ceramic piece. An analysis of some of these impressions demonstrates that the weaving of Late Woodland peoples was very intricate and took great amounts of time to produce. Consequently, Benn argued that there are complex styles present on Late Woodland ceramics and that this culture, previously thought to be relatively less complex than its contemporaries, may in fact have been at least as complex. More important, all three cultures may have shared a greater number of beliefs than previously thought, because each culture made extensive use of elaborate designs representing a single figure, the thunderbird. As with ceramic sociology, ethnoarchaeology is controversial and does not always produce clear results, especially when there is no ethnographic information available about what various symbols may have meant.

SUMMARY

Ceramics represent an important and abundant category of material culture that archaeologists must deal with. Because of the frequency with which ceramics occur in the archaeological record, the breakable nature of entire pieces but durability of individual sherds, and the ability of potters to embellish their products with socially meaningful or preferable elements, archaeologists find the analysis of pottery very productive. The analysis of the physical properties of ceramics through technologically sophisticated processes, as well as the analysis of their stylistic elements, is informed by ethnographic and ethnoarchaeological research. Such work places the interpretation of ceramics within known social systems and allows archaeologists to formulate interpretive models. Such models can help account for a wide variety of human behaviors associated with the acquisition of raw materials, methods of production of wares, and distribution of these wares, as well as the use and ultimate deposition of these materials in the archaeological record.

FOR FURTHER INFORMATION

Arnold, D. 1985. *Ceramic theory and cultural process.* Cambridge: University of Cambridge.

Benn, D. W. 1995. Woodland people and the origins of Oneota. In *Oneota archaeology: Past, present, and future,* edited by W. Green, pp. 91–140. Report 20, Iowa City: Office of the State Archaeologist of Iowa.

Bronitsky, G., ed. 1989. *Pottery technology: Ideas and approaches.* Boulder, CO: Westview Press.

Cottrell, A. 1981. *The first emperor of China, the greatest archeological find of our time.* New York: Holt, Rinehart & Winston.

Cunliffe, B. 1984. Ceramics. *World Archaeology* 15 (whole no. 3).

Deal, M. 1985. Household pottery disposal in the Maya highlands: An ethnoarchaeological interpretation. *Journal of Anthropological Archaeology* 4: 243–91.

Deetz, J. 1968. The inference of residence and descent rules from archaeological data. In *New perspectives in archaeology,* edited by S. R. Binford and L. R. Binford, 41–48. Chicago: Aldine.

Greene, K. 1992. *Roman pottery.* Berkeley: University of California.

Hurley, W. M. 1979. *Prehistoric cordage, identification of impressions on pottery.* Washington, D.C.: Taraxacum.

Kennet, D. H. 1986. *Anglo-Saxon pottery.* Princes Risborough, England: Shire Archaeology.

Kingery, W. D., ed. 1985. *Ceramics and civilization: Vol. I, From ancient technology to modern science.* Columbus, Ohio: American Ceramic Society.

———, ed. 1986. *Ceramics and civilization: Vol. II, Technology and style.* Columbus, Ohio: American Ceramic Society.

Longacre, W. A., ed. 1991. *Ceramic ethnoarchaeology.* Tucson: University of Arizona.

Orton, C., P. Tyers, and A. Vince. 1993. *Pottery in archaeology.* Cambridge: Cambridge University Press.

Plog, S. 1978. Social interaction and stylistic similarity: A reanalysis. In *Advances in archaeological method and theory,* Vol. 1, edited by M. B. Schiffer, 143–82. New York: Academic Press.

———. 1980. *Stylistic variation in prehistoric ceramics.* Cambridge: Cambridge University Press.

———. 1983. Analysis of style in artifacts. *Annual Review of Anthropology* 12: 125–42.

Rice, P. M. 1987. *Pottery analysis: A sourcebook.* Chicago: University of Chicago Press.

8

METALS AND GLASS
IN THE ARCHAEOLOGICAL
RECORD

*When I look at these rusted heaps of metal, discarded in this thing we call a junk yard,
it tells me a lot about us, our ideas. Every piece has a story, every piece has a history,
and it is all bound together here so that we can collectively forget about it.*

—*Paul Vaughn*

Human societies have been producing metal and glass materials for thousands of years. Because metals such as copper occur naturally, it is not surprising to learn that the use of such materials predates the first formation of glass, which is an amalgam of raw materials and is human produced. Yet both metal and glass have been predominant in many areas of the world's material culture, especially from approximately 1200 B.C. to A.D. 1970, when plastics began to dominate most phases of consumer packaging and hence material culture. During this period metals and glass also share an increasing technological sophistication that saw a shift from the specialized production of such materials for decoration and elite classes of societies to the production of metal and glass designed for use by millions of consumers. This is in itself significant because most of these materials are synthetic and represent cultural innovations that circumvent the limitations placed on people by their environments. Because of this shift and of the durable nature of glass and many metals, archaeologists can use them to identify changes in technologies, markets, and social preferences in past societies. As with ceramics, glass and metal objects can provide important insights into past societies.

METALS

Copper, an Ancient Medium

Copper occurs naturally in many locations throughout the world. In central Europe, for example, copper is typically found along the dykes and sills (geologic features associated with the interface of multiple rock formations). In North America copper can be found in cobbles along the shores of the Great Lakes, as well as in the moraines deposited by the advance of the last glaciation (the Wisconsinan) and its subsequent melting. Typically, though, copper-bearing stone is quarried by digging simple shafts into areas of earth where such material has been found on the surface. Such quarrying can be dangerous and hard work, but it yields a raw material that, when processed, provides a special and unique form of material culture.

Once quarried, the stone containing the copper veins is soaked in a stream or river for several weeks. The soaking saturates the material and allows imperfections in the stone to swell. In a process sometimes called **drawing,** the rock is then typically placed next to a high-temperature open fire. The heat splits the rock open along the saturated imperfections, and as the copper reaches its melting point (about 1083°C) it begins to flow outward along these routes. In this manner copper is effectively "drawn" from its natural place of deposition and collected in a usable form. The extracted metal can then be heated over an open fire and hammered into a variety of shapes with simple tools, including pebbles and even wood or antler. Should a crack develop in the item under construction, the piece can be reheated and the crack sealed through a process called **annealing.** In this process the two sides of the crack are heated and hammered together until they effectively meld together. This same process can be used to join two smaller pieces of copper together in order to form a single larger piece. It was only after the development of very high temperature techniques that people could melt copper and pour it into prepared molds. Most ancient copper was produced in the manner described here.

Copper can be processed into a variety of forms ranging from tubes for hair ornaments to large axe heads, such as the one carried by the famous Iceman of the Alps (Box 8.1). Between about 3000 and 2500 B.C., along the western shores of the Great Lakes, a society developed that today we call the Old Copper Culture. The people of this society used the abundantly available natural copper resources to produce metal projectile points, awls, drills, and a number of personal decorative items. Few, if any, items were restricted in society, so it appears that the copper items were available to everybody. In practical terms, however, copper is a soft metal and tends to suffer damage rapidly when used to perform arduous tasks. Although the people of the Old Copper Culture had the technological sophistication to produce metal implements, these tended to be inferior in many respects to the chert implements available elsewhere in the western Great Lakes region.

drawing The process of extracting copper from ore-bearing rocks by heating the rock and liquefying the copper.

annealing The process of heating copper over an open flame and then hammering together pieces of the metal to mend cracks or to form a single item.

By the time the Hopewell Interaction Sphere developed in the last centuries B.C. (see Chapter 7), copper had ceased to be used to make most tools. The metal was still used to produce sociotechnic items such as small copper cones used as hair ornaments, as well as decorative and ceremonial headdresses. Its most elaborate use, however, was in the form of decorative, embossed tablets that expressed socially and perhaps ideologically significant images. Such tablets were highly prized and widely traded as prestige items; to possess one, or perhaps to make a gift of it to an ally or trading partner, was a socially powerful and acceptable method of enhancing one's social position. Such uses of copper plaques continued from the Adena culture, which existed in what would become the heartland of Ohio Hopewell society at the time of the rise of the Hopewell Interaction Sphere, into the historic era, when they were known to be used in the Pacific Northwest **potlatch** ceremonies.

Bronze and Brass

By about 4000 B.C. in the Old World, pottery technology had developed, and kilns were in widespread use throughout many areas. The use of this firing technology was adapted by metalworkers to melt copper. It was quickly observed that some coppers turned out to be harder and seemingly more dense than others. Observation led early craftsmen to note that copper mixed with tin produced one such **alloy.** Today we call this alloy bronze. Somewhat later zinc was discovered to have a similar effect, though the resulting alloy is somewhat harder and more brittle than bronze. This mixture of material is known today as brass.

The technology to smelt copper and produce bronze and later brass had profound effects on the production of metals. Craftsmen working with these metals needed enough resources to own and operate a kiln capable of consistently reaching temperatures in excess of 1200°C. This meant that the technology for producing such metals was restricted to a relatively few people, and these people required large amounts of resources to undertake such work. Only two ways exist to acquire sufficient quantities of resources on a regular basis—through the patronage of a powerful person or organization, such as a government, or by trading the products of this sort of work for the necessary resources. Moreover, the knowledge and skills required to produce desired materials became increasingly difficult to master. The net result of these changes was to transfer the production of copper alloys to specialists who spent most or all of their time working at their craft (Box 8.2).

One of the effects of this specialization was a blossoming of different decorative techniques. Such techniques include repoussé, engraving, chasing, matting, gilding, inlay, and filigree. **Repoussé** is the systematic raising of metal from the interior or underside of a metal plate in order to produce a pattern or image. Copper bowls and cups with raised parallel ribs, a repoussé form of decoration, were found in the royal graves of Ur by Sir Leonard Wooley.

potlatch An elaborate competitive and alliance feast in which the host gives away massive quantities of both utilitarian and prestige items in order to cement alliances and to obligate rivals to give away even more material at their own potlatches.

alloy A combination of two or more metals.

repoussé The raising of a pattern or decorative element on the surface of a metal item.

BOX 8.1

OTZI: A NEOLITHIC TRAVELER AND HIS COPPER AXE

The summer of 1991 had been particularly warm in the Alps. On September 19, 1991, a German couple, Helmut and Erika Simon, decided to take a hike into the passes between Italy and Austria, a series of scenic valleys made more accessible than usual by the warm weather. Along the way Erika Simon caught sight of something protruding from the ice. On investigating they discovered the head and shoulder of a human body projecting out of the ice. They dutifully informed the authorities, and all parties assumed that it was a hiker or skier who had been caught in an avalanche or other alpine disaster. What they had in fact found, just south of the Otzal Valley, were the remains of a five-thousand-year-old man, a traveler who had been caught in inclement weather sometime about 3000 B.C. The body was quickly labeled Otzi, and his remains have provided archaeologists a unique window into life during the Neolithic era of central Europe. In fact, the body represents the oldest largely intact human remains ever found in the Old World, and among the oldest in the world. (Only the Chinchorro mummies of Chile's arid west coast surpass Otzi in age, being almost seven thousand years old.)

Otzi's story is remarkable. He was apparently traveling between Austrian settlements and those in northern Italy, probably participating in some sort of trade. Although most discussions of his demise emphasize that he traveled alone, we really don't know if this is so. What we do know is that he died in a small depression along a hillside. This area is sheltered, and he may have been taking refuge from the cold or other inclement weather. Whatever his problems, he died in this place and was soon covered by a blanket of snow. No scavengers found his remains, which were gradually frozen. As the glacier moved over the area during periods of intensive cold, Otzi was spared because of his position in the depression. Hundreds of tons of ice passed within inches of his body, scouring the stone and all material beneath it, but not touching Otzi in his sheltered depression. He stayed in that depression until

The Iceman, here shown still locked in glacial ice as he was found in September 1991.

Reconstruction of the Iceman's axe. The axe was likely mounted in a solid wooden haft and lashed fast with natural pitch and sinew or leather.

that uncommonly warm summer and his chance encounter with the Simons.

Once Otzi had survived his initial misidentification as a modern accident victim and a less-than-scientific recovery by rescue workers, his body was moved to Innsbruck, Austria. There, archaeologist Konrad Spindler examined the body and the artifacts that had been brought back with him. Within seconds Spindler had identified the axe as belonging to the early Bronze Age, or about 2000 B.C. The axe appeared to be a classic example of an early bronze axe, and there was little reason

for Spindler or anyone else to suspect otherwise. Fortunately, scientists like to check their assumptions, so a team of scholars set to work identifying all of the many things that Otzi had carried with him on the day that he died, as well as determining Otzi's physical condition.

Otzi carried with him a backpack attached to a wooden frame made of larch and hazel, along with an unfinished yew bow and the copper axe critical to Spindler's initial assessment of Otzi's age. He wore a tightly woven grass cape, grass-lined shoes to keep out the cold, and a leather belt with a variety of tools. He also carried two dried mushrooms hung on leather thongs. That particular type of mushroom is known to produce a form of antibiotic and has been used in folk medicine for centuries, if not longer.

The idea that Otzi may have been carrying the mushrooms for medicinal purposes gained credibility after his body was analyzed. Dieter Zur Nedden of the University of Innsbruck has identified significant wear in the Iceman's joints, especially in his legs. Otzi also seemed to have chronic problems in his feet as a result of an old case of frostbite. An analysis of his fingernails also revealed periods of interrupted development approximately 60, 80, and 120 days before his death. This suggested to scientists that Otzi may have suffered from some systemic, recurring illness that he had been battling just two months before his death.

Similarly, the Iceman may have suffered from acute arsenic poisoning. Analyses of Otzi's hair identified a
(continued)

Fragments of Otzi's pack. Two larchwood branches serve as evidence for the Iceman's careful selection of natural material for his gear, in this case the frame of his pack.

BOX 8.1 (continued)

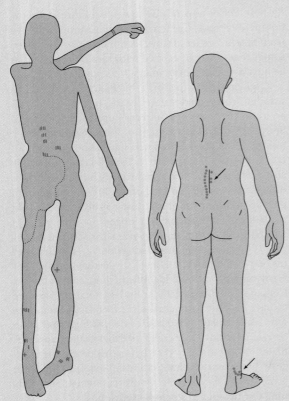

Tattoos on the Iceman's back and legs are the oldest known evidence for body art of this sort. The tattoos may have served a magical or curative purpose for their owner because they are associated with areas where the man may have been injured or suffered from ailments.

areas of pain endured by the Iceman and likely reflect some sort of ritual treatment of his ailments. Such uses for tattoos are known ethnographically and ethnohistorically, so it seems a plausible explanation. Without better contextual evidence, however, it is impossible to tell if this was indeed the case.

Despite all the knowledge researchers had gained, Otzi still had a few surprises in store for them. Radiocarbon assays by two independent laboratories provided Spindler and his colleagues with unexpected results: The wood associated with Otzi was dated by both laboratories to between 3500 and 3000 B.C., between one thousand and fifteen hundred years older than the axe's date. Spindler double-checked the axe, and it still appeared to him and others to be a typical example of early Bronze Age technology. The only option left to them was to check the axe itself, to determine if it was really bronze. Spectographic analyses were subsequently run on the axe, and they failed to identify any significant amounts of tin. This could only mean one thing: that the axe was made from nearly pure copper and represented a forerunner of the styles that would become popular in the region by 2000 B.C.

The presence of the copper axe raised some interesting questions. First, copper is not terribly effective for heavy chopping and battering work. It would seem that such an object might be more a symbol of social or ideological factors than a strictly functional item. Also, the fact that the axe so closely resembled later types of tools caused speculation about connections between Otzi's people and the people who would come after. Questions arose about where the copper was extracted and what peoples had the technology to create such a large and dense copper tool. Other copper items of this time tend to be small and decorative; none match the size of Otzi's axe. No sites from the era have yet been found that contain evidence for the production of comparable items. So archaeologists are left to ponder the meaning of the axe. How did it fit into the society in which Otzi lived? Where did Otzi come from? These questions are still being addressed, but now researchers have narrowed down what type of additional questions need to be asked in their research.

high concentration of copper on the surface of his hair and high concentrations of arsenic inside his hair strands. Diane De Kerchove and Geoff Grime of Oxford University have explored the presence of these materials and concluded that the absence of these elements in the animal hairs of Otzi's clothing make it likely that the Iceman himself was exposed to high levels of dust from metalworking (copper and arsenic are closely related to the production of tools such as the copper axe).

The last clue to his health came from his tattoos. Spindler suggests that these markings correspond to

A craftsman can cut into the surface of the metal with a sharp implement, a technique called **engraving,** or hammer a pattern into the metal using a blunt instrument, a technique called **chasing.** Engraving removes metal, whereas chasing deforms the metal. Both typically occur on precious metals such as gold and silver, though examples are known to occur on other metals.

Another way to define a field on a metal surface is to abrade the surface with a hard object to form a crosshatched or similar pattern. This technique, known as **matting,** is particularly striking on precious metals or on those that were typically polished to a sheen. The hatched pattern creates a dull area and can be used to highlight decorative fields or figures. Another way to achieve marked contrast on a metal surface is to gild the surface, or portions of it, with another metal. **Gilding** is simply the adhesion of one metal, usually precious, over a less precious metal. **Inlay** is a similar process, though this involves insetting one metal into a predefined, prepared area in the surface of another metal. This is not to be confused with the twining or interlacing of fine strands of gold or silver that are then soldered onto the surface of another metal. This technique, called **filigree,** adds only a pattern of wire, whereas inlay adds solid, plaque-like areas (Box 8.3).

Iron and Steel in the Ancient World

Iron is a naturally occurring ore that can be extracted from the rock matrix in which it is found through heating and hammering. **Steel,** on the other hand, is an alloy of iron and carbon that is produced only at very high temperatures (above 1370°C). It has been only in the past seven hundred years or so, since the fourteenth century A.D., that steel could be produced at will in sizeable amounts. Prior to this, steel was manufactured in small amounts, though possibly as often by accident as by intent. Most of the alloys created by artisans prior to the development of high-temperature furnace systems would today be classified as wrought irons. Yet, because of the variety of alloys that can be created, it is useful to view them not as discrete materials but as items produced along a continuum of possibilities, ranging from roughly processed iron ores on one extreme to high-carbon steels on the other.

Although the two terms are sometimes used interchangeably in older literature, there are important differences in the characteristics of steel and iron. Steel can be fashioned into harder, more durable implements than can iron, which tends to be more malleable even when cold. The greatest advantages of steel, however, are that tools weigh less and tend to last longer than comparable iron tools. Iron implements, on the other hand, were less expensive to produce in antiquity and did not suffer from brittleness, as did most early steels. These traits, combined with the difficulty involved in making steel, made this metal exceptionally valuable in the ancient world. For example, small amounts of steel were known in Egypt from about 3000 B.C. onward. The metal was more prized than gold by the elite classes because it was more rare than gold and because to possess steel reflected a special sort of power

engraving The removal of metal from the surface of an item in order to create a decorative pattern or the use of hard bits or wheels to cut a pattern into glass.

chasing The deformation of the surface of a metal item, usually with a fine, blunt instrument, in order to create a decorative pattern.

matting The technique of incising a cross-hatched pattern on metal to create a dull area.

gilding The application of one metal, usually gold, over another.

inlay The placement of one material, either glass or metal, into a prepared depression (or reservoir) on the surface of an item for decorative purposes.

filigree The application of wire to the surface of a metal object in order to create a decorative pattern.

iron A naturally occurring metallic ore that can be extracted from a rock matrix.

steel An alloy of iron and carbon that is produced at very high temperatures (above 1370°C).

BOX 8.2

THE GUNS OF THE *MARY ROSE*

The *Mary Rose* was one of the finest vessels of her age, and she was the flagship of no less a monarch than England's Henry VIII. Her architecture and guns were state of the art for the first half of the sixteenth century, sporting both bronze and wrought-iron cannon ranging in size from those designed to fire 2-pound metal shot up through those capable of hurling 50-pound stone balls that would explode into tens of thousands of sharp fragments on impact. Her armament has been described as innovative against the backdrop of naval weaponry of the era. Contemporary observers considered her among the most powerful warships in the world. Yet, on June 19, 1545, she sank to the bottom after having rolled violently and apparently taken on water. Only forty of her company of approximately seven hundred survived the disaster, and with the wreck went the secrets of her advanced arsenal.

The location of the wreck along The Solent channel was identified in 1968 by Alexander McKee and Harold Edgerton using side- and bottom-scanning sonar. The sonar sweeps revealed a suspicious mound covering what appeared to be a W-shaped feature. Although optimistic about their findings, McKee and Edgerton were unable to confirm that this was the *Mary Rose* until 1971. This confirmation opened the way for the largest maritime excavations undertaken in the United Kingdom. Beginning in 1979, Margaret Rule, a terrestrial archaeologist who learned to dive just for this project, supervised more than 24,640 dives. The culmination of the work occurred on October 11, 1982, when the hull of the mighty warship was raised to the surface and conservation work began to preserve and display her now-fragile form.

For archaeologists and historians alike, the material from the *Mary Rose* proved spectacular. A total of ten

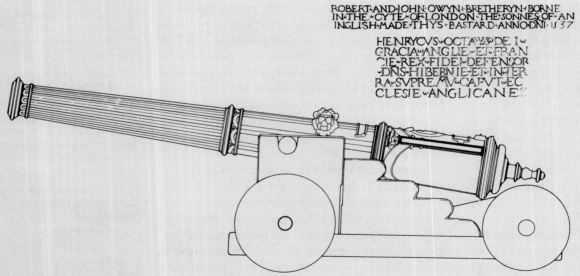

A bronze bastard. A cast bronze gun of a type known as a bastard from the *Mary Rose*.
This piece bears an inscription stating it was built by the Owen brothers, Robert and John, in 1537.

loaded, gunners had to be able to reach and work around the muzzle of the weapon. When fired, the gun recoiled with massive force, reeling backward until arrested by ropes or blocks attached to the gun deck. The carriages proved to be the essential component in making such guns viable at sea. The carriage could be retracted to allow the cannon to be loaded and then wheeled forward to the very edge of the deck, the massive bronze barrel projecting through a gun port in the vessel's side. A fuse was set and detonated, and a massive stone or iron projectile, in one case up to 65 pounds, was hurled forth. The recoil of the shot sent the carriage rolling backward until it was stopped by the lines or blocks, leaving it in position to be reloaded and readied for action. These massive weapons were supported by a variety of smaller wrought-iron artillery pieces set throughout the vessel.

Artistically the bronze weapons were beautiful. They boasted cast lion's heads as decoration and finely cast grooved barrels. In this respect they reflected the artistry of the specialists who produced them; politically they embodied the ideas set forth by the English monarchy. The deadly and impressive nature of the cannons was enhanced by the expensive and fine craftsmanship of their construction, exhibiting the combined military and social affluence of the English crown. Thus, when the *Mary Rose* entered port with her guns exposed and the elaborate carvings on her hull glistening in the sunlight, she was more than a warship; she reflected the ideas put into her design by the royalty of England.

A spoked wheel from the wreck of the *Mary Rose*. This particular wheel was part of the carriage supporting one of the warship's massive wrought-iron cannon.

of the fifteen bronze guns employed on the vessel were recovered, most dating to between 1535 and 1542. They were made by men such as Francisco Arcanus, an Italian military engineer who had entered the service of Henry VIII in 1522, and John and Robert Owens, brothers also in the employ of the English monarchy. These guns were comparable to the massive siege weapons used on land, and each was mounted on four-wheeled wooden carriages. Each of the carriages was specifically designed for the gun it would support, and they are among the earliest examples of this application of technology. Because guns of this size had to be muzzle-

BOX 8.3

THE POWER OF GOLD: MOCHE METALWORK

In addition to exceptionally fine ceramics, Moche artisans were extraordinary metalsmiths. Working in gold, silver, and alloys, the Moche produced elaborate ear ornaments, nose flares, back plates, necklaces, pins, and effigies. Gold was particularly important to the Moche, perhaps because it represented the power of the sun and, as such, reflected an important aspect of their religion. Often, stones such as turquoise and lapis lazuli were set into gold ornaments as eyes and teeth.

But the Moche were not content to work in raw metals alone. They devised a technique called *depletion annealing*. Gold was dissolved in a solution of corrosive salts and minerals. Copper was subsequently dipped into the solution and became both an anode and a cathode. This created a basic system of electroplating, as the gold adhered to the copper when heated to about 800°C. The result was an object that glistened with a pure gold coating, though the object itself was lighter because its core was copper.

Moche artisans also used the lost-wax method of casting to create the same quality of exquisitely detailed effigies that were produced by their counterparts working in ceramics.

A miniature golden face with lapis lazuli eyes from the site of Sipán, the only site to produce a major, unlooted Moche burial.

A golden necklace from Sipán. The value of such pieces of art, as well as the value of the materials, have made Moche sites targets for aggressive looting for centuries.

and prestige. The young pharaoh Tutankhamun (King Tut), for example, was buried in a series of sarcophagi, the innermost of which contained the most powerful and personal symbols of his position. The sarcophagus itself was solid gold, and on the pharaoh's chest, in the innermost layers of the cloth that bound his mummy, was placed a small piece of steel. Thus steel was so valued that it featured prominently in one of the most symbolic places in Tutankhamun's entire mortuary complex.

In Europe iron played a pivotal role in the spread of Celtic culture across the continent. During the Hallstatt period (1200 to 600 B.C.) in central Europe, Celtic metalworkers successfully developed techniques to extract and form iron ores. The Celts were among the most sophisticated metalworkers in the world at this time, and their craft abilities in this medium were not to be equaled by the classical civilizations of Rome and Greece until several hundred years later.

Iron and steel were used in two very different ways by Hallstatt and other Celtic peoples. Utilitarian implements for agriculture, cooking, processing, and hunting were widely used and proved more efficient than the bronze and copper implements that preceded them. At Butser Iron Age Farm in southern England, scholars and archaeologists have experimented with Celtic technology as it existed on the eve of the Roman invasion in 43 A.D. Based on historic documents and their experimental studies, they have calculated that Iron Age farming produced a higher average yield per acre than did modern farming techniques in the United Kingdom prior to the widespread introduction of pesticides in the 1950s. Likewise, these techniques seem to be more efficient than previously used techniques throughout Europe, though it is difficult to ascertain this for certain (Figure 8.1).

The more prominent use of iron and steel among Celtic peoples was in warfare. Each village supplied food and material to equip a warrior elite, primarily men with high social standing who were probably related to the ruling lineages of the village and perhaps the larger tribe or chiefdom. A small number of Celtic women were also known to have engaged in warfare, one of whom was Queen Boudicca, who, in A.D. 60, led a rebellion that nearly drove the Romans out of England. For the Celts warfare was a social act, one that bestowed honor and prestige on those individuals who accomplished daring deeds. Warfare was endemic between different tribes and chiefdoms in the Iron Age, though among the Celts this warfare tended to focus on raiding and feuds rather than on wars of conquest and annihilation.

Celtic warriors went to battle armed with long iron swords and a unique form of armor, called maille. This sort of armor was formed by linking one iron ring with four other rings, thus weaving a flexible iron fabric. This armor was more effective than other contemporary armors, especially against sword cuts, because it covered a large part of the wearer's body and still allowed the wearer flexibility. In addition, those Celts who chose to wear armor (some fought nude as a sign of their faith and courage) also carried into battle elaborately decorated bronze helmets, sometimes ornamented with gold

FIGURE 8.1
Detail of the Gunderstrup cauldron, Denmark. This cauldron is a masterpiece of Celtic art and craftsmanship.

and silver. For the Celts, it was as important to impress your allies and foes as it was to defeat your enemies on the battlefield. In many respects, then, steel was integrated into a display of wealth and power and served both technomic and sociotechnic roles. Yet, unlike in ancient Egypt, iron and steel increasingly fulfilled utilitarian functions and were spread through larger portions of society.

Iron and Steel in the Historic Era

The use of iron and steel reached its height in the modern world. By the early eighteenth century machinery was being built that dramatically increased the rate at which craftsmen could produce finished products. Similarly, the human population was beginning to grow exponentially as families grew larger and death rates slowed, situations that persist today. As a consequence of these changes, demand increased for more consumer goods, and craftspeople developed new methods to meet these demands. Many of the goods in great de-mand were made of iron or steel and were designed to meet the needs of the common people. Although many of the items produced seem commonplace in the modern world, understanding the history of their development and distribution helps archaeologists to understand the means, timing, and na-ture of Euroamerican expansion across the globe.

The development of nails and their distribution may seem almost plebeian to many modern people. After all, we reason, one nail is much the same as an-other nail. Yet a survey of nails in use today would reveal a variety of special-ized forms and sizes, each designed, though not necessarily used, to perform a specific type of task. In the past this diversity was even greater, with nails being produced individually by hand and therefore more expensive than they are today.

There are three basic types of nails: hand-wrought, machine-cut, and wire-drawn. Although each of these forms of nails is still produced today, the dates these methods were developed and the numbers in which they were produced are all significant. Prior to the late eighteenth century all nails were hand forged by smiths. Each nail was individually heated, formed, and finished and was therefore relatively expensive. These nails show a great variety of forms, as one might expect, but typically they have four sides tapering to a point. The heads were either L-shaped, being nothing more than the shank of the nail folded perpendicular, or applied by hand. These heads tend to be rela-tively high at the center and taper toward the edges and to be either square or roughly oval. Variants of hand-forged nails have been recovered from every-thing from sunken Roman ships to door frames in medieval Kiev. Because of the expense of producing nails by hand, though, they were often salvaged from previous constructions and reused. It is therefore difficult to ascertain the original place of construction and intended purpose of hand-wrought nails. By 1800 such nails were falling from favor in most eastern and western North American communities, though they persisted in significant numbers in the sparsely populated plateau and mountain regions of western North America (Figure 8.2).

By 1790 the technology for producing nails by machine had developed and spread to the east coast of North America. This method relied on cutting sheets of metal into tapering strips and then making heads by heating and hammering one end. The shanks of nails could be produced rapidly, and be-cause smiths had only to finish the heads, production of nails increased. Such nails tend to begin in flat shanks immediately beneath the head and then taper about a third of the way down the shaft toward a point. Only two sides of the nail, though, show this pattern, because the cutting only takes place on these edges. The other two edges are often flat, reflecting the flat plate from which the nails were cut. The heads of such nails tend to be flat and either rectangu-lar or oval.

By about 1835, water-powered machines had been developed that both cut the nails and powered a hammer that applied a head to the shank. As this

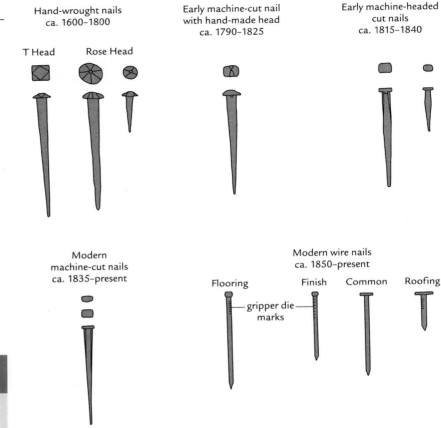

TABLE 8.1
Nail Weights

1″	2d*
1¼″	3d
1½″	4d
1¾″	5d
2″	6d
2¼″	7d
2½″	8d
2¾″	9d
3″	10d
3¼″	12d
3½″	14d
4″	20d
4½″	30d
5″	40d
5½″	50d
6″	60d

*Note: d = pennyweight or
penny.

technology improved, the heads on cut nails became more uniform, squarer, and notably flatter than heads produced by earlier machines. Cut nails were popular across most of the United States and Canada until about 1890, when wire nails came to prominence.

Wire nails began to be produced in France during the early to middle nineteenth century. These nails were produced by drawing a round wire shank and then applying a head, usually round or oval. The shanks were then ground to a point by hand and given heads individually, a slow and expensive process. Machines developed in midcentury, however, automated the process entirely, and by about 1855 French manufacturers were mass producing wire-drawn, machine-headed nails in great quantities. Because of American trade policies and the expenses involved in importing these items, machine-cut nails continued to dominate the North American market. By the 1880s, though, American industry had successfully copied the French technique for mass-producing wire nails, and wire nails began to appear with great frequency. By 1900 wire nails were produced at a rate of nearly six times that of machine-cut nails (Table 8.1).

FUNCTIONAL CATEGORIES:
THE CASE OF MUNITIONS

Another way to look at metals is by considering the intended use of the items made from metal. Rather than working through specific raw materials, archaeologists sometimes have the luxury of easily recognizing certain categories of artifacts that were designed for specific purposes but that include items made from a variety of raw materials. Ammunition is one such category. There is little argument over why ammunition is produced; it is designed to be fired from a firearm of some nature, and certain types of munitions, such as those issued to soldiers, typically are designed to be fired at opposing soldiers.

There are two primary metallic components of modern firearms, the projectile and the cartridge, which houses the powder. When the base of the cartridge is struck by the firing pin of the firearm, the resulting spark ignites the gunpowder, which, in turn, forces gases out of the cartridge at great velocity. These expanding gases force the projectile from its resting position atop the cartridge, down the weapon's barrel, and out into the surrounding environment. In the case of a rifle or most modern handguns, the barrel has been tooled with a corkscrew-like pattern that imparts a spin to the projectile. This has the effect of making the path of the projectile more stable and more accurately sending the projectile toward its intended target. Muskets and similar early weapons, however, did not have such rifling and consequently were considerably less accurate.

This two-part system is about three hundred years old. Paper cartridges were developed first, whereas metal cartridges have been used only for the past one hundred fifty years or so. Prior to the cartridge system, a projectile was loaded directly into the barrel of a weapon and on top of a wad of cloth and a small pan of gunpowder. The operator of the firearm ignited the powder in one of two ways. In one method, those associated with flintlock and wheel-lock weapons, the operator pulled a trigger, which caused a mechanical mechanism to spring closed and in the process drive a **gunflint** (literally a fragment of chert, often in blade or spawl form) across a metallic striking platform to produce a spark and hopefully ignite the powder. The older, more direct method required the operator to touch a smoldering fuse to the powder in order to ignite it. Both methods were difficult in adverse weather conditions, and both required the operator to carry dangerous amounts of gunpowder in a single container. This last issue was significant because, in the early years of firearms, large numbers of handgunners (hande gonners, as they were called) were killed when their powder bags were inadvertently ignited. Today ammunition is classified according to the caliber system in the United States and according to the metric system in most of the rest of the world (Table 8.2).

Munitions manufacturing has important ramifications in archaeology. Like ceramics makers, manufacturers often stamped identifying marks on

gunflint A chert or flint fragment, sometimes produced from a prismatic blade, that is used in the striking mechanisms of flintlock firearms to strike a spark and thus ignite gunpowder to fire the weapon.

TABLE 8.2   Standard Cartridge Dimensions for Common Historic Rifles Used in North America

Cartridge	Max Length (inches)	Base Width (inches)	Aperture Width (inches)	Marketed as Caliber/MM	Date Introduced Commercially	Common Use
.22 Hornet	1.403	.350	.2425	.22c	1932	Sport
.222 Remington	1.700	.3325	.253	.22c	1950	Sport
.243 Winchester	2.045	.4000	.276	.22c	1955	Sport
.25-35 Winchester	1.980	.506	.2816	.22	1895	Sport
.30-06	2.494	.409	.3397	.30c	1906	Sport
.30-40 Krag	2.314	2.314	.338	.30c	1892	Military (U.S.)
.303 British	.545	.460	.338	.30c	1888	Military (U.K.)
8mx57mm JS Mauser	2.240	.400	.3493	8mm	1888	Military (German)
.375 Holland & Holland Magnum	2.850	.480	.404	.375	1912	Sport/ Big Game
.38-40 Winchester	1.305	.525	.4167	.38	1874	Sport
.44-40 Winchester	1.305	.525	.443	.44	1873	Sport
.45-70 U.S. Government	2.105	.495	.480	.45	1873	Military (U.S.)

*Note that the caliber of a weapon is not rigidly defined and varies by manufacturer. In general, the caliber of a slug can be estimated by subtracting .030 from the maximum aperture width of the casing.

** Note that the .44-40 Winchester was used in quantity with the repeating round Model 1873 Winchester rifle by the Native American forces at Little Big Horn while the .45-70 U.S. Government made primary use of the .45-70 U.S. Government cartridge in its single shot Springfield rifle.

***Data after Barnes (1980).

their products, here cartridge cases. These marks allow archaeologists to identify not only the type of weapon that the munition may have come from but also when the munition was manufactured and, in some cases, where that munition was distributed and by whom. Military ammunition is particularly informative in this way, though some civilian arms manufacturers also kept sufficiently detailed distribution records to be of some use in this vein (Box 8.4).

GLASS

flux An element or compound with a low melting point that is combined with another element or compound with a high melting point. The flux lowers the melting point of the entire mixture.

Glass is typically defined as "an inorganic product of fusion which has cooled to a rigid condition without crystallizing" (Jones and Sullivan 1989: 10). Its primary component is silica, usually drawn from sand, quartz, or flint (chert). The melting point of silica is so high, however, that it must be mixed with an alkali, which works as a **flux** and allows the material to liquefy at lower temperatures. To counteract the physical properties of the alkaline flux, however, a nonalkaline base such as lime is also added to stabilize the mixture. If this base is not added, the glass produced from the mixture typically suffers from *crizzling*, a cracking effect that distorts the finish of the item.

The Making of Glass

With this in mind, glass was produced using soda (an alkali) derived by burning seaweed and kelp. This typically produced a greenish tint, and so this type of glass was known as **soda-lime glass.** Because this sort of glass is light and sets quickly, it was favored for producing elaborate forms and complex projects. The method for deriving soda was refined several times, most significantly by William Leighton in 1864. His process featured a higher ratio of lime to flux and this allowed the production of hard, lustrous glass that was well suited for mold production. It was less expensive than European crystal and glass (produced from potash and known as **potash-lime glass**) and therefore was substantially more marketable in the increasingly industrialized world. It became commonly used in producing bottles and is typified by dark green spirits (alcohol) bottles. Another type of glass, **potash-lead glass,** was developed in England in 1676 by Georges Ravenscroft. This glass is heavy, lustrous, and more refractive than other forms of glass. It was originally favored for medicine vials, condiment bottles, and lamp chimneys. Today it is still used to produce fine tableware and cut glassware.

In many respects the development of glass parallels the development of metallurgy. By 4000 B.C. Egyptian craftspeople were producing **faience** beads. These beads consisted of quartz pebbles or other naturally occurring items that were covered with melted silica. Faience is not considered a true glass by most scholars, but its presence demonstrates the beginnings of the development of glass technology. By 2000 B.C. Old World civilizations such as Egypt were familiar with the techniques for producing glass beads and similar objects and, by 1500 B.C., the ability to produce glass containers of a variety of shapes was possessed by specialists across much of the Classical world. These earliest vessels, and indeed most of those produced prior to the development of the Phoenician and Roman glass industries, were made without the aid of the blowpipe. Instead, most vessels were produced with the *core technique.* This involved forming a **mold** of the interior shape of the vessel by packing a mixture of clay and dung onto a metal rod. This core was dipped into a vat of molten glass and pulled out. The glass adhering to the core was then smoothed on a flat stone. When the glass cooled beyond the point at which it could be usefully worked, the entire mass was reheated, and the process continued until, after several such repetitions, the final vessel was created. As a last step, the remnants of the core were picked out and the interior finished. Only small vessels, such as cosmetic bottles and small vases, were typically produced in this way. By the sixth century B.C., the Greeks had revised the core technique and were able to produce larger objects, though in basically the same manner.

Other forms of ancient glassmaking also existed. Perhaps the simplest method involved creating a solid globule of glass, letting it cool, and then carving it. Or, molten glass could be poured into prepared molds to produce statuettes and open-mouthed jars. All of these forms could be decorated by applying strips of molten glass. These strips were usually created by first pre-

soda-lime glass Glass produced using soda (an alkali) derived by burning seaweed and kelp.

potash-lime glass Glass produced using potash derived from burning wood.

potash-lead glass Glass based on potash as a flux with high concentrations of lead, it is heavy, lustrous, and more refractive than other forms of glass.

faience An early Egyptian glaze for coating a pebble with a layer of melted silica. Faience is not generally considered to be a true glass.

molds Prepared receptacles used to impart specific shapes to materials such as glass, clay, or metals.

BOX 8.4

MUNITIONS AND THE LAST STAND AT LITTLE BIG HORN

One of the most informative and provocative studies of munitions was headed by Richard Fox at the Little Big Horn battlefield. On June 25, 1876, General George Armstrong Custer led the Seventh Cavalry in a raid on a substantial Native American village along the Little Big Horn River in Montana. Before the day was over, Custer and a significant portion of his command, including all soldiers who rode directly under his command (Custer had dispatched two officers and some troopers to accomplish other tasks related to his attack), were dead. Because there were no survivors on the government side of the battle who rode with Custer for the duration of the battle and because Euroamerican historians have been either unwilling or unable to piece together sufficient detail from accounts of the Native Americans who opposed Custer that day, the progress of the battle has largely been a mystery.

Custer's death was elevated to epic proportions as the myth of a last stand formed, an image that portrayed Custer and the Seventh Cavalry fighting to the last man and last bullet, all the while on the defensive and besieged by overwhelming odds. This image has found its way into films, with such notable actors as Errol Flynn and Robert Shaw portraying Custer as a gallant but doomed hero.

Some historians have sought to reconstruct the battle based on the location of monuments placed fourteen years after the battle on the sites at which federal soldiers were thought to have been killed. However, most of the actual remains, except for those of George Custer, who was buried at West Point in New York, were buried in a mass grave immediately after the battle, and doubt has always been cast on the accuracy of models of the battle that were based on these monuments. Still, historians had little to go on save the scattered accounts of Native Americans who fought in the battle and the accounts of those troopers in other parts of the Seventh Cavalry who survived the ordeal.

Most historians depicted the battle as following the same basic course. According to this version Custer had split his command into three regiments, one under Major Marcus Reno, a second under Captain Frederick Benteen, and the third under the direction of Custer himself. Reno's unit was sent to attack the village from the south, and Benteen was to support him. Custer, with roughly half of the Seventh Cavalry, was then to attack the northern edge of the village. Reno's attack, how-

Crew members recover munitions from the Custer Battlefield Site during the 1984–1985 field season. Metal detectors were used to identify the position of spent rounds. These were subsequently excavated and analyzed by project members.

A reenactment of the battle at Little Big Horn based on the testimony of Native American warriors.

ever, was either ill timed or weak, according to many historians, and his unit was driven back, eventually taking shelter in some fallen trees and then rejoining Benteen's unit later in the day. This combined unit was then pinned down by sporadic Native American attacks for the rest of the day and most of the next. Reno was court-martialed, though he was ultimately exonerated of any wrongdoing or incompetence.

While Reno's attack was faltering, Custer prepared to launch his attack on the northern edge of the village. Historians argue that, before he could do so, he was attacked by a group of Northern Cheyenne, who were late moving to battle Reno, and then by the full weight of the assembled warriors in the village. Against these odds, Custer was assumed to have retreated to high ground, today known as Custer Hill, from which he led his troops in a long and arduous struggle that was ultimately doomed to fail. Other historians were less willing to accept that Custer ever made it to the high ground himself and argued that he was one of the first men killed when the warriors returned to face him after fending off Reno's abortive attack. In either event, Custer and his men died as heroes according to most Euroamerican historians.

During the early 1980s a series of wildfires at the battlefield provided an opportunity for the government administrators to undertake archaeology as part of an ongoing cultural resource management program designed to preserve the area. Richard Fox was brought in to lead the survey, and his initial findings suggested that archaeology could contribute a great deal to the understanding of what really took place that June day. The government agreed, and Fox was given the opportunity to conduct an extensive archaeological survey on the battlefield grounds.

Using metal detectors and numerous volunteers to support his staff, Fox conducted a pedestrian survey along defined transects across the battlefield. Whenever the metal detectors indicated the presence of a metal object, the location was marked with a surveying flag and recorded on a master map with the aid of a laser theodolite, which emits a laser that reflects off a prism mounted on top of a pole. The beam reflects to the unit, and this allows an onboard computer to calculate the distance, angle, and elevation to the prism relative to the theodolite. This information was recorded on a computer and then downloaded into a GIS soft-

(continued)

BOX 8.4 (continued)

ware package. The resulting map recorded the detailed provenience for all finds.

At the site of each positive metal detector reading, an archaeologist excavated a small subsurface test to determine what caused the reading. Though many of the metal detector "hits" turned out to be modern refuse, Fox and his team were able to locate artifacts specifically related to the battle. The most important of these artifacts proved to be spent projectiles, those fired at a target, and the cartridge cases from which the projectiles came. Fox was able to identify the unique **firing pin signature** left on the base of the cartridges by individual weapons. With this information he could trace the movement across the battlefield of specific weapons, presumably in the hands of people involved in the battle. By also identifying the types of weapons involved in the battle on each side and then comparing this information with the survey map that his team produced, Fox was able to identify specific events on the battlefield.

Another piece of the puzzle of what happened to Custer's command came from historical documents and testimonies detailing how federal cavalry troops were trained to fight in battle and how people reacted to adverse conditions on a battlefield. Cavalry troopers were taught to form skirmish lines with about 5 yards separating troopers in each squad (a small group of troopers working together) and 20 yards separating different squads along the line. As long as the soldiers maintained this organization and fought in a disciplined manner, Fox reasoned that he would find distributions of federal shell casings that reflected this arrangement. On the other hand, if this tactical stability, as Fox called it, began to break down, there would be evidence of a behavior he called bunching. In this behavior troopers tend to cluster close together, and this leads to a different pattern of casings on the battlefield. Bunching was dangerous because it could lead to the failure of unit stability and the eventual flight of people from their positions.

When Fox brought this knowledge to the distribution of artifacts, it began to become clear what had happened to Custer and his command. The battle began as

historians had pieced together: Custer separated the Seventh Cavalry into three components, and both Benteen and Reno performed as reported in documents related to the battle. However, Custer, according to Fox, operated much differently than historians surmised. He moved to the north as expected but left half of his force on a ridge overlooking the Little Big Horn River. Custer led the remainder of his troopers, about eighty men in all, even farther north and skirted the village entirely. According to Fox, Custer had observed that the women and children in the village had run to the northwest when Reno launched his attack. Custer apparently intended to capture them in order to force the Native American warriors to surrender. Surprised by the number of people fleeing the village, Custer turned back to retrieve more of his troopers. It was then that he saw that the unit he left behind was under intense pressure from warriors who had moved to the northern edge of the battlefield after repulsing Reno along the southern edge. Custer rode to the high ground, Custer Hill, and there was joined by the remains of the unit that had been stationed along the ridge. Only about twenty men made it to Custer's position, and they soon found themselves in the same position they had been in previously, heavily outnumbered and under intense pressure.

The archaeological record demonstrates that the Seventh Cavalry was decimated within minutes. There are relatively few federal shell casings in the area and a large number of projectiles from Native American weapons. What was once interpreted as a final skirmish line, known as the south skirmish line, based on the position of grave monuments, proved to be a path of retreat for the final members of the federal force. Some twenty-eight troopers found their way into a ravine, where they were eventually shot. Native American accounts of this last phase of the battle suggest that fighting was opportunistic, that individual warriors and soldiers fought one another independently rather than as part of a larger unit. With the death of the last trooper rose the myth of the last stand, a myth that has endured for more than a century.

paring rods of glass and then melting these onto the surface of the object to be decorated.

The technique of blowing glass into shapes originated along the eastern Mediterranean coast, in the area that is now Lebanon, Israel, Syria, and Palestine, during the first century B.C. In this method a hollow pipe is inserted in a vat of molten glass and a globule of the desired size is removed. The glassmaker then blows through the pipe while spinning it in order to give the globule the desired shape. This method takes great skill and patience but was generally much faster than the already existing core and mold methods; mold production continued to be practiced, however.

The Roman glass industry became renowned for its ability to cast effigy forms that were turned on lathes to provide threads, inlaid with gold or precious stones, and even made into cameo scenes. Practicality also played a role in Roman glassmaking. British archaeologists working at a variety of Roman sites in the United Kingdom have uncovered fragments of window glass. This glass was produced in oval kilns, such as the one excavated at Wilderspool, Cheshire, that were capable of consistently high temperatures, 1000° to 1200°C. Window glass also seems to have been produced by pouring molten glass into carefully sanded molds, as well as by shaping glass into cylinders in molds and then cutting and flattening the cylinders while still hot.

The Roman Empire played a significant role in shaping the material culture of much of Europe. Craftspeople of all sorts, including glassworkers, were drawn to areas in which the Romans had successfully established towns. Even after the Roman Empire collapsed, these towns continued to be locations for innovation and craft production. Some areas, such as Venice, took Roman traditions in glassmaking and other crafts and developed them to even higher technological and artistic planes. The Roman commercial and market system helped transform glass production from an art possessed by the elite, as in Egypt, to an industry that transcended all levels of the social spectrum in many cultures (Box 8.5).

During the late nineteenth century, as the industrial revolution reached new heights, glassmaking became increasingly machine dominated. New technology was developed to automate and standardize the production of all varieties of glass products, especially containers designed to hold products for resale. As with metal manufacture, the transition to fully mechanized glass production developed in stages, and there is no uniform chronology. Yet a general trend can be described, such as those provided by Jones and Sullivan (1989) and by Sutton and Arkush (1998; Table 8.3).

Blown and mold-made glass was produced by hand-blowing prior to the late nineteenth century. *Semi-automatic machines* (machines that performed a forming task under the direct control of a person, with the person introducing the molten glass to the machine) for producing bottles and other containers with narrow mouths were introduced commercially by 1893. The operator worked the machine by introducing a globule of molten glass into a mold; the

firing pin signature The manufacturer's mark on the base of a munitions cartridge.

BOX 8.5

A VIEW FROM THE BOTTOM: AN UNDERWATER LOOK AT THE ELEVENTH CENTURY A.D. GLASS TRADE

One hundred feet beneath the surface of Serce Limani (Sparrow Harbor), Turkey, divers under the direction of George Bass and Fred Van Doorninck (both of Texas A & M) were probing the sand for evidence of a shipwreck they suspected to be in the area. As they proceeded, some of the divers noticed a slight burning sensation in their hands, and they noticed they had come out of the sand bleeding. Gently clearing away the sediments by waving their hands, they found the culprit that had caused their minor wounds—glass, lots of glass. In fact, they had found part of the cargo of a vessel that sank nearly one thousand years ago.

Excavations were conducted between 1977 and 1979. Literally tons of glass were recovered from the wreck, nearly all of it broken and mixed together. By carefully mapping their finds (a key difference between underwater archaeologists, who record everything they find in great detail, and treasure hunters, who wantonly take material from its historical and archaeological contexts without recording), Bass and Van Doorninck were able to show that the glass had been broken before the vessel sank. Indeed, it seems to have been loaded on board in its fragmentary state. Painstaking reconstruction by Turkish students and the Texas A & M staff identified more than one hundred complete containers, as well as partially completed glass items and what appeared to be glass globules that were abandoned during construction. The material was typical of the glass being produced by Islamic craftsmen during the early eleventh century A.D. and seems to represent a load of scrap being transported to glass workshops elsewhere in the eastern Mediterranean.

Also of interest to archaeologists were Greek amphorae (large ceramic urns), as well as Greek coins and a Byzantine scale. It would appear that the owner of the ship made his living by trading across national and cultural boundaries all through the eastern Mediterranean. This was an interesting theory, because warfare between the various Islamic states and Christian Byzantium was endemic during this era. Perhaps this finding reflected that although states might combat one another, the fluid nature of the people in the region tolerated and perhaps thrived on trade across political boundaries. Somewhat sinisterly, however, Bass observed that the sailors aboard the Serce Limani vessel were heavily armed and may actually have been the victims of piracy.

An Islamic glass vase recovered from the Serce Limani wreck.

The "great bottle" from the Serce Limani wreck. This bottle, one of the largest known from archaeology, required archaeologists to sort through over a million fragments of glass and took over a year to reconstruct.

The glass-sorting workshop for members of the Serce Limani laboratory crew.

TABLE 8.3   Generalized Chronology of Major Methods for Bottle Manufacturing

Bottle Form

To ca. 1860	Hand-blown/Hand-formed
1790–1810	Dip Mold
1870–1910	Three-part Mold
1870–1925	Turn Mold
1904–Present	Automatic Bottle Machinery

Lip Form

To ca. 1810	Hand formed as part of bottle
1810–1840	Sheared Lip
1840–1860	Hand-applied Lip
1840–1920	Mechanically applied Lip
1904–Present	Lip molded as part of bottle

Dates reflect the periods when the indicated technology was popular. Some forms of bottle manufacture, such as hand-blowing, continue even today but are responsible for only a small percentage of the total number of bottles produced and circulated. Note also that some techniques existed alongside of one another, sometimes for extended periods of time.
Source: After Jones and Sullivan 1989, and Sutton and Arkush 1998

machine pressed it into a rough shape and then mechanically blew it into its final shape. These machines are sometimes referred to as *press and blow machines*. Similar machines for producing wide-mouthed jars and comparable items were introduced in commercial production six years later. These machines were at their height of use in about 1917 but were largely obsolete by 1926.

Fully automated Owens machines for glass container production were first introduced for commercial purposes in 1904. These machines worked in five basic steps. First, a globule of molten glass was introduced by suction into a mold. Second, the neck was formed while the base was simultaneously sheared off. Third, the still-hot globule was mechanically transferred to a full-sized mold. Fourth, air was introduced and the globule was blown into the final shape of the product. Fifth, the container was removed from the mold as a finished product. By 1917 this method of container production equaled the production runs from semiautomatic machines, with fully half of the glass containers in the United States being produced by Owens machines. By the late 1920s advances in technology were beginning to make the Owens machine obsolete, though it continued to have a productive life until about 1950.

The emphasis on 1917 is because it was at this time that production techniques allowed molten glass to be directly introduced into semiautomatic machines. This *flow and feed* process enabled producers to compete with the Owens machine by turning out large quantities of containers inexpensively.

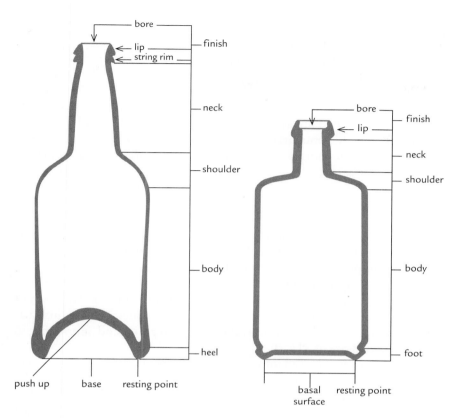

FIGURE 8.3

The generalized anatomy of a bottle, shown here in two different forms.

The products of both these machines and other semiautomated production processes, as well as the Owens machine, resembled one another in appearance and quality. A seam connects the top of the lip to the rest of the finish, which is in turn connected to the neck of the container by a second seam. A third seam runs from the base of the finish to the base of the vessel and is sometimes paralleled by a "ghost seam," a by-product of the mold. A fourth seam connects the base to the body of the container (Figure 8.3).

In 1925 the individual section machine was introduced as an alternative to these production methods. These machines produced discrete segments of the container and then joined them. The bottles seen today on supermarket shelves are typical examples of this technology. These bottles have a single seam running down opposite sides of the container and a single seam that joins the base to the body of the container. Such containers are less expensive to produce than all previous forms of containers because there are fewer steps in the production process. Arguably, such containers are also more durable and subject to fewer flaws because there are fewer seams that might be misjoined or cracked during manufacture.

TABLE 8.4
Glass Colors

Finished Color	Chemical Contents
amber (brown)	carbon, nickel
amethyst (purple)	manganese, nickel
black (dark green)	iron
blue	cobalt, copper
green	soda-lime, copper, chromium
red/pink	copper, selenium
white/ milk glass	tin, zinc

tableware A category of glass items commonly used on tables, including plates, glasses, goblets, and serving bowls.

closures All items used to seal glass containers, including both glass and nonglass items such as metal and ceramic bottle caps.

superimposition The application of glass on top of other glass surfaces, including methods such as threading, banding, quilting and casing.

contact mold A mold used to produce a full-sized, or a portion of a full-sized, glass item.

It would be wrong to assume that all glass was produced using the machine processes set forth here. There are numerous additional manufacturing processes and a variety of ways in which alterations can be introduced into many of these procedures. Consequently the study of glass, especially in the historic era, can become quite complicated. Jones and Sullivan (1989), for example, list two classes of molds and note variations within each, whereas Sutton and Arkush (1998) divide the list into ten types of molds. And these categories apply only to containers, not to **tableware** (glasses, plates, and similar items), **closures** (items used to seal containers), and various *flat glasses* (window and plate glasses).

Decorations

Perhaps even more than ceramics, glass products lend themselves to decoration. Glass can be decorated by color, molding, inclusions (such as air bubbles), **superimposition** (glass applied on glass), etching, engraving, cutting, gilding, enameling, painting, staining, and silvering. Moreover, because glass is so widely distributed in the modern world, there is a market for each of these treatments, as well as many other less common ones. Despite this variety, it is important to define at least the major categories and approaches to decorating glassware of all sorts.

Colors can be introduced into glass either deliberately or as a by-product of the manufacturing process. At one point archaeologists tried to classify glass by color, but this was problematic because of the variety of colors possible. Certainly color can be a useful characteristic to record, but not all green glass fragments, for example, will belong to the same type of glass product; indeed, they may not even be the same sort of glass. Table 8.4 lists some of the common colors produced in glass and the chemicals associated with them. The coloration can be functional, as in the case of certain medical or chemical containers, or purely decorative (Box 6.4).

Mold production for decoration is similar to that used to produce utilitarian glassware and ceramics. Molten glass is forced into a prepared mold and then detached, producing a potentially complex decoration. With glass, however, this sort of technique subsumes embossing, punctation, and most other specific decorative techniques used on ceramics. For example, a flower image that could be produced by any of the ceramic decorative techniques is likely to have been produced in great numbers by mold in glass, especially in the historic era. Because of the liquid nature of molten glass, the mold techniques available for glassworking are significantly more varied than those available for ceramic production.

Contact molding is one of the most common processes associated with utilitarian and decorative glass production. In this method a full-sized object or a portion of a full-sized object is produced in a mold: The molten glass is introduced into the mold, and then air, either mechanically supplied or blown by a worker, is used to form the glass into the mold. This is the principle underlying most of the machines discussed previously.

Pattern molding involves blowing molten glass into a small pattern of shapes, such as diamonds, stars, circles, and so forth. The glass is allowed to fill the mold but is then removed and free-blown (by a person using a blowpipe) into a final form. This technique allows the creation of repetitive geometric patterns but frees the craftsperson to create a unique shape for the final product.

Optic molding is the mechanical counterpart to pattern molding. In this process molten glass is introduced into a pattern mold. The patterned glass is then removed, placed into a contact mold, and blown into its final shape. This method allows the mass production of standardized shapes, each with a repetitive pattern derived from the pattern mold.

Another molding technique is **press molding.** In this system a globule of molten glass is introduced into a sealed mold. Any pattern to be imparted to the exterior of the piece is imposed by the shape of the chamber into which the glass is introduced. A plunger is forced into the globule, thus imparting its shape to the interior of the item being formed. The plunger is then removed and the finished piece taken from the mold.

Inclusions can be deliberately introduced into the glass piece as a form of decoration. For example, air bubbles can be left in the walls of the vessel. These bubbles can also be manipulated by twisting the glass. Metallic inclusions or glass rods can also be introduced into the vessel's walls and left in place or twisted as desired.

Another common technique for decorating glass is the superimposition of glass on top of an already completed glass shape. For example, a completed bottle could be wrapped in threadlike ribbons of glass (*threading*) or bands could be applied vertically or horizontally (*banding*) or formed into a cross-hatched pattern (*quilting*). More elaborate techniques include *casing,* in which layers of glass of approximately equal thickness are fused together so that the interior and exterior surfaces of the item are different. This can be done over the entire item or it can be done in part (*partial casing*). Yet another form of decoration is the addition of **prunts** (globules of glass) to the surface of a glass item. These prunts can also be tooled or otherwise formed into shapes, such as flowers or leaves.

Glass can also be *engraved, cut,* or *etched* either by mechanical or chemical means. Diamond-tipped gravers can be used to introduce patterns on glass by hand or under the guidance of machinery, as can abrasive wheels. Specialized saw blades and abrasive belts can also be used to cut glass into desired shapes, such as is done with expensive cut crystals. **Acid etching** is a caustic but effective way to impart complex patterns to glass. A glass object is encased in a layer of wax, except for a portion of the surface that will carry the pattern. The entire object is then sprayed with hydrofluoric acid, which is allowed to chemically burn the glass. After sufficient time has elapsed to impart a pat-

pattern mold A mold used to impart a decorative pattern to a sheet of glass, which is then manually blown into a final shape.

optic mold A mold used to impart a decorative pattern to a sheet of glass, which is then pressed into a contact mold in order to produce a finished item.

press mold A mold used to shape the exterior of a glass item while a plunger shapes the interior of the item.

prunts Globules of glass that may or not be molded or cut into shapes but that are attached to an otherwise complete glass object.

acid etching The use of hydrofluoric acid to etch a pattern onto a glass surface.

BOX 8.6

THE ARCHAEOLOGY OF CONSUMERISM: BITTERS AND PATENT MEDICINES

A distinctive category of bottles is associated with the production of bitters and patent medicines. These products had their origin in herbal cures passed on through the folk traditions of many different societies. Bitters originally contained mixtures of water, roots, barks, and spices for flavoring. These were distributed as cure-alls for a wide variety of ailments for both people and animals. As folklore would have it, in the eighteenth century King George II placed a heavy tax on gin. In order to circumvent this tax, gin was added to bitters and sold as medicine. The ruse apparently worked, because the business of bitter production increased dramatically. Regional variations of these products developed, some of which petitioned for and received proprietary status, essentially becoming patented. These then became known as patent medicines, a term that has in most usages replaced the term bitters when referring to this class of potions.

With the addition of alcohol to the original mixture, makers of these medicines discovered they had stumbled into a range of untapped markets. Many people found it more socially acceptable to drink bitters than alcohol clearly labeled as such. Women, for example, found that although they were expected not to drink or to purchase alcohol, they could acquire and consume medicines. Industries that frowned on alcohol use, such as in winter logging camps in the early twentieth century, allowed individual workers to bring patent medicines but not alcohol.

The archaeological study of the bottles and their distribution is sometimes telling. Although written documents describe prohibitions against alcoholic beverages in certain American towns and locations, the recovery of the remains of a thriving patent medicine industry sheds a different light on the real behaviors of the people in these places. Moreover, because many of these products have historically known dates of production and distribution, archaeologists find the presence of containers for bitters useful in dating occupations. In many respects the containers for these medicines function much like coins in helping to establish TPQ and TAQ.

Some of the more colorful names include "Moxie Nerve Food," "Allen's Nerve and Bone Liniment," "Pierce's Golden Discovery," and "Morse's Invigorating Cordial." Literally thousands of products were produced and continued to be popular until the eventual action by the United States government in passing laws about truth in advertising and instituting tough taxation of products containing alcohol ended the heyday of this industry.

---

tern into the glass, the entire object is washed in hot water to remove both the acid and the remaining wax.

Glass can also be covered with a decorative coating. Gold (gilding) and silver (silvering) both can be applied to glass in a liquid matrix resembling paint. The item is then fired to set and polished to shine the metallic finish. Paints and enamels (powders) are similarly applied to glass and fired on. These processes are particularly common in jewelry or other ornamentation, though tableware featuring decorations produced by one or more of these methods is known. Such items are typically very expensive and are usually associated with the economically affluent classes of a society.

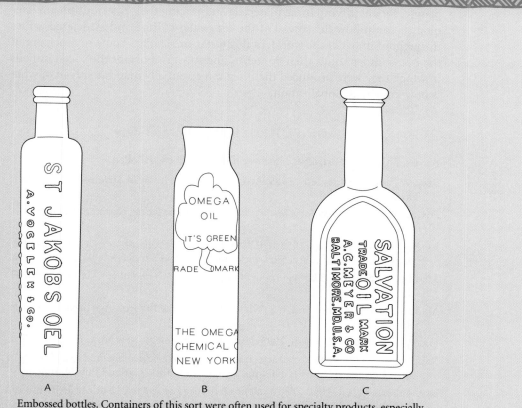

Embossed bottles. Containers of this sort were often used for specialty products, especially patent medicines. These bottles from the Drake site in northern Illinois reveal some of the marketing and variation of glass containers during the industrial revolution.

SUMMARY

The rise of industrialization and consumerism had a profound effect on the production and distribution of material culture. Trends associated with this shift are well illustrated by following the development of metallurgy and glass manufacturing. Both began producing exotic items possessed only by the elite and produced only by specially trained craftspeople. As techniques for producing metals and glass improved and wider applications became economically viable, items made from these materials spread into ever widening uses. Some rare items, such as gold or lead crystal, remained associated with elite classes of society, but more utilitarian items have become increasingly available to all people. By identifying these materials and tracing their distribution, archaeologists can follow the spread of the consumer culture and associated values throughout much of the world. In this instance, scholars know so much about the items under study, their contents, and most important the social milieus in which they were produced that they can essentially map the spread of what is now known as globalization.

FOR FURTHER INFORMATION

Barnes, F. C. 1980. *Cartridges of the world,* 4th ed. Chicago: Follett.

Bray, W., and N. Seeley, eds. 1989. Archaeometallurgy. *World Archaeology* 20 (whole no. 3).

Fox, R. A. 1993. *Archaeology, history, and Custer's last battle.* Norman: University of Oklahoma.

Jones, O., and C. Sullivan. 1989. *The Parks Canada glass glossary,* rev. ed. Ottawa: National Historic Parks and Sites and Canadian Parks Service.

Maddin, R., ed. 1988. *The beginning of the use of metals and alloys.* Cambridge: MIT Press.

Maddin, R., J. D. Muhly, and T. S. Wheeler. 1977. How the Iron Age began. *Scientific American* 237 (4): 122–31.

Orser, C. E., and B. M. Fagan. 1995. *Historical archaeology.* New York: HarperCollins.

Rapp, G., Jr., 2000. Metals, characterization. In *Archaeological method and theory: An encyclopedia,* edited by L. Ellis, pp. 364–67. New York: Garland Publishing.

Rothenberg, B., ed. 1990. *The ancient metallurgy of copper.* London: Institute for Archaeo-Metallurgical Studies.

Shimada, I., and J. F. Merkel. 1991. Copper-alloy metallurgy in ancient Peru. *Scientific American* 265 (1): 80–86.

Spindler, K. 1985. *The man in the ice: The discovery of a 5,000-year-old body reveals the secrets of the Stone Age.* New York: Harmony Books.

Sutton, M. Q., and B. S. Arkush. 1998. *Archaeological laboratory methods,* 2nd ed. Dubuque, Iowa: Kendall/Hunt.

Swart, P., and B. D. Till. 1984. Bronze carriages from the tomb of China's first emperor. *Archaeology* 37 (6): 18–25.

9

ORGANIC MATERIALS IN THE ARCHAEOLOGICAL RECORD

[The problem is] the mummies don't come with letters in their pockets.

—*James Mallory*

This chapter discusses fundamentally different material from that discussed previously. Here we will focus on the sorts of organic material that archaeologists work with. Although stone tools, pottery, metal, and glass are major categories of material culture, they are exclusively products of human activity. Organic materials, on the other hand, can be either *artifacts,* as in the case of a carved antler or a bone harpoon, or *ecofacts,* as in the case of pollen or naturally occurring bone deposits. Both artifacts and ecofacts serve to provide archaeologists with information on past human activities. They do so, however, in different ways. At the technological and functional levels, many organic materials tell us less about direct human actions than they do about the environment in which these activities took place. Once these materials are brought into a social context, though, they often can provide researchers with data comparable to those afforded by other types of material culture.

Organic materials can be divided into three major categories: plant material, insect material, and animal material, including such creatures as shellfish and snails (Table 9.1). Each of these categories can usually be further subdivided into two subcategories: those things handled or directly worked by humans and those that are unmodified but nonetheless provide information on past human activities. This chapter introduces these organic materials and the more common types of research related to them.

TABLE 9.1 Divisions of Organic Remains and Examples of Each

Material	Cultural Occurrence	Natural Occurrence
Plant	Gourds used for food or containers	Pollen
	Cereal remains (corncobs, wheat hulls)	Phytoliths
	Woven flax, cotton	
	Shaped wood (beams, planks)	
Insect	Food remains (U.S. Great Basin)	Internal parasites
	By-products of dye production (Europe)	Insect larvae
Animal	Butchered bone	Rodents exploiting middens
	Worked antler or bone	Incidental animal death
	Woven wool or other hair	

PLANTS

Macrobotanical Remains

A variety of **macrobotanical remains,** that is, preserved fragments of actual plant tissue, are encountered in archaeology (Figure 9.1). As a general rule, the better the preservation at a site, the more likely that botanical remains of all sorts will be present. Unlike microbotanical remains, many forms of macrobotanical materials can be retrieved through careful excavation and immediate conservation efforts. Materials such as wood, seeds, woven fibers, and leaves are usually badly eroded and in delicate states. Once they are removed from the depositional environment that preserved them, they tend to degrade rapidly. Because such remains carry a great deal of potential for identifying rarely seen aspects of past human behaviors, such as the way in which a beam was cut or the changes in seed sizes brought about by domestication, archaeologists need to be aware of what can be done with such remains and how best to go about doing these things.

Wood is one of the most common forms of macrobotanical remains encountered by archaeologists. In extraordinarily arid environments, such as in deserts or in permafrost, and in exceptionally wet, anaerobic environments, such as bogs, mud beds, or deep water, details on wood, as well as the structure of the wood itself, may be well preserved. Some of the significant things we can learn about ships and their construction through analyses of preserved wood include the type of wood used, when it was cut, and when it was used. Likewise, the way in which past craftsmen worked the wood, whether they cut mortises and tenons, whether they covered small mistakes in carving, and whether the vessel suffered from chronic structural problems are all useful in understanding both the history of the vessel and the world in which it functioned.

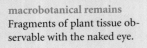

macrobotanical remains
Fragments of plant tissue observable with the naked eye.

FIGURE 9.1

A wide range of macrobotanical remains are often preserved at archaeological sites on the arid Peruvian coast. Here a researcher displays three fragments of ancient maize, and a number of other remains are visible in the background.

A series of three nautical wrecks in the Mediterranean Sea provides a vivid example of the value of preserved woods. The first is the wreck of a Roman era merchant vessel near Kyrenia, off of the coast of Cyprus (Figures 9.2 and 9.3). George Bass began working on the remains of the vessel in 1967, and, in 1986, a reconstructed version of the vessel (*Kyrenia II*) based primarily on data recovered archaeologically sailed from Athens to Cyprus. Of particular interest to our discussion is that this vessel, which sank in about 288 B.C., was built using mortise and tenon joins. In this method the keel of the vessel and the hull are constructed first and only then reinforced with an internal frame (called **hull-first construction**). The careful work of Richard Steffy showed archaeologists that great care was taken to make each join in the vessel both functional and attractive. Untold additional hours were spent covering small mistakes and refining details by the shipwright in charge of producing this vessel.

The Serce Limani vessel (discussed in Chapter 8) showed a very different method of construction. By about A.D. 1000, when this vessel was constructed, both wood and labor were in short supply. Unlike ship construction during the classical Greek era, when wood was cheap and labor was provided by trained slaves, ship construction in the Byzantine era relied on wood imported from Lebanon, and therefore sometimes subject to interdiction by Arab sultans, and labor was provided by free laborers. As a consequence vessels were produced using an innovative method known as **frame-first construction.** In this

hull-first construction The method of constructing a ship by erecting its shell before supporting it with a frame. This method is more labor and time intensive than frame-first construction.

frame-first construction The method of first constructing a ship's frame and then enclosing it with a hull. This method is faster than hull-first construction and saves on both labor and materials.

FIGURE 9.2

A schematic representation of the amphorae carried by the Kyrenia vessel. The vessel sank and came to rest on its side. As the wooden hull rotted, it began to collapse, spilling the cargo from the high side of the vessel across the seafloor while holding the material on the bottom side of the vessel in neat piles.

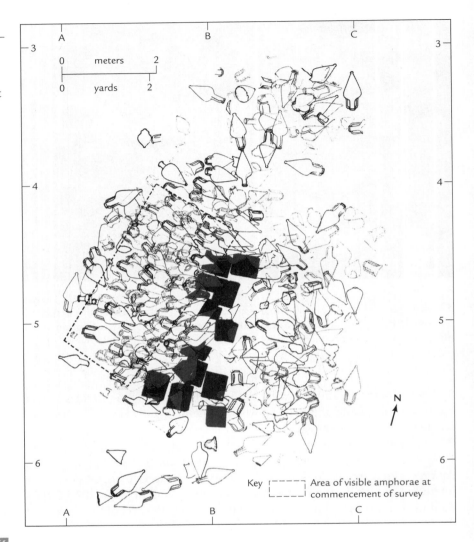

Key ⌐‒‒‒‒⌐ Area of visible amphorae at
     ⌐‒‒‒‒⌐ commencement of survey

open market system A method of exchange in which artisans are free to provide their products to anyone capable of meeting their asking price.

closed market system A method of exchange in which artisans provide their products only to their patrons or to an exclusive group of people.

method the keel of the vessel is laid down and a frame is built on top of it. Planks are then fitted to the sides of the frame using nails. This method uses less wood and fewer workers and can be completed more rapidly than vessels built using hull-first methods. The Serce Limani vessel was the product of an **open market system,** one in which craftspeople produced material for a wide range of consumers. The Kyrenia vessel, on the other hand, was a product of a **closed market system,** one in which some materials were sold openly but in which many items, such as ships, were produced exclusively for wealthy patrons by workers laboring solely on behalf of a single patron (Box 9.1).

By about 1100 A.D., the wreck of another frame-first vessel near Pelago Nisos in the Sporades Islands shows even more innovations. The planking of the

FIGURE 9.3

A member of the under-water archaeological team that surveyed and excavated the Kyrenia wreck swims past part of the cargo spilled from the collapse of the main hold as the vessel rotted.

vessel is quite thin and demonstrates that the ship had been refitted and re-paired many times before she eventually sank. Peter Throckmorton and Harry Kistas, the excavators of the ship, characterized her construction as one in which the planking served to keep the water out, whereas the Kyrenia vessel's plank-ing served as an integral structural element of the vessel. The Serce Limani vessel is an intermediary form, showing frame-first construction but relying on thicker, more durable planking than in vessels made just a century later.

Rarer than preserved wood are preserved **textiles,** that is, fibrous material from either plant tissue or animal hairs that are bound together, usually but not always by weaving (Figure 9.4). Plants from a wide range of species have been utilized by humans across the globe to create a broad range of textiles designed to perform numerous purposes. For instance, woven reeds and bark have been used to produce hats, cloaks, baskets, mats, and even roofing mate-rial for structures. Flax, cotton, and similar plants have also been woven into fabrics from which clothing, ornamentation, packaging material (bags), and still more items have been produced. In general, though, such products tend to decay rapidly in acidic, basic, or moist soils. They are subject to chemical erosion, physical erosion, and destruction by biological organisms.

textiles Fibrous material from either plant tissue or animal hairs that are bound together, usually but not always by weaving.

BOX 9.1

HUMAN ECONOMIC SYSTEMS

Economic systems are rules that control the distribution of resources in human societies. Archaeologists and cultural anthropologists have identified three basic economic systems common to humankind. Though countless variations of these three systems exist, all systems can be grouped into one of these primary categories: reciprocity, redistribution, and market exchange.

Reciprocity is the oldest economic system and works best among relatively small social groups, those that function primarily through face-to-face interactions. In such societies resources are usually transferred from one person to another in a form of gift exchange. Such exchanges can be informal or highly ritualized, depending on the social connection between the giver of the goods and the recipient.

Between close friends and family this exchange usually takes the form of **generalized reciprocity**: gifts are given without the expectation of an immediate or equal return of the gift. In some cases, although no return gift is expected, one may be given to reaffirm friendship or kinship.

In more formal settings, especially in situations in which allies from different groups meet, gift exchange often takes the form of **balanced reciprocity**. In this method of exchange, social rules dictate that a gift of equal or greater value must be returned to the original gift giver within a prescribed amount of time or when a predetermined event, such as a feast, will take place. In this way the allies reaffirm their mutual respect for one another and create social obligations that unite their groups.

Not all exchanges are considered beneficial, though. In circumstances in which unallied groups of people meet or in which opposing groups come into contact, **negative reciprocity** can take place. In this method of

---

reciprocity An economic system in which gifts are exchanged in order to create and reinforce social relationships between people and groups.

generalized reciprocity A subsystem of reciprocity in which gifts are exchanged between individuals without the expectation of an immediate or equal return.

balanced reciprocity A subsystem of reciprocity in which allied individuals provide gifts of equal or slightly greater value to each other at predetermined times or events.

Despite these problems, textiles provide archaeologists with glimpses into the daily lives of peoples. A simple look at how modern people dress reveals some of the great complexity inherent in both the production and display of textiles. Anthropologists have repeatedly documented that dress is one of the primary methods of signaling group identity and, subsequently, ideologies. Today, in large parts of Latin America, each village within cultures such as the Maya, Inca, and others produces specific patterns of textiles. The patterns, coupled with the choice of colors, shapes of the finished products, and even the way the finished item is worn or used, distinguishes people from the different villages. This system seems to extend back into prehistory in the portions of the world from which we have recovered substantial amounts of textiles (Box 9.2).

The production of textiles is a time-consuming and labor-intensive process. Moreover, there are numerous opportunities in the production process to add variety to textiles. The result is that these common and frequently poorly preserved items are among the most complex forms of material culture, both in terms of their production and what they can be used to represent.

The first step in the production of textiles is to procure the raw material. This means collecting, perhaps even growing, plants useful for textile manu-

exchange one trader or gift giver seeks to acquire more than he gives. Negative reciprocity can also be extended to include such human behaviors as feuding, vendettas, or raiding, though such violent activities also have special terminological categories and meanings among cultural anthropologists.

Redistribution tends to occur in societies that have large populations and more complex resource bases. In such instances a central authority or group often emerges and assumes the responsibility of ensuring that all people in the society receive required goods and services. In order to do this, a portion, perhaps even the whole, of all resources is collected and brought to the central authority. The material is then reallocated as the central authority sees fit. Such management systems are easily modified, and in many cases the central authority acquires more wealth and prestige than do other members of society. Nonetheless, as long as their efforts are perceived to benefit the society as a whole, this is usually tolerated, perhaps even encouraged.

Market exchange occurs only in societies in which there are many people who specialize in the production of specific goods and services. These people make at least a portion of their living by trading these goods for other resources that they need to survive. In the simplest systems people are only part-time craft specialists; they also work in the fields, hunt, or tend animals. However, for part of their time, they produce materials or provide services to others in exchange for additional resources. When craft specialists can acquire all of their goods through market exchange, they may become full-time craft specialists and abandon their other subsistence activities. In general, full-time craft specialization and market exchange only appear when societies reach populations numbering in the tens of thousands.

facture. Flax, representing a family of plants, has been used for the production of textiles for at least ten thousand years and possibly many tens of thousands more. The earliest datable evidence of flax comes from impressions of textiles from wetlands and clays at Pavlov in the Czech Republic and date minimally to 23,000 B.C. However, few intact fragments of textiles survive from the area. One of the oldest is from a Neolithic-era burial at Kremela I in the eastern portion of the Czech Republic. Here, fabric was charred, apparently as part of a cremation ritual. The burning helped preserve the fabric, which has been identified as linen, made from flax, and dated to approximately 4000 B.C. More often, textiles are preserved in arid environments, such as on the western coast of South America, portions of the Near East, and in arctic and tundra conditions.

The second step in the process, once the raw material has been obtained, is to process the material and make it ready for use. This typically involves a spinning process, often using a stone or ceramic weight called a spindle whorl (prior to the advent of spinning machines). The fiber is threaded into the weight while the other end of the fiber is held in the hand. The weight is allowed to hang and is then spun. The fibers stretch and intertwine, producing a sort of yarn. This process is repeated until sufficient quantities of

negative reciprocity A subsystem of reciprocity in which gifts or resources are exchanged between individuals seeking to gain an advantage from their trade.

redistribution An economic system in which a percentage of all goods and resources produced in a community are given to a central authority for redistribution to members of the community who need these resources.

market exchange An economic system in which artisans provide their products to others in exchange for those items or services that the artisan needs or desires.

FIGURE 9.4

A woolen brocade recovered from Tomb 4 at Cherchen, western China. The outstanding preservation at the site allows archaeologists to examine the fiber, type of weave, and pattern of these textiles.

fiber have been processed to facilitate weaving, braiding, or other production techniques. Fibers that are particularly rough may need to be combed and separated before spinning. Some fibers, such as most barks, simply cannot be spun.

When fiber is spun, it develops a specific twist. Researchers refer to these twists as **Z-twists** and **S-twists,** the letters referring to the direction in which the fiber is turned (Figure 9.5). S-twist cordage turns from the left to the right and is sometimes referred to as a right-handed twist. The central portion of the letter "S" describes this turn. A Z twist, on the other hand, turns from the right to the left and is sometimes called a left-handed twist. The central portion of the letter "Z" is like this turn.

Life would be relatively easy for textile specialists if cordage was left only in these basic forms. However, multiple strands of fibers can be wrapped together in numerous ways, with each strand potentially representing a different twist. Consequently, archaeologists sometimes have to describe fibers as Z^s, S^z, or even Z^s_z, with the second and subsequent letters referring to the twists of individual fiber strands wrapped around the base strand.

Various plants, shellfish, minerals, and insect material can be used to color the fibers. Ocher in the form of hematite, for example, is among the most abundant minerals in the world. It contains substantial amounts of iron and can be crushed into a reddish-brown powder. This powder is then mixed with liquid and used to dye textiles. Lichens can be similarly processed, with those indigenous to northern Italy producing a rich purple tint. Unsurprisingly, it is the combination of differently colored and sometimes different weaves of fabric that allows textile workers to produce such a wide range of products.

Z-twist The turn of fibers from the top right toward the bottom left.

S-twist The turn of fibers from the top left to the bottom right.

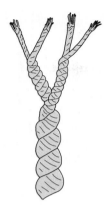

FIGURE 9.5

Examples of S- and Z-twisted cords, as well as an illustration of the number of strands, or ply, involved in weaving textiles.

2-ply, "Z-twist" cordage   2-ply, "S-twist" cordage   4-ply, "Z-twist" rope

Once a thread or yarn has been prepared, the fibers can be shaped into form by hand or through the use of a number of different looms. One of the oldest and simplest looms is nothing more than an anchor point mounted on a tree or wall to which the yarn is attached. The other end of the yarn is then worked by a person who intertwines the strands to produce the desired object. As textile production became more specialized through history, more elaborate looms were developed, each designed to meet the needs and desires of the societies that developed them. In the Old World, weaving had become a specialization by 3000 B.C. in Egypt and Mesopotamia. Looms as we know them today are really products of the past one thousand years, with the basic principles of weaving evolving little in that time.

Microbotanical Remains

Pollen   Microbotanical remains are small, often microscopic, fragments of plants. **Pollen,** among the most common microbotanical remains studied in archaeology, is the common term applied to male gametophytes, the reproductive organs of plants (Figure 9.6). Pollen is transmitted from the stamen of a plant to the stigma of a plant of the same species. There the pollen lodges and grows a tube, which eventually introduces sperm into the ovules (immature seeds) of the plant. Of particular importance to archaeologists are the facts that (1) the pollen of each genera of plants is unique in its size, shape, and surface features; (2) pollen is very durable and can be preserved for thousands of years; and (3) pollen is produced in great amounts and typically finds its way into archaeological deposits.

Pollen is moved through the environment in several ways, depending on the nature of the plant producing the material. Pine trees and other evergreens distribute their pollen by wind. As a result, pollen from a single plant may be transported miles, even hundreds of miles, away from its point of

pollen The common term applied to male gametophytes, the reproductive organs of plants.

BOX 9.2

MAGIC IN MOTION? THE PARACAS TEXTILES

The southern coast of Peru is one of the driest places on earth. It is not an exaggeration to state that rain is a special event in this region because it falls infrequently and rarely in quantities that do more than minimally dampen the ground. The moist, warm air from the Pacific Ocean rises rapidly, forming clouds that roll up the west slope of the Andes. There, as the air cools, rain falls in the highlands and is channeled back to the coast in rivers that traverse deeply cut valleys. These rivers provide the vital freshwater that allows humans to form permanent settlements and to irrigate the fertile but dry soils adjacent to the rivers.

It was here, between approximately 600 and 150 B.C., that the settlement now known as Paracas thrived. People moved to this growing town to take advantage of the rich marine resources of the Pacific Ocean and enjoy the benefits of a permanent flow of freshwater. The combination of crop production in the form of modest agriculture with fishing in the cold, oxygen-rich waters of the Humboldt Current was instrumental in the formation of this and other west coast settlements. The process has been described by Michael Moseley and named the "maritime foundations hypothesis." According to this view settlements could support larger populations than would normally be possible because of the rich and predictable resources provided by the Humboldt Current. Consequently, craft specialization could be supported, and society could grow increasingly more complex.

Excavations at Paracas have supported this hypothesis. The dry climate has preserved a special class of data that is usually inaccessible to archaeologists but that was undoubtedly important, especially in pre-Hispanic South America. That information is in the form of textiles—elaborately woven and brightly colored shawls, ponchos, and a host of other items. Human remains are also well preserved, so that archaeologists can begin to examine the connection between human populations and textiles. Across the western coast of South America and into the highlands, textiles do more than provide a convenient canvas for weavers to express themselves. Specific areas, even specific towns,

have distinct styles that can be seen archaeologically. It seems that at Paracas people paid their taxes or made offerings to a central authority in the form of textiles. This may reflect the same sort of system that was in place on the northern coast of Peru in the Moche Valley, only slightly later in time.

In addition to being symbols of social identity, the Paracas textiles are filled with colorful depictions of the spirit world. A common theme in the weavings centers around a figure called the Ecstatic Shaman. A shaman serves as an intermediary between humans and the spirit world, often for the purposes of diagnosing illness and effecting cures. The image of the Ecstatic Shaman depicts a human with his eyes wide open, his hair tumbled, his limbs thrown back, and his mouth

A woven owl. The owl is sometimes associated with warfare in coastal South Africa.

A depiction of what some have termed "the ecstatic shaman" from Paracas.

in a grimace or toothy grin. Such effects are parallel to those known in depictions of other trance states, including those associated with hallucinogenic substances. Mescaline derivatives and similar substances, ranging from peyote to more exotic substances known in South America as the "Tail of the Jaguar" and the "Rope of the Corpse," have effects similar to those depicted in the imagery. Mescaline derivatives, for example, cause the user to purge himself and to be unable to focus his eyes clearly, often resulting in seeing images in a rainbow of patterns. Muscle stiffness, especially of the neck and back, as well as of the face, are also reported for some hallucinogens. The San Pedro cactus, which is associated with mescaline, is still used in sacraments by modern shamans. Hence the textiles of Paracas may reflect both social ideas (functioning on Binford's sociotechnic level) and religious and ideological ideas (functioning on Binford's ideotechnic level).

Examples of magnified
pollen grains from several
common species of plants.
Note the distinctive shapes
that palynologists look for
when working with such
material.

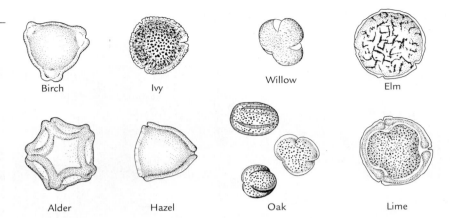

Birch   Ivy   Willow   Elm

Alder   Hazel   Oak   Lime

origin on prevailing winds. Other plants, including many flowers, spread their
pollen on the feet and bodies of insects, such as bees. Because such insects
tend to have restricted ranges, their distribution of pollen is localized.

Pollen is best preserved in bogs or the sediments of similar wet environments, though it is also well preserved in mildly acidic soils not subject to heavy
erosion or abrasion. In wetland deposits, archaeologists and palynologists
(people who study pollen) typically use augers to recover sediment samples
from the muck at the bottom of standing bodies of water. Such deposits are
ideal for sampling because the pollen sinks to the bottom and is quickly buried
by sediments also moved into the wet environment. This process limits the
opportunity for pollen from later years to mix with more ancient pollens and
to potentially skew the distribution of plant species found in the sample. In
more open environments and on archaeological sites, pollen is retrieved by
the systematic recovery of soil samples (see Chapter 4). In all cases, however,
it is important for archaeologists to sample both their sites and the surrounding environment for pollen. This sampling establishes a pattern of naturally
occurring pollen and provides a baseline for interpreting pollen samples from
archaeological deposits (Figure 9.7).

Once an archaeologist has retrieved a soil sample from the field, usually
by removing sediments from one or more of the profile walls and being sure
to exclude the surface exposed during excavations, the sample is transported
to a laboratory specializing in **palynology** (the study of pollens). There, a
tiny sample will be prepared on slides and examined under a microscope.
Using a series of counters, a palynologist systematically examines each grain
of pollen on the slide and records its presence. Because of the similarity in
related forms, in most cases it is possible to identify only the genera of the
pollen grains rather than the species. Experimentation with scanning electron microscopy, however, has produced promising results, though such

palynology The systematic
study of pollen, often useful in reconstructing past
environments.

FIGURE 9.7

Workers extract a pollen core from a swamp at Burrell Boom, Belize.

work is typically more time-consuming and costly than analyses using optical microscopes.

Once a series of samples from the soils has been examined, the counts of the different sorts of pollens are tabulated and plotted on a graph (Figure 9.8). Along the bottom axis are listed the various types of pollen identified, and on the dependent axis (the vertical axis) are listed the dates corresponding to the strata from which the samples were taken. The relative percentage of each species is then plotted through time. In this way archaeologists can view at a glance the comparative proportions of each type of plant identified from a site at any particular point in time. The distribution of these plants can reveal a great deal about human activities, as well as the sorts of resources available to people in a given place and time.

The case of the Maya collapse in the valley of Copán, Honduras, is a useful example of the benefits of palynology. In this area the presence of naturally occurring hardwoods, which take a long time to mature, is associated with the reforestation of the region. This means that people were not present in sufficient numbers to clear large areas of forest for farming, the standard **subsistence strategy** (plan for getting food) for the Maya of this time. Until the 1980s the standard explanatory model for the collapse of the Maya state of Copán was that people had largely left the valley by about 900 A.D. because of endemic warfare, climatic change, plague, or other disastrous events. Pollen cores taken from bogs in the valley, however, revealed the presence of signifi-

subsistence strategy A general plan for obtaining food and vital resources. The four traditional strategies are hunting and gathering, horticulture, pastoralism, and agriculture.

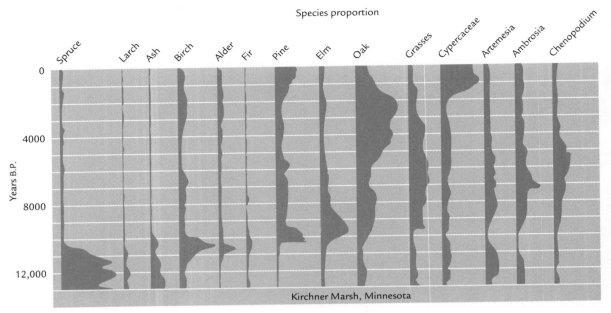

Species proportion

Kirchner Marsh, Minnesota

FIGURE 9.8

Frequency of pollen from the Tuskegee Pond, Alabama. The date ranges and corresponding archaeological periods appear on the left; the frequency of each type of pollen is displayed on the graph itself.

cant amounts of *Zea mays* (corn) in the samples until almost A.D. 1200. Only then did pollen from hardwoods begin to dominate the samples, indicating the demise of extensive farming in the region. In fact, archaeologists now have dismissed the idea of a rapid depopulation in the valley, instead arguing for a long period of decline as a result of the extensive cultivation of uplands during the height of the Copán kingdom. This practice resulted in extensive erosion, which eventually made large-scale cultivation in the valley untenable.

Phytoliths   **Phytoliths** are fragments of plant opal (silica). Silicates are very long lasting: Phytoliths have been recovered in sediments millions of years old, making these materials excellent markers that are of interest to both archaeologists and paleontologists. In a general sense, phytolith analysis is similar to palynology; both fields of study use plant remains to identify and study the distribution of past plant communities. Unlike pollen, however, plants that produce phytoliths (grasses, rushes, coniferous, and deciduous trees) sometimes produce multiple forms of phytoliths. When combined, palynology and phytolith analysis can produce useful and detailed results, providing a more complete view of past plant communities than either analysis would individually. The inclusion of macrobotanical remains further adds to the portrait of past environments.

Deborah Pearsall of the University of Missouri has used data from each of these forms of analysis to develop a chronology for the domestication of plants in South America. Phytoliths from the Vegas site near the west coast of Ecua-

phytoliths Fragments of plant opal (silica) derived from plant cells. Because they are silicates, they are very long lasting.

TABLE 9.2 Archaeological Remains of Cultivated Plants from Ecuador and Venezuela

Site	Cultivated Plant	First Appearance
Ecuador, coast		
Vegas (OGSE 80)	*Zea mays*	6000–4500 B.C.
Real Alto	*Canavalia plagiosperma* *Gossypium* spp. *Zea mays*	3300–1500 B.C.
	Canna spp.	2300–1500 B.C.
San Pablo	*Zea mays*	2000–1800 B.C.
Loma Alta	*Canavalia* spp. *Zea mays*	3000–2700 B.C.
San Isidro	*Zea mays* *Canavalia* spp. *Lagenaria siceraria*	1700–1500 B.C.
	Zea mays *Canavalia* spp.	500 B.C.–A.D. 1500
La Ponga	*Zea mays* *Canavalia* spp.	1200–800 B.C.
Rio Perdido	*Zea mays*	1200–800 B.C.
Vessel looted near Chacras site	*Zea mays*	ca. 800 B.C.
Ecuador, sierra		
Cerro Narrio	*Zea mays*	2000–1800 B.C.
Nueva Era	*Zea mays*	670–500 B.C.
Cotocollao	*Zea mays* *Phaseolus* spp.	1500–500 B.C.
Site 48, Quito	*Phaseolus vulgaris* *Zea mays*	150 B.C.
Ecuador, Amazon		
Ayauchi Lake core	*Zea mays*	3300 B.C.
Venezuela		
Parmana area, various sites	*Zea mays*	800 B.C.–A.D. 400
	Zea mays *Canavalia ensiformis* *Manihot esculenta*	A.D. 400–1500
El Tiestal	*Zea mays*	200 B.C.

Deborah Pearsall. 1992. The origins of plant cultivation in South America. In *The origins of agriculture*, ed. C. W. Cowan & P. V. Watson, pp. 173–205. Washington, D.C.: Smithsonian.

dor document the presence of *Zea mays* between 6000 and 4500 B.C., considerably earlier than previously thought. Combining this data with other lines of evidence, Pearsall presents a chronology for the development of plant cultivation in Ecuador and surrounding regions (Table 9.2).

ANIMALS

Animal material appears in three basic forms archaeologically: as bone, shell, and teeth; as hair; and most rarely as tissue. Given moderately good depositional environments, bone survives for substantial periods of time, as can hair. Nonetheless, chemical, physical, and biological agents take their toll on these materials, and they tend to eventually disappear from archaeological sites completely. Tissue, as you might imagine, degrades very quickly in most depositional environments, being preserved only in extremely arid (including frozen) and anaerobic waterlogged conditions. Perhaps ironically, it is the very rare finds of tissue samples that receive the most attention in the popular press and draw the most media attention even though most archaeologists work with less romanticized and more common faunal remains on a regular basis. Nonetheless, the entire range of material adds to the range of evidence archaeologists have to work with.

Nonhuman Bone

Humans and their immediate predecessors have been consuming parts of animals for millions of years. Primatologists have recorded meat-eating behavior among chimps as well, some populations of chimps regularly pursue, kill, and eat monkeys. Of course some animals also die of natural causes, sometimes in the middle or on top of archaeological remains. Rodents, for example, are frequently attracted to the food waste left by humans and spend portions of their lives in and around such deposits. They sometimes die in such places as well. The net result of such activities is a set of remains of animal tissue and bone that has the potential to be recovered by archaeologists (Figure 9.9).

The study of animal remains from archaeological sites is called **zooarchaeology,** sometimes also referred to as **faunal analysis.** Such research has a number of basic goals, including (1) the identification of the animal species present, (2) the quantification of the animal species present, and (3) the interpretation of how, or even if, the animals represented by the bones were used by humans at this site. Depending on the context of the excavations, a fourth goal can sometimes be added, that is, to identify how the remains of the animals were deposited at the site. These are branches of the area of study called **taphonomy,** which is the study of animal remains from the time a creature died to the time the remains were recovered by scientists. This is often an important area of study because it involves determining whether the remains were deposited on the site by natural forces, such as nonhuman predators or floodwaters, or left by humans. If the latter, taphonomy can help archaeologists to understand the methods used to acquire, transport, and process the animals (Figure 9.10).

In some respects zooarchaeologists operate like pathologists and forensic scientists. From the evidence left behind, they must identify what animals

zooarchaeology The scientific study of animal remains from archaeological sites.

faunal analysis Another term for zooarchaeology.

taphonomy The study of animal remains and what happened to them from the time they entered the archaeological record to the time they were recovered and analyzed.

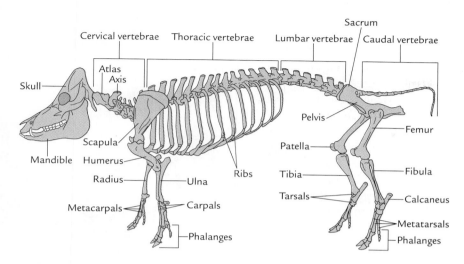

Skull

Mandible   Humerus

Cervical vertebrae   Thoracic vertebrae

Atlas
Axis

Scapula

Radius   Ulna

Metacarpals   Carpals

Phalanges

Sacrum

Lumbar vertebrae   Caudal vertebrae

Ribs

Pelvis

Patella

Femur

Tibia   Fibula

Tarsals   Calcaneus

Metatarsals

Phalanges

FIGURE 9.9

A lateral view of the skeleton of a pig. Note the different shape of the pelvis in the pig, a quadruped, and in a human (Figure 9.11).

were at the site, what happened to these animals, and how people were using the animals. Usually, the first order of business for a zooarchaeologist is to sort through the faunal assemblage and identify each piece of bone as accurately as possible. The name of the bone, the species and side of the animal it comes from, the age of the animal, and even the sex and health of the animal all need to be assessed. Likewise, any pathologies on the bone must be noted, including evidence of trauma, butchering, and burning. The tabulation of all remains from the sites and the organization of this data into a database enables archaeologists to work through large amounts of data and identify patterns of human and animal activity.

Researchers can turn to a variety of resources for data. Chief among these resources are **comparative collections.** These are assemblages of bones of known animals, including all the pertinent age, sex, and health data, that the researcher can compare with the archaeologically recovered samples. Comparative collections often include multiple examples of different sorts of animals so that zooarchaeologists can better account for the sometimes subtle but ever present genetic variations that exist among all living creatures. Although the overall form of an animal does not vary much from one population to another, specific shapes of foramena (holes in bone for nerves and blood vessels) and similar features do vary. Comparative collections tend to be ever growing and, consequently, can be both expensive and difficult to curate as new material is added. Nonetheless, there really is no substitute for such a collection.

In the field, though, or in the absence of a good comparative collection, field manuals with drawings and data on different animal bones can be very helpful. Although these books cannot provide the same level of comparative data as real bones, they can still be useful in helping to sort and identify bones.

comparative collections
Collections of identified bones used for comparison with archaeologically recovered remains.

FIGURE 9.10

A schematic illustration of taphonomic processes.

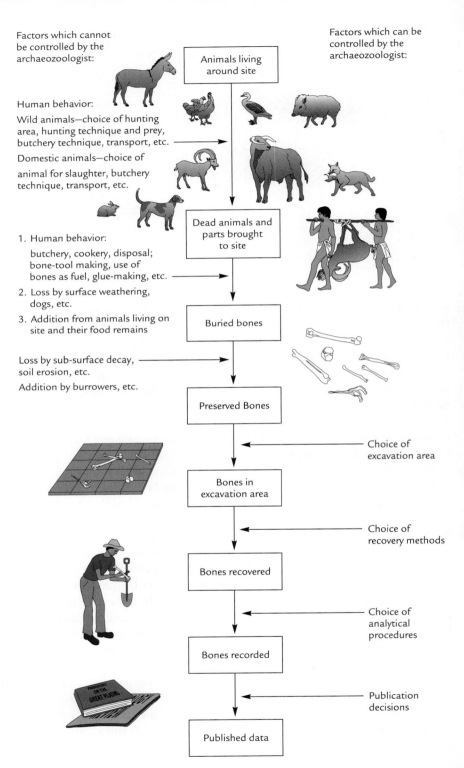

Factors which cannot be controlled by the archaeozoologist:

Human behavior:

Wild animals—choice of hunting area, hunting technique and prey, butchery technique, transport, etc.

Domestic animals—choice of animal for slaughter, butchery technique, transport, etc.

1. Human behavior:
   butchery, cookery, disposal; bone-tool making, use of bones as fuel, glue-making, etc.

2. Loss by surface weathering, dogs, etc.

3. Addition from animals living on site and their food remains

Loss by sub-surface decay, soil erosion, etc.

Addition by burrowers, etc.

Factors which can be controlled by the archaeozoologist:

Animals living around site

Dead animals and parts brought to site

Buried bones

Preserved Bones

Bones in excavation area

Bones recovered

Bones recorded

Published data

Choice of excavation area

Choice of recovery methods

Choice of analytical procedures

Publication decisions

They are also much less expensive to acquire and maintain, thus making them a good alternative in situations in which space and funds are an issue.

Some branches of zooarchaeology focus on the pattern of cell growth in different animals to help identify them. Called **histology,** this research identifies the patterns of development and cell growth in different bones in a variety of species by taking thin sections of the bones and magnifying them. This method can be very specific, and it is often more specific than macroscopic identification of bones from closely related species, such as sheep and goats. Histology, however, is limited in that the researcher needs a large catalog of histological thin sections, and, even with these, little can be determined about the use and processing of the animals by humans.

Once archaeologists identify and count the remains present on a site, they need to determine how many animals may be represented in the assemblage. Perhaps the most common way to do this is to calculate the **minimum number of individuals,** or **MNI,** in the assemblage. To do this, researchers select a single bone from a single species that occurs with great frequency in the assemblage. Often this bone is large, dense, and easily identified, such as a femur or humerus. Because such bones occur in pairs, though, the zooarchaeologist needs to be able to sort them by the side of the body from which they come. Likewise, the researcher must be aware that bones might be broken, so she may only count a specific part of the bone that is unlikely to break, such as the proximal or distal ends of the bone. Hence, a researcher may elect to count all the left femurs in the assemblage, using either the proximal or distal end to make sure that the bone is not counted twice. When all of the bones have been counted, the zooarchaeologist can state that at least as many animals from the species under study are represented at the site as there are left femurs in the assemblage. If there are twenty-five left femurs from white-tailed deer, then at least twenty-five deer are represented in the assemblage.

This method tends to underestimate the total number of individuals represented in the assemblage because it is possible, perhaps even likely, that one or more of the *index elements* (the sections of bone being used to calculate MNI) is missing. As a double-check and to help offset this underestimate, the researcher might calculate the MNI for a species using several different bones and then compare the tabulations. For example, if there are twenty-five left femurs and thirty right humeri, then there are at least thirty animals.

Another common method of calculating the number of animals on a site is to use the **number of identified specimens,** or **NISP,** as a measure. This method is somewhat easier to calculate than MNI because the researcher needs only to calculate the number of total bones of a given sort from a single species present in the assemblage. This measure simply gives a list of bones and animal species recovered, something basic to archaeological study, and does little to help archaeologists understand the different ways the animals may have been exploited. However, NISP can be calculated and then divided by the number of bones of that sort that naturally occur in animals of that species, thus calculating MNI in a different way. For example, instead of counting just

histology The scientific study of the formation and distribution of cells in animal bones.

minimum number of individuals (MNI) Minimum number of individual animals present at a specific location as calculated in zooarchaeology.

number of identified specimens (NISP) Number of specimens of bone from a single species as identified in zooarchaeology.

left femurs of deer, the researcher counts all femurs and then divides the total by two, the number of femurs present in each deer. This method is faster but sometimes tends to overestimate the number of individuals present on a site because it does not take into account broken bones being counted twice. Careful identification and database management, however, can help mitigate this problem, though like MNI, NISP yields only an estimate of the number of animals of any given species present in the assemblage.

Calculations of this sort are useful because they provide archaeologists with a rough idea of how much food was being brought to a given site. In turn, archaeologists can use estimates of how much usable meat is available from modern forms of each kind of animal to estimate how much energy is represented by animals of those sorts in the archaeological assemblage. Then, turning to estimates from ethnographically known peoples, archaeologists can estimate how many calories an average person who lived primarily by hunting and gathering needed to eat to stay alive. This number and the estimate of calories from the faunal remains can be compared in order to calculate the number of person-days of food represented by the meat assumed to be associated with the faunal assemblage. Thus, if enough calories are calculated to be present to feed 150 people for one day, the archaeologists can state that there were 150 person-days of food available from the faunal assemblage. What the researcher cannot identify this way, but may be able to through careful excavation of living areas, is how many people lived on the site at any one time. The total person-days of energy could feed seventy-five people for two days, fifty people for three days, fifteen people for ten days, and so on. This sort of analysis provides only an approximation of numbers of calories and people and more specific estimates of populations and diet must be supported by further analyses.

These estimates also only account for calories obtained from average, adult animals and do not take into account variation in animal size, health, or the completeness of the animals in the sample. Scavenged animals, for example, provide fewer calories than do whole animals. Fortunately, patterns of bone distribution often provide good clues as to whether an animal was scavenged or not, as do animal gnaw marks (see the Original Essay by Marie M. Selvaggio, following this chapter). It is difficult to identify, however, how much meat was left on the bones after other animals got to the carcass. Another issue of concern is that the calculation of calories from animal sources ignores food sources not represented in the faunal assemblage. Plant foods and even animals killed and eaten off-site are not accounted for in this method, although ethnographic sources can help archaeologists estimate the amount of plant foods eaten compared with the amount of animal foods eaten. Even though human behavior and available resources vary through time and space, archaeologists are at least able to begin to estimate the amount of energy available to past humans at a given point in time and location on the landscape.

Human Remains

Issues Archaeology and physical anthropology overlap most strongly when human remains are encountered. Humans, like all creatures, die, and sometimes their remains find their ways into the archaeological record. In many cases human remains are found in the context of important human activities and often reflect powerful and intangible factors of human culture, such as spirituality and kinship. The analysis of human remains, the materials that sometimes accompany these remains, and the distribution of the remains and associated material culture are among the most powerful ways archaeologists have of identifying and interpreting high-order cultural beliefs. On a biological level, the study of human remains is often the only way for archaeologists to explore the health and population demographics of past peoples.

Such research is not without controversy. Although the scientific importance of human remains and burials is undeniable, archaeologists must also be aware of the social systems in which they themselves operate. Some living cultures find the excavation and analysis of human remains offensive, indeed, sometimes repugnant. The dead may be believed to be spiritually charged and to be avoided or believed to be the remains of honored ancestors and to be left alone. This situation is exacerbated when the remains in question are believed to be related, even in unspecified ways, to living peoples. In these cases issues of political activism, human rights, and legal maneuvering can also arise. Added to this is the notion among some groups of people that archaeologists represent the very political establishment (the United States federal government, for example) that is responsible for conquests, wars, and sometimes unspeakable acts of cruelty to indigenous peoples. The resulting political and social tensions can create situations in which archaeologists find themselves torn between their work as scientists, their support of and friendships with specific indigenous peoples, and current political legislation. Such issues are particular volatile in North America, Australia, New Zealand, Tasmania, and Israel. Such issues tend to be largely nonexistent in parts of the world, such as Europe and Asia, where colonial histories are more distant or absent.

In the United States, the federally mandated **Native American Graves Protection and Repatriation Act (NAGPRA),** as well as parallel state and local legislation, seeks to apply order to this sometimes chaotic situation. NAGPRA, which became law in 1990 (see also Chapter 10), requires all archaeological collections to be assessed for human remains associated with federally recognized Native American tribes, and for these remains to be repatriated to the appropriate tribes on request. Items of cultural patrimony, those clearly associated with known Native American tribes, are also to be identified and returned. The intended purpose of this law is to ensure respect for Native American remains and to return them for reburial.

Native American Graves Protection and Repatriation Act (NAGPRA) Enacted in 1990, this law requires federal agencies and repositories for federal archaeological material to identify and, if possible, repatriate human remains and items of cultural patrimony to appropriate Native American groups.

Unfortunately, the legislation has had unforeseen, sometimes negative, results. Scientific researchers have systematically been deprived of opportunities to undertake meaningful and significant research on human diversity, as well as on issues of paleopathology and disease: the reburial of the human remains effectively eliminates the data that support some research. So there is a clear tension between the religion, opinions, and emotions of some Native Americans and the interests, opinions, and emotions of some segments of the scientific community.

On an unforeseen front, however, NAGPRA and parallel legislation have also polarized some segments of both the Native American community and the scientific community. For example, some tribes have been criticized by others for being too passive in asserting claims to human remains that may be associated with their heritage. An answer to this charge has come from some tribes, such as the Dené (Navajo), who have made it clear that they feel strongly about the spiritual importance of the dead and are equally concerned not to repatriate any remains that are not their own. Other tribes have been criticized for trying to repatriate too many remains, of laying claim to everybody and anybody's ancestors. Such charges have created potentially bitter relations between some Native American groups. Scientists have been similarly polarized in some arenas, as careers and avenues of research into human remains have come under increasing stress as a result of NAGPRA and parallel legislation.

Despite this, Native Americans and researchers both acknowledge that such legislation has many benefits. These laws ensure a measure of protection and respect for the remains of people who have largely been treated as study subjects by science for centuries. The legislation has forced scientists and Native Americans to work together to meet the needs and interests of both groups. In many cases the interests of both groups have been met, and both groups have received useful and valuable insights into the other group's work. Only time will tell what the legacy of this sort of legislation will ultimately be. For now, however, it seems that both scientists and indigenous peoples are just reaching the point at which real cooperation and collaboration can begin.

Material and Studies   Perhaps ironically, the subject at the center of the debates between research and respect is material that is present in every human being. Yet, because humankind is genetically and culturally diverse, and because this diversity exists through space and time, the value in such studies is associated with understanding human diversity across long spans of both space and time. The study of human remains and their distribution has the potential to provide archaeologists and physical anthropologists with essential information about past populations, including information on diet, genetic diversity, kinship, marriage patterns, health, life spans, violent conflicts, and, sometimes, spirituality and social beliefs (Figure 9.11).

The most common sorts of human remains encountered by archaeologists are the larger, more dense portions of the skeleton. Bones and teeth tend to be

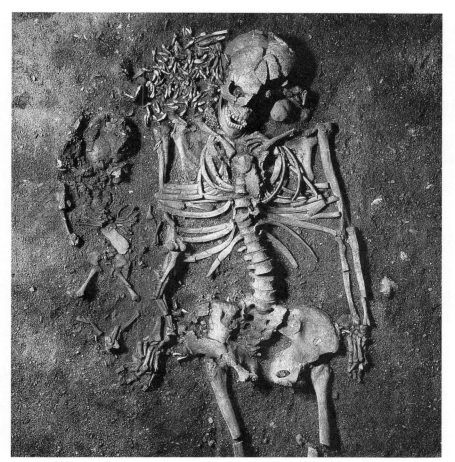

FIGURE 9.11

The 7000-year-old remains of a mother and her infant, from the Mesolithic site of Vedbaek, Denmark. Not only do the remains provide archaeologists with important information including nutrition and pathology, but they also provide poignant insights into past worlds. Here the infant has been laid to rest next to its mother on the wing of a swan and is accompanied by a flint knife. The presence of the knife, typically associated with males, suggests that the child was likely a boy.

harder and more dense than soft tissue and are therefore more resistant to decay and erosion. Nonetheless, these materials do decay and, if not fossilized, will eventually disappear completely from the archaeological record. In some cases, such as in arid areas not subject to human or animal disturbance, this may take millennia, whereas in more temperate climates and in soil systems that are basic or acidic, even bones and teeth may disappear in decades (Figure 9.12).

Both bones and teeth are readily used to study **paleopathology,** that is, the study of abnormal physiological conditions in the remains of past peoples. Human pathological conditions can range from genetic to varying effects of nutrition or physical wear on the body. Genetic conditions such as spina bifida have been encountered archaeologically. In one form of spina bifida, the bone of the spinal column does not completely close, thus exposing the spinal column to stress and degeneration. The condition becomes clear early in life and may render victims unable to take care of themselves (Figure 9.13).

paleopathology The study of trauma or abnormal conditions in animal remains, usually human.

FIGURE 9.12

A generalized view of the human skeleton. Note the broad, basin-shaped pelvis, which has evolved to support the weight of the torso.

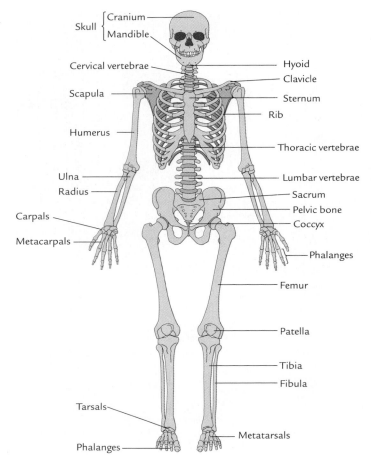

At the Windover site in Florida, advancing construction encroached on a seven-thousand-year-old burial site. The site is archaeologically important because the people who buried their dead there did so by wrapping the remains in fabric and then pinning these remains under the surface of a shallow lake. The water concealed the remains from scavengers and proved to be an excellent matrix for preserving the human remains. In this context, archaeologists were able to identify a teenager who had suffered from spina bifida but who had been nursed through a longer, more painful, life than the condition would normally allow. Other remains were also well preserved, one skull even containing a partial human brain. Taken together, the human remains from this site painted a surprising portrait of good health and long lives, with some individuals living into their seventies. This sort of evidence is important because it contradicts the popular picture that all premodern humans lived short,

FIGURE 9.13

An example of *spina bifida occulta* in a human sacrum. Note the opening in the posterior area of the sacrum.

brutal, and often painful lives. Although some did, others clearly did not. It falls to archaeologists to explain why some populations suffered and others did not. Such sorts of studies are sometimes called **paleodemographics.**

Trauma is another area of interest to paleopathologists. Trauma reflects the damage done to humans through such activities as work, repetitive motion, and injuries. Archaeologists and physical anthropologists studying the remains of the Early Kingdom Egyptians who built the pyramids have provided outstanding insights into the effects of such hard, physical labor on humans. They discovered that substantial towns grew around pyramid construction sites, especially around the Sphinx. Here, laborers, artisans, and administrators tended to the details of constructing the largest structures ever seen on earth in the ancient world. Although slaves may have been present, it seems that much of the work was accomplished by peasant laborers who spent substantial portions of their lives working in the quarries and assembling the gigantic stone edifices. When these people died they were buried in and around these towns, and archaeologists have recovered substantial numbers of their bodies. Many reflect extreme forms of osteoarthritis in the major limb joints and in the spine, the result of regular stress caused by lifting and moving heavy loads.

Excavations in and around the shell mounds lining the Green River in Kentucky reveal another set of pathologies. Here, William Webb excavated Indian Knoll, as well as a large series of shell middens dating to about forty-five hundred years ago. In these middens he found a large number of human burials: Indian Knoll yielded the remains of approximately one thousand individuals.

paleodemographics The study of the distribution of past humans across the landscape. This work is usually closely intertwined with the analysis of human biological remains.

The rear of a human skull from the Anglo-Saxon period in the United Kingdom showing blunt force trauma, likely from an edged weapon. Such evidence, while often grisly, is important in the reconstruction of past human societies and events.

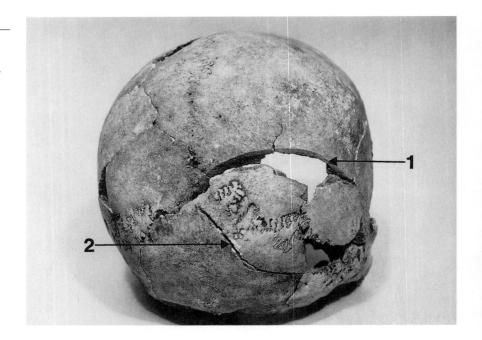

Of special significance, though, was the number of individuals with broken bones in their left forearms. The radius, and sometimes the ulna, was broken by a sharp blow that apparently first struck the inside of the arm (the side on which the little finger is located). Such breaks are known as parry fractures and are the result of the application of large amounts of blunt force. Although such fractures can result from falls and accidents, they are also caused by blows directed toward the victim's head that are blocked by the victim's raised arm. The large number of both healed and unhealed fractures—the unhealed ones suggesting that the victim died shortly after the injury occurred—suggested to Webb that violence may have been endemic in the societies along the Green River and that it was a function of increasing population levels. This, he suggested, was indeed the case, because 23% of people buried at Indian Knoll had projectile points embedded in their bodies, suggesting intergroup conflict. According to this model, as human populations grew, different groups staked claims to areas of rich resources, such as those along the rivers. Occasionally, groups would come into conflict over these resources, and this resulted in violence (Figure 9.14).

Nutritional stress is well represented on bones and teeth. Humans build new layers of material on both their bones and teeth as part of the regular growth process. When an individual receives adequate nutrition for normal growth, these layers appear as continuous growth, and the bones and teeth are strong and, in terms of the different areas of growth, essentially homogenous. During periods of an individual's life in which inadequate nutrition for normal growth is received, these growth patterns are interrupted. In long bones, for example, hard, dark lines, called Harris lines, are deposited. These mark a period during which bone either was not properly deposited or was, in fact, reabsorbed as the body sought to compensate for the lack of nutrition. The appearance of such lines can help paleopathologists document the life history of an individual or groups of individuals.

The presence of porous lesions in the skull can be a sign of iron deficiency anemia. In these cases, although an individual might be eating sufficient calories to sustain life, the person is not receiving enough food with essential minerals, especially iron. The lack of iron affects the efficiency of red blood cell production, as well as the health of bone. Archaeologists studying the decline of the Maya kingdom of Copán, in western Honduras, have documented the increasing presence of iron deficiency anemia in both elite and peasant classes beginning in the ninth century A.D. This was probably a function of the increasing environmental degradation of the valley and the difficulties associated with acquiring a diet sufficiently complete for sustaining life. Indeed, although some of the individuals identified as suffering from this form of anemia recovered, others died as a result of this and related conditions.

Beyond paleopathology, the distribution of human remains within a community often provides insight to archaeologists. Archaeologists working in the Upper Midwest region of the United States have identified three general archaeological traditions for the period between A.D. 300 and 1650: the Late Woodland, Oneota, and Mississippian traditions. People living in the Late Woodland tradition were primarily hunters and gatherers, although they also grew squash, beans, and some maize to supplement their diets. The people living in the Oneota tradition were also hunters and gatherers but relied more heavily on their gardens, and they seemed to produce greater quantities of maize (corn). People of the Mississippian tradition relied heavily on corn, supplemented with other crops and some hunting and gathering. The skeletal remains from these three populations are readily differentiated on the basis of stature, dental health, and bone pathology. People of the Late Woodland tradition are typically noticeably taller than people of the other two traditions, they have generally good dental health, and they show little evidence of interrupted growth. These conditions result from a more balanced diet than those found in the other two populations. This balanced diet resulted in less dietary stress and less wear on teeth. On the other extreme, all but the elite members of societies in the Mississippian tradition tend to be relatively short, have high incidences of dental caries (cavities and abscesses), and frequently show periods of extended nutritional stress. This pattern results from a heavy emphasis on maize culture, which limited the total range of nutrients consumed. Regular consumption of ground maize also results in a rapid destruction of dental enamel, which contributes to increased incidents of caries and abscesses (Figure 9.15). Falling in between these two profiles are the skeletal remains of people associated with the Oneota tradition.

FIGURE 9.15

Pathological attrition of the palate and maxillary (upper jaw) in a late Anglo-Saxon individual from the United Kingdom. This sort of information provides important clues about the health and genetic composition of past communities.

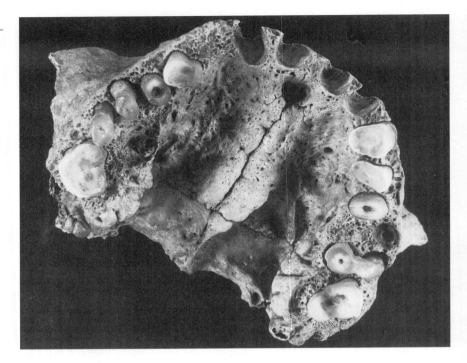

In rare instances archaeologists recover human remains with substantial portions of soft tissue intact. This usually occurs when the remains are recovered in an arid situation, including icebound conditions in which water freezes and therefore preserves the tissue rather than helping to facilitate its decomposition. More rarely, remains were naturally tanned or chemically preserved in bogs, though humans also preserved bodies artificially through mummification. Finds of these sorts have made headlines over the past several decades, with the late 1980s and 1990s witnessing astonishing discoveries of human remains in the Andes, in China's western provinces, and also in Egypt.

The best evidence of human tissue comes from the frozen remains of past peoples. Such remains preserve not only skeletal data, as discussed previously, but also DNA, internal parasites, hair color, and body decoration. For example, Otzi the Iceman has a series of tattoos on his back, ankles, and knees. The Pazyryk horsemen of Siberia, who lived about two thousand years ago, were also extensively tattooed. Sergei Rudenko, one of the Soviet archaeologists involved in the excavation of a series of Pazyryk burials, observed that both men and women were heavily tattooed, especially on their faces, arms, and hands (Figure 9.16). He suspects that such markings served to identify the individuals as important members of their social groups, probably elites. We cannot postulate the same for Otzi because we know little of the sociopolitical organization of the group he may have come from. What we do know of such groups, however, has led researchers to suggest that his tattoos served to

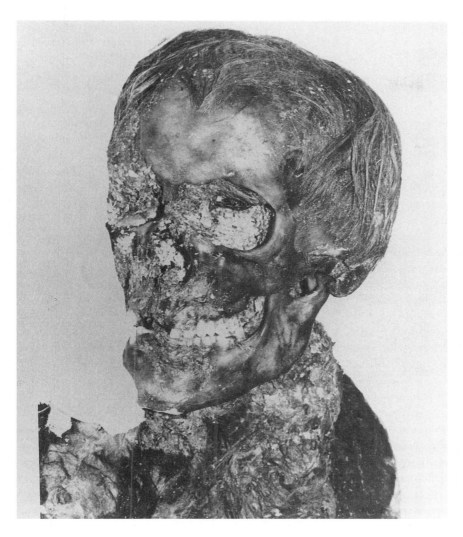

FIGURE 9.16

Sergei Rudenko's excavation of Pazyryk tombs in Siberia was among the first to produce frozen mummies from premodern populations. The individuals were preserved in blocks of ice beneath a layer of permafrost in southern Siberia.

mark him as a member of a cult or other social group and that, because they were not visible to others when he wore clothing, these tattoos did not serve as marks of his prestige.

Tattoos might be used to indicate lineages and kinship, as seems to be the case with the Greenland Inuit mummies. Eight individuals were buried in two separate graves at the rockshelter of Qilakitsoq around A.D. 1475. Two of the women, who (based on tissue analysis) may have been sisters, possessed identical facial tattoos, probably made by the same artist. A third woman, who (based on skeletal morphology and other analyses) appears to be unrelated to the others, possessed very different facial markings. It seems that she may have married into the group from a different region, as perhaps did the two sisters (Figure 9.17).

FIGURE 9.17

FIGURE 9.17

Distinctive and socially important tattoos on the face of a woman from the Qilakitsoq site. Similar tattoos on the faces of some of the women from Qilakitsoq suggest that they may have been related or members of the same social group.

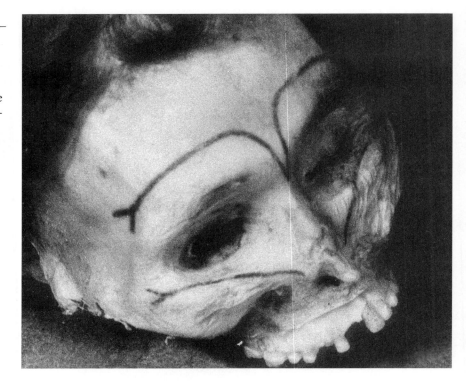

Besides social marking of the bodies, the remains from Qilakitsoq also provide archaeologists with information on the diet and health of the individuals. The women, for example, had high amounts of soot in their lungs, probably as a result of working in confined, poorly ventilated shelters around fires and lamps that burned oil rendered from seal blubber. The diet of these people, as one might expect, was high in marine resources; marine mammals and fish accounted for nearly three-fourths of the food identified by analyses of the skin collagen and digestive tracts of the individuals. The remaining one-fourth of the stomach contents identified in the individuals came from terrestrial resources, such as reindeer, arctic hare, and even some plants. This suggests that these people practiced more varied resource procurement strategies than some researchers had predicted and that they had technologies capable of efficiently extracting material resources from both earth and sea (Box 9.3).

Not all information about diet and health comes from human bodies. In particularly rare circumstances, human excrement may be preserved and, although it sounds offensive to many casual readers, the analysis of these remains can yield a wealth of information about human health and behavior. Excavations in the Anglo-Scandinavian levels in the English city of York have yielded such information: The potential for the analysis of fecal remains was

FIGURE 9.18

The "Lloyd's Bank turd" is a segment of human fecal material from the Lloyd's Bank site, York, United Kingdom. Although such remains are often the subject of much questionable humor, they also contain a tremendous amount of data about the diet and health of the person from which the material originated.

first observed at the Lloyd's Bank site by archaeologists excavating in advance of urban renewal projects in the city. Here researchers recovered "a single fusiform mass of organic debris, concreted by mineral deposition," more readily referred to as the "Lloyd's Bank turd." Indeed, the mass was preserved human feces and analysis of it helped to alert archaeologists to look for such remains (Figure 9.18). The material contained evidence of human diet, as well as the eggs of two particularly aggressive forms of parasites: whip worm and maw worm. It is likely that the worms caused some mild but chronic level of stomach upset similar to mild ulcers and perhaps bowel problems, such as diarrhea. This type of information has been taken into account in other archaeological reconstructions, such as that at the Jorvik Viking Center in York, where painstaking reconstruction at a level seldom equaled anywhere in the world has gone into displaying life as it was in Anglo-Scandinavian York (Figure 9.19). Part of the exhibit includes a tour past a manikin defecating inside an outhouse. The particular effect of the exhibit comes from the discomfort clearly portrayed on the man's face as a result of his intestinal conditions. Although this might seem trite, the detail with which scholars can recreate the fabric of life in such communities can sometimes be astonishing.

PUTTING IT ALL TOGETHER: ENVIRONMENTAL RECONSTRUCTION

These different, seemingly disparate lines of evidence come together when archaeologists ask questions about what past environments were like and how people interacted with these environments. By assembling the evidence of plants, animals, and people in a given place and time, archaeologists can begin to assemble a profile of both what resources were available to past people and how these people elected to extract and utilize such resources.

BOX 9.3

FOR THE SINS OF THE EMPEROR: INCAN SACRIFICES

Few people thought much of the first find. In 1954 miners searching for a fabled lost Inca treasure stumbled across the frozen remains of a young boy. No one thought much about his presence atop a frozen mountain, nor that he might represent something more than a wayward youth who paid with his life for his curiosity.

More than forty years later, though, archaeologists made a series of discoveries that brought a great deal of attention to the remains of this young boy and to the young woman (now called Sara Sara) who was found near the top of the frozen peak. She lay curled in a fetal position, wrapped in a shawl, atop a stone platform. She was approximately nine years old when she left this world for that of the spirits. With her were three gold and silver statuettes and a small bundle of cocoa. Two other sacrificial victims, a young male and another female, were found about 100 feet below Sara Sara on the platform. Archaeologists Johan Reinhard and Jose Antonio Perez specialized in exploring the use of high-altitude areas by past peoples, and to them these discoveries were not surprises but verification that the Inca viewed such summits as spiritually charged places, places at which sacrifices of the most sacred kind were to be made. Both the young woman, dubbed by some Sarita, and the young man discovered four decades before were sacrifices to the gods. Likely enough, so too were the young couple found below the summit and another young woman, about fourteen years old when she died, found on another peak, and dubbed the "Ice Maiden" by the media.

Reinhard has found other forms of offerings and sacrifices as well. The most common were of textiles, though sometimes animals, such as guinea pigs, and llamas, and precious statuary were also offered to the spirit world. Together they are called *capacochas*, or "royal sins." For the Inca the fortunes of all people were tied to that of the emperor, who was himself the offspring of the sun. Yet, despite his divine being, he was responsible for his wrongdoings, and the fate of his people depended on his making amends for any mis-

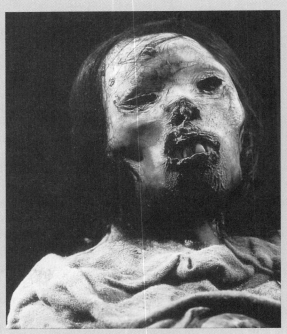

The face of an Incan child, apparently sacrificed in connection to the concept of *capacochos*.

One of the most common forms of environmental work involves studying the seasonal availability of resources and the human uses of those resources. Different archaeological situations require different approaches, so that researchers addressing the lifeways of hunters and gatherers inevitably must focus their attentions on different sorts of archaeological deposits than do re-

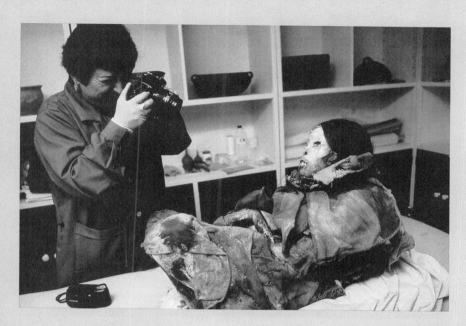

The bundled mummy of a young woman sacrificed in a high-altitude shrine.

deeds. Thus sacrifices were made to the mountains themselves, from the peaks of which water flowed each wet season to irrigate the Incan agricultural fields. In this system sacrifices were considered precious and, in the case of humans, pure. To be selected as a sacrifice was to be elevated to the gods themselves and to earn an eternal place in the spirit world. To the Inca, to sacrifice a person was to ensure them a measure of immortality and sacredness that few could ever dream of achieving.

It is in this context of the sacred that Reinhard and Perez offered wine over the grave of the young woman found atop Ampato. According to Inca belief, if something is taken from the mountain, something else should be given back; hence the offering in accordance with what were probably the young girl's own beliefs. Her body was then carefully transported to the Catholic University in Arequipa, where she will be closely studied. Her DNA may be compared with that of living populations, as well as with that of other sacrifices, in order to determine where sacrifices originated. A study of her health, diet, and other physical characteristics will help shed new light on the connections between the pre-Hispanic Inca, their environment, and their spiritual worlds.

searchers studying horticulturalists, pastoralists, or agriculturalists. Hunters and gatherers extract naturally occurring resources from the environment in systematic ways, whereas people employing the other three subsistence strategies control to a great extent the timing and placement of at least a portion of the resources they rely on. Consequently, it is often easier to get a good

Excavations by the York Archaeological Trust at 16-22 Coppergate, York, United Kingdom. The site, which has been reconstructed as part of the Jorvik Interpretive Center, yielded a great deal of information about daily life in Anglo-Scandinavian York during the tenth and eleventh centuries A.D.

human ecology The systematic study of the dynamic interrelationships between humans and their environments.

seasonal rounds The action of foragers who move from one environment to another following the seasonal availability of desired resources. The group tends to move through the same territories on an annual basis.

view of their subsistence activities and **human ecology** (the study of human-environment interactions) than it is to identify the same information for hunters and gatherers.

For example, Mount Sandal is an archaeological site adjacent to the river Bann in extreme northern Ireland. It is well known for its Iron Age earthen fortress but is also the location of what may prove to be one of Ireland's earliest year-round settlements. Peter Woodman of the University of Cork undertook a study of the Mesolithic component at Mount Sandal in the early 1970s. During this era, from about 7000 to 3500 B.C., people were thought to be predominantly mobile hunters and gatherers who occupied sites seasonally but never lived on them throughout the year. Such a subsistence strategy is often referred to as a **seasonal round.** The logic of this strategy seemed especially strong for sites on the often cold, windswept northern Irish coast.

Woodman's work, however, revealed the presence of a sequence of wild resources that would make habitation of the site feasible year-round. Because much of the material was recovered from Mount Sandal, it seemed as though people visited this site, if not lived on it, throughout the year. During the late spring, summer, and into the fall a variety of plant foods were available in the region. Hazelnuts, in particular, seemed to be a favorite food of the Mesolithic people during their season of peak availability in October. Also during this time, Atlantic salmon visited the region in large numbers and were easily

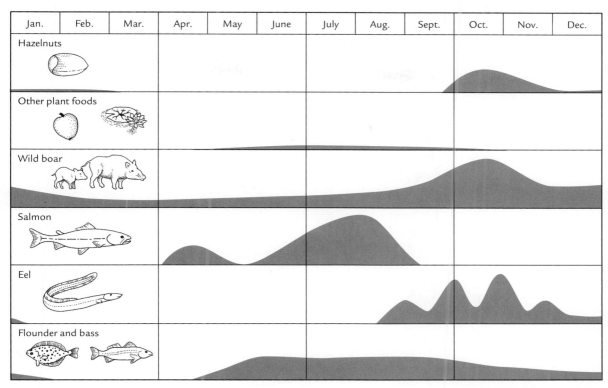

	Jan.	Feb.	Mar.	Apr.	May	June	July	Aug.	Sept.	Oct.	Nov.	Dec.
Hazelnuts												
Other plant foods												
Wild boar												
Salmon												
Eel												
Flounder and bass												

FIGURE 9.20

A table illustrating the seasonal resources available to the occupants of Mount Sandal, Ireland, during the Mesolithic. Note that there are resources available throughout the year even though the site is located near the extreme northern tip of Ireland.

acquired in the waters of the Bann. As the salmon run dwindled, eels either became increasingly available or were more frequently taken and processed on archaeological sites. Coupled with the near year-round availability of flounder, bass, and wild boar, a modest population of humans could indeed survive at Mount Sandal throughout the year. Whether they actually did so, however, remains unknown (Figure 9.20).

The fifth century A.D. Anglo-Saxon village at Bishopstone, overlooking the English Channel in southeastern England, represents a more complex subsistence system. The Anglo-Saxons grew grains, such as barley, and tended herd animals, such as sheep and cattle. They also fished in the nearby English Channel and hunted locally available red deer and wild boar. Archaeologists have recovered a wide range of resources in the waste pits and middens at Bishopstone and have been faced with the challenge of deciphering how all of these resources were integrated. By calculating the percentages of the different resources present in domestic waste deposits, such as middens, archaeologists have created a profile of the different resources available to the Anglo-Saxons. Analysis of other resources, such as clays for pottery, can also be added to this sort of analysis to develop a composite portrait of Anglo-Saxon human ecology (Figure 9.21).

FIGURE 9.21

A diagram of the range of resources used by the Anglo-Saxon community at Bishopstone, Sussex, United Kingdom. Note a small but important amount of the community's resources were acquired from the sea and associated estuaries.

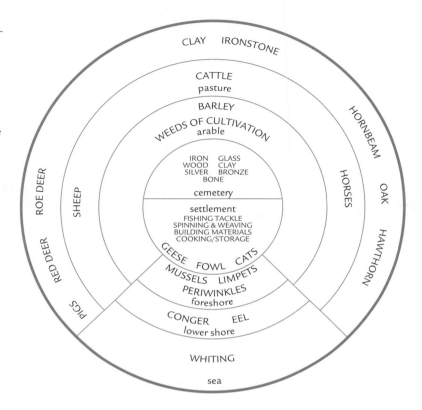

SUMMARY

Plant and animal remains provide important information to archaeologists interested in reconstructing the connections between people and their environments. Plant remains in a variety of forms, such as pollen, phytoliths, fibers, and fragments of plant tissue, help researchers identify the specific botanical communities in which past peoples lived and also help reconstruct the climate of the region. Changes in the profiles of plant remains through time are usually indicative of changing ecological conditions and therefore can be used to help identify different impetuses for changes in human behavior. Unsurprisingly, there is a general correlation between changes in ecological conditions and changes in material culture.

Animal remains, usually in the form of bones, provide similar information. Small mammals (voles, mice, and such) are especially sensitive indicators of local environmental and ecological conditions. Larger animal remains help archaeologists identify the preferred prey species of humans, as well as the ways in which humans acquired, processed, and utilized these animals. Research into the patterns of kills can help archaeologists understand both the structure of local animal populations and how humans exploited these structures for their own uses.

Human remains are particularly useful in understanding the health and life histories of past peoples. Pathologies of all sorts help archaeologists and physical anthropologists identify everything from marriage patterns to genetic affiliation. Yet, although this material is of vital importance to some scientific research, human remains are also at the center of controversy. Archaeologists and physical anthropologists are mandated both legally and ethically to treat human remains with respect and care. Sometimes situations develop that prevent research from taking place at all, though in most cases scientists are afforded the opportunity to conduct their work. Nonetheless, the rift between the interests of science and the interests of various indigenous groups are often in conflict, and negotiated compromise, sometimes mandated by law, is necessary.

Taken together, information from plants, nonhuman animals, and human remains can be used to develop detailed understandings of past human activities. Armed with such information, archaeologists are able to pursue other questions related to the ways in which humans interact with the environment and each other to construct complex societies and abstract ideologies. Hence, the study of the materials discussed here represents a range of research that is fundamental to interpreting past human behaviors. Without understanding how humans fit into their physical environments, there is little that can be learned about how past peoples constructed and manipulated their societies within those environments.

FOR FURTHER INFORMATION

Adovasio, J. M. 1977. *Basketry technology: A guide to identification and analysis.* Chicago: Aldine.

Barber, E. J. W. 1999. *The mummies of Urumchi.* New York: W. W. Norton.

Brothwell, D. R. 1981. *Digging up bones,* 3d ed. Ithaca, N.Y.: Cornell University Press.

Bryant, V. M., Jr., and R. G. Holloway. 1983. The role of palynology in archaeology. In *Advances in archaeological method and theory,* Vol. 6, edited by M. B. Schiffer, 191–224. New York: Academic Press.

Claasen, C. P. 1991. Gender, shellfishing, and the Shell Mound archaic. In *Engendering archaeology: Women and prehistory,* edited by J. M. Gero and M. W. Conkey, 276–300. Oxford: Blackwell.

————. 1998. *Shells.* Cambridge: Cambridge University Press.

Crabtree, P. J. 1990. Zooarchaeology and complex society: Some uses of faunal analysis for the study of trade, social status, and ethnicity. In *Advances in archeological method and theory,* Vol. 2, edited by M. B. Schiffer, pp. 155–205. Tucson: University of Arizona Press.

Crowfoot, E., F. Pritchard, and K. Staniland. 1996. *Medieval finds from excavations in London: Textiles and clothing.* London: Museum of London.

Davis, S. J. M. 1987. *The archaeology of animals.* New Haven, Conn.: Yale University Press.

Dimbleby, G. W. 1967. *Plants and archaeology.* London: John Baker.

———. 1985. *The palynology of archaeological aites.* Orlando, Fla.: Academic Press.

Flenley, J. R., and S. M. King. 1984. Late Quaternary pollen records from Easter Island. *Nature* 307: 47–50.

Gilbert, B. M. 1973. *Mammalian osteoarchaeology.* Missouri Archaeological Society Special Publications. Columbia: Missouri Archaeological Society.

Gilbert, R. I., Jr., and J. H. Mielke, eds. 1985. *The analysis of prehistoric diets.* Orlando, Fla.: Academic Press.

———. 1984. *Quantitative zooarchaeology: Topics in the analysis of archaeological faunas.* New York: Academic Press.

Hart Hansen, J. P., and H. C. Gullov. 1989. *The mummies from Qilakitsoq: Eskimos from the 15th century.* Copenhagen: Commission for Scientific Research in Greenland.

Hart Hansen, J. P., J. Melgaard, J. Nordqvist. 1991. *The Greenland mummies.* Washington D.C.: Smithsonian Institution.

Horne, P. D. 1985. A review of the evidence of human endoparasitism in the pre-Columbian New World through the study of coprolites. *Journal of Archaeological Science* 12: 299–310.

Issac, G. L. 1983. Bones in contention: Competing explanations for the juxtaposition of early Pleistocene artifacts and faunal remains. In *Animals and archaeology: Vol. 1. Hunters and their prey,* edited by J. Clutton-Brock and C. Grigson, pp. 3–19. British Archaeological Reports International Series 163. Oxford: British Archaeological Reports.

Klein, R. G., and K. Cruz-Uribe. 1984. *The analysis of animal bones from archaeological sites.* Chicago: University of Chicago Press.

Lyman, R. L. 1982. Archaeofaunas and subsistence studies. In *Advances in archaeological method and theory,* Vol. 5, edited by M. B. Schiffer, pp. 331–93. New York: Academic Press.

———. 1994. *Vertebrate taphonomy.* Cambridge: Cambridge University Press.

Mallory, J. P. 2000. *The Arim mummies: Ancient China and the mystery of the earliest people from the west.* New York: Thames & Hudson.

Reinhard, K. 2000. Archaeoparasitology. In *Archaeological method and theory: An encyclopedia,* ed L. Ellis, pp. 52–60. New York: Garland.

———. 2000. Coprolite analysis. In *Archaeological method and theory: An encyclopedia,* ed L. Ellis, pp. 124–32. New York: Garland.

Reitz, E. J., and E. S. Wing. 1999. *Zooarchaeology.* Cambridge: Cambridge University Press.

Rudenko, S. I. 1953. *Kul'tura Naseleniia Gornogo Altaia v Skifskie Vremia.* Moscow: Akademii Nauk (translations available).

Stirland, A. 1999. *Human bones in archaeology,* 2nd ed. Princes Risborough, England: Shire Archaeology.

———. 2000. *Raising the dead: The skeleton crew of Henry VIII's great ship, the Mary Rose.* New York: John Wiley.

PURSUING THE PAST WITH MIDDLE RANGE THEORY

Marie M. Selvaggio

Marie M. Selvaggio (Ph.D., Rutgers University) is Associate Professor of Anthropology and currently chair of the department at Southern Connecticut State University. She works in Africa and analyzes faunal remains.

As a child I was captivated by anything ancient. I fantasized that someday I would follow in the footsteps of Mary Leakey and make a discovery of a very early human. Instead, I married my childhood sweetheart and had three wonderful children. But my desire to learn about the past never completely disappeared. I returned to college when the youngest of my children was four years old. Although I knew it would not be easy, I decided to pursue my childhood dream and become an archaeologist. My husband and children supported my decision. They pitched in with extra chores around the house and cheered me on as I grappled with subjects I had not thought about in years.

When I made my decision, I did not realize that I was one of thousands of women who were returning to college to pursue their dreams, change careers, or just learn more about a particular subject. Many of us had grown up in the 1960s, a decade in which nonconformity was celebrated. As nontraditional students, we challenged traditional ideas and fostered changes in the conventional academic environment. It is no accident that the establishment of Women's Studies Programs, day care centers, and human diversity courses accompanied the increase in college enrollments of nontraditional students. As part of this group, I was intrigued by new methodologies that could provide a way to test ideas about the past.

The textbooks I read during my undergraduate years stressed that the hunting way of life was the basis of human behavior. Hunting appeared to offer a complete explanation for the development of bipedalism, language, brain expansion, tool use, and modern gender roles. By the time I became a graduate student, some theorists were stating that the stone tools found at early archaeological sites were not weapons but butchery tools. They argued that the tools and bones indicated that hominids scavenged the remains of abandoned carnivore kills. I found their arguments for scavenging compelling. I decided that in my dissertation research project I would use middle range theory to model faunal assemblages scavenged from abandoned carnivore kills.

In middle range theory, the causal relationship between the agencies that formed the archaeological record and the traces that remain are understood through the study of living systems in which both the dynamics and the results can be observed. The methods of this theory are based on two of Lyell's principles of geologic uniformity: (1) natural laws are constant in space and time, and (2) processes that are in operation now were operating in the past. With respect to living East African carnivores, my assumption was that their hunting and feeding behavior was similar to that of their ancestors who inhabited East Africa 2 million years ago. This supposition is justified because of the similarities in the skeleton and dentition of modern carnivores and their ancient ancestors.

I hypothesized that one of the key differences between bones from carcasses hunted by ancient hominids and those scavenged by them would be the frequency and anatomical patterning of carnivore tooth marks. This hypothesis was based on my observations of captive East African carnivores.

Captive animals often chew bones longer than their free-ranging relatives out of boredom. This increases the number of tooth marks on bones and the extent of bone damage. Therefore, I knew that I needed to study free-ranging carnivores to have an accurate picture of the carnivore contribution to an archaeological assemblage.

Based on my observations of captive carnivores, I decided to focus my research on one body part of prey animals, limb bones. The feeding behavior of free-ranging carnivores should differ from that of their well-fed, yet rather bored, captive relatives.

I inferred that limb bones from carcasses defleshed by free-ranging carnivores should exhibit a very high frequency of tooth marks because the carnivores would con-

FIGURE 1

Marie Selvaggio surveys the Serengeti for free-ranging carnivores.

Inferred Distribution of Carnivore Tooth Marks	
Scavenged carcasses	Tooth marks present on all areas of flesh-bearing limb bones (ends and shafts).
Hunted carcasses	Tooth marks present primarily on areas of limb bones that contained a source of nutrition (ends).

sume flesh from all areas of the bones, and sometimes they would disarticulate them from the carcass. In contrast, when hyenas found bones discarded from carcasses that hominids had hunted, a different distribution of tooth marks should be evident. With flesh and marrow removed from limb bones through butchery, only grease would be left as a source of nutrition in the fragmented bone ends (epiphyses).

Seven years after becoming a nontraditional student, I was on the Serengeti conducting an archaeological research project based on middle range theory (Figure 1).

My research on the Serengeti began by learning the home ranges of the resident carnivores in the areas surrounding the Serengeti Research Station. Most carnivores hunt at night or during the cool hours just after dawn. I woke up before dawn each day and tried to locate carnivores making a kill or consuming one that they had hunted that night. On average, I was successful one day out of three.

A mother leopard in my study area (Figure 2) was quite an active hunter, because she had two growing cubs to feed. Her favorite place was along the Wandamu River.

FIGURE 2

A leopard with her kill.

288

FIGURE 3

Hyena with limb bone.

FIGURE 4

Hyena kill near water.

Here there were many trees in which she could store her kills and not have them stolen by larger predators. After two days of feeding, she and her cubs would abandon a carcass that had little flesh remaining, but usually all the limb bones, rich with marrow, were intact.

One of the lion prides in my study area was hunting mainly buffalo. A buffalo carcass was usually consumed by the pride over a three-day period. Sometimes, if all members of the pride were present, it was picked clean and abandoned after only one day. Carcasses abandoned by lions were usually left with only a few small scraps of flesh. However, complete head contents and marrow within the limb bones were often available.

When hyenas located an abandoned carcass, there was a feeding frenzy, and subordinate hyenas were chased away from the carcass (Figure 3). During the chase, sometimes bones were lost in the high grass. After the hyenas left the area, I was often able to collect some abandoned intact limb bones for my study.

Hyenas not only scavenge from predators but also actively hunt. When hunting was good for several days, hyenas stored a carcass, or parts of it, in a local water hole or shallow lake (Figure 4). The horns of the prey animals bobbing in the water make these carcasses easy to locate.

The bones I collected were butchered with stone tools of the same materials that were used by hominids millions of years ago (Figure 5). Remaining flesh scraps and marrow were removed. After butchery, bones from the right side of carcasses were cleaned by boiling, air dried, and stored. These bones bore tooth marks left by the predator(s) who had defleshed the carcass.

Bones from the left side of carcasses were set out on the landscape in different environments (Figure 6). In almost all cases, the butchered bones were located by hyenas who removed or consumed the only remaining food, the greasy ends of the limb bones. These experiments simulated archaeological sites abandoned by hominids after

FIGURE 5

Stone tools used in butchering.

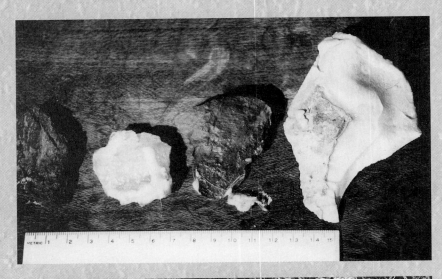

FIGURE 6

Butchered bones set out on landscape for scavengers.

FIGURE 7

Bones the scavengers left behind.

they had fed on a scavenged carcass. The tooth marks in these experiments were left not only by the original predator, most frequently a felid, but also by hyenas.

Almost all of the epiphyseal fragments were consumed or removed by the hyenas. As Figure 7 shows, the hyenas ignored the midshaft fragments, which had been depleted of flesh and marrow in butchery. However, the tooth marks of the carnivores that defleshed the carcass were present on the midshaft fragments I recovered. This pattern is quite different from that in experiments that model a hunting scenario.

I conducted a few experiments in which hyenas were given limb bones from complete carcasses in which all the flesh and marrow was removed by butchery. This type of experiment modeled carcasses hunted by hominids. Again the hyenas removed the epiphyseal fragments and ignored the midshafts because they contained no flesh, marrow, or grease (Figure 8). When I collected the bones I found only a few midshaft fragments, and less than 15% of them bore tooth marks. These were most likely inflicted when a hyena was crunching a bone end that was attached to part of a shaft. As the bone end shattered, one or more

FIGURE 8

Hyena with bone.

FIGURE 10

A close-up of one of the bones from *Zinjanthropus* showing tooth marks, cut marks, and percussion marks.

FIGURE 9

Midshaft bones from the *Zinjanthropus* site.

pieces of the shaft broke away—and often these shaft fragments were tooth marked.

In the assemblage associated with the *Zinjanthropus* site, prey species are mainly represented by midshaft fragments such as these (Figure 9). If hominids were hunting animals, we would expect less than 15% of the midshaft fragments to bear tooth marks. However, like my experi-

mental bone assemblages from abandoned carnivore kills, over 50% of the midshaft fragments in this assemblage bear tooth marks (Figure 10). This evidence supports the hypothesis that hominids at the *Zinjanthropus* site were scavenging carcasses from abandoned carnivore kills.

Butchery marks and carnivore tooth marks can be distinguished using a hand lens. However, a scanning elec-

FIGURE 11

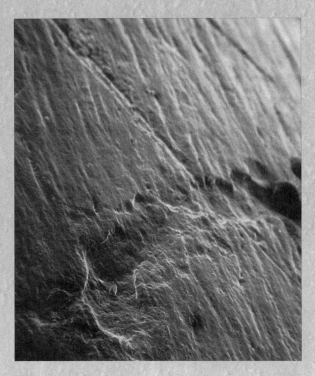

Scanning electron photomicrograph showing cut marks in addition to tooth marks.

tron microscope illuminates tiny details of bone modifications. As the scanning electron photomicrograph in Figure 11 shows, midshaft fragments in the *Zinjanthropus* assemblage also bear cut marks, as well as tooth marks. The cuts appear to have been inflicted during the removal of small scraps of flesh.

Although my research supports the hypothesis that hominids scavenged carcasses, science depends on repeated experiments that duplicate the method and procedures of previous investigations. Similar experiments have been conducted recently; unfortunately, my methods and procedures were not duplicated by the researchers. Original research rather than replication has been the tradition in archaeology. The new generation of archaeologists can change this practice. Experiments based on middle range theory, when replicated by other researchers, will provide an important step in the growth of archaeology as a mature science.

10

THE PRESERVATION OF THE ARCHAEOLOGICAL RECORD

The Court sees it as a vicious circle. You think you are not doing anything improper and there is nothing wrong with collecting. . . . What that does is encourage people to go out and gather by whatever means so that you can buy it. . . . That is the problem as I perceive it throughout the country.

—U.S. District Court Judge Gene Brooks, to the defendants

in the General Electric mounds looting case

Archaeological sites and materials represent nonrenewable resources. The loss of such materials has increased exponentially in much of the world during the past fifty years, and there is no sign that the causes of such losses will relent. Simply put, this happens because most site losses are related to population increase and developing economies. People need places to live and jobs that support them. This inevitably leads to development and sprawl, forces that are difficult, if not impossible, to stop. Other sites are lost as a result of the increasing number of regional wars and revolutions. As weapons become more destructive, both people and their material culture, from all ages, tend to suffer more. There is also a seeming increase in the rate of looting of archaeological sites, coupled with wanton vandalism (Figure 10.1).

The first two forces are related to the social and political needs of human populations. It is difficult to argue that people should be made to live in squalor or that economies should be stifled in order to preserve all archaeological remains. Instead, it is the role of archaeologists to seek solutions that do not negatively affect societies in significant ways while also preserving as much of the archaeological record as possible. This is the focus of the fifth goal of archaeology as defined early in this book. It is also at the heart of cultural resource management industries and legislation.

FIGURE 10.1

The remains of Karlsburg Castle, northeastern Moravia, Czech Republic, a fourteenth-century property of the Holy Roman Emperor Charles IV. This site was dynamited in 1960 at the behest of local bureaucrats, who were desperate for stone to continue state-funded road construction projects.

Looting and generic vandalism are another matter. These activities are issues in both the legislative and cultural resource management communities, but such destructive ignorance is also a matter for local, state, federal, and international policy authorities. Increasingly, nations that have seen their cultural heritage disappear through theft and looting have adopted a get-tough policy. In nations such as Tanzania, game poaching is more of a problem than archaeological looting, which has led to the increased militarism of game wardens and an escalation of violence. Similar policies are being adopted or are already in place in nations such as Peru, where looting has led to armed conflict between thieves and government authorities. In this arena, the preservation of archaeological sites takes on new and sometimes frightening aspects. This chapter discusses the methods designed to preserve the record of past human societies for all future generations.

CULTURAL RESOURCE MANAGEMENT

Cultural resource management, or CRM, is a broad term developed in 1974 at the first Cultural Resource Management Conference, held in Denver, Colorado. It is deliberately broad so that it includes the protection and management of all cultural resources, including archaeological sites, historic buildings, social institutions, and even social groups. In practice, however, the term is most closely associated with the protection and management of physical remains, including archaeological resources. The term is also often applied to the industry that has developed to accomplish these ends, an industry also referred to as contract archaeology, though this term is probably too narrow to adequately characterize the range of functions fulfilled by workers in this area.

The development of CRM as a private industry began in the late 1960s. The industry developed in a niche opened by federal legislation that mandated that cultural resources that might be affected by the development of federally funded projects, such as dams and roadways, should be assessed. The expansion of the federal interstate system, for example, initiated many concerns over the loss of cultural resources. Archaeologists had become increasingly concerned that attempts to salvage threatened archaeological remains through a process sometimes called **rescue** or **salvage archaeology** was leading to the loss of data and to the unnecessary destruction of archaeological remains. Although salvage work had the best intentions—saving the past— limited funds and outlets for reporting results meant that this type of work was too often unsystematic and lacked scientific rigor. Arguments were made that a better system for managing and protecting threatened resources and for mitigating potential damage to such resources was required. In particular, it was noted that if archaeologists were made a part of the planning and assessment process in federal developments, then a great deal of time, money, and archaeological resources could be saved.

Most modern CRM archaeology is undertaken as a result of the **National Historic Preservation Act (NHPA),** first passed in 1966 and subsequently amended in 1976 and in 1980. The NHPA is designed to protect important cultural sites. It lists eligible sites in the National Register of Historic Places and also serves to integrate local and state agencies into a nationwide program designed to preserve sites. Once listed on the National Register, sites cannot be disturbed if an alternative to doing so can be found. Moreover, if any research or disturbance might affect the site, such work must first be evaluated and authorized by appropriate local, state, and federal agencies, and any work undertaken must proceed according to specific guidelines. Specifically, the NHPA requires the employment of professional archaeologists to undertake the archaeological research and specifies that the archaeological resources be accounted for in development plans (Figure 10.2).

Section 106 of the NHPA usually determines when and if archaeological research is required in advance of any planned development. This section requires archaeological and historical assessment of all properties that are currently in or that might be eligible for inclusion in the National Register of Historic Places. This process typically involves hiring a cultural resource management firm to make an assessment on behalf of the agency or company proposing the development. The CRM typically takes responsibility for conducting all of the historic and archaeological surveys pertinent to the project and for preparing a report to the contracting company and all appropriate

rescue/salvage archaeology
A term once used to refer to archaeology done in advance of construction or other destructive processes.

National Historic Preservation Act (NHPA) This act was first passed in 1966 and subsequently amended in 1976 and 1980. The act is designed to protect important cultural sites by placing them on a master list called the National Register of Historic Places. The act also serves to integrate local and state agencies into a nationwide program designed to preserve sites.

FIGURE 10.2

Salvage work underway at the Mitchell site, southern Illinois, 1960.

government agencies detailing the results of their research and making recommendations as to whether the proposed disturbance should be allowed, modified, or stopped altogether.

The actual research proceeds along a series of steps, each designed to assess the presence and significance of any historic material in the path of the project. Phase I is a survey of known records about the project area and a program of archaeological reconnaissance in that area. The purpose of this phase is to determine if potentially significant resources exist in the pathway of development. If not, then the CRM team typically recommends that the work be allowed to proceed. If resources that might be eligible for the National Register of Historic Places are encountered, however, additional research may be recommended.

Phase II research is designed to assess the extent and significance of specific sites identified in Phase I. Phase II often involves vertical sampling of sites, as well as other archaeological testing such as remote sensing designed to provide information about the extent of the cultural deposits. The results of this research enable the archaeologists to make further recommendations about the fate of the site being assessed. If the materials are found to be significant, that is, potentially eligible for inclusion in the National Register, then the archaeologists will likely recommend that any adverse impact to the site be mitigated. This moves the research to Phase III. If the materials from the site do not seem significant, then the archaeologist may elect to recommend that no further research be done and that the proposed project be allowed to proceed.

Phase III represents the most extensive form of CRM work. The purpose of this phase is to mitigate all adverse effects on the site. Mitigation can range from suggesting that the proposed development be cancelled or that it be relocated away from the site. Mitigation might also include designing a method that would enable the development to proceed yet avoid the adverse effects. For example, if a park is being developed on top of an archaeological site so that the construction of benches, rest facilities, and parking lots would disturb the cultural resources, it may be sufficient to cover the site with a thick layer of sediment. This would effectively seal the archaeological deposits under the sediments, protecting them from damage and preserving them for future research.

Another alternative in mitigation is to excavate the endangered material. In many ways this is the last resort, although it is closest to what archaeologists have traditionally been trained to do. In excavating the material, archaeologists take on the responsibility of forever removing the cultural materials from their places of deposition—without the guiding design of an ongoing research project. Most archaeologists agree that the best way to excavate a site is as part of a specific research program that provides a context in which to undertake recovery, interpretation, and assessment. In most cases, CRM archaeology is limited in the scope of research that it can undertake. The extent of the research undertaken on any project is defined by the **scope of work,** a document that defines the area to be investigated and details what must be done, as well as any restrictions on methods or approaches. In CRM, these things are almost exclusively defined by the area to be affected by proposed development and only rarely by larger, ongoing research programs (Box 10.1).

By most popular accounts CRM archaeology accounts for approximately 70% of the archaeology undertaken in the world today. Whether this figure is accurate or not depends on whether one measures archaeology in terms of total dollars spent, total number of projects begun, total number of projects completed, or total number of workers employed. No matter how the figure is calculated and what the precise ratio is of CRM to more traditional archaeological research, there is no doubt that CRM accounts for the majority of employment opportunities in archaeology today.

As you know by now, archaeologists can develop numerous skills and often employ a wide range of specialists to undertake some areas of research. Yet this range of skills is expanded even further in the world of CRM. Because many archaeologists conduct CRM as a business, issues of bidding on contracts, managing accounts, payrolls, and office equipment all become important. Because CRM archaeologists usually both write and publish their reports by themselves, even if in limited form, they must also become adept at photography, cartography, expositions, and desktop publishing. Although some of these skills also emerge in more traditional archaeology, the fact that people's livelihoods and

scope of work Definition of the amount, type, extent, and location of work that can be done under a given contract.

BOX 10.1

CRM AND THE FAI-270 PROJECT

Most archaeological investigations done under the auspices of cultural resource management tend to be relatively modest in size and scope. There have been some exceptions, of course, such as the Abbott Farm Project in New Jersey and the Tellico Dam Project in Tennessee. Of all such large projects, few have come close to matching the size, scope, and number of publications associated with the FAI-270 project in southern Illinois.

FAI-270 is the project name for the Federal Aid Interstate-270 Archaeological Mitigation Project. The project has since been redesignated FAI-255 because of changes to the specific highway numbers associated with the interchanges of Interstates 55 and 70 west of Collinsville, Illinois, though most people still refer to the project by its original designation. The area is adjacent to the massive archaeological site known as Cahokia, which was home to somewhere between ten thousand and forty thousand Native Americans at about A.D. 1050. Under section 106 of the National Historic Preservation Act, the area was deemed likely to have multiple sites eligible for the National Register, and therefore archaeological survey, assessment, and finally mitigation of damage were in order. When the project was first developed in 1975, approximately one thousand acres of land were scheduled to undergo the impact of the construction of the new roadways, and the proximity of the affected area to Cahokia had many cultural resource specialists anticipating that several new sites would be identified and made eligible for inclusion on the National Register. As it turned out, the number of sites eligible for inclusion on that list far exceeded most people's expectations; a total of fifty-nine were identified based on the surveys conducted under the direction of John Kelly, now of Washington University in St. Louis.

The Illinois Department of Transportation (IDOT) contracted the University of Illinois at Urbana-Champaign to supervise and conduct Phase I and II operations on these sites. The University of Illinois at Chicago, Southern Illinois University at Edwardsville, Western Illinois University, and the Illinois State Museum were also brought into the project to assist with this monumental task. By 1982 all fifty-nine sites had been explored and assessed. Twenty of these sites required some level of mitigation (Phase III work). Perhaps not surprisingly, the announcement of the new roadway had sparked increased industrial development in the area, which resulted in the identification and assessment of another forty-three sites adjacent to the original one-thousand-acre project area. A total of 102 archaeological sites were now either directly or indirectly tied to the highway development. It is remarkable that all of these sites were explored and evaluated within approximately seven years of the initiation of archaeological research.

The archaeologists charged with developing a research design for the area began their work by defining and delimiting their research interests in the project area. The scope of work was significantly large and the project area so big as to allow for the inclusion of a greater than usual range of interests. Four general categories of research interests were first defined. These centered on the shift from Late Archaic to Early Woodland lifeways, the nature of the Late Woodland and Mississippian communities in the region, how the rise and fall of the Mississippian occupation at Cahokia was reflected on sites in the region, and the significance of climate in the region over the past three thousand years.

These interests then had to be melded with the realities of the project's scope of work, finances, and logistics in order to generate a research design. The design developed by the University of Illinois to address the investigation of these sites therefore included three additional factors. The first of these was the nature of the American Bottom, the geophysical region the project area is in. This area is adjacent to the Mississippi River floodplain just south of the confluence of the Missouri and Mississippi Rivers. This area has unique environmental conditions even today, and the presence of the major rivers offered ample opportunity for transportation during the prehistoric era.

(continued)

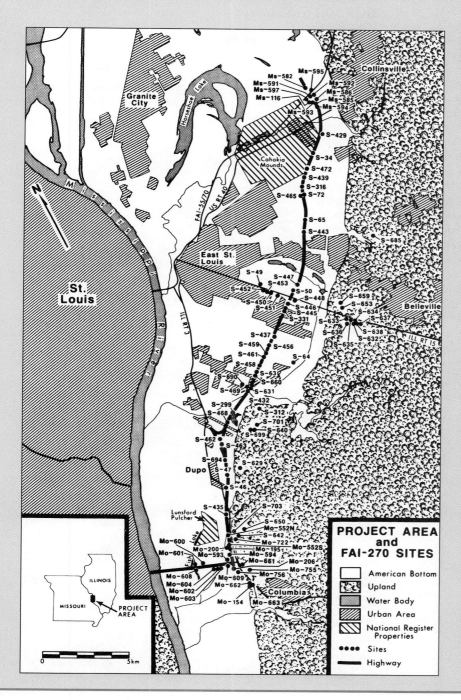

The American Bottom and
project area for the FAI-270
Highway Project.

BOX 10.1 (continued)

The second major factor affecting the research design was the sheer number and size of the archaeological sites in the area. Undoubtedly, the presence of a major center such as Cahokia attracted large numbers of people to the area between about A.D. 900 and 1250. The outstanding opportunities for hunting, gathering, and, later, agriculture in the region also attracted people to the project area both before the rise and after the decline of Cahokia. This archaeological richness also included important historic sites relating to the westward expansion of Europeans and Americans in the Midwest.

The third major factor in developing the research design was the exact location of the highway to be built. Some sites would be destroyed by the construction, whereas other sites were likely to be affected but not destroyed. Distinguishing these two groups of sites helped archaeologists to develop priorities for their limited resources and energies.

When all was said and done in the planning stage, twelve general questions were developed. These questions would subsequently be used to generate specific hypotheses for each site explored and combine the massive corpus of data into a meaningful interpretive synthesis for the project area. The twelve questions are summarized by Charles Bareis and James Porter (1984: 8–9), the editors of the final report, as follows:

1. What is the nature of the Late Archaic community plans and recovered artifactual debris?

Large-scale excavation of the Turner site, southern Illinois. The disturbed plow zone has been removed mechanically to allow archaeologists to concentrate their resources on the intact material beneath.

Aerial view of the horizontal approach adopted by the archaeologists of the FAI-270 Project. Here, the Mississippian-era Range site is under excavation. The rectangular structures are prehistoric trenches that define the outlines of buildings, and the round pits are storage and refuse pits.

2. What is the composition of Early Woodland community plans? Does the introduction of Marion Thick pottery [the first pottery in the region] represent a major cultural change in the American Bottom or merely one technological innovation in a continuation of Archaic lifeways?

3. Where do the entirely new and buried Florence Street [a discrete sequence of pottery] ceramics and structural features fit in the Early Woodland to Middle Woodland continuum?

(continued)

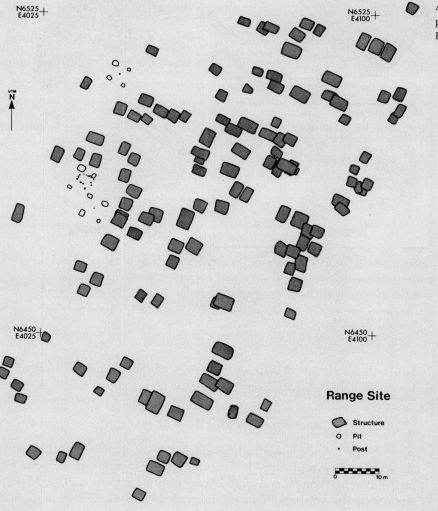

A drawing of the Lindeman phase of occupation at the Range site, southern Illinois.

N6525
E4025

N6525
E4100

UTM
N

N6450
E4025

N6450
E4100

Range Site

⬠ Structure
○ Pit
• Post

0   10 m

BOX 10.1 (continued)

4. Do the buried Middle Woodland data . . . represent a totally new view of the importance of Middle Woodland occupations in American Bottom prehistory?

5. Can we detect the transition from Middle Woodland to Late Woodland in the American Bottom area? What does it represent in terms of cultural dynamics?

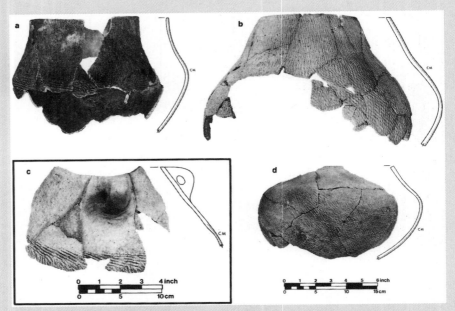

Emergent Mississippian pottery recovered by archaeologists at the Range site. In addition to exposing community plans, the FAI-270 project increased archaeological awareness of the diversity and sequences of material cultural developments throughout the project area.

Antiquities Act of 1906 The act that gave the president of the United States authority to declare areas national monuments and required that any archaeology undertaken on federal properties administered by the departments of Interior, Agriculture, and War be done so by permit.

large sums of money often depend largely on the ability to perform all of these functions effectively reinforces the importance of such skills.

LAWS AND ARCHAEOLOGY

In the United States, laws effecting archaeological resources can be traced to the **Antiquities Act of 1906** (Table 10.1). This act sought to preserve archaeological materials on federal lands. Passage of this act was spurred in part by the systematic mining of known archaeological sites, such as those in and around Chaco Canyon, New Mexico, to extract material that could then be

6. Are there detectable differences in the community plans for the Late Woodland sequence?

7. What is the nature of the Mississippian community plans and how do these compare to those of the preceding Late Woodland and Emergent Mississippian periods?

8. What are the detectable changes that reflect the increasing dependence on agriculture in late prehistoric times and the rise of Cahokia?

9. How is the fall of Cahokia in the thirteenth century reflected at other sites on the American Bottom?

10. What is the nature of Oneota [a later material culture reflecting a number of different social groups] occupation in the American Bottom?

11. For the Historic period, what phases will be represented within highway right-of-way and what does this mean for research in historical archaeology?

12. What archaeological evidence is revealed that can be used to judge the significance of climatic changes on cultures in the American Bottom over the past 3000 years?

Clearly, the archaeologists had chosen to define a challenging and important set of questions. Methodology had to be established to allow researchers to test the various sites in ways that would yield data that helped to answer these questions. Given the temporal constraints and the fact that much of the area had been plowed, heavy machinery was frequently used to remove disturbed layers of sediments overlying intact archaeological deposits. Although this method sometimes damaged the underlying material culture, every effort was made to insulate the in situ cultural remains from the impact of the archaeologists' work. The use of heavy equipment also allowed archaeologists to open broad expanses of area more quickly and inexpensively than would otherwise be possible. In turn, these large open areas allowed fieldworkers to identify, map, and excavate features that defined the physical layout of the community. Statistical sampling could be employed in meaningful ways to help select what precisely was excavated and what was left intact. Soil samples, from which pollen and other botanical remains could be extracted, and material for radiocarbon dating were collected regularly. Material remains were sent to specialists in such fields as archaeological dating, palynology, zooarchaeology, paleoethnobotany, and biological anthropology. These researchers compiled reports that were sent to the principal investigators at each site. The data and results from these reports were synthesized with other data obtained in the field in order to assess the specific hypotheses that were unique to each site and that fit into the twelve categories of research questions common to the entire project. Final reports were then produced from the work, as were journal articles, popular news stories, and monographs providing overviews of the entire project.

sold to collectors and in part by the increasing interest in antiquities generated by the 1890 World Columbian Exposition. The act gave the president of the United States the authority to declare some areas national monuments and national parks, thus making them eligible for federal protection. It further required that any archaeology undertaken on federal properties administered by the departments of Interior, Agriculture, and War be done so by permit and that the results of these works be placed in public repositories, such as museums. Unfortunately, the act was worded in such a way that made the prosecution of violators difficult, if not impossible. This problem was painfully illustrated in a series of court decisions in favor of looters who had been charged with violating the Antiquities Act on federal properties in the American Southwest. Two cases proved particularly problematic for archaeologists when the courts ruled that the Antiquities Act of 1906 was too vague to be legally enforceable. In effect, the court decisions mandated new laws because the Antiquities Act was rendered nearly useless by the courts' decisions.

The **Historic Sites Act of 1935** expanded on the Antiquities Act of 1906. The 1935 law enabled the government to declare national historic landmarks, in addition to national monuments and national parks. The act reinforced and clarified the requirements for archaeological surveys to be conducted in situations in which cultural resources might be irreparably damaged or lost by federally funded development projects. Also, any federal agency sponsoring construction that threatened archaeological resources was required to allocate funds up to 1% of the total cost of the project for the archaeological survey and testing.

The 1960s saw the passage of two major legislative acts that influenced cultural resource management. The National Historic Preservation Act of 1966, discussed previously, organized state, local, and national programs for archaeological preservation. In 1969, the federal government also enacted the **National Environmental Protection Act (NEPA).** This act expanded on the Historic Sites Act of 1935 by requiring all federal agencies to file environmental impact statements on proposed development projects. Significantly, cultural resources were included as part of the environment, so that the impact of the development was also assessed for historic and archaeological sites in the area slated for development. For the first time, the entire federal government was placed under the umbrella of what would eventually be known as cultural resource management.

Unfortunately, it was not until 1979 that agencies charged with enforcing the laws protecting historic and archaeological resources were given the legal means to actively pursue prosecutions. The **Archaeological Resource Protection Act (ARPA)** provided enforceable punishments on both civil and criminal levels for vandalizing or looting cultural resources. Punishments can range from monetary fines to actual jail time. Among the most effective penalties, though, is the confiscation of all personal materials used to perpetrate the offending acts. This provision can result in the confiscation of everything from excavation equipment used to remove archaeological materials to the vehicles used to transport these materials to the buildings used to store and process the stolen materials. In this respect, these laws mirror the laws designed to combat organized crime and drug trafficking.

The battle against the theft of cultural properties became international for Americans in 1982 with the passage by Congress of the Convention of Cultural Property. This enabled the United States to participate in the 1970 United Nations Convention on the Means of Prohibiting and Preventing Illicit Import, Export, and Transfer of Ownership of Cultural Property. This convention was designed to prevent the legalized importation of material cul-

Historic Sites Act of 1935 This act expanded the Antiquities Act of 1906. It enabled the government to declare some properties national historic landmarks while reinforcing and clarifying the requirements for archaeological survey. It also required any federal agency sponsoring construction that threatened archaeological resources to allocate funds in an amount of up to 1% of the total cost of the project, for archaeological survey and testing.

National Environmental Protection Act of 1969 (NEPA) Expanded on the Historic Sites Act of 1935 by requiring all federal agencies to file environmental and cultural resource impact statements on proposed development projects.

Archaeological Resource Protection Act (ARPA) Enacted in 1979, this provided the government with civil and criminal outlets to pursue individuals vandalizing or looting cultural resources on federal properties.

TABLE 10.1	Timeline of Legislation
Antiquities Act of 1906	This act gave the president of the United States the authority to declare some areas national monuments, thus moving archaeological materials on these properties into the caretakership of the federal government.
Historic Sites Act of 1935	This act enabled the establishment of national historic landmarks, in addition to national monuments, while also clarifying the need for archaeological survey to be undertaken on federal properties where cultural resources might be threatened.
National Historic Preservation Act of 1966	This act organized local, state, and federal programs for cultural resource management through the creation of the National Register of Historic Places. This act also defined the need and requirements for professional archaeologists to be involved with any sites on or eligible for inclusion on this register.
National Environmental Protection Act of 1969	This legislation required all federal agencies to conduct cultural resource and environmental impact studies of proposed developments on federal land.
Archaeological Resource Protection Act of 1979	This act provided the federal government with a series of civil and criminal outlets for the prosecution of individuals who vandalized or looted archaeological sites on federal property.
Convention of Cultural Property	Passed by the U.S. Congress, 1982. Passage of this statement brought the United States into agreement with other countries to participate in the international efforts to stop the import and export of looted cultural materials. The original convention was initiated in other parts of the world as early as 1970.
Convention of Cultural Property of 1983	Passage of this convention provided the United States with the ability to impose legal sanctions against the import and export of stolen cultural property.
Native American Graves Protection and Repatriation Act of 1990	This legislation compels museums and federal agencies to report and then seek to return human remains and items of cultural patrimony to appropriate indigenous groups.

ture from countries that had not knowingly and officially allowed the material to leave its boundaries. All countries participating in the U.N. convention agreed that it was inappropriate and unethical to violate the tenets of the statement, though it did not provide for any penalties for violations. The convention stated that it was unethical for participating countries to import cultural materials from any country illegally occupied by a foreign power. This provision was explicitly designed to deter the wholesale theft of antiquities and national treasures such as occurred in occupied France during World War II. The Convention of Cultural Property was followed in 1983 by the passage of the **Cultural Property Act,** which provided legal sanctions against the import or export of stolen cultural property. As we shall see, though, dramatic finds in northern Peru and the smuggling of ancient Peruvian antiquities into the United States would soon challenge many of these laws (Box 10.2).

Maritime archaeological sites present a special problem for proponents of cultural resource management. Long-standing marine salvage laws tend to allow anyone who recovers material from wrecks to keep that material, especially in international waters. The reasoning has been that the individual or group incurring the expenses of salvage should have the right to recover their investment and perhaps make a profit as well. Unfortunately, salvage activities destroy archaeological sites in the form of the wrecks themselves, as does the uncontrolled sport diving that sometimes follows the discovery of many wrecks.

This situation was exemplified by the activities of the late Mel Fisher and his Treasure Salvors company. Fisher was an avid treasure hunter, and through painstaking trial and error he located the remains of the *Atocha,* a sixteenth-century Spanish galleon lost in a storm off the coast of Florida. Fisher was attracted to the *Atocha* because historic documents recorded that the vessel was transporting a load of gold from the New World back to Spain when she was lost. Treasure Salvors invested millions of dollars in searching for the wreck and endured near bankruptcy, violence from competitors, and scorn from those dubious of their chances to succeed. Yet succeed the company eventually did, finding the wreck and systematically removing its treasure. In the process, an unknown but doubtlessly significant amount of archaeological data was lost. Some material that was recovered underwent conservation processes and was placed on exhibit at the Treasure Salvors Museum. What alarmed archaeologists and cultural resource managers alike was that significant portions of the treasure were auctioned off to the public or used to repay investors in the search. This process divided the archaeological assemblage into an unknown number of parts and scattered significant portions of it across the globe in the hands of private collectors. Therefore, research on the material as a whole is not possible, leaving historians and archaeologists trying to piece together data about exactly what the *Atocha* carried, where it came from, how it was shipped, and what variations existed within the material culture of the era.

The state of Florida and eventually the federal government became involved in litigation and subsequent legislation designed to protect wrecks of archaeological significance. In the case of the *Atocha,* after lengthy court proceedings Fisher was allowed to keep his salvaged material, but further salvage work of this nature was prohibited. To Fisher's and Treasure Salvors' credit, archaeologists eventually became involved in the research, and the company now sponsors material conservation and works with a number of students and professionals exploring marine archaeology. For some, however, this was too little, too late.

Cultural Property Act of 1983 (CPA) Provided legal sanctions against the import or export of stolen cultural properties into or out of the United States.

Activities such as those associated with the *Atocha*'s salvage led to the passage of the Federal Abandoned Shipwreck Act in 1988. This law explicitly removes marine wrecks of archaeological interest from the jurisdiction of marine salvage laws. It also localizes the protection of such sites, giving states jurisdiction over their nautical cultural resources. Although this has not prevented all salvage activities from disturbing archaeological sites, it has led to a dramatic decrease in the number of treasure hunters who actively pursue major research and recovery projects such as those illustrated by the actions of Treasure Salvors.

As you know by now, archaeology does not exist in a vacuum. The actions of archaeologists are viewed in different lights by different segments of societies. One of these segments is the descendants of the people who deposited most of the archaeological material in North America prior to the arrival of great numbers of Europeans beginning in the late seventeenth century. Collectively referred to as Native Americans, these people represent several hundred different tribes and groups, ranging from Native Hawaiians to the Inuit (inappropriately referred to as Eskimo) and the various tribes and peoples of continental North America. At times, but certainly not always, there have been disputes over archaeologists excavating the material culture of and, sometimes, human remains of people that may be the ancestors of some living Native Americans.

Concerns over these activities have led to a variety of state laws and culminated in the enactment of the Native American Graves Protection and Repatriation Act (NAGPRA; see Chapter 9) in 1990. This act has several goals. First, human remains and closely associated material culture housed in museums and federal depositories are to be returned to the social groups most closely associated with these remains. Museums and federal agencies holding human remains and any cultural material associated with graves and funeral activities are therefore compelled to inventory their holdings and then consult with Native American groups that may be connected to the human and material remains, concerning repatriation or other arrangements: Depending on the cultural and political views of the groups that may be affiliated with the material identified through NAGPRA, the remains might be returned to the Native American group to which the remains belong, where such affiliations can be ascertained, reburied in another cemetery, or be allowed to remain at the institution for a set period of time.

A second major goal of NAGPRA is to afford increased protection to Native American burials and sacred sites. The act requires that indigenous groups be consulted whenever archaeological research on federal or tribal lands encounters or is likely to encounter human remains. In the terms of the act, the ideal outcome of such consultations is to foster the preservation of the remains in situ, essentially preventing the remains from being excavated. Some physical anthropologists and archaeologists point out that this essentially prevents analyses such as paleodemographics, paleopathology, and a host of allied

BOX 10.2

THE ROYAL GOLD OF SIPÁN

The village of Sipán lies in the Lambayeque River Valley of northern Peru, almost one hundred miles north of the Moche River Valley and the splendid civilization that flourished there during the first millennium A.D. Near the village are a Moche cemetery and three earthen pyramids similar to, but smaller than, those at the capital city of the Moche culture. Many local residents regularly looted the cemetery for pottery, gold, or other valuables that they could sell on the black market. They represent a class of person known widely in Latin America as *huacareos*, or looters of special places.

By the end of 1986 the cemetery at Sipán had essentially been destroyed; there was nothing left to loot. One small group of *huacareos* turned their attention to the smallest of the three pyramids at the site. They dug at night to avoid detection by the local authorities and began extensive mining operations inside the pyramid. On the night of February 16, 1987, they hit pay dirt, and their lives would never be the same. Indeed, for at least one of the looters, life would end abruptly in the near future. The *huacareos* broke into an intact burial chamber of a Moche noble, possibly even a king. The tomb was filled with gold, silver, and other precious objects of art. The *huacareos* believed they would finally be rich, but it was not to be so.

The local police discovered the illegal activities of the looters and arrested many of them. One was killed in a violent gun battle with authorities who sought to arrest him and his brother. Unfortunately, the authorities were too late to recover all of the material that had been stolen; much had already been sold to local collectors. These people, in turn, sold the material for a profit to other collectors and so on, until the material

An aerial view of the Moche site of Sipán, northern Peru. The smallest of the three pyramids (left) was the focus of the looting that led Walter Alva to the burial chambers.

Some of the magnificent gold ornaments and craft work recovered from the tombs at Sipán. Prior to these finds, such material was largely unknown to archaeologists, though some material had made its way through *huacareos* into private collections.

was eventually smuggled out of Peru into Canada, the United States, and the United Kingdom. It is likely that other material made its way to continental Europe and to Japan as well.

The trail of artifacts and smugglers eventually found its way to a former U.S. government employee living in Peru and to a young and socially prominent art dealer in southern California. Along the way the trail of illegal activities included attaching false bottoms to the artifacts so that they appeared to be modern replicas. One

particular shipment had been sent from Peru to Bolivia, where the false bottoms were attached. The material was then shipped to Canada with the intent of transporting the material into the United States across the Canadian border. Canadian customs officials, however, quickly spotted the false bottoms and arrested the culprits, who eventually avoided any substantial jail time. Another shipment made by the same individuals went from Peru to England, where there were no import laws covering archaeological materials. There the material was packed into a trunk and exported to the United States as the personal effects of a recently deceased resident of the United Kingdom. Items sent in this manner are not subject to search, and only a small fee must be paid to claim the material from the U. S. customs warehouses to which such materials are shipped. This is precisely what happened—the looted artifacts were successfully smuggled into California and into the hands of a waiting art dealer.

This process of smuggling might have continued indefinitely except for two factors: First, the Peruvian government was systematically protecting the source of the items, the pyramids at Sipán. Second, the Englishman who had been used to smuggle the trunk into the United States and who was a trained museum specialist contacted federal authorities and reported the activity. In a carefully orchestrated investigation, the art dealers involved were identified and arrested. Unfortunately, in a series of court appeals, they were able to successfully argue that United States law did not apply to material from archaeological sites in other countries and that the material was their rightful property. The stolen artifacts, much to the chagrin of American and Peruvian authorities, were returned to the thieves. For all intents and purposes, the pipeline for looted artifacts had been reopened, at least on the American side. In order to prevent an international incident, then-President George Bush intervened and issued an executive order banning the importation of archaeological material from Peru into the United States without official documents from the Peruvian government supporting such activity. The pipeline was again plugged.

(continued)

BOX 10.2 (continued)

The looted artifacts, however, remained in the hands of the very people who ultimately paid for the theft, one man with his life.

At Sipán things have changed. The government now monitors the site closely, and archaeologists have access to the site. Walter Alva, who first identified the stolen artifacts confiscated by the police, leads the Peruvian archaeologists working there. He explains that the site represents the only largely intact Moche ceremonial center and royal necropolis known. The information obtained from the site may very well represent our last and best window into reconstructing and interpreting Moche life. Alva also points out that all of the attention focused on the looting of Sipán has produced some positive results. The public, as well as government agencies, are much more aware of the problems presented by looting and the smuggling of artifacts across national boundaries. It has become more diffi-cult, though by no means impossible, to obtain stolen material.

The people of the village of Sipán have benefited also. The ongoing archaeological work has meant jobs for many unemployed and underemployed workers. Local schools have seen the benefit of archaeologists and others coming into classrooms to teach students about their past and how to curate it. Still others bene-fit from the dramatic increase in tourists, as well as ar-chaeologists, soldiers, and government employees, who work at or near the site. Such benefits are sustainable and are less destructive and significantly less danger-ous than those from looting. They are also legal and serve to instill a sense of place and pride to the people who live in the shadow of this great site. Perhaps it is the latter benefit that outweighs all others, because it links living people with the past in a way that benefits both the past and the present.

approaches. Moreover, although NAGPRA does not specifically prohibit the excavation of human remains, it creates a political situation in which it is dif-ficult to pursue archaeological research in many regions. Even the analysis of house structures may be difficult because some Native American cultures buried their dead under the floors of their homes. Under NAGPRA, research on the settlement patterns of such groups becomes problematic because human remains are likely to be encountered. On the other hand, many Native American groups have observed that NAGPRA provides very little real pro-tection to ancient burial areas but does at least require that archaeologists consult with them before pursuing research covered by the act.

The ultimate impact of NAGPRA will be measured only in the future. In the meantime, though, a benefit of the act has been to increase the dialogue between many Native American groups and archaeologists. Although some factions in each group still refuse to deal with the other group, most people interested in the past in the New World have been drawn into discussions about the needs and concerns of both science and native peoples. These dis-cussions have resulted in some novel solutions to the problems of dealing with human remains in archaeology. Likewise, these discussions have en-hanced the understanding of both scientists and Native Americans about the ideas and issues driving the concerns of each group.

It is important to note that not all Native Americans support NAGPRA, though the majority do, and that not all archaeologists resent NAGPRA, though some certainly resent some of the results of the law. The situation is more complex than can be treated in this book, and it would be a mistake to characterize one group as pro-NAGPRA and another group anti-NAGPRA. Moreover, issues of constitutional and treaty law, as well as issues of ethics and philosophical bias, all intertwine in addressing NAGPRA. As a result, much of the work affected by NAGPRA is proceeding slowly, cautiously, as personnel at the various agencies and in different Native American groups assess their own needs and learn the needs of those they now must work with (Box 10.3).

LOOTING AND ARCHAEOLOGY

Looting is one of the greatest threats to archaeological resources today. Looting ranges from the casual removal of artifacts or even human bone by curious, often well-intentioned people to the systematic theft of material remains by organized profit-seeking criminals. In some cases this theft involves international rings of smugglers, unethical art dealers, and wealthy private collectors. It also pits governments against one another, as those countries routinely victimized by looters, such as Guatemala and Peru, seek support and aid from countries known as active markets for looted antiquities, such as the United States and Japan.

The size and the power of the antiquities trade can be quickly assessed by a brief search on the World Wide Web. A single query using a readily available Internet search engine yielded over one hundred sites selling antiquities or replicas of antiquities in one form or another. Although the sites selling replicas pose little threat to archaeology, and indeed may make it more approachable to the public, the number of sites offering items claimed to be genuine archaeological specimens is disturbing. The problem is not restricted to small vendors or difficult-to-find websites. Companies such as Amazon.com and eBay.com have listings for a variety of artifacts. Specialty sites such as www.antiquities.net and www.medusa-art.com also offer archaeological items at auction or through direct sales.

There is an even more insidious side to the electronic trafficking of artifacts. Because most websites earn additional income by selling their client lists, databases of people interested in the purchase of antiquities can be easily obtained. Companies specializing in such trade can then contact potentially interested individuals and offer items for direct sale. Similar effects are also achieved by linking advertising databases to specific topics that people might search for on the Internet. For example, Alex Barker of the Dallas Museum of Natural History searched Amazon.com for an archaeological book on mound building. The database quickly responded with the expected publication data and pricing information, as well as the opportunity to pursue an Internet link that provided information on related topics. As expected, the link connected to advertisements for other products and services generally related to archaeology. One of these ads, however, suggested people buy "guaranteed authentic"

BOX 10.3

THE KENNEWICK CONTROVERSY

It was July 28, 1996, and both Dave Deacy and Will Thomas were home from college. They were attending the hydroplane races on the Columbia River near West Richmond and Kennewick, Washington. Something caught their attention in the shallow water near the shore: parts of a human body eroding from the shoreline. The two contacted the authorities and an investigation began. It was quickly determined that the remains were likely quite old, and cultural resource management archaeologists were called in to rescue the skeleton from its precarious position. This incident set in motion a still unresolved saga of litigation, allegation, and scientific questioning that has tempers and emotions running high in Native American, government, and scientific communities alike.

Anthropologist James Chatters was granted an Archaeological Resource Protection Act permit on July 31, 1996, to recover the remains. The permit was made retroactive to July 28, however, to legally justify the original collection of the skeleton from the river. Police originally thought the skeleton was of recent origin; later it was potentially identified as a late-nineteenth or early-twentieth-century person based on artifacts found nearby. Therefore the procedure seemed both appropriate and logical. Certainly, no one seems to have acted inappropriately in recovering the remains.

The uproar began to develop when it was discovered that the pelvis of the individual contained a segment of a prehistoric projectile point usually dated to between 9500 and 4000 B.C. The individual, a male, had survived the injury, and the hip bone healed around the fragment of the tool. This discovery prompted scientists to use radiocarbon dating to determine more precisely the age of the individual. The results came back from R. Ervin Taylor, Jr., of the University of California at Riverside as a surprising 8,410 (±60 years) before present. Kennewick Man, as the remains became known, was one of the early inhabitants of North America and was therefore presumed to be Native American (Mongoloid, in physical anthropological terms). His remains, though, showed strong Caucasoid features, suggesting to some that he might represent a previously undocumented group of early immigrants to the New World.

Before the scientific debate could reach fever pitch and the remains could be more fully examined, they became subject to NAGPRA provisions. All tribal groups that might be reasonably associated with the remains, or more precisely with the territory on which the remains were found, were notified according to law. The tribes included the Umatilla tribes, the Yakama, the Colville, and the Nez Perce. Together with a fifth tribe, the Wanapum, these groups filed a joint claim for the remains. Armand Minthorn of the Umatilla wrote that the remains belonged to the Native American communities based on religious beliefs. He wrote, "If this individual

General and detailed maps of the Kennewick area.

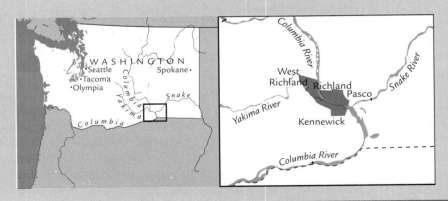

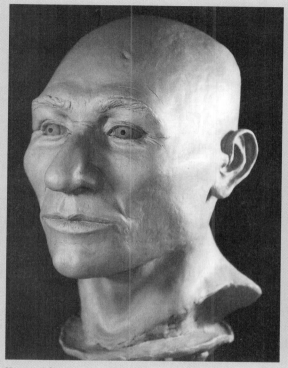

Kennewick Man reconstructed face.

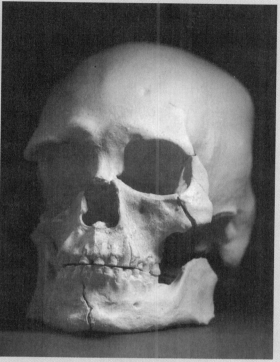

The skull of Kennewick man.

is truly over 9,000 years old, that only substantiates our belief that he is Native American. From our oral histories, we know that our people have been part of this land since the beginning of time. . . ." Further, Minthorn stated, "some scientists say that if this individual is not studied further, we, as Indians, will be destroying evidence of our history. We already know our history. It is passed on to us through our elders and through our religious practices" (Minthorn, in Slayman 1997: 3).

The Army Corps of Engineers, which has federal jurisdiction over the navigable Columbia River waterway, accepted this claim and announced its intention to repatriate the remains according to the provisions of NAGPRA. A rift in the coalition of tribes requesting repatriation soon developed, though. The Umatilla and the Nez Perce planned on reburying the remains

as soon as possible, effectively ending all scientific inquiry into the age and affiliation of the remains. The Colville, however, supported reburying the remains only after they had been analyzed through nondestructive means and the sampling of DNA extracted from small amounts of bone. Such work had begun shortly after the material was first recovered, but the Army Corps of Engineers had ordered the work stopped and confiscated the samples that scientists had already taken.

At about the same time, numerous concerned citizens and scientists began asking that permission be granted for a physical anthropological analysis of the material before it was reburied. The Army Corps of Engineers rejected these requests and continued with its plans for repatriation. On October 16, 1996, this re-

(continued)

BOX 10.3 (continued)

fusal precipitated a suit filed on behalf of eight prominent scientists seeking to study the remains.

On June 2, 1997, Judge John Jelderks denied the scientists' motion to permit immediate study, as well as the government's motion to dismiss the suit outright. Instead, he ordered the Army Corps of Engineers to make up its mind about the final disposition of the remains. The Corps had rescinded its decision to repatriate the remains immediately and now found itself in the middle of a complex debate involving science, knowledge for the benefit of society, religious beliefs, and federal legislation that is not always clear on precisely how to interpret repatriation guidelines.

For now, Kennewick Man remains locked away. The remains are in limbo as our society and its legal system wrestle with the merits, constitutionality, and legalities of what should happen to them. In the meantime, no studies are being done and no burial ceremonies are scheduled. What we know is simply that the remains are those of a muscular man, probably between forty-five and fifty-five years old at the time of his death, whose teeth were worn to the roots. Although he had suffered a traumatic injury to his hip, he had survived the spear wound and continued his life, though likely in at least occasional discomfort. He was intentionally buried shortly after death, likely by his friends and family. His precise relationship to living Native Americans or to another group of Asian, Eurasian, or European descent remains unknown.

Taino artifacts dated to between A.D. 700 and 900 (Barker 2000:15). Barker correctly observes that the hard work of dedicated archaeologists, those who authored the book on mound building, is being used without their knowledge to support the trade in antiquities. Moreover, people who may be just becoming interested in archaeology might be led to believe that such sales were both legal and sanctioned by archaeologists.

The power and now pervasiveness of the antiquities market raises serious concerns for cultural resource specialists. If the advertisements succeed in cultivating expanding markets for the sale of antiquities, then prices for them will rise. Archaeological artifacts cannot be manufactured in the sense that radios or softballs are manufactured. Although it is feasible for some unscrupulous dealers to sell fakes, that is, modern forgeries of genuine artifacts, it seems more likely that people will turn to looting more archaeological sites. In North America, such efforts are relatively inexpensive and can be done on the weekends and evenings. They also have the potential to yield tens of thousands of dollars or more. The net effect may be the rapid loss of archaeological sites as more people turn to selling antiquities as a form of cottage industry. A second search of the World Wide Web yielded more than forty sites selling antiquities. Of these, nearly one-third were selling materials that had either obviously originated in archaeological contexts and were therefore probably stolen or were outright forgeries and were therefore worthless. Among the items offered for sale were Maya ceramics, mummified animals allegedly from ancient Egypt, coins, buckles, and jewelry from Roman, Celtic, Anglo-

Saxon, and Byzantine contexts, and hundreds of North American projectile points.

The most prestigious looted artifacts, however, tend to be collected by wealthy individuals. The sale of this category of looted materials can occur in a number of ways but usually involves auctions or private sales. Well-known auction houses such as Sotheby's regularly hold pre-Columbian auctions. Most of these auction houses accept the word of their clients that the items placed for sale were legally obtained. A simple statement to this effect is usually all that most auction houses request as verification. If an individual were selling illegal antiquities and had already violated state and federal laws in one or more countries, falsifying such a statement would likely be easily done.

Moreover, these same auction houses have had a tendency to require any individual or agency, including foreign governments, to prove that a particular item was stolen from a specific location on a specific date. This is an impossible standard to meet in most instances because the material being stolen could come from any number of looted sites, even some that have yet to be recorded. It is generally impossible to trace a single artifact to a single episode of looting, especially in remote areas where looting is not discovered quickly. Although the situation seems obviously incongruous to cultural resource specialists, American federal law has also tended to support the position of the auction houses, especially when the resources in question were not obtained from American archaeological sites covered by one or more of the laws discussed previously. Fortunately, federal laws now prevent the legal importation of archaeological materials from several countries, but the flow of illegally smuggled objects into the United States seems to continue.

Extensive looting is not restricted to foreign soil. Items such as late prehistoric Native American ceramics can bring tens of thousands of dollars at both private and public auctions. The market is particularly strong for the painted and elaborately decorated ceramics of the American Southwest and Southeast, especially material from cultures such as Anasazi and Mississippian. In 1988 the prominent archaeologist Brian Fagan published a column in *Archaeology Magazine* discussing recent events at a place called Slack Farm. The farm is located on the Kentucky side of the confluence of the Wabash and Ohio Rivers, two known major avenues for communication and travel by Native Americans for millennia. Known artifacts from the site suggested late prehistoric and early historic occupation, sometime between about 1450 and 1600 A.D. The site is one of the few major habitation sites that spans the gap between the prehistoric and historic eras. The owners of the site, the Slack family, had long made efforts to protect the site from looters, although some people nevertheless stole onto the property at night and brazenly excavated looters' pits.

When the property was sold, however, all protection was lost. The new owners cared little about the archaeology; nor did the tenant farmers who leased the property. Organized looters learned of the change in ownership and paid a fee of $10,000 to the new owners for exclusive rights to "excavate"

FIGURE 10.3

The Slack Farm site, northern Kentucky, after looters irrevocably destroyed significant portions of the site in order to recover materials for sale and for personal collections.

the site. What they in fact did was to bulldoze large portions of the site in order to find pottery and other items they could then sell. This went on for two months before neighbors became outraged and asked the authorities to do something. Finally, the Kentucky State Police intervened and arrested the looters for violating a law that prevented the desecration of venerated objects, such as graves. No one knows how many graves the looters violated, but bones littered the surface of the farm, as did crude pits and trenches. Archaeologists estimate, conservatively, that at least seven hundred graves were unearthed and looted by the thieves. However, because the events took place on private land, the charges filed against the looters, to which they pleaded innocent, amounted only to misdemeanors: The looters got away with destroying a large part of one of the most important sites in the Midwest (Figure 10.3).

The situation was turned on other would-be excavators in the area just a few years later. The General Electric Company owns substantial amounts of land on the Indiana side of the confluence of the Wabash and Ohio Rivers. On some of these properties mounds were being systematically excavated without permission by people claiming to be avocational archaeologists. In fact, they were also antiquities dealers and collectors.

The furor over the events at Slack Farm led to renewed public outcries to protect the past, and the offending parties were arrested and tried, this time for violation of the Archaeological Resource Protection Act. During well-documented legal proceedings, one of the accused, Arthur Gerber, testified that he had sold artifacts from the site and destroyed photographs that would have incriminated him as a looter. Nonetheless, he maintained that he was just a concerned citizen trying to rescue the past from others who had also looted the site. The individuals indicted for their actions in the incidents arranged plea bargains. The leader of the looters, Gerber, agreed to a plea bargain on five misdemeanor counts of violating ARPA. Two of his personal vehicles were confiscated because they were used to transport artifacts stolen from the General Electric mounds; he received a $5,000 fine and was sentenced to five 12-month prison terms, to run concurrently. Gerber eventually challenged this agreement, but his appeal was denied.

In a summary of his decision, U.S. District Court Judge Gene Brooks rejected the notion that Gerber and his cohorts were avocational archaeologists. He described the actions of the collectors as part of a vicious circle of destruction.

SUMMARY

Archaeological materials and sites are finite resources. Once excavated, for better or worse, they can never be returned to their places of origin in spatially useful ways. The United States, along with Canada, Mexico, and much of the rest of the world, has developed laws and cultural resource management protocols to protect these valuable pieces of human heritage. These laws are not always successful, and unscrupulous people regularly ignore legislation for personal profit and satisfaction.

Fortunately, laws coupled with widespread education are making a difference in the battle with the thieves of time. As more people understand what archaeology really is and why it is important, they cultivate an interest in the various chapters in the story of humankind. Moreover, they come to understand that the world's heritage belongs to all people, to share and perpetuate across time. No one can possess the past. Indeed, archaeologists have come to consider what they do as a public trust. It is only through the careful performance of our jobs and the pursuit of the five general goals of archaeology that we not only serve our scholarly interests but also contribute to humankind's understanding of itself and its common history. Civilizations may come and civilizations may go, but the stories that archaeology tells are forever.

FOR FURTHER INFORMATION

Alva, W. 1988a. Discovering the New World's richest unlooted tomb. *National Geographic Magazine* 174 (4): 510–14.

———. 1988b. Into the tomb of a Moche lord. *National Geographic Magazine* 174 (4): 516–49.

Barker, A.W. 2000. Ethics, e-commerce, and the future of the past. *Society for American Archaeology Bulletin* 18 (1): 15.

Cleere, H., ed. 1984. *Approaches to the archaeological heritage: A comparative study of world cultural resource management systems.* Cambridge: Cambridge University Press.

———, ed. 1989. *Archaeological heritage management in the modern world.* London: Unwin Hyman.

Fagan, B. M. 1988. Black day at Slack Farm. *Archaeology* 41 (8): 15–16, 73.

Fowler, D. D. 1982. Cultural resources management. In *Advances in archaeological method and theory,* vol. 5, ed. M. B. Schiffer, pp. 1–50. New York: Academic Press.

Friedman, J. L., ed. 1985. A history of the Archaeological Resources Protection Act: Law and regulations. *American Archaeology* 5: 82–119.

Harrington, S. P. M. 1991. The looting of Arkansas. *Archaeology* 44 (3): 22–30.

MacDonald, W. K., ed. 1976. *Digging for gold: Papers on archaeology for profit.* Ann Arbor: University of Michigan, Museum of Anthropology.

McManamon, F. P. 2000a. Abandoned Shipwreck Act. In *Archaeological method and theory: An encyclopedia,* edited by L. Ellis, pp. 1–2. New York: Garland.

———. 2000b. Antiquities Act of 1906. In *Archaeological method and theory: An encyclopedia,* edited by L. Ellis, pp. 33–35. New York: Garland.

———. 2000c. Archeological and Historical Preservation Act. In *Archaeological method and theory: An encyclopedia,* edited by L. Ellis, pp. 60–62. New York: Garland.

———. 2000d. Archaeological Resource Protection Act. In *Archaeological method and theory: An encyclopedia,* edited by L. Ellis, pp. 62–64. New York: Garland.

———. 2000e. National Historic Preservation Act. In *Archaeological method and theory: An encyclopedia,* edited by L. Ellis, pp. 385–86. New York: Garland.

———. 2000f. Native American Graves Protection and Repatriation Act. In *Archaeological method and theory: An encyclopedia,* edited by L. Ellis, pp. 386–88. New York: Garland.

Munson, C. A., M. M. Jones, and R. E. Fry. 1990. Forum: GE mounds: An ARPA test case. *American Antiquity* 60 (1): 171–85.

Schiffer, M. B., and G. J. Gumerman, eds. 1977. *Conservational archaeology: A guide for cultural resource management studies.* New York: Academic Press.

Schiffer, M. B., and J. H. House. 1977. Cultural resource management and archaeological research: The Cache Project. *Current Anthropology* 18: 43–68.

Shelton, D. 1986. Law and looting. *Archaeology* 39 (4): 80.

GLOSSARY

acid etching The use of hydrofluoric acid to etch a pattern onto a glass surface.

active style Expressions of meaning that are deliberately created and transmitted by an individual or group.

adaptation The development of specified cultural responses designed to cope with the natural and social environments of a given people in a given place and time.

alloy A combination of two or more metals.

annealing The process of heating copper over an open flame and then hammering together pieces of the metal to mend cracks or to form a single item.

anthropological archaeology The study of the human past, principally through material culture.

antiquarianism Collecting materials made by people of past eras for the sake of possessing, displaying, and/or feeling a connection with the past. Antiquarianism often emphasizes the most spectacular and finest examples of past material culture rather than the everyday material culture used by most people.

Antiquities Act of 1906 The act that gave the president of the United States authority to declare areas national monuments and required that any archaeology undertaken on federal properties administered by the departments of Interior, Agriculture, and War be done so by permit.

applique The addition of paste to an otherwise finished or nearly finished ceramic item in order to create a definable, discrete element, decorative or functional, to the piece.

arbitrary unit size The selection of a standard size for an excavation unit based on personal preferences.

archaeological cultures The definition of generally similar phases across a wide geographic region and long spans of time.

archaeological reconnaissance The process of searching for archaeological sites.

archaeological record All things left behind by past peoples and preserved in or on the earth.

Archaeological Resource Protection Act (ARPA) Enacted in 1979, this provided the government with civil and criminal outlets to pursue individuals vandalizing or looting cultural resources on federal properties.

archaeometry The combination of natural scientific disciplines with archaeological issues and problems.

archaeoparasitology The study of parasites in archaeological, and consequently human, contexts.

architectural unit method In this method observable architectural zones of predefined structures are excavated as a single horizontal provenience. Thus a room within a palace or other sort of structure would be treated as its own excavation area. The idea is to try to correlate archaeological units with the divisions of space constructed by past peoples.

artifacts The materials deliberately produced by past peoples.

attributes Specific, measurable elements, such as length, width, or weight, that combine to define a specific artifact or feature.

balanced reciprocity A subsystem of reciprocity in which allied individuals provide gifts of equal or slightly greater value to each other at predetermined times or events.

baseline A line placed on a site at a 90-degree angle from at least one other such line. These lines together allow archaeologists to identify their position on a site quickly and easily. Such baselines are invaluable tools when mapping a site.

baulk excavation method The excavation of an area of a site leaving vertical pillars or walls in place, thus enabling archaeologists to better correlate excavations with already defined strata.

billet An antler, bone, or wooden implement used to strike flakes from a core.

bioturbation Disturbance of sediments related to the archaeological record by animals such as moles and gophers.

block excavation method The excavation of an area of a site without leaving intervening walls or pillars in the area. This method allows archaeologists to expose contiguous areas of floors better than does a baulk method.

burin An Upper Paleolithic stone tool with a sharpened corner or projection specifically designed to engrave wood or bone. This tool is closely associated with the production of decorative art.

burnishing Polishing a ceramic using a simple abrasive in order to harden or add sheen to the surface.

chasing The deformation of the surface of a metal item, usually with a fine, blunt instrument, in order to create a decorative pattern.

chert A microcrystalline metamorphic stone commonly used as a stone tool. Sometimes used as a synonym for flint.

chipped stone tools Tools that have been produced through direct or indirect percussion, or a combination of these, or through pressure flaking.

closed market system A method of exchange in which artisans provide their products only to their patrons or to an exclusive group of people.

closures All items used to seal glass containers, including both glass and nonglass items such as metal and ceramic bottle caps.

coil construction The building of a ceramic piece by rolling strands of paste and then combining these to form a single piece of pottery.

comparative collections Collections of identified bones used for comparison with archaeologically recovered remains.

component A single zone within an archaeological site that represents the actions of past peoples, often presumably within a relatively short span of time.

compositional studies The study of the elemental composition of ceramics, usually through technologically sophisticated archaeometric techniques.

conspicuous consumption The use or display of excessive resources for a given task in order to display affluence, prestige, power, and/or identity.

contact mold A mold used to produce a full-sized, or a portion of a full-sized, glass item.

coprolite Any formed fecal mass, including fossilized, frozen, or mummified forms.

core The parent stone from which flakes are struck.

corporate lineage group A group of direct descendants and ancestors who combine efforts and work to benefit the lineage as a whole, usually under the leadership of a senior kinsman or lineage chief.

cortex Sometimes also called *rind,* the weathered exterior of a stone.

craft specialization The ability of part of a population to work at a single task to the exclusion or near exclusion of other forms of work.

crop marks Differences in the health and distribution of crops that reflect buried archaeological materials; usually used in conjunction with forms of remote sensing.

cross dating The process of assigning a date from a dated archaeological sequence to an undated sequence based on similarities in material culture between the sequences.

C-transforms The movement and redistribution of material culture by human agencies.

cultural evolution The theory that all cultures tend to move from simple to complex as they grow in size.

Cultural Property Act of 1983 (CPA) Provided legal sanctions against the import or export of stolen cultural properties into or out of the United States.

culture All of the beliefs and customs that we learn as members of society and that bind members of any given society together. It is the sharing of these customs and beliefs that allows people to anticipate and understand what other people are doing.

culture area A broad geographic region defined by similar natural resources in which the humans who live there tend to develop related or parallel cultural adaptations to exploit these resources.

decal A transferable decoration added to the surface of pottery beginning in the middle of the nineteenth century.

decorations One or more of a series of modifications performed on pottery for purposes that were primarily nonfunctional.

dendrochronology The analysis of growth rings in trees in order to determine the age of the wood being studied.

depositional environment The physical setting in which material culture is found. Depositional environments include such things as sediment types, soil pH, the amount of water in the sediment, and similar physical factors.

diachronic Across or through time.

diffusion The spread of material or ideas from a point of origin into other places.

digital elevation model (D.E.M.) A three-dimensional representation of the landscape within a defined area.

direct dating The use of a dating technique directly on the object being discussed, such as the charcoal from a fireplace or a piece of obsidian.

direct historical approach The tracing of material culture backward in time from known historical points using changes in typologies as guides.

direct percussion Striking a core directly with a hammer or billet in order to drive off a flake or the use of an anvil on which a core is directly struck to drive off a flake.

documentary archaeology The use of documentary sources to generate or enhance perspectives on the past, even in the absence of known archaeological materials.

drawing The process of extracting copper from ore-bearing rocks by heating the rock and liquefying the copper.

earthenware Ceramic usually composed of relatively dense, heavy clays, sometimes with noticeable inclusions, and fired at temperatures between approximately 800 and 1200°C.

ecofacts Naturally occurring materials such as pollen and phytoliths that can provide information about past human behaviors.

electron spin resonance (ESR) A technique best suited for the analysis of tooth enamel, shells, and burnt stone, it uses a spectrometer to measure the amount of energy released from an object when bombarded with microwaves.

emblemic style Expressions of meaning through associations with a socially known emblem

embossing The raising of portions of a ceramic piece to form decorative or functional patterns.

engraving The removal of metal from the surface of an item in order to create a decorative pattern, or the use of hard bits or wheels to cut a pattern into glass.

enumerative methods Dating techniques based on the observation and counting of measurable events, such as the growth of tree-rings or deposition of sediments.

ethnoarchaeology The study of living or ethnohistorically known peoples for the purposes of generating archaeologically useful data.

excavation unit A defined horizontal area that will be systematically excavated; a unit defines the horizontal location of a sampling location on an archaeological site.

expedient tools Tools that are formed quickly and for immediate use. Such tools often do not conform to typological standards and are often made using a flake.

faience An early Egyptian glaze for coating a pebble with a layer of melted silica. Faience is not generally considered to be a true glass.

faunal analysis Another term for zooarchaeology.

feature A combination of artifacts and/or ecofacts that create a single, definable item, such as a fireplace or burial.

filigree The application of wire to the surface of a metal object in order to create a decorative pattern.

firing pin signature The manufacturer's mark on the base of a munitions cartridge.

fission track dating A dating technique based on the observation and measurement of fission tracks in crystalline material created by the fissioning of 238U atoms.

flakes The pieces of stone struck off a rock in the reduction sequence, each usually having a striking platform, bulb of percussion, and similar identifying features.

flintknapping The process of chipping stone into shapes usable as tools or for expressive purposes.

flotation The use of water or air pressure and sometimes chemicals to cause light materials such as seeds and charcoal to rise to the surface in a container of water, where they can be collected.

flux An element or compound with a low melting point that is combined with another element or compound with a high melting point. The flux lowers the melting point of the entire mixture.

frame-first construction The method first constructing a ship's frame and then enclosing it with a hull. This method is faster than hull-first construction and saves on both labor and materials.

functional typology An archaeological typology based on the manners in which the objects under study were actually employed in the past.

generalized reciprocity A subsystem of reciprocity in which gifts are exchanged between individuals without the expectation of an immediate or equal return.

geographic information system (GIS) A database linked to a spatial component capable of displaying data on a projected landscape.

gilding The application of one metal, usually gold, over another.

glaze A vitreous (glassy) coating that is melted into the outer layers of a ceramic piece in order to make that piece watertight.

greenware state The state of a ceramic after it has been formed and allowed to air dry but prior to it being fired.

grinding platform, or **metate** Usually a substantial slab of abrasive stone on which grains and other plant materials are pulverized.

grinding stone, or **mano** Usually a hand-sized block or cylinder of abrasive stone designed to pulverize grains or other plant materials on a grinding platform.

ground penetrating radar A form of remote sensing that emits radar signals into the earth and then registers their return, thus plotting patterns of buried materials and sediments.

ground stone tools Tools that are produced by pecking and grinding stones into desired shapes.

gunflint A chert or flint fragment, sometimes produced from a prismatic blade, that is used in the striking mechanisms of flintlock firearms to strike a spark and thus ignite gunpowder to fire the weapon.

hammerstone The stone used to strike a core in order to detach flakes.

hard hammer technique The use of a percussive instrument that is as hard as or harder than the core to strike a flake from that core.

heavy fraction The portion of material that sinks in a flotation tank.

heliocentrism The belief in an extreme form of diffusionism popular among some English scholars in the late nineteenth and early twentieth centuries, according to which all culture developed in Egypt and spread outward through space and time.

histology The scientific study of the formation and distribution of cells in animal bones.

Historic Sites Act of 1935 This act expanded the Antiquities Act of 1906. It enabled the government to declare some properties national historic landmarks while reinforcing and clarifying the requirements for archaeological survey. It also required any federal agency sponsoring construction that threatened archaeological resources to allocate funds in an amount of up to 1% of the total cost of the project, for archaeological survey and testing.

holism The notion that anthropology encompasses the study of all aspects of human behavior, past and present.

horizontal approach A strategy of excavation designed to open large areas of a component to facilitate better understanding of that particular area.

hull-first construction The method of constructing a ship by erecting its shell before supporting it with a frame. This method is more labor and time intensive than frame-first construction.

human ecology The systematic study of the dynamic interrelationships between humans and their environments.

ideotechnic A category of material culture inferred to have served to display or communicate ideological statements, such as connections to spirits or religious tenets.

in situ In place.

incision The carving of lines into ceramics.

inclusion Any object other than clay or water present in the paste of a ceramic; items used specifically as temper are a special form of inclusion.

indirect dating The application of a date obtained for one item, through one or more of the methods discussed here, to a second object thought to be associated with the dated material. For example, the application of a date obtained on the charcoal in a fireplace to the rocks in that same fireplace, or

any tools mixed into the fireplace, would be indirect dating.

indirect percussion The use of an intermediary punch to focus the power of a blow on a specific point of a core.

inference A determination arrived at by reasoning.

inlay The placement of one material, either glass or metal, into a prepared depression (or reservoir) on the surface of an item for decorative purposes.

intuitive sampling The use of personal preferences in locating archaeological tests and excavation units.

iron A naturally occurring metallic ore that can be extracted from a rock matrix.

journal A serialized scholarly publication, such as *Antiquity, American Antiquity,* and the *Journal of Field Archaeology.*

kiln firing The use of a prepared structure for the process of hardening ceramics by creating high temperatures.

Levallois technology A Paleolithic technique common to archaic forms of the genus *Homo* in which a tortoise-shaped core is struck against an anvil in order to produce a long, broad flake.

light fraction The portion of the material that rises to the surface in a flotation tank.

linguistic anthropology The study of the human use of language and how it is both developed by and helps to develop meaning within culture.

lithics The full range of stone material related to or resulting from human activity.

logical positivism The philosophical position that there is an objectively knowable past that can be discovered through rigid adherence to scientific methods.

looting The uncontrolled excavation and effective theft of material culture for personal satisfaction or gain.

macrobotanical remains Fragments of plant tissue observable with the naked eye.

magnetometer Usually a highly mobile unit designed to measure changes in magnetic fields and/or gravitational fields.

market exchange An economic system in which artisans provide their products to others in exchange for those items or services that the artisan needs or desires.

material culture The material remains of the past; the actual things people made, used, and altered, and then left behind.

matrix A general term applied to the sediments and other material, such as boulders, gravel, or stone, in which archaeological materials are found.

matting The technique of incising a cross-hatched pattern on metal to create a dull area.

Mesolithic An Old World term for the period of time that represents regional diversification in human adaptations following the abandonment of big-game hunting but prior to the development of domestication and horticulture.

metal detector A simple tool that emits a cycling magnetic field and receives electrical signals resulting from distortions of these fields. When a detector passes over a metal object, including buried ones, the cycling field that it emits is distorted. This distortion produces an electrical signal, which triggers the beeper in the detector.

middle range theory Bridging theory that enables archaeologists to link excavated data with their interpretations about past human lifeways.

Midwest Taxonomic System A classificatory system developed by W. C. McKern based on foci, phases, and traditions.

mineral Naturally formed chemical elements or compounds, each possessing a specific chemical composition and usually appearing in crystal form.

minimum number of individuals (MNI) Minimum number of individual animals present at a specific location as calculated in zooarchaeology.

mold construction Pressing paste into a prepared form, or mold, which imparts its shape to the paste.

molds Prepared receptacles used to impart specific shapes to materials such as glass, clay, or metals.

monogenesis The belief in a single divine creation of humankind.

morphological typology An archaeological typology based on the shape and related physical characteristics of material culture.

National Archaeological Database (NADB) Contains references to archaeological reports from across the country and is particularly useful when searching for cultural resource management reports.

National Environmental Protection Act of 1969 (NEPA) Expanded on the Historic Sites Act of 1935 by requiring all federal agencies to file environmental and cultural resource impact statements on proposed development projects.

National Historic Preservation Act (NHPA) This act was first passed in 1966 and subsequently amended in 1976 and 1980. The act is designed to protect important cultural sites by placing them on a master list called the National Register of Historic Places. The act also serves to integrate local and state agencies into a nationwide program designed to preserve sites.

Native American Graves Protection and Repatriation Act (NAGPRA) Enacted in 1990, this law requires federal agencies and repositories for federal archaeological material to identify and, if possible, repatri-

ate human remains and items of cultural patrimony to appropriate Native American groups.

negative reciprocity A subsystem of reciprocity in which gifts or resources are exchanged between individuals seeking to gain an advantage from their trade.

Neolithic A term popular in the Old World applied to the era beginning roughly ten thousand years ago when humans began to domesticate plants and animals. The hallmark of this era is ground stone tools designed for plant processing.

normal curve The standard bell-shaped distribution of statistics in which approximately two-thirds of all points under the curve fall within 1 standard deviation of the mean value.

N-transforms The movement and reposition of cultural material on an archaeological site by natural agencies, such as animals or freeze-thaw action.

number of identified specimens (NISP) Number of specimens of bone from a single species as identified in zooarchaeology.

obsidian Sometimes referred to as volcanic glass, this is a form of stone that has no internal blocky structure. Consequently, it can be made to have an exceptionally sharp edge, though it is typically brittle.

obsidian hydration A dating technique that can be both relative and absolute. Fractures on the edge of obsidian pieces are examined under a microscope to identify the thickness of the hydration (bonded hydrogen atoms) layer that has accumulated. The thicker the level, the longer that fracture has been exposed to the atmosphere.

open market system A method of exchange in which artisans are free to provide their products to anyone capable of meeting their asking price.

open-air firing The heating and hardening of ceramics in pits or simple, above-earth, temporary structures.

optic mold A mold used to impart a decorative pattern to a sheet of glass, which is then pressed into a contact mold in order to produce a finished item.

optically stimulated luminescence (OSL) and thermoluminescence (TL) Related dating techniques which attempt to measure the amount of energy trapped in sediments (in the case of OSL) or heated clays and stones (in the case of TL) by reheating the material and then measuring the amount of energy released in the process.

oral history Traditions and tales passed from generation to generation by word of mouth.

paleoanthropologist A person who specializes in the study of hominid evolution and related disciplines, including archaeology, anatomy, and ecology.

paleodemographics The study of the distribution of past humans across the landscape. This work is usually closely intertwined with the analysis of human biological remains.

Paleolithic A term popular in the Old World defining the "Old Stone Age," the period prior to the last glacial epoch.

paleopathology The study of trauma or abnormal conditions in animal remains, usually human.

palynology The systematic study of pollen, often useful in reconstructing past environments.

paradigm Philosophical and scientific points of view that help structure the nature of thought and research. For all intents and purposes, paradigms are lenses through which a researcher sees information and constructs data.

passive style Expressions of meaning through stylistic displays that are the unintentional result of everyday activities

paste The mixture of clay, water, and inclusions, including temper, used to create ceramics.

pattern mold A mold used to impart a decorative pattern to a sheet of glass, which is then manually blown into a final shape.

pecking and grinding A combination of direct percussion and abrasion used to produce ground stone items.

Pecos Classification An archaeological sequence for the American Southwest proposed by A. V. Kidder based on his work at the Pecos Pueblo using the direct historical approach.

petrological studies The study of the physical structure of the rocks and minerals in ceramics.

phase I The initial stage in cultural resource management research, assessing the likely presence of cultural resources within a defined area.

phase II In cultural resource management, refers to the testing and assessment of cultural resources on an already-discovered archaeological site.

phases Tightly defined categories of time and space that refer only to a specific range of material culture in a small geographic area across a limited span of time, ideally no more than a few hundred years at most.

physical anthropology The study of humans as biological creatures, including their genetic diversity and evolution.

phytoliths Fragments of plant opal (silica) derived from plant cells. Because they are silicates, they are very long lasting.

pinching The creation of a ceramic item by hand forming a ball of paste without the use of a mold, wheel, slabs, or coils.

point counting Categorizing individual grains of sediment exposed by thin sectioning by size and sometimes by shape and then counting.

point proveniencing/piece plotting The precise three-dimensional measurement of a single piece of material culture in relation to an archaeological site.

pollen The common term applied to male gametophytes, the reproductive organs of plants.

polygenesis The belief in multiple divine creations of humankind.

polyhedral core A specially prepared many-sided core from which prismatic blades may be struck.

porcelain White kaolin clays fired at extremely high temperatures, usually somewhere between approximately 1300° and 1400°C.

potash-lead glass Glass based on potash as a flux with high concentrations of lead, it is heavy, lustrous, and more refractive than other forms of glass.

potash-lime glass Glass produced using potash derived from burning wood.

potlatch An elaborate competitive and alliance feast in which the host gives away massive quantities of both utilitarian and prestige items in order to cement alliances and to obligate rivals to give away even more material at their own potlatches.

pottery All forms of human-made products constructed from clay.

press mold A mold used to shape the exterior of a glass item while a plunger shapes the interior of the item.

pressure flaking The controlled application of increasing pressure to a core in order to strike off a flake.

primary clays Clays formed in place by the chemical and physical weathering of rock.

primary flake A flake that has substantial amounts of cortex on it and that was one of the first flakes removed from the core when the stone was initially broken open.

prismatic blade A flake struck from a polyhedral core, at least twice as long as it is wide, with steep, parallel sides, and trapezoidal (prismatic) in cross section.

provenience The precise three-dimensional location of an object on an archaeological site.

prunts Globules of glass that may or not be molded or cut into shapes but that are attached to an otherwise complete glass object.

pseudoscience The presentation of untested or untestable statements as fact. Such claims also reject scientific methodology and often emphasize fantastic or overly romanticized notions of natural and cultural behavior.

punctation Pressing nodes or other shapes into the surface of pottery, usually one shape at a time.

radiometric dating techniques A range of dating techniques based on principles of radioactive decay and change among specific materials, such as bone, wood, and certain forms of stone.

random sampling The use of random number methods in selecting locations for archaeological testing and exploration.

reciprocity An economic system in which gifts are exchanged in order to create and reinforce social relationships between people and groups.

reconnaissance (or site survey) The systematic search for archaeological sites and remains.

redistribution An economic system in which a percentage of all goods and resources produced in a community are given to a central authority for redistribution to members of the community who need these resources.

reduction sequence The various stages that a stone tool goes through from the point at which it is first struck to the point at which it is worked for the last time.

refitting The reconstruction of a core by fitting all of the flakes struck from that core back together.

remote sensing The application of technology to identify cultural resources without having to ground proof or otherwise excavate.

replication An example of middle range theory based on the production and use of modern stone tools to identify patterns of wear and breakage directly comparable to those found on archaeologically observed material culture.

repoussé The raising of a pattern or decorative element on the surface of a metal item.

rescue/salvage archaeology A term once used to refer to archaeology done in advance of construction or other destructive processes.

research design The plan for answering a series of research questions through the application of archaeological techniques and strategies.

research questions The specific questions that archaeologists ask when preparing a research program and seek to answer when executing that program.

rock An aggregate of one or more minerals that can be defined by both physical properties and mineral content. The three forms are igneous, rock that has cooled from a molten state; sedimentary, rock that has formed through the accretion of sediments; and metamorphic, rock formed from preexisting rocks subjected to extreme heat, pressure, or chemical change.

scope of work Definition of the amount, type, extent, and location of work that can be done under a given contract.

seasonal rounds The action of foragers who move from one environment to another following the seasonal availability of desired resources. The group tends to move through the same territories on an annual basis.

secondary clays Clays deposited in secondary locations, usually by erosion and the flow of streams.

secondary context The position in which material culture is found after it has undergone either or both C-transforms and N-transforms.

secondary flake A flake that may have some cortex on its surface (usually less than 20%) and that was struck during the rough shaping of a stone tool.

shadow marks Comparable to crop marks, shadow marks are the distribution of shadows created by cultural resources on an archaeological site that are identified through aerial photography.

sideways-looking-airborne-radar (SLAR) Projects electromagnetic (radar) pulses from an aircraft. These pulses are differentially reflected by various soil, sediment, and stone types and can be used to identify cultural resources.

site datum The master control point on an archaeological site into which all measurements are eventually tied.

site locality A large geographic area, such as a valley or gorge, in which many separate sites are clustered.

sites Spatially discrete places in which evidence for past human activity is found.

slab construction The construction of ceramics by preparing flattened slabs of clay and then joining them together.

slip A thin coating of fine, watery clay that can sometimes be made to resemble paint.

sociocultural anthropology The study of living or historically recorded societies with the goal of understanding the mechanisms of interpersonal and intergroup interaction.

sociotechnic A category of material culture in which items are inferred to have served social roles, such as identity marking.

soda-lime glass Glass produced using soda (an alkali) derived by burning seaweed and kelp.

soft hammer technique or **cylindrical hammer technique** The use of a percussive instrument that is softer than the core to strike a flake from that core.

soil marks Comparable to crop marks and shadow marks, soil marks are the distribution of differential sediments on an archaeological site that can indicate the presence of buried cultural resources.

sonar A form of remote sensing in which a data collecting unit sends an electromagnetic signal outward, usually into water. The signal penetrates through the water at a known rate; when it encounters something that it cannot penetrate, it is reflected back to the data collector. The time it takes the ping to return and the pattern of the return is collected by the sonar unit and is subsequently displayed in a readout.

sondage A term popular in Europe, a sondage is an area of intensive testing, often in the form of trenches or contiguous archaeological units.

stamping The use of a prepared, multitined or pictorial image on clay to impress a pattern into the surface of pottery.

state historic preservation officer (SHPO) The person charged with reviewing archaeological reports and helping to mitigate potential damage to archaeological sites as a result of approved development.

steel An alloy of iron and carbon that is produced at very high temperatures (above 1370°C).

stoneware A ceramic made from medium- to coarse-sized clay particles, fired at approximately 1200° to 1350°C. The combination of particle size and high heat results in a grey to brown, partially vitrified body.

stratified random sampling A method of sampling by which an archaeological site is first divided into zones or sections and a fixed number of excavation units are assigned to be placed at random in each zone. Thus, by defining a section of the site that is obviously important to the archaeologist, such as a cluster of buildings or a courtyard, as a zone and then deciding how many units to assign to that area, the archaeologist makes certain that at least some excavation will take place in that area.

stratigraphy The systematic study of layers of sediments, usually to determine the sequence in which past human acitvities took place.

strict random sampling The use of random number methods in the selection of locations for archaeological testing and exploration to the exclusion of all other methods.

S-twist The turn of fibers from the top left to the bottom right.

subsistence The means by which people acquire essential resources, such as food.

subsistence strategy A general plan for obtaining food and vital resources. The four traditional strategies are hunting and gathering, horticulture, pastoralism, and agriculture.

subsurface testing The process of excavating small, controlled tests in search of buried cultural resources.

superimposition The application of glass on top of other glass surfaces, including methods such as threading, banding, quilting and casing.

surface treatments Modifications made to the surface of pottery for either technological or functional purposes.

synchronic Within time or within a limited span of time.

tableware A category of glass items commonly used on tables, including plates, glasses, goblets, and serving bowls.

taphonomy The study of animal remains and what happened to them from the time they entered the archaeological record to the time they were recovered and analyzed.

technomic A category of material culture inferred to have served principally technological ends, such as cutting or piercing.

temper Coarse inclusions deliberately added to a paste for purposes of improving the firing characteristics of that paste.

terminus ante quem Refers to the date before which something must have happened.

terminus post quem Refers to the date after which something must have happened.

terra-cotta Ceramics fired at under 900°C. Such wares tend to be porous and somewhat delicate.

tertiary flake A flake that has no or very little cortex on it and that was struck during the final shaping of a stone tool.

test pitting The placement of single or small groups of excavation units across a site in order to acquire as much localized data as possible from the site being explored. Such data helps archaeologists define both the vertical and horizontal distribution of archaeological materials on the site.

test trenches Isolated or small groups of trenches excavated to preliminarily determine the natural and cultural distribution of materials across the site.

textiles Fibrous material from either plant tissue or animal hairs that are bound together, usually but not always by weaving.

three-age approach The method pioneered by C. J. Thomsen that linked stone, bronze, and iron material culture together in three successive periods. The basic concept of this method was adopted throughout much of the world.

transect A predetermined, usually straight path used in archaeological reconnaissance.

transfer printing Colored paper impressions derived from inked templates applied to the surface of unfired or partially fired pottery.

typology The formal description of all of the attributes that characterize most, if not all, of the artifacts that archaeologists recognize as clustering together.

unit datum point The control point from which all measurements in a specific excavation unit are made.

United States Geologic Survey (USGS) The government agency charged with the recording and dissemination of information related to the geology of the United States and its holdings.

utilized flakes Flakes that have been used as tools without further modification, such as sharpening or grinding.

varve analysis The study of the patterned, seasonal deposition of sediments in lakes adjacent to glaciers.

vertical approach The excavation of deep but relatively narrow units, usually employed to identify the type of natural and cultural deposits present on an archaeological site.

viewshed The area that can be seen from a given point on the landscape.

water screening The application of water under pressure to force sediments through screens.

wheel construction The construction a ceramic form through the use of a mechanical wheel that turns the developing form at varying speeds.

Zooarchaeology The scientific study of animal remains from archaeological sites.

Z-twist The turn of fibers from the top right toward the bottom left.

BIBLIOGRAPHY

Adams, E. C. 1989. Changing form and function in Western Pueblo ceremonial architecture from A.D. 1000 to A.D. 1500. In *The architecture of social integration in prehistoric pueblos,* edited by W. Lipe and M. Hegmon, 155–60. Occasional Paper no 1. Cortez, Colo.: Crow Canyon Archaeological Center.

Adams, J. L. 1988. Use-wear analysis on manos and hide process stones. *Journal of Field Archaeology* 15:307–15.

Adams, R. E. W., and F. Valdez, Jr. 1998. Stratigraphy. In *Field methods in archaeology.* 7th ed., edited by T. R. Hester, H. J. Shafer, and K. L. Feder, 147–62. Mountain View, Calif.: Mayfield.

Adams, R. E. W., W. E. Brown, Jr., and T. P. Culbert. 1981. Radar mapping, archaeology, and ancient Maya land use. *Science* 213:1457–63.

Adams, R. M. 1966. *The evolution of urban society.* Chicago: Aldine-Atherton.

———. 1974. Anthropological perspectives on ancient trade. *Current Anthropology* 15:239–58.

Adams, R. M., and H. Nissen. 1972. *The Uruk countryside.* Chicago: University of Chicago Press.

Adams, W. Y. 1968. Invasion, diffusion, evolution? *Antiquity* 42:194–215.

———. 1988. Archaeological classification: Theory versus practice. *Antiquity* 62:40–56.

Adams, W. Y., and E. W. Adams. 1991. *Archaeological typology and practical reality: A dialectical approach to artifact classification.* Cambridge: Cambridge University Press.

Addington, L. R. 1985. *Lithic illustration.* Chicago: University of Chicago Press.

Adkins, L., and R. Adkins. 1989. *Archaeological illustration.* Cambridge: Cambridge University Press.

Adovasio, J. M. 1977. *Basketry technology: A guide to identification and analysis.* Chicago: Aldine.

Aitken, M. J. 1960. Magnetic dating. *Archaeometry* 3:41–44.

———. 1985. *Thermoluminescence dating.* Orlando, Fla.: Academic Press.

———. 1990. *Science-based dating in archaeology.* London: Longman.

———. 2000a. Luminescence dating. In *Archaeological method and theory: An encyclopedia,* edited by L. Ellis, 222. New York: Garland.

———. 2000b. Optical dating. In *Archaeological method and theory: An encyclopedia,* edited by L. Ellis, 414–15. New York: Garland.

———. 2000c. Radiocarbon dating. In *Archaeological method and theory: An encyclopedia,* edited by L. Ellis, 505–8. New York: Garland.

———. 2000d. Thermoluminescence dating. In *Archaeological method and theory: An encyclopedia,* edited by L. Ellis, 630–34. New York: Garland.

Aldenderfer, M. S. 1983. Review of *Essays on archaeological typology,* edited by R. Whallon and J. A. Brown. *American Antiquity* 48:652–54.

———. 1991. The analytical engine: Computer simulation and archaeological research. In *Advances in archaeological method and theory.* Vol. 3, edited by M. B. Schiffer, 195–247. Tucson: University of Arizona Press.

Alexander, D. 1983. The limitations of traditional surveying techniques in a forested environment. *Journal of Field Archaeology* 10:133–44.

Alexander, J. 1970. *The directing of archaeological excavations.* London: Baker.

Allen, K. M. S., S. W. Green, and E. B. W. Zubrow, eds. 1990. *Interpreting space: GIS and archaeology.* London: Taylor & Francis.

Allen, R. O., ed. 1989. *Archaeological chemistry IV.* Advances in Chemistry Series, no. 220. Washington, D.C.: American Chemical Society.

Allen, W. L., and J. B. Richardson III. 1971. The reconstruction of kinship from archaeological data: The concepts, the methods, and the feasibility. *American Antiquity* 36:41–53.

Allman, J. C. 1968. The incinerator village site. *Ohio Archaeologist* 18:50–55.

Altman, J., J. P. Dwyer, M. R. Beckes, and R. D. Hake. 1982. ASP: A simplified computer sampling package for the field archaeologist. *Journal of Field Archaeology* 9:136–40.

Alva, W. 1988a. Discovering the New World's richest unlooted tomb. *National Geographic* 174 (4):510–14.

———. 1988b. Into the tomb of a Moche lord. *National Geographic* 174 (4):516–49.

———. 1990. New tomb of royal splendor. *National Geographic* 177 (6):2–15.

Ammerman, A. J. 1981. Surveys and archaeological research. *Annual Review of Anthropology* 10:63–88.

———. 1985. Plow-zone experiments in Calabria, Italy. *Journal of Field Archaeology* 8:151–65.

Ammerman, A. J., and M. W. Feldman. 1978. Replicated collection of site surfaces. *American Antiquity* 43:734–40.

Anderson, D. D. 1985. Reburial: Is it reasonable? *Archaeology* 38 (5):48–51.

Anderson, K. M. 1969. Ethnographic analogy and archaeological interpretation. *Science* 163:133–38.

Angel, J. L. 1969. The bases of paleodemography. *American Journal of Physical Anthropology* 30:427–38.

Arden, H. 1989. Who owns our past? *National Geographic* 175 (3):376–92.

Arnold, C. J. 1997. *An archaeology of the early Anglo-Saxon kingdoms.* 2d ed. London: Routledge.

Arnold, D. 1985. *Ceramic theory and cultural process.* Cambridge: Cambridge University Press.

Arnold, J. R., and W. F. Libby. 1949. Age determinations by radiocarbon content: Checks with samples of known age. *Science* 110:678–80.

Aronoff, S. 1989. *Geographic information systems: A management perspective.* Ottawa: WDL.

Arzigian, C. 1987. The emergence of horticultural economies in southwestern Wisconsin. In *Emergent horticultural economies of the Eastern Woodlands,* edited by W. Keegan, 217–42. Southern Illinois University Center for Archaeological Investigations, Occasional Paper 7. Carbondale: Southern Illinois University.

Ascher, M., and R. M. Ascher. 1963. Chronological ordering by computer. *American Anthropologist* 65:1045–52.

Ascher, R. M. 1961a. Analogy in archaeological interpretation. *Southwestern Journal of Anthropology* 17:317–25.

———. 1961b. Experimental archaeology. *American Anthropologist* 63:793–816.

———. 1968. Time's arrow and the archaeology of a contemporary community. In *Settlement archaeology,* edited by K. C. Chang, 43–52. Palo Alto, Calif.: National Press.

Ashmore, W. 1980. Discovering early classic Quiriguá. *Expedition* 23 (1):35–44.

———. 1991. Site-planning principles and concepts of directionality among the ancient Maya. *Latin American Antiquity* 2:199–226.

———, ed. 1981. *Lowland Maya settlement patterns.* School of American Research Advanced Seminar Series. Albuquerque: University of New Mexico Press.

Aveni, A. F. 1980. *Sky watchers of ancient Mexico.* Austin: University of Texas Press.

———. 1981. Archaeoastronomy. *Advances in archaeological method and theory.* Vol. 4, edited by M. B. Schiffer, 1–77. New York: Academic Press.

———, ed. 1982. *Archaeoastronomy in the New World.* Cambridge: Cambridge University Press.

———, ed. 1989. *World archaeoastronomy.* Cambridge: Cambridge University Press.

Bada, J. L., and P. M. Helfman. 1975. Amino acid racemization dating of fossil bones. *World Archaeology* 7:160–73.

Bahn, P. G., and J. Vertut. 1988. *Images of the Ice Age.* New York: Facts on File.

Baillie, M. G. L. 1982. *Tree-ring dating and archaeology.* Chicago: University of Chicago Press.

———. 2000. Dendrochronology. In *Archaeological method and theory: An encyclopedia,* edited by L. Ellis, 150–54. New York: Garland.

Baker, C. M. 1978. The size effect: An explanation of variability in surface artifact assemblage content. *American Antiquity* 43:288–93.

Baker, J., and D. R. Brothwell. 1980. *Animal diseases in archaeology.* New York: Academic Press.

Bamforth, D. B., and A. C. Spaulding. 1982. Human behavior, explanation, archaeology, history, and science. *Journal of Anthropological Archaeology* 1:170–95.

Bannister, B. 1962. The interpretation of tree-ring dates. *American Antiquity* 27:508–14.

———. 1970. Dendrochronology. In *Science in archaeology.* 2d edited by D. Brothwell and E. S. Higgs, 191–205. New York: Praeger.

Bannister, B., and T. L. Smiley. 1955. Dendrochronology. In *Geochronology,* edited by T. L. Smiley, 177–95. Physical Science Bulletin, no. 2. Tucson: University of Arizona.

Barber, E. J. W. 1999. *The mummies of Urumchi.* New York: Norton.

Bareis, C. J., and J. W. Porter. 1984. Research design. In *American Bottom archaeology: A summary of the FAI-270 project contribution to the culture history of the Mississippi River Valley,* edited by C. J. Bareis and J. W. Porter, 1–14. Urbana: University of Illinois Press.

Bareis, C. J., and J. W. Porter, eds. 1984. *American Bottom archaeology: A summary of the FAI-270 Project.* Urbana: University of Illinois.

Barker, A. W., and T. R. Pauketat. 1992. Introduction: Social inequality and the native elites of Southeastern North America. In *Lords of the Southeast: Social inequality and the native elites of Southeastern North America,* edited by A. W. Barker and T. Pauketat, 1–10. Archaeological Papers of the American Anthropological Association, no. 3. Washington, D.C.: American Anthropological Association.

Barker, G. 1985. *Prehistoric farming in Europe.* Cambridge: Cambridge University Press.

Barker, P. 1993. *The techniques of archaeological examination.* London: Batsford.

Barnes, F. C. 1980. *Cartridges of the world.* 4th ed. Chicago: Follett.

Bartel, B. 1982. A historical review of ethnological and archaeological analyses of mortuary practice. *Journal of Anthropological Archaeology* 1:32–58.

Bass, G. F. 1966. *Archaeology under water.* London: Thames & Hudson.

———. 2000. Sonar. In *Archaeological method and theory: An encyclopedia,* edited by L. Ellis, 582–84. New York: Garland.

Bass, G. F., and P. Throckmorton. 1961. Excavating a Bronze Age shipwreck. *Archaeology* 14:78–87.

Bass, W. M. 1986. *Human osteology: A laboratory and field manual of the human skeleton.* Columbia: Missouri Archaeological Society.

Bassett, C. A. 1986. The culture thieves. *Science* 867 (6):22–29.

Bator, P. M. 1983. *The international trade in art.* Chicago: University of Chicago Press.

Bawden, G. 1982. Community organization reflected by the household. *Journal of Field Archeology* 9:165–81.

Beadle, G. W. 1980. The ancestry of corn. *Scientific American* 242 (1):112–19.

Beaudry, M. C., ed. 1989. *Documentary archaeology in the New World.* Cambridge: Cambridge University Press.

Beck, C., and G. T. Jones. 1989. Bias and archaeological classification. *American Antiquity* 54:244–62.

Beck, C. W., ed. 1974. *Archaeological chemistry.* Advances in Chemistry Series, no. 138. Washington, D.C.: American Chemical Society.

Behrensmeyer, A. K. 1984. Taphonomy and the fossil record. *American Scientist* 72:558–66.

Behrensmeyer, A. K., and A. P. Hill. 1980. *Fossils in the making: Vertebrate taphonomy and paleoecology.* Chicago: University of Chicago Press.

Bellhouse, D. R. 1980. Sampling studies in archaeology. *Archaeometry* 22:123–32.

Benner, S. M., and R. S. Brodkey. 1984. Underground detection using differential heat analysis. *Archaeometry* 26:21–36.

Bennett, C. L., R. P. Beukens, M. R. Clover, H. E. Grove, R. B. Liebert, A. E. Litherland, K. H. Purse, and W. E. Sondheim. 1977. Radiocarbon dating using electrostatic accelerators: Negative ions provide the key. *Science* 198:508–10.

Bennett, M. A. 1974. *Basic ceramic analyses.* Contributions in Anthropology, no. 6. Portales: Eastern New Mexico University.

Bertalanffy, L. von. 1968. *General system theory: Foundations, development, applications.* New York: Barziller.

Betancourt, J. L., T. R. Van Devender, and P. S. Martin, eds. 1990. *Packrat middens: The last 40,000 years of biotic change.* Tucson: University of Arizona Press.

Bewley, R. 2000. Aerial photography for archaeology. In *Archaeological method and theory: An encyclopedia,* edited by L. Ellis, 3–9. New York: Garland.

Biddle, M., ed. 1977. Architecture and archaeology. *World Archaeology* 9 (whole no. 2).

Binford, L. R. 1961. A new method of calculating dates from kaolin pipe stem samples. *Southern Archaeological Conference Newsletter* 9 (1):19–21.

———. 1962. Archaeology as anthropology. *American Antiquity* 28:217–25.

———. 1964. A consideration of archaeological research design. *American Antiquity* 29:425–41.

———. 1967. Smudge pits and hide smoking: The use of analogy in archaeological reasoning. *American Antiquity* 32:1–12.

———. 1968a. Archeological perspectives. In *New perspectives in archaeology,* edited by S. R. Binford and L. R. Binford, 5–32. Chicago: Aldine.

———. 1968b. Post-Pleistocene adaptations. In *New perspectives in archaeology,* edited by S. R. Binford and L. R. Binford, 313–41. Chicago: Aldine.

———. 1971. Mortuary practices: Their study and their potential. In *Approaches to the social dimensions of mortuary practices,* edited by J. A. Brown, 6–29. Memoir no. 25. Washington, D.C.: Society for American Archaeology.

———. 1972a. *An archaeological perspective.* New York: Seminar Press.

———. 1972b. Archaeological reasoning and smudge pits—revisited. In *An archaeological perspective,* edited by L. R. Binford, 52–58. New York: Seminar Press.

———. 1973. Interassemblage variability—the Mousterian and the "functional" argument. In *The explanation of culture change: Models in prehistory,* edited by C. Renfrew, 227–54. Pittsburgh: University of Pittsburgh Press.

———. 1978. *Nunamiut Ethnoarchaeology.* New York: Academic Press.

———. 1981a. Behavioral archaeology and the "Pompeii premise." *Journal of Anthropological Research* 37:195–208.

———. 1981b. *Bones, ancient men and modern myths.* New York: Academic Press.

————. 1982. The archaeology of place. *Journal of Anthropological Archaeology* 1:5–31.

————. 1983. *Working at archaeology*. New York: Academic Press.

————. 1985. Human ancestors: Changing views of their behavior. *Journal of Anthropological Archaeology* 4: 292–327.

————. 1987. Data, relativism and archaeological science. *Man* 22:391–404.

————. 1989. *Debating archaeology*. San Diego: Academic Press.

————, ed. 1977. *For theory building in archaeology*. New York: Academic Press.

Binford, L. R., S. R. Binford, R. Whallon, and M. A. Hardin. 1970. *Archaeology at Hatchery West*. Memoir no. 24. Washington, D.C.: Society for American Archaeology.

Binford, S. R. 1968. Ethnographic data and understanding the Pleistocene. In *Man the hunter,* edited by R. B. Lee and I. DeVore, 274–75. Chicago: Aldine.

Binford, S. R., and L. R. Binford, eds. 1968. *New perspectives in archeology*. Chicago: Aldine.

Bintleff, J. L., and C. F. Gaffney, eds. 1986. *Archaeology at the interface: Studies in archaeology's relationships with history, geography, biology and physical science*. British Archaeological Reports International Series, no. 300. Oxford: British Archaeological Reports.

Bishop, R. L., R. L. Rands, and G. R. Holley. 1982. Ceramic compositional analysis in archaeological perspective. In *Advances in archaeological method and theory*. Vol. 5, edited by M. B. Schiffer, 275–330. New York: Academic Press.

Blanton, R. E. 1976. Anthropological studies of cities. *Annual Review of Anthropology* 5:249–64.

Bleed, P. 1983. Management techniques and archaeological fieldwork. *Journal of Field Archaeology* 10:494–98.

Blumenschine, R. J. 1986. *Early hominid scavenging opportunities: Implications of carcass availability in the Serengeti and Ngorongoro ecosystems*. British Archaeological Reports International Series, no. 283. Oxford: British Archaeological Reports.

Blumenschine, R. J., and M. M. Selvaggio. 1988. Percussion marks on bone surfaces as a new diagnostic of hominid behavior. *Nature* 333:763–65.

Bodner, C. C., and R. M. Rowlett. 1980. Separation of bone, charcoal, and seeds by chemical flotation. *American Antiquity* 45:110–16.

Bonnichsen, R., and M. G. Sorg, eds. 1989. *Bone modification*. Orono: University of Maine, Center for the Study of the First Americans.

Bordaz, J. 1970. *Tools of the Old and New Stone Age*. Garden City, N.Y.: Natural History Press.

Bordes, F. 1968. *The Old Stone Age*. New York: McGraw-Hill.

————. 1969. Reflections on typology and techniques in the Paleolithic. *Arctic Anthropology* 6:1–29.

Bordes, F., and D. de Sonneville-Bordes. 1970. The significance of variability in Paleolithic assemblages. *World Archaeology* 2:61–73.

Bourdieu, P. 1977. *Outline of a theory of practice*. Cambridge: Cambridge University Press.

Bowden, M. 1999. Augustus Pitt Rivers. In *Encyclopedia of archaeology: The great archaeologists*. Vol. 1, edited by T. Murray, 127–40. Santa Barbara, Calif.: ABC-CLIO.

Bowman, S. 1990. *Radiocarbon dating*. Berkeley and Los Angeles: University of California Press.

Brain, C. K. 1981. *Hunters or the hunted: An introduction to African cave taphonomy*. Chicago: University of Chicago Press.

Brainerd, G. W. 1951. The place of chronological ordering in archaeological analysis. *American Antiquity* 16:301–13.

Braun, D. P., and S. Plog. 1982. Evolution of "tribal" social networks: Theory and prehistoric North American evidence. *American Antiquity* 47:504–25.

Bray, W., ed. 1973. Trade. *World Archaeology* 5 (whole no. 2).

————, ed. 1976. Climatic change. *World Archaeology* 8 (whole no. 2).

Bray, W., and N. Seeley, eds. 1989. Archaeometallurgy. *World Archaeology* 20 (whole no. 3).

Brew, J. O. 1946. The use and abuse of taxonomy. In *The archaeology of Alkali Ridge, Southern Utah,* by J. O. Brew, 44–66. Papers of the Peabody Museum, no. 21. Cambridge: Harvard University Press.

————, ed. 1968. *One hundred years of anthropology*. Cambridge: Harvard University Press.

Brodrick, A. H. 1949. *Lascaux: A commentary*. London: Benn.

Bronitsky, G., ed. 1989. *Pottery technology: Ideas and approaches*. Boulder, Colo.: Westview Press.

Brothwell, D. R. 1971. Paleodemography. In *Biological aspects of demography,* edited by W. Brass, 111–30. London: Taylor & Francis.

————. 1981. *Digging up bones*. 3rd ed. Ithaca, N.Y.: Cornell University Press.

Brothwell, D. R., and A. T. Sandison, eds. 1967. *Diseases in antiquity*. Springfield, Ill.: Thomas.

Browman, D. L. 1981. Isotopic discrimination and correction factors in radiocarbon dating. In *Advances in archaeological method and theory*. Vol. 4, edited by M. B. Schiffer, 241–95. New York: Academic Press.

Brown, J. A. 1981. The search for rank in prehistoric burials. In *The archaeology of death,* edited by R. Chapman, I. Kinnes, and K. Randsborg, 25–37. Cambridge: Cambridge University Press.

———, ed. 1971. *Approaches to the social dimensions of mortuary practices.* Memoir no. 25. Washington, D.C.: Society for American Archaeology.

Brown, J. A., and S. Struever. 1973. The organization of archaeological research: An Illinois example. In *Research and theory in current archaeology,* edited by C. L. Redman, 261–80. New York: Wiley-Interscience.

Bruce-Mittford, R. L. S. 1979. *The Sutton Hoo ship-burial: Reflections after thirty years.* York: University of York.

Bryant, V. 2000. Flotation. In *Archaeological method and theory: An encyclopedia,* edited by L. Ellis, 216–18. New York: Garland.

Bryant, V. M., Jr., and R. G. Holloway. 1983. The role of palynology in archaeology. In *Advances in archaeological method and theory.* Vol. 6, edited by M. B. Schiffer, 191–224. New York: Academic Press.

Buikstra, J. E. 1976. *Hopewell in the Lower Illinois Valley: A regional study of human biological variability.* Evanston, Ill.: Center for American Archaeology Press.

———. 1981a. Mortality practices, paleodemography, and paleopathology: A case study from the Koster site (Illinois). In *The archaeology of death,* edited by R. Chapman, I. Kinnes, and K. Randsborg, 123–32. Cambridge: Cambridge University Press.

———, ed. 1981b. *Prehistoric tuberculosis in the Americas.* Evanston, Ill.: Center of American Archaeology Press.

Buikstra, J. E., and D. C. Cook. 1980. Paleopathology: An American account. *Annual Review of Anthropology* 9:433–70.

Buikstra, J. E., and L. W. Konigsberg. 1985. Paleodemography: Critiques and controversies. *American Anthropologist* 88:316–33.

Bunn, H. T. 1981. Archaeological evidence for meateating by Plio-Pleistocene hominids from Koobi Fora and Olduvai Gorge. *Nature* 29:574–77.

———. 1983. Evidence on the diet and subsistence patterns of Plio-Pleistocene hominids at Koobi Fora, Kenya, and Olduvai Gorge, Tanzania. In *Animals and archaeology.* Vol. 1, *Hunters and their prey,* edited by J. Clutton-Brock and C. Grigson, 21–30. British Archaeological Reports International Series, no. 163. Oxford: British Archaeological Reports.

Bunn, H. T., J. W. K. Harris, G. Isaac, Z. Kaufulu, E. Kroll, K. Schick, N. Toth, and A. K. Behrensmeyer. 1980. FxJj50: An early Pleistocene site in northern Kenya. *World Archaeology* 12:109–36.

Burnett, A. 1991. *Coins.* Berkeley: University of California.

Burnham, B. C., and J. Kingsbury, eds. 1979. *Space, hierarchy and society: Interdisciplinary studies in social area analysis.* British Archaeological Reports Inter-

national Series, no. 59. Oxford: British Archaeological Reports.

Butler, W. B. 1987. Significance and other frustrations in the CRM process. *American Antiquity* 52:820–29.

Butzer, K. W. 1982. *Archaeology as human ecology: Method and theory for a contextual approach.* New York: Cambridge University Press.

Byrd, B. 1980. A standardized system for recording survey-project information. *Journal of Field Archaeology* 8:381–83.

Cahan, D., L. H. Keeley, and F. L. Van Noten. 1979. Stone tools, toolkits and human behavior in prehistory. *Current Anthropology* 20:661–83.

Callen, E. O. 1970. Diet as revealed by coprolites. In *Science in archaeology.* 2d ed., edited by D. Brothwell and E. S. Higgs, 235–43. New York: Praeger.

Callender, D. W., Jr. 1976. Reliving the past: Experimental archaeology in Pennsylvania. *Archaeology* 29:173–77.

Cann, J. R., and C. Renfrew. 1964. The characterization of obsidian and its application to the Mediterranean region. *Proceedings of the Prehistoric Society* 30:111–33.

Carneiro, R. L. 1970. A theory of the origin of the state. *Science* 169:733–38.

Carr, C. 1982. *Handbook on soil resistivity surveying.* Evanston, Ill.: Center for American Archaeology Press.

———. 1984. The nature of organization of intra-site archaeological records and spatial analytic approaches to their investigation. In *Advances in archaeological method and theory.* Vol. 7, edited by M. B. Schiffer, 103–222. Orlando, Fla.: Academic Press.

Carr, D. R., and J. L. Kulp. 1957. Potassium-argon method of geochronometry. *Bulletin of the Geological Society of America* 68:763–84.

Carter, G. F., ed. 1978. *Archaeological chemistry II.* Advances in Chemistry Series, no. 171. Washington, D.C.: American Chemical Society.

Carter, H. [1922] 1972. *The tomb of Tutankhamen.* Reprint. New York: Excalibur Books.

Carver, M. 1998. *Sutton Hoo: Burial ground of kings?* Philadelphia: University of Pennsylvania.

Casteel, R. W. 1970. Core and column sampling. *American Antiquity* 35:465–66.

———. 1976. *Fish remains in archaeology and paleoenvironmental studies.* New York: Academic Press.

Caton-Thompson, G., ed. 1931. *The Zimbabwe culture: Ruins and reactions.* Oxford: Clarendon.

Cavallo, J. A. 1984. Fish, fires, and foresight: Middle Woodland economic adaptations in the Abbott Farm National Landmark. *North American Archaeologist* 5:111–38.

Chamberlain, T. C. 1897. The method of multiple working hypotheses. *Journal of Geology* 39:155–65.

Champe, J. D., D. S. Byers, C. Evans, A. K. Guthe, H. W. Hamilton, E. B. Jelks, C. W. Meighan, S. Olafson, G. I. Quimby, W. Smith, and F. Wendorf. 1961. Four statements for archaeology. *American Antiquity* 27:137–38.

Champion, S. 1980. *A dictionary of terms and techniques in archaeology.* Oxford: Phaidon Press.

Chang, C., and H. A. Koster. 1986. Beyond bones: Toward an archaeology of pastoralism. In *Advances in archaeological method and theory.* Vol. 9, edited by M. B. Schiffer, 97–148. Orlando, Fla.: Academic Press.

Chang, K. C. 1958. Study of the Neolithic social groupings: Examples from the New World. *American Anthropologist* 60:298–334.

———. 1967. Major aspects of the interrelationship of archaeology and ethnology. *Current Anthropology* 8: 227–43.

———. 1972. *Settlement patterns in archaeology.* Modules in Anthropology, no. 24. Reading, Mass.: Addison-Wesley.

———. 1983. *Art, myth and ritual: The path to political authority in ancient China.* Cambridge: Harvard University Press.

———, ed. 1968. *Settlement archaeology.* Palo Alto, Calif.: National Press Books.

Chaplin, R. E. 1971. *The study of animal bones from archaeological sites.* New York: Seminar Press.

Chapman, R., I. Kinnes, and K. Randsborg, eds. 1981. *The archaeology of death.* Cambridge: Cambridge University Press.

Charles, D. K., and J. E. Buikstra. 1983. Archaic mortuary sites in the Central Mississippi Drainage: Distribution, structure, and implications. In *Archaic hunters and gatherers,* edited by J. Philips and J. Brown, 117–45. New York: Academic Press.

Charleton, T. H. 1981. Archaeology, ethnohistory, and ethnology: Interpretive interfaces. In *Advances in archaeological method and theory.* Vol. 4, edited by M. B. Schiffer, 129–76. New York: Academic Press.

Chartkoff, J. L. 1978. Transect interval sampling in forests. *American Antiquity* 43:46–53.

Chenhall, R. G. 1975. *Museum cataloging in the computer age.* Nashville, Tenn.: American Association for State and Local History.

Childe, V. G. 1929. *The Danube in prehistory.* Oxford: Oxford University Press.

———. 1954. *What happened in history.* Rev. ed. Harmondsworth, England: Penguin Books.

———. 1956. *A short introduction to archaeology.* London: Muller.

Christenson, A. L., ed. 1989. *Tracing archaeology's past: The historiography of archaeology.* Carbondale: Southern Illinois University Press.

Claasen, C. P. 1991a. Gender, shellfishing, and the Shell Mound archaic. In *Engendering archaeology: Women and prehistory,* edited by J. M. Gero and M. W. Conkey, 276–300. Oxford: Blackwell.

———. 1991b. Normative thinking and shell-bearing sites. In *Advances in archaeological method and theory.* Vol. 3, edited by M. B. Schiffer, 249–98. Tucson: University of Arizona Press.

———. 1998. *Shells.* Cambridge: Cambridge University Press.

Clark, G. A. 1982. Quantifying archaeological research. In *Advances in archaeological method and theory.* Vol. 5, edited by M. B. Schiffer, 217–73. New York: Academic Press.

Clark, G. A., and C. R. Stafford. 1982. Quantification in American archaeology: A historical perspective. *World Archaeology* 14:98–119.

Clark, J. G. D. 1952. *Prehistoric Europe: The economic basis.* London: Methuen.

Clarke, D. L. 1968. *Analytical archaeology.* London: Methuen.

———. 1972a. Models and paradigms in contemporary archaeology. In *Models in archaeology,* edited by D. L. Clarke, 1–60. London: Methuen.

———. 1972b. A provisional model of an Iron Age society. In *Models in archaeology,* edited by D. L. Clarke, 801–69. London: Methuen.

———. 1973. Archaeology: The loss of innocence. *Antiquity* 47:6–18.

———. 1978. Introduction and polemic. In *Analytical archaeology.* 2d ed., edited by D. L. Clarke, 1–41. London: Methuen.

———, ed. 1977. *Spatial archaeology.* New York: Academic Press.

Clay, R. B. 1976. Typological classification, attribute analysis, and lithic variability. *Journal of Field Archaeology* 3:303–11.

Cleere, H., ed. 1984. *Approaches to the archaeological heritage: A comparative study of world cultural resource management systems.* Cambridge: Cambridge University Press.

———, ed. 1989. *Archaeological heritage management in the modern world.* London: Unwin Hyman.

Clutton-Brock, J., and C. Grigson, eds. 1983. *Animals and archaeology.* Vol. 1, *Hunters and their prey.* British Archaeological Reports International Series, no. 163. Oxford: British Archaeological Reports.

———, eds. 1984. *Animals and archaeology.* Vol. 3, *Early herders and their flocks.* British Archaeological Reports International Series, no. 203. Oxford: British Archaeological Reports.

Coe, M. D., and K. V. Flannery. 1964. Microenvironments and Mesoamerican prehistory. *Science* 143:650–54.

Coggins, C. C. 1972. Archaeology and the art market. *Science* 175:263–66.

Coggins, C. C., and O. G. Shane, III, eds. 1984. *Cenote of sacrifice.* Austin: University of Texas Press.

Cohen, M. N. 1977. *The food crisis in prehistory.* New Haven: Yale University Press.

Cohen, M. N., and G. J. Armelagos, eds. 1984. *Paleopathology at the origins of civilization.* Orlando, Fla.: Academic Press.

Cole, J. R. 1980. Cult archaeology and unscientific method and theory. In *Advances in archaeological method and theory.* Vol. 3, edited by M. B. Schiffer, 1–33. New York: Academic Press.

Coles, B., and J. M. Coles. 1986. *Sweet track to Glastonbury: The Somerset levels in prehistory.* New York and London: Thames & Hudson.

———. 1989. *People of the wetlands: Bog, bodies and lake-dwellers.* New York: Thames & Hudson.

Coles, J. M. 1973. *Archaeology by experiment.* New York: Scribner's.

———. 1984. *The archaeology of wetlands.* Edinburgh: Edinburgh University Press.

———. 1989. The world's oldest road. *Scientific American* 261 (5):100–106.

Collingwood, R. G. 1946. *The idea of history.* Oxford: Oxford University Press.

Collon, D. 1990. *Near Eastern seals.* Berkeley: University of California.

Conkey, M. W. 1984. To find ourselves: Art and social geography of prehistoric hunter gatherers. In *Past and present in hunter-gatherer studies,* edited by C. Schrire, 253–76. Orlando, Fla.: Academic Press.

———. 1985. Ritual communication, social elaboration, and the variable trajectories of Paleolithic material culture. In *Prehistoric hunter gatherers. The emergence of cultural complexity,* edited by T. D. Price and J. A. Brown, 299–323. Orlando, Fla.: Academic Press.

———. 1987. New approaches in the search for meaning? A review of research in "Paleolithic art." *Journal of Field Archaeology* 14:413–30.

Conkey, M. W., and J. Spector. 1984. Archaeology and the study of gender. In *Advances in archaeological method and theory.* Vol. 7, edited by M. B. Schiffer, 1–38. Orlando, Fla.: Academic Press.

Conkey, M. W., and C. Hastorf, eds. 1990. *The uses of style in archaeology.* Cambridge: Cambridge University Press.

Cook, B. F. 1991. The archaeologist and the art market: Policies and practice. *Antiquity* 65:533–37.

Cook, D. C. 1981. Mortality, age-structure and status in the interpretation of stress indicators in prehistoric skeletons: A dental example from the lower Illinois valley. In *The archaeology of death,* edited by R. Chapman, I. Kinnes, and K. Randsborg, 133–44. Cambridge: Cambridge University Press.

Cook, S. F. 1972. *Prehistoric demography.* Modules in Anthropology, no. 16. Reading, Mass.: Addison-Wesley.

Cooper, M. A., and J. D. Richards, eds. 1985. *Current issues in archaeological computing.* British Archaeological Reports International Series, no. 271. Oxford: British Archaeological Reports.

Coote, G. 2000. Fluorine-uranium-nitrogen dating. In *Archaeological method and theory: An encyclopedia,* edited by L. Ellis, 218–26. New York: Garland.

Cordell, L. S. 1979. Prehistory: Eastern Anasazi. In *Handbook of North American Indians.* Vol. 9, edited by W. C. Sturtevant and A. Ortiz, 131–51. Washington, D.C.: Smithsonian Institution.

———. 1984a. *Prehistory of the Southwest.* Orlando, Fla.: Academic Press.

———. 1984b. Southwestern archaeology. *Annual Review of Anthropology* 13:301–32.

Cordell, L. S., and F. Plog. 1979. Escaping the confines of normative thought: A reevaluation of Puebloan prehistory. *American Antiquity* 44:405–29.

Cornwall, I. W. 1970. Soil, stratification and environment. In *Science in archaeology.* 2d ed., edited by D. R. Brothwell and E. S. Higgs, 120–34. New York: Praeger.

Costin, C. L. 1991. Craft specialization: Issues in defining, documenting, and explaining the organization of production. In *Advances in archaeological method and theory.* Vol. 3, edited by M. B. Schiffer, 1–56. Tucson: University of Arizona Press.

Cottrell, A. 1981. *The first emperor of China: The greatest archeological find of our time.* New York: Holt, Rinehart & Winston.

Courty, M. A., P. Goldberg, and R. Macphail. 1989. *Soils and micromorphology in archaeology.* Cambridge: Cambridge University Press.

Cowan, C. W., and P. J. Watson, eds., 1992. *The origins of agriculture.* Washington, D.C.: Smithsonian Institution.

Cowgill, G. L. 1964. The selection of samples from large sherd collections. *American Antiquity* 29:467–73.

———. 1968. Archaeological applications of factor, cluster and proximity analysis. *American Antiquity* 33:367–75.

———. 1974. Quantitative studies of urbanization at Teotihuacan. In *Mesoamerican archaeology: New approaches,* edited by N. Hammond, 363–97. Austin: University of Texas Press.

————. 1977. The trouble with significance tests and what we can do about it. *American Antiquity* 42:350–68.

————. 1986. Archaeological applications of mathematical and formal methods. In *American archaeology past and future: A celebration of the Society for American Archaeology 1935–1985*, edited by D. J. Meltzer, D. D. Fowler, and J. A. Sabloff, 369–93. Washington, D.C.: Smithsonian Institution Press.

Crabtree, D. E. 1972. *An introduction to flintworking*. Part 1, *An introduction to the technology of stone tools*. Occasional Paper no. 28. Pocatello: Idaho State University.

Crabtree, P. J. 1990. Zooarchaeology and complex society: Some uses of faunal analysis for the study of trade, social status, and ethnicity. In *Advances in archeological method and theory*. Vol. 2, edited by M. B. Schiffer, 155–205. Tucson: University of Arizona Press.

Cronyn, J. M. 1990. *The elements of archeological conservation*. London: Routledge.

Crowfoot, E., F. Pritchard, and K. Staniland. 1996. *Medieval finds from excavations in London: Textiles and clothing*. London: Museum of London.

Crumley, C. 1979. Three locational models: An epistemological assessment for anthropology and archaeology. In *Advances in archaeological method and theory*. Vol. 2, edited by M. B. Schiffer, 141–73. New York: Academic Press.

Crumley, C. L., and W. H. Marquardt, eds. 1987. *Regional dynamics: Burgundian landscapes in historical perspective*. San Diego: Academic Press.

————. 1990. Landscape: A unifying concept in regional analysis. In *Interpreting space: GIS and archaeology*, edited by K. M. S. Allen, S. W. Green, and E. B. W. Zubrow, 73–79. Bristol, Pa.: Taylor & Francis.

Cunliffe, B., ed. 1978. Landscape archaeology. *World Archaeology* 9 (whole no. 3).

————. 1984. Ceramics. *World Archaeology* 15 (whole no. 3).

————. 1999. Sir Mortimer Wheeler. In *Encyclopedia of archaeology: The great archaeologists*. Vol. 1, edited by T. Murray, 371–84. Santa Barbara: ABC-CLIO.

Curtis, G. H. 1975. Improvements in potassium-argon dating: 1962–1975. *World Archaeology* 7:198–209.

Custer, J. F., T. Eveleigh, V. Klemas, and I. Wells. 1986. Application of LANDSAT data and synoptic remote sensing to predictive models for prehistoric archaeological sites: An example from the Delaware coastal plain. *American Antiquity* 51:572–88.

Dabas, M., A. Hesse, and A. Tabbagh. 2000. Electrical and electromagnetic prospecting. In *Archaeological method and theory: An encyclopedia*, edited by L. Ellis, 165–70. New York: Garland.

Dales, G. F. 1966. The decline of the Harappans. *Scientific American* 214 (5):92–100.

Daniel, G. 1943. *The three ages: An essay on archaeological method*. Cambridge: Cambridge University Press.

————. 1962. *The idea of prehistory*. Baltimore: Penguin Books.

————. 1967. *The origins and growth of archaeology*. Baltimore: Penguin Books.

————. 1971. From Worsaae to Childe: The models of prehistory. *Proceedings of the Prehistoric Society* 38:140–53.

————. 1976a. *A hundred and fifty years of archaeology*. Cambridge: Harvard University Press.

————. 1976b. Stone, bronze and iron. In *To illustrate the monuments: Essays on archaeology presented to Stuart Piggott*, edited by J. V. S. Megaw, 35–42. London: Thames & Hudson.

————. 1981a. *A short history of archaeology*. London: Thames & Hudson.

————, ed. 1981b. *Towards a history of archaeology*. New York: Thames & Hudson.

Daniels, S. G. H. 1972. Research design models. In *Models in archaeology*, edited by D. L. Clarke, 201–229. London: Methuen.

Dart, R. A. 1949. The predatory implemental technique of the australopithecines. *American Journal of Physical Anthropology* 7:1–16.

————. 1957. The *Osteodontokeratic culture of Australopithecus Prometheus*. Memoir no. 10. Pretoria, South Africa: Transvaal Museum.

Darwin, C. R. 1859. *On the origin of species*. London: Murray.

Davies, D. D. 1985. Hereditary emblems: Material culture in the context of social change. *Journal of Anthropological Archaeology* 4:149–76.

Davies, M. 1987. The archeology of standing structures. *Australian Journal of Historical Archaeology* 5:54–64.

Davis, H. A. 1972. The crisis in American archeology. *Science* 175:267–72.

————. 1982. Professionalism in archaeology. *American Antiquity* 47:158–62.

Davis, J., and A. P. Sullivan. 2000. Surveys, multistage and large-scale. In *Archaeological method and theory: An encyclopedia*, edited by L. Ellis, 610–12. New York: Garland.

Davis, S. J. M. 1987. *The archaeology of animals*. New Haven: Yale University Press.

Davis, W. 1986. The origins of image making. *Current Anthropology* 27:193–215.

Deagan, K. 1982. Avenues of inquiry in historical archaeology. In *Advances in archaeological method and the-*

ory. Vol. 5, edited by M. B. Schiffer, 151–77. New York: Academic Press.

Deal, M. 1985. Household pottery disposal in the Maya highlands: An ethnoarchaeological interpretation. *Journal of Anthropological Archaeology* 4:243–91.

Dean, J. S. 1978. Independent dating in archaeological analysis. In *Advances in archaeological method and theory.* Vol. 1, edited by M. B. Schiffer, 223–55. New York: Academic Press.

De Atley, S. P., and F. J. Findlow, eds. 1984. *Exploring the limits: Frontiers and boundaries in prehistory.* British Archaeological Report International Series, no. 223. Oxford: British Archaeological Reports.

Deetz, J. 1965. *The dynamics of stylistic change in Arikara ceramics.* Illinois Studies in Anthropology, no. 4. Urbana: University of Illinois Press.

———. 1967. *Invitation to archaeology.* Garden City, N.Y.: Natural History Press.

———. 1968. The inference of residence and descent rules from archaeological data. In *New perspectives in archaeology,* edited by S. R. Binford and L. R. Binford, 41–48. Chicago: Aldine.

———. 1977. *In small things forgotten: The archaeology of Early American life.* Garden City, N.Y.: Doubleday/Anchor.

———. 1988a. History and archaeological theory: Walter Taylor revisited. *American Antiquity* 53:13–22.

———. 1988b. American historical archeology: Methods and results. *Science* 239:362–67.

Deetz, J., and E. Dethlefsen. 1965. The Doppler effect and archaeology: A consideration of the spatial aspects of seriation. *Southwestern Journal of Anthropology* 21:196–206.

———. 1967. Death's head, cherub, urn and willow. *Natural History* 76 (3):28–37.

Delgado, J. P. 1998. *Encyclopedia of underwater and maritime archaeology.* New Haven: Yale University Press.

Dethlefsen, E., and J. Deetz. 1966. Death's heads, cherubs, and willow trees: Experimental archaeology in colonial cemeteries. *American Antiquity* 31:502–10.

Diamant, S. 1979. Archaeological sieving at Franchthi cave. *Journal of Field Archeology* 6:203–19.

Dillon, B. 1989. *Practical archaeology: Field and laboratory techniques and archaeological logistics.* Rev. ed. Archaeological Research Tools 2. Los Angeles: UCLA Institute of Archaeology.

———, ed. 1985. *Student's guide to archaeological illustrating.* Rev. ed. Archaeological Research Tools 1. Los Angeles: UCLA Institute of Archaeology.

Dimbleby, G. W. 1967. *Plants and archaeology.* London: Baker.

———. 1985. *The palynology of archaeological sites.* Orlando, Fla.: Academic Press.

Donley, L. W. 1982. House power: Swahili space and symbolic markers. In *Symbolic and structural archaeology,* edited by I. Hodder, 63–73. Cambridge: Cambridge University Press.

Doran, J. 1970. Systems theory, computer simulations and archaeology. *World Archaeology* 1:289–98.

Dorrell, P. G. 1989. *Photography in archaeology and conservation.* Cambridge: Cambridge University Press.

Douglas, M. 1972. Symbolic orders in the use of domestic space. In *Man, settlement and urbanism,* edited by P. J. Ucko, R. Tringham, and G. W. Dimbleby, 513–21. London: Duckworth.

Doumas, C. 1974. The Minoan eruption of the Santorini volcano. *Antiquity* 48:110–15.

Dower, M.S. 1999. Sir William Flinders Petrie. In *Encyclopedia of archaeology: The great archaeologists.* Vol. 1, edited by T. Murray, 221–32. Santa Barbara: ABC-CLIO.

Dowman, E. A. 1970. *Conservation in field archaeology.* London: Methuen.

Drennan, R. D. 1976. Religion and social evolution in formative Mesoamerica. In *The Early Mesoamerican village,* edited by K. V. Flannery, 345–68. New York: Academic Press.

Dumond, D. E. 1977. Science in archaeology: The saints go marching in. *American Antiquity* 42:33–49.

Dunnell, R. C. 1971. *Systematics in prehistory.* New York: Free Press.

———. 1980. Evolutionary theory and archeology. In *Advances in archaeological method and theory.* Vol. 3, edited by M. B. Schiffer, 35–99. New York: Academic Press.

———. 1982. Science, social science, and common sense: The agonizing dilemma of modern archaeology. *Journal of Anthropological Research* 38:1–25.

———. 1986. Methodological issues in Americanist artifact classification. In *Advances in archaeological method and theory.* Vol. 9, edited by M. B. Schiffer, 149–207. Orlando, Fla.: Academic Press.

———. 2000a. Archaeometry. In *Archaeological method and theory: An encyclopedia,* edited by L. Ellis, 47–52. New York: Garland.

———. 2000b. Seriation. In *Archaeological method and theory: An encyclopedia,* edited by L. Ellis, 549–50. New York: Garland.

———. 2000c. Type-variety system. In *Archaeological method and theory: An encyclopedia,* edited by L. Ellis, 638–40. New York: Garland.

Dunnell, R. C., and W. S. Dancey. 1983. The siteless survey: A regional scale data collection strategy. In *Advances in archaeological method and theory*. Vol. 6, edited by M. B. Schiffer, 267–88. New York: Academic Press.

Dyer, J. 1992. *Hillforts of England and Wales*. Princes Risborough, England: Shire Archaeology.

Earle, T. K., and J. E. Ericson, eds. 1977. *Exchange systems in prehistory*. New York: Academic Press.

Earle, T. K., and R. W. Preucel. 1987. Processual archaeology and the radical critique. *Current Anthropology* 28:501–38.

Ebert, J. I. 1984. Remote sensing applications in archaeology. In *Advances in archaeological method and theory*. Vol. 7, edited by M. B. Schiffer, 293–362. Orlando, Fla.: Academic Press.

Eddy, J. A. 1974. Astronomical alignment of the Big Horn Medicine Wheel. *Science* 184:1035–43.

Edgerton, H. E. 1976. Underwater archaeological search with sonar. *Historical Archaeology* 10:46–53.

Edwards, S. W. 1978. Nonutilitarian activities in the lower Paleolithic: A look at the two kinds of evidence. *Current Anthropology* 19:135–37.

Ehrich, R. W., ed. 1990. *Chronologies in Old World archaeology*. 3d ed. Chicago: University of Chicago Press.

Eidt, R. C. 1977. Detection and examination of anthrosols by phosphate analysis. *Science* 197:1327–33.

———. 1985. Theoretical and practical considerations in the analysis of anthrosols. In *Archaeological geology*, edited by G. Rapp, Jr., and J. A. Gifford, 155–90. New Haven: Yale University Press.

Eighmy, J. L., and R. S. Sternberg, eds. 1990. *Archaeomagnetic dating*. Tucson: University of Arizona Press.

Elachi, C. 1982. Radar images of the earth from space. *Scientific American* 247 (6):54–61.

Ericson, J. E., and T. K. Earle, eds. 1982. *Contexts for prehistoric exchange*. New York: Academic Press.

Ericson, J. E., and B. A. Purdy, eds. 1984. *Prehistoric quarries and lithic production*. Cambridge: Cambridge University Press.

Ester, M. 1981. A column-wise approach to seriation. *American Antiquity* 46:496–512.

Estes, J. E., J. R. Jensen, and L. R. Tinney. 1977. The use of historical photography for mapping archaeological sites. *Journal of Field Archaeology* 4:441–47.

Fagan, B. M. 1975. *The rape of the Nile*. New York: Scribner's.

———. 1978. *Quest for the past: Great discoveries in archaeology*. Reading, Mass.: Addison-Wesley.

———. 1985. *The adventure of archaeology*. Washington, D.C.: National Geographic Society.

———. 1988. Black day at Slack Farm. *Archaeology* 41 (8):15–16, 73.

Falk, L., ed. 1991. *Historical archaeology in global perspective*. Washington, D.C.: Smithsonian Institution Press.

Feder, K. L. 1998. *Frauds, myths, and mysteries: Science and pseudoscience in archaeology*. 3d ed. Mountain View, Calif.: Mayfield.

Fehon, J. R., and S. C. Scholtz. 1978. A conceptual framework for the study of artifact loss. *American Antiquity* 43:271–73.

Feinman, G., and J. Neitzel. 1984. Too many types: An overview of prestate societies in the Americas. In *Advances in archaeological method and theory*. Vol. 7, edited by M. B. Schiffer, 39–102. Orlando, Fla.: Academic Press.

Fell, B. 1976. *America B.C.* New York: Pocket Books.

Findlow, F. J., and J. E. Ericson, eds. 1980. *Catchment analysis: Essays on prehistoric resource space*. Anthropology UCLA, Vol. 10, nos. 1 and 2. Los Angeles: University of California Press.

Finley, M. I. 1971. Archaeology and history. *Daedalus* 100:168–86.

Finney, B. R. 1977. Voyaging canoes and the settlement of Polynesia. *Science* 196:1277–85.

Fish, S. K., P. R. Fish, and J. H. Madsen. 1990. Analyzing regional agriculture: A Hohokam example. In *The archaeology of regions: A case for full-coverage survey*, edited by S. K. Fish and S. A. Kowalewski, 189–218. Washington, D.C.: Smithsonian Institution Press.

Fish, S. K., and S. A. Kowalewski, eds. 1990. *The archaeology of regions: A case for full-coverage survey*. Washington, D.C.: Smithsonian Institution Press.

Fitting, J. E., ed. 1973. *The development of North American archaeology: Essays in the history of regional traditions*. Garden City, N.Y.: Doubleday/Anchor.

Fladmark, K. R. 1982. Microdebitage analysis: Initial considerations. *Journal of Archaeological Science* 9:205–20.

Flannery, K. V. 1965. The ecology of early food production in Mesopotamia. *Science* 147:1247–56.

———. 1967. Culture history vs. cultural process: A debate in American archaeology. *Scientific American* 217 (2):119–22.

———. 1968. Archaeological systems theory and early Mesoamerica. In *Anthropological archaeology in the Americas*, edited by B. J. Meggers, 67–87. Washington, D.C.: Anthropological Society of Washington.

———. 1969. Origins and ecological effects of early domestication in Iran and the Near East. In *The domestication and exploitation of plants and animals*, edited by P. J. Ucko and G. W. Dimbleby, 73–100. Chicago: Aldine-Atherton.

———. 1972a. The cultural evolution of civilizations. *Annual Review of Ecology and Systematics* 2: 399–426.

———. 1972b. The origins of the village as a settlement type in Mesoamerica and the Near East: A comparative study. In *Man, settlement and urbanism,* edited by P. J. Ucko, R. Tringham, and G. W. Dimbleby, 23–53. London: Duckworth.

———. 1973. Archaeology with a capital S. In *Research and theory in current archaeology,* edited by C. L. Redman, 47–53. New York: Wiley-Interscience.

———. 1982. The Golden Marshalltown: A parable for the archaeology of the 1980s. *American Anthropologist* 84:265–78.

———. 1986. A visit to the master. In *Guilá Naquitz, Archaic foraging and early agriculture in Oaxaca, Mexico,* edited by K. V. Flannery, 511–19. Orlando, Fla.: Academic Press.

Flannery, K. V., and J. Marcus. 1976. Evolution of the public building in Formative Oaxaca. In *Cultural change and continuity: Essays in honor of James Bennett Griffin,* edited by C. E. Cleland, 205–21. New York: Academic Press.

Fleming, S. J. 1979. *Thermoluminescence techniques in archaeology.* Oxford: Clarendon Press.

Flenley, J. R., and S. M. King. 1984. Late quaternary pollen records from Easter Island. *Nature* 307:47–50.

Flenniken, J. J. 1984. The past, present, and future of flintknapping: An anthropological perspective. *Annual Review of Anthropology* 13:187–203.

Flint, R. N. 1971. *Glacial and quaternary geology.* New York: Wiley.

Foley, R. 1981. Off-site archaeology: An alternative approach for the short-sited. In *Pattern of the past,* edited by I. Hodder, G. Isaac, and N. Hammond, 157–83. Cambridge: Cambridge University Press.

Forbes, R. J. 1963. *Studies in ancient technology.* Vol. 7. Leiden, Netherlands: Brill.

Ford, J. A. 1954. The type concept revisited. *American Anthropologist* 56:42–53.

———. 1962. *A quantitative method for deriving cultural chronology.* Pan American Union, Technical Manual 1. Washington, D.C.: Organization of American States.

———. 1969. *A comparison of formative cultures in the Americas.* Smithsonian Contributions to Anthropology. Vol. 11. Washington, D.C.: Smithsonian Institution.

Ford, R. I. 1977. The state of the art in archeology. In *Perspectives on anthropology,* edited by A. F. C. Wallace, J. L. Angel, R. Fox, S. McLendon, R. Sady, and R. J.

Sharer, 101–15. Special Publication 10. Washington, D.C.: American Anthropological Association.

———. 1979. Paleoethnobotany in American archeology. In *Advances in archaeological method and theory.* Vol. 2, edited by M. B. Schiffer, 285–336. New York: Academic Press.

———. 1983. The Archaeological Conservancy, Inc.: The goal is site preservation. *American Archaeology* 3: 221–24.

Fowler, D. D. 1982. Cultural resources management. In *Advances in archaeological method and theory.* Vol. 5, edited by M. B. Schiffer, 1–50. New York: Academic Press.

———. 1987. Uses of the past: Archaeology in the service of the state. *American Antiquity* 52:229–48.

Fowler, M. L. 1974. *Cahokia: Ancient capital of the Midwest.* Modules in Anthropology, no. 48. Reading, Mass.: Addison-Wesley.

———. 1989. *The Cahokia atlas.* Studies in Illinois Archaeology, no. 6. Springfield: Illinois Historic Preservation Agency.

Fowler, P. J. 1988–89. The experimental earthworks 1958–88. *Annual Report of the Council for British Archaeology* 39:83–98.

Fox, C. 1922. *The archaeology of the Cambridge region.* Cambridge: Cambridge University Press.

Fox, R. A. 1993. *Archaeology, history, and Custer's last battle.* Norman: University of Oklahoma.

Fried, M. H. 1967. *The evolution of political society.* New York: Random House.

Friedman, I., and R. L. Smith. 1960. A new dating method using obsidian. Part 1, The development of the method. *American Antiquity* 25:476–93.

Friedman, I., and F. W. Trembour. 1978. Obsidian: The dating stone. *American Scientist* 66:44–51.

———. 1983. Obsidian hydration dating update. *American Antiquity* 48:544–47.

———. 2000. Obsidian hydration dating. In *Archaeological method and theory: An encyclopedia,* edited by L. Ellis, 409–13. New York: Garland.

Friedman, J. L., ed. 1985. A history of the Archaeological Resources Protection Act: Law and regulations. *American Archaeology* 5:82–119.

Frink, D. S. 1984. Artifact behavior within the plow zone. *Journal of Field Archaeology* 11:356–63.

Fritz, J. M. 1978. Paleopsychology today: Ideational systems and human adaptation in prehistory. In *Social archaeology: Beyond subsistence and dating,* edited by C. L. Redman, M. J. Berman, E. V. Curtin, W. T. Langhorne, Jr., N. M. Versaggi, and J. C. Wanser, 37–59. New York: Academic Press.

———. 1986. Vijayanagara: Authority and meaning of a South Indian imperial capital. *American Anthropologist* 88:44–55.

Fritz, J. M., G. Michell, and M. S. N. Rao. 1986. Vijayanagara: The city of victory. *Archaeology* 39 (2):22–29.

Fry, R. E. 1980. *Models and methods in regional exchange.* SAA Paper, no. 1. Washington, D.C.: Society for American Archaeology.

Gallatin, A. 1836. A synopsis of the Indian tribes within the United States east of the Rocky Mountains, in the British and Russian possessions in North America. *Archaeologia Americana* 2:1–422.

Gardin, J.-C. 1980. *Archaeological construct: An aspect of theoretical archaeology.* Cambridge: Cambridge University Press.

Gathercole, P., and D. Lowenthal, eds. 1989. *The politics of the past.* London: Unwin Hyman.

Gero, J. M. 1991. Genderlithics: Women's roles in stone tool production. In *Engendering archaeology: Women and prehistory,* edited by J. M. Gero and M. W. Conkey, 163–93. Oxford: Blackwell.

Gero, J. M., and M. W. Conkey, eds. 1991. *Engendering archaeology: Women and prehistory.* Oxford: Blackwell.

Gibbon, G. 1984. *Anthropological archaeology.* New York: Columbia University Press.

———. 1989. *Explanation in archaeology.* Oxford: Basil Blackwell.

Gibbons, A. 1991. A "new look" for archaeology. *Science* 252:918–20.

Giesecke, A. G. 1985. Shipwrecks, states and the courts. *Archaeology* 38 (5):80.

Gifford, D. P. 1981. Taphonomy and paleoecology: A critical review of archaeology's sister disciplines. In *Advances in archaeological method and theory.* Vol. 4, edited by M. B. Schiffer, 365–438. New York: Academic Press.

Gilbert, B. M. 1973. *Mammalian osteoarchaeology.* Columbia: Missouri Archaeological Society, Special Publications.

Gilbert, R. I., Jr., and J. H. Mielke, eds. 1985. *The analysis of prehistoric diets.* Orlando, Fla.: Academic Press.

Gillard, R. 2000. Amino acid racemization/epimerization dating. In *Archaeological method and theory: An encyclopedia,* edited by L. Ellis, 13–17. New York: Garland.

Givens, D. R. 1999. Alfred Vincent Kidder. In *Encyclopedia of archaeology: The great archaeologists.* Vol. 1, edited by T. Murray, 357–70. Santa Barbara: ABC-CLIO.

Gladfelter, B. G. 1981. Developments and directions in geoarchaeology. In *Advances in archaeological method and theory.* Vol. 4, edited by M. B. Schiffer, 343–64. New York: Academic Press.

Glassie, H. 1975. *Folk housing in Middle Virginia: A structural analysis of historic artifacts.* Knoxville: University of Tennessee Press.

Glassow, M. A. 1977. Issues in evaluating the significance of archaeological resources. *American Antiquity* 42:413–20.

———. 1978. The concept of carrying capacity in the study of culture process. In *Advances in archaeological method and theory.* Vol. 1, edited by M. B. Schiffer, 31–48. New York: Academic Press.

Glob, P. V. 1969. *The bog people: Iron Age man preserved.* Translated by R. Bruce-Mitford. Ithaca, N.Y.: Cornell University Press.

Glover, I., and D. Griffiths, eds. 1989. Ceramic technology. *World Archaeology* 21 (whole no. 1).

Goodman, A. H., R. B. Thomas, A. C. Swedlund, and G. J. Armelagos. 1988. Biocultural perspectives on stress in prehistoric, historical and contemporary population research. *Yearbook of Physical Anthropology* 31:169–202.

Goodwin, A. J. H. 1960. Chemical alteration (patination) of stone. In *The application of quantitative methods in archaeology,* edited by R. F. Heizer and S. F. Cook, 300–312. Viking Fund Publications in Anthropology, no. 28. New York: Wenner-Gren Foundation for Anthropological Research.

Goodyear, A. C., L. M. Raab, and T. C. Klinger. 1978. The status of archaeological research design in cultural resource management. *American Antiquity* 43:159–73.

Gordon, R. 2000. Industrial archaeology. In *Archaeological method and theory: An encyclopedia,* edited by L. Ellis, 301–305. New York: Garland.

Gorenstein, S. 1977. History of American archaeology. In *Perspectives on anthropology,* edited by A. F. C. Wallace, J. L. Angel, R. Fox, S. McLendon, R. Sady, and R. J. Sharer, 86–100. Special Publication no. 10. Washington, D.C.: American Anthropological Association.

Gould, R. A. 1980a. *Living archaeology.* Cambridge: Cambridge University Press.

———, ed. 1978. *Explorations in ethnoarchaeology.* Albuquerque: University of New Mexico Press.

———, ed. 1980b. *Shipwreck anthropology.* School of American Research Advanced Seminar Series. Albuquerque: University of New Mexico Press.

Gould, R. A., and M. B. Schiffer, eds. 1981. *Modern material culture: The archaeology of us.* New York: Academic Press.

Gould, R. A., and P. J. Watson. 1982. A dialogue on the meaning and use of analogy in ethnoarchaeological reasoning. *Journal of Anthropological Archaeology* 1:355–81.

Gowlett, J. A. J. 1987. The archaeology of radiocarbon accelerator dating. *Journal of World Prehistory* 1:127–70.

Graham, I., ed. 1985a. Ethnoarchaeology. *World Archaeology* 17 (whole no. 2).

———, ed. 1985b. Water-craft and water transport. *World Archaeology* 16 (whole no. 3).

Graham, I., P. Galloway, and I. Scollar. 1976. Model studies in computer seriation. *Journal of Archaeological Science* 3:1–30.

Grayson, D. K. 1979. On the quantification of vertebrate archaeofaunas. In *Advances in archaeological method and theory*. Vol. 2, edited by M. B. Schiffer, 199–237. New York: Academic Press.

———. 1983. *The establishment of human antiquity*. New York: Academic Press.

———. 1984. *Quantitative zooarchaeology: Topics in the analysis of archaeological faunas*. New York: Academic Press.

Green, E. L., ed. 1984. *Ethics and values in archaeology*. New York: Free Press.

Green, J. 1990. *Maritime archaeology: A technical handbook*. London: Academic Press.

Green, S. W. 1980. Toward a general model of agricultural systems. In *Advances in archaeological method and theory*. Vol. 3, edited by M. B. Schiffer, 311–55. New York: Academic Press.

Green, S. W., and S. M. Perlman, eds. 1985. *The archaeology of frontiers and boundaries*. Orlando, Fla.: Academic Press.

Greene, K. 1992. *Roman pottery*. Berkeley: University of California.

Greenfield, J. 1989. *The return of cultural treasures*. Cambridge: Cambridge University Press.

Griffin, J. B. 1959. The pursuit of archaeology in the United States. *American Anthropologist* 61:379–88.

———. 1999. James Alfred Ford. In *Encyclopedia of archaeology: The great archaeologists*. Vol. 2, edited by T. Murray, 635–52. Santa Barbara: ABC-CLIO.

Grigson, C., and J. Clutton-Brock, eds. 1983. *Animals and archaeology*. Vol. 2, *Shell middens, fishes, and birds*. British Archaeological Reports International Series, no. 183. Oxford: British Archaeological Reports.

Grinsell, L., P. Rahz, and D. P. Williams. 1974. *The preparation of archaeological reports*. 2d ed. London: Baker.

Grün, R. 2000a. Electron spin resonance dating. In *Archaeological method and theory: An encyclopedia*, edited by L. Ellis, 174–78. New York: Garland.

———. 2000b. Uranium-series dating. In *Archaeological method and theory: An encyclopedia*, edited by L. Ellis, 645–51. New York: Garland.

Gumerman, G. J., and T. R. Lyons. 1971. Archaeological methodology and remote sensing. *Science* 172:126–32.

Gumerman, G. J., and D. A. Phillips, Jr. 1978. Archaeology beyond anthropology. *American Antiquity* 43:184–91.

Gurfinkel, D. M., and U. M. Franklin. 1988. A study of the feasibility of detecting blood residue on artifacts. *Journal of Archaeological Science* 15:83–98.

Gyrisco, G. M. 1983. Tools suggested and coalitions to preserve archaeological resources. *American Archaeology* 3:224–27.

Hadingham, E. 1984. *Early man and the cosmos*. New York: Walker.

Hall, R., 1995. *Viking age archaeology in Britain and Ireland*. Princes Risborough, England: Shire Archaeology.

Hall, R. L. 1977. An anthropocentric perspective for eastern United States prehistory. *American Antiquity* 42: 499–518.

———. 1989. The material symbols of the Winnebago sky and earth moieties. In *The meaning of things: Material culture and symbolic expression,* edited by I. Hodder, 178–84. London: Unwin Hyman.

Hamilton, D. L., and R. Woodward. 1984. A sunken 17th-century city: Port Royal, Jamaica. *Archaeology* 37 (1):38–45.

Hammil, J., and L. J. Zimmerman, eds. 1983. *Reburial of human skeletal remains: Perspectives from Lakota holy men and elders*. Indianapolis, Ind.: American Indians Against Desecration.

Hardestry, D. L. 1980. The use of general ecological principles in archaeology. In *Advances in archaeological method and theory*. Vol. 3, edited by M. B. Schiffer, 157–87. New York: Academic Press.

Harlan, J. R. 1967. A wild wheat harvest in Turkey. *Antiquity* 20:197–201.

Harp, E., Jr., ed. 1975. *Photography in archaeological research*. School of American Research Advanced Seminar Series. Albuquerque: University of New Mexico Press.

Harré, R., and P. F. Secord. 1972. *The explanation of social behavior*. Oxford: Blackwell.

Harrington, J. C. 1954. Dating stem fragments of seventeenth and eighteenth century clay tobacco pipes. *Bulletin of the Archaeological Society of Virginia* 9 (1):9–13.

Harrington, S. P. M. 1991. The looting of Arkansas. *Archaeology* 44 (3):22–30.

Harris, D. M., and G. Hillman, eds. 1989. *Foraging and farming*. London: Unwin Hyman.

Harris, E. C. 1975. The stratigraphic sequence: A question of time. *World Archaeology* 7:109–21.

———. 1989. *Principles of archaeological stratigraphy*. 2d ed. London: Academic Press.

Harris, M. 1968. *The rise of anthropological theory: A history of theories of culture*. New York: Crowell.

Hart Hansen, J. P., and H. C. Gullov. 1989. *The mummies from Qilakitsoq: Eskimos from the 15th century.* Copenhagen: Commission for Scientific Research in Greenland.

Hart Hansen, J. P., J. Melgaard, and J. Nordqvist. 1991. *The Greenland mummies.* Washington D.C.: Smithsonian Institution.

Hassan, F. A. 1978. Demographic archaeology. In *Advances in archaeological method and theory.* Vol. 1, edited by M. B. Schiffer, 49–103. New York: Academic Press.

Hastings, C. M., and M. E. Moseley. 1975. The adobes of Huaca del Sol and Huaca de la Luna. *American Antiquity* 40:196–203.

Hastorf, C. A., and V. S. Popper, eds. 1988. *Current paleoethnobotany: Analytical methods and cultural interpretations of archaeological plant remains.* Chicago: University of Chicago Press.

Hawley, F. M. 1937. Reverse stratigraphy. *American Antiquity* 2:297–99.

Hayden, B., ed. 1979. *Lithic use-wear analysis.* New York: Academic Press.

Haynes, G. 1983. Frequencies of spiral and green-bone fractures on ungulate limb bones in modern surface assemblages. *American Antiquity* 48:102–14.

Hecker, H. M. 1982. Domestication revisited: Its implications for faunal analysis. *Journal of Field Archaeology* 9:217–36.

Hedges, R. E. M., and J. A. J. Gowlett. 1986. Radiocarbon dating by accelerator mass spectrometry. *Scientific American* 254 (1):100–107.

Hempel, C. G. 1966. *Philosophy of natural science.* Englewood Cliffs, N.J.: Prentice-Hall.

Henderson, J., ed. 1989. *Scientific analysis in archaeology and its interpretation.* Archaeological Research Tools 5/Monograph 19. Los Angeles and Oxford: UCLA Institute of Archaeology and Oxford University.

Henry, D. O., and G. H. Odell, eds. 1989. *Alternative approaches to lithic analysis.* Archaeological Papers of the American Anthropological Association, no. 1. Washington, D.C.: American Anthropological Association.

Herscher, E. 1989. A future in ruins. *Archaeology* 42: (1):67–70.

Hess, B., and P. Wapnish. 1985. *Animal bone archaeology: From objectives to analysis.* Washington, D.C.: Taraxacum.

Heyerdahl, T. 1950. *The Kon-Tiki expedition: By raft across the South Seas.* London: Allen & Unwin.

Hietala, H. J., ed. 1984. *Intrasite spatial analysis in archaeology.* Cambridge: Cambridge University Press.

Higgenbotham, C. D. 1983. Native Americans versus archaeologists: The legal issues. *American Indian Law Review* 10:91–115.

Higgs, E. S., ed. 1972. *Papers in economic prehistory.* Cambridge: Cambridge University Press.

———, ed. 1975. *Paleoeconomy.* Cambridge: Cambridge University Press.

Hill, A. P. 1979. Butchery and natural disarticulation: An investigatory technique. *American Antiquity* 44: 739–44.

Hill, J. N. 1966. A prehistoric community in eastern Arizona. *Southwestern Journal of Anthropology* 22:9–30.

———. 1970. *Broken K Pueblo: Prehistoric social organization in the American Southwest.* Anthropological Paper no. 18. Tucson: University of Arizona Press.

———, ed. 1977. *Explanation of prehistoric change.* School of American Research Advanced Seminar Series. Albuquerque: University of New Mexico Press.

Hill, J. N., and R. K. Evans. 1972. A model for classification and typology. In *Models in archaeology,* edited by D. L. Clarke, 231–73. London: Methuen.

Hill, J. N., and J. Gunn, eds. 1977. *The individual in prehistory.* New York: Academic Press.

Hillson, S. 1986. *Teeth.* Cambridge: Cambridge University Press.

Hindle, B. P. 1990. *Medieval town plans.* Princes Risborough, England: Shire Archaeology.

Hinton, D. A., 1993. *Archaeology, economy, and society.* London: Seaby.

Hirth, K. G. 1978. Problems in data recovery and management in settlement archaeology. *Journal of Field Archaeology* 5:125–31.

———, ed. 1984. *Trade and exchange in Early Mesoamerica.* Albuquerque: University of New Mexico Press.

Hodder, I. 1982b. *Symbols in action: Ethnoarchaeological studies of material culture.* Cambridge: Cambridge University Press.

———. 1982c. *The present past: An introduction to anthropology for archaeologists.* New York: Pica Press.

———. 1985. Postprocessual archaeology. In *Advances in archaeological method and theory.* Vol. 8, edited by M. B. Schiffer, 1–26. Orlando, Fla.: Academic Press.

———. 1990. *The domestication of Europe: Structure and contingency in Neolithic societies.* Oxford: Blackwell.

———. 1991a. *Reading the past: Current approaches to interpretation in archaeology.* 2d ed. Cambridge: Cambridge University Press.

———. 1991b. Interpretive archaeology and its role. *American Antiquity* 56:7–18.

———, ed. 1978a. *Simulation studies in archaeology.* Cambridge: Cambridge University Press.

————, ed. 1978b. *The spatial organisation of culture.* Pittsburgh: University of Pittsburgh Press.

————, ed. 1982a. *Symbolic and structural archaeology.* Cambridge: Cambridge University Press.

————, ed. 1989. *The meaning of things: Material cultural and symbolic expression.* London: Unwin Hyman.

Hodder, I. R., and M. Hassall. 1971. The non-random spacing of Romano-British walled towns. *Man* 6:391–407.

Hodder, I. R., and C. Orton. 1976. *Spatial analysis in archaeology.* Cambridge: Cambridge University Press.

Hodges, H. 1964. *Artifacts: An introduction to early materials and technology.* London: Baker.

Hole, B. 1980. Sampling in archaeology: A critique. *Annual Review of Anthropology* 9:217–34.

Hole, F., K. V. Flannery, and J. A. Neely. 1969. *Prehistoric human ecology of the Deh Luran Plain: An early village sequence from Khuzistan, Iran.* Memoirs of the Museum of Anthropology, no. 1. Ann Arbor: University of Michigan.

Hole, F., and M. Shaw. 1967. *Computer analysis of chronological seriation.* Rice University Studies, no. 53. Houston: Rice University.

Holland, T. 1999. Kathleen Mary Kenyon. In *Encyclopedia of archaeology: The great archaeologists.* Vol. 2, edited by T. Murray, 481–90. Santa Barbara: ABC-CLIO.

Hope-Simpson, R. 1984. The analysis of data from surface surveys. *Journal of Field Archaeology* 11:115–17.

Horne, P. D. 1985. A review of the evidence of human endoparasitism in the pre-Columbian New World through the study of coprolites. *Journal of Archaeological Science* 12:299–310.

Hurley, W. M. 1979. *Prehistoric cordage, identification of impressions on pottery.* Washington, D.C.: Taraxacum.

Huss-Ashmore, R., A. H. Goodman, and G. J. Armelagos. 1982. Nutritional inference from paleopathology. In *Advances in archaeological method and theory.* Vol. 5, edited by M. B. Schiffer, 395–474. New York: Academic Press.

Issac, G. L. 1967. Towards the interpretation of occupation debris: Some experiments and observations. *Kroeber Anthropological Society Papers* 37:371–75.

————. 1971. Whither archaeology? *Antiquity* 45:123–29.

————. 1983. Bones in contention: Competing explanations for the juxtaposition of early Pleistocene artifacts and faunal remains. In *Animals and archaeology:* Vol. 1, *Hunters and their prey,* edited by J. Clutton-Brock and C. Grigson, 3–19. British Archaeological Reports International Series 163. Oxford: British Archaeological Reports.

Jackson, T. L. 1991. Pounding acorn: Women's production as social and economic focus. In *Engendering archaeology: Women and prehistory,* edited by J. M. Gero and M. W. Conkey, 301–25. Oxford: Blackwell.

Jakes, K. A., and A. Angel. 1989. Determination of elemental distribution in ancient fibers. In *Archaeological chemistry IV,* edited by R. O. Allen, 451–64. Advances in Chemistry Series, no. 220. Washington D.C.: American Chemical Society.

Jarman, M. R., C. Vita-Finzi, and E. S. Higgs. 1972. Site catchment analysis in archaeology. In *Man, settlement and urbanism,* edited by P. J. Ucko, R. Tringham, and G. W. Dimbleby, 61–66. London: Duckworth.

Jelinek, A. J. 1976. Form, function, and style in lithic analysis. In *Cultural change and continuity: Essays in honor of James Bennett Griffin,* edited by C. E. Cleland, 19–34. New York: Academic Press.

Jochim, M. A. 1979. Breaking down the system: Recent ecological approaches in archaeology. In *Advances in archaeological method and theory.* Vol. 2, edited by M. B. Schiffer, 77–117. New York: Academic Press.

Johnson, A. W., and T. Earle. 1987. *The evolution of human societies: From foraging group to agrarian state.* Stanford, Calif.: Stanford University Press.

Johnson, E. 1985. Current developments in bone technology. In *Advances in archaeological method and theory.* Vol. 8, edited by M. B. Schiffer, 157–235. Orlando, Fla.: Academic Press.

Johnson, G. A. 1972. A test of the utility of central place theory in archaeology. In *Man, settlement and urbanism,* edited by P. J. Ucko, R. Tringham, and G. W. Dimbleby, 769–86. London: Duckworth.

————. 1973. *Local exchange and early state development in Southwestern Iran.* Anthropological Papers, no. 51. Ann Arbor: University of Michigan.

————. 1977. Aspects of regional analysis in archaeology. *Annual Review of Anthropology* 6:479–508.

Johnson, J. K., T. L. Sever, S. L. H. Madry, and H. T. Hoff. 1988. Remote sensing and GIS analysis in large scale survey design in north Mississippi. *Southeastern Archaeology* 7 (2):124–31.

Johnstone, P. 1980. *The sea-craft of prehistory.* Cambridge: Harvard University Press.

Joukowsky, M. 1980. *A complete manual of field archaeology.* Englewood Cliffs, N.J.: Prentice-Hall.

Jovanovic, B. 1980. The origins of copper mining in Europe. *Scientific American* 242 (5):152–67.

Karata, H. M., ed. 1989. *Non-topographic photogrammetry.* 2d ed. Falls Church, Va.: American Society for Photogrammetry and Remote Sensing.

Keeley, L. H. 1974. Technique and methodology in microwear studies: A critical review. *World Archaeology* 5:323–36.

————. 1977. The functions of Paleolithic stone tools. *Scientific American* 237 (5):108–26.

————. 1980. *Experimental determination of stone tool uses: A microwear analysis.* Chicago: University of Chicago Press.

Keeley, L. H., and M. H. Newcomer. 1977. Microwear analysis of experimental flint tools: A test case. *Journal of Archaeological Science* 4:29–62.

Keesing, R. M. 1974. Theories of culture. *Annual Review of Anthropology* 3:71–97.

Kehoe, A. B., and T. F. Kehoe. 1973. Cognitive models for archaeological interpretation. *American Antiquity* 38:150–54.

Kelley, J. H., and M. P. Hanen. 1988. *Archaeology and the methodology of science.* Albuquerque: University of New Mexico Press.

Kennedy, D., ed. 1989. *Into the sun: Essays in air photography in archaeology in honour of Derrick Riley.* Sheffields: University of Sheffields.

Kennedy, D., and D. Riley. 1990. *Rome's desert frontier from the air.* Austin: University of Texas Press.

Kennet, D. H. 1986. *Anglo-Saxon pottery.* Princes Risborough, England: Shire Archaeology.

Kent, K. P. 1983. *Prehistoric textiles of the Southwest.* School of American Research. Albuquerque: University of New Mexico Press.

Kent, S. 1984. *Analyzing activity areas: An ethnoarchaeological study of the use of space.* Albuquerque: University of New Mexico Press.

————, ed. 1987. *Method and theory for activity area research: An ethnoarchaeological approach.* New York: Columbia University Press.

————, ed. 1990. *Domestic architecture and the use of space.* Cambridge: Cambridge University Press.

Kenyon, J. L., and B. Bevan. 1977. Ground penetrating radar and its application to a historical archaeological site. *Historical Archaeology* 11:48–55.

Kenyon, K. M. 1931. Sketch of the exploration and settlement of the East Coast of Africa. In *The Zimbabwe culture: Ruins and reactions,* edited by G. Caton-Thompson, 260–74. Oxford: Clarendon.

————. 1961. *Beginning in archaeology.* Rev. ed. London: Phoenix House.

Kidder, A. V. 1932. *The artifacts of Pecos.* Papers of the Southwestern Expedition, no. 6. Andover, Mass.: Phillips Academy.

King, T. F., P. P. Hickman, and G. Berg. 1977. *Anthropology in historic preservation: Caring for culture's clutter.* New York: Academic Press.

Kingery, W. D., ed. 1985. *Ceramics and civilization.* Vol. 1, *From ancient technology to modern science.* Columbus, Ohio: American Ceramic Society.

————, ed. 1986. *Ceramics and civilization.* Vol. 2, *Technology and style.* Columbus, Ohio: American Ceramic Society.

Kings, M. E. 1978. Analytical methods and prehistoric textiles. *American Antiquity* 43:89–96.

Kings, T. F. 1971. A conflict of values in American archaeology. *American Antiquity* 36:255–62.

————. 1978. *The archaeological survey: Methods and uses.* Washington, D.C.: U.S. Department of the Interior, Heritage Conservation and Recreation Service.

————. 1983. Professional responsibility in public archaeology. *Annual Review of Anthropology* 12:143–64.

Kintigh, K. W. 1988. The effectiveness of subsurface testing: A simulation approach. *American Antiquity* 53: 686–707.

Kintigh, K. W., and A. J. Ammerman. 1982. Heuristic approaches to spatial analysis in archaeology. *American Antiquity* 47:31–63.

Kirch, P. V. 1980. The archaeological study of adaptation: Theoretical and methodological issues. In *Advances in archaeological method and theory.* Vol. 3, edited by M. B. Schiffer, 101–56. New York: Academic Press.

————. 1984. *The evolution of the Polynesian chiefdoms.* Cambridge: Cambridge University Press.

Klein, J., J. C. Lerman, P. E. Damon, and E. K. Ralph. 1982. Calibration of radiocarbon dates: Tables based on the consensus data of the workshop on calibrating the radiocarbon time scale. *Radiocarbon* 24:103–50.

Klein, L. S. 1977. A panorama of theoretical archaeology. *Current Anthropology* 18:1–42.

————. 1982. *Archaeological typology.* Translated by P. Dole. British Archaeological Reports International Series, no. 153. Oxford: British Archaeological Reports.

Klein, R. G., and K. Cruz-Uribe. 1984. *The analysis of animal bones from archaeological sites.* Chicago: University of Chicago Press.

Klejn, L. 1999a. Gustaf Kossina. In *Encyclopedia of archaeology: The great archaeologists.* Vol. 1, edited by T. Murray, 233–46. Santa Barbara: ABC-CLIO.

————. 1999b. Heinrich Schliemann. In *Encyclopedia of archaeology: The great archaeologists.* Vol. 1, edited by T. Murray, 109–26. Santa Barbara: ABC-CLIO.

Klindt-Jensen, O. 1975. *A history of Scandinavian archaeology.* London: Thames & Hudson.

Knudson, R. 1989. North America's threatened heritage. *Archaeology* 42 (1):71–73, 106.

Kopper, J. S., and G. Rossello-Bordoy. 1974. Megalithic quarrying techniques and limestone technology in eastern Spain. *Journal of Field Archaeology* 1:161–70.

Kraft, J. C., S. E. Aschenbrenner, and G. Rapp, Jr. 1977. Paleogeographic reconstructions of coastal Aegean archaeological sites. *Science* 195:941–47.

Krakker, J. J., M. J. Shott, and P. D. Welch. 1983. Design and evaluation of shovel-test sampling in regional archaeological survey. *Journal of Field Archaeology* 10:469–80.

Kramer, C., and M. Stark. 1988. The status of women in archaeology. *Anthropology Newsletter* (American Anthropological Association) 29 (9):1, 11–12.

Krieger, A. D. 1944. The typological concept. *American Antiquity* 9:271–88.

———. 1946. *Culture complexes and chronology in Northern Texas with extension of Puebloan datings to the Mississippi Valley.* Publication no. 4640. Austin: University of Texas.

———. 1960. Archaeological typology in theory and practice. In *Selected papers of the Fifth International Congress of Anthropological and Ethnological Sciences,* edited by A. F. C. Wallace, 141–51. Philadelphia: University of Pennsylvania Press.

Kroeber, A. L. 1939. *Cultural and natural areas of Native North America.* Berkeley and Los Angeles: University of California Press.

Kroll, E. M., and G. Isaac. 1984. Configurations of artifacts and bones at early Pleistocene sites in East Africa. In *Intrasite spatial analysis in archaeology,* edited by H. J. Hietala, 4–31. Cambridge: Cambridge University Press.

Kroll, E. M., and T. D. Price, eds. 1991. *The interpretation of archaeological spatial patterning.* New York: Plenum.

Kuhn, T. S. 1970. *The structure of scientific revolutions.* 2d ed. Chicago: University of Chicago Press.

Kvamme, K. L. 1989. Geographic information systems in regional archaeological research and data management. In *Advances in archaeological method and theory.* Vol. 1, edited by M. B. Schiffer, 139–203. Tucson: University of Arizona Press.

———. 2000. Geographic information systems. In *Archaeological method and theory: An encyclopedia,* edited by L. Ellis, 244–51. New York: Garland.

Lamberg-Karlovskly, C. C., ed. 1988. *Archaeological thought in America.* Cambridge: Cambridge University Press.

Lambert, J. B., ed. 1984. *Archaeological chemistry III.* Advances in Chemistry Series, no. 205. Washington, D.C.: American Chemical Society.

Lawrence, R. A. 1979. Experimental evidence for the significance of attributes used in edge-damage analysis. In *Lithic use-wear analysis,* edited by B. Hayden, 113–21. New York: Academic Press.

Layton, R., ed. 1989a. *Conflict in the archaeology of living traditions.* London: Unwin Hyman.

———, ed. 1989b. *Who needs the past? Indigenous values and archaeology.* London: Unwin Hyman.

LeBlanc, S. A. 1975. Micro-seriation: A method for fine chronologic differentiation. *American Antiquity* 40: 22–28.

———. 1976. Archaeological recording systems. *Journal of Field Archaeology* 3:159–68.

Lee, R. B. 1968. What hunters do for a living, or, how to make out on scarce resources. In *Man the hunter,* edited by R. B. Lee and I. DeVore, 30–48. Chicago: Aldine.

Lee, R. B., and I. DeVore, eds. 1968. *Man the hunter.* Chicago: Aldine.

———, eds. 1976. *Kalahari hunter-gatherers.* Cambridge: Harvard University Press.

Leone, M. P. 1972. Issues in anthropological archaeology. In *Contemporary archaeology,* edited by M. P. Leone, 14–27. Carbondale: Southern Illinois University Press.

———. 1977. The new Mormon temple on Washington, D.C. In *Historical archaeology and the importance of material things,* edited by L. Ferguson, 43–61. Lansing, Mich.: Society for Historical Archaeology.

———. 1982. Some opinions about recovering mind. *American Antiquity* 47:742–60.

———. 1986. Symbolic, structural, and critical archaeology. In *American archaeology past and future: A celebration of the Society for American Archaeology 1935–1985,* edited by D. J. Meltzer, D. D. Fowler, and J. A. Sabloff, 415–38. Washington, D.C.: Smithsonian Institution Press.

Leone, M. P., and P. B. Potter, eds. 1988. *The recovery of meaning.* Washington, D.C.: Smithsonian Institution Press.

Leroi-Gourhan, A. 1975. The flowers found with Shanidar IV, a Neanderthal burial in Iraq. *Science* 190:562–64.

———. 1982. *The dawn of European art.* Cambridge: Cambridge University Press.

Levin, A. M. 1986. Excavation photography: A day on a dig. *Archaeology* 39 (1):34–39.

Lewarch, D. E., and M. J. O'Brien. 1981. The expanding role of surface assemblages in archaeological research. In *Advances in archaeological method and theory.* Vol. 4, edited by M. B. Schiffer, 297–342. New York: Academic Press.

Libby, W. F. 1955. *Radiocarbon dating.* 2d ed. Chicago: University of Chicago Press.

Lightfoot, K. 1986. Regional surveys in the Eastern United States: The strengths and weaknesses of implementing subsurface testing programs. *American Antiquity* 51:484–504.

———. 1989. A defense of shovel-test-sampling: A reply to Shott. *American Antiquity* 54:413–16.

Limp, W. F. 1974. Water separation and flotation processes. *Journal of Field Archaeology* 1:337–42.

Lipe, W. D. 1974. A conservation model for American archaeology. *Kiva* 39:213–45.

———. 1984. Value and meaning in cultural resources. In *Approaches to the archaeological heritage: A comparative study of world cultural resource management systems,* edited by H. Cleere, 1–11. Cambridge: Cambridge University Press.

Little, B. J., ed. 1991. *Text-aided archaeology.* Boca Raton, Fla.: CRC Press.

Lock, G., and J. Wilcock. 1987. *Computer archaeology.* Aylesbury, England: Shire.

Longacre, W. A. 1970. *Archaeology as anthropology: A case study.* Anthropological Paper no. 17. Tucson: University of Arizona Press.

———. 1981. Kalinga pottery: An ethnoarchaeological study. In *Pattern of the past: Studies in honour of David Clarke,* edited by I. Hodder, G. Isaac, and N. Hammond, 49–66. Cambridge: Cambridge University Press.

Longacre, W. A., and J. E. Ayres. 1968. Archaeological lessons from an Apache wickiup. In *New perspectives in archaeology,* edited by S. R. Binford and L. R. Binford, 151–59. Chicago: Aldine.

Longworth, I., ed. 1971. Archaeology and ethnography. *World Archaeology* 3 (whole no. 2).

———, ed. 1984. Mines and quarries. *World Archaeology* 16 (whole no. 2).

Lovis, W. A., Jr. 1976. Quarter sections and forests: An example of probability sampling in the northeastern woodlands. *American Antiquity* 41:364–72.

Loy, T. H. 1983. Prehistoric blood residues: Detection on tool surfaces and identification of species of origin. *Science* 220:1269–71.

Lubbock, J. (Lord Avebury). 1865. *Prehistoric times.* London: Williams & Norgate.

Luckenbach, A. H., C. G. Holland, and R. O. Allen. 1975. Soapstone artifacts: Tracing prehistoric trade patterns in Virginia. *Science* 187:57–58.

Lyell, C. 1830–1833. *Principles of geology.* London: Murray.

Lyman, R. L. 1982. Archaeofaunas and subsistence studies. In *Advances in archaeological method and theory.* Vol. 5, edited by M. B. Schiffer, 331–93. New York: Academic Press.

———. 1994. *Vertebrate taphonomy.* Cambridge: Cambridge University Press.

Lynch, B. D., and T. F. Lynch. 1968. The beginnings of a scientific approach to prehistoric archaeology in 17th and 18th century Britain. *Southwestern Journal of Anthropology* 24:33–65.

Lynch, B. M. 1980. Site artifacts density and the effectiveness of shovel probes. *Current Anthropology* 21:516–17.

MacDonald, W. K., ed. 1976. *Digging for gold: Papers on archaeology for profit.* Ann Arbor: University of Michigan, Museum of Anthropology.

MacNeish, R. S. 1964a. Ancient Mesoamerican civilization. *Science* 143:531–37.

———. 1964b. The origins of New World civilization. *Scientific American* 211 (5):29–37.

———. 1967. An interdisciplinary approach to an archaeological problem. In *The prehistory of the Tehuacán Valley.* Vol. I, edited by D. S. Byers, 14–24. Austin: University of Texas Press.

———. 1974. Reflections on my search for the beginnings of agriculture in Mexico. In *Archaeological researches in retrospect,* edited by G. R. Willey, 207–34. Cambridge, Mass.: Winthrop.

MacNeish, R. S., M. L. Fowler, A. G. Cook, F. A. Peterson, A. Nelken-Terner, and J. A. Neely. 1972. *Excavations and reconnaissance: The prehistory of the Tehuacán Valley.* Vol. 5. Austin: University of Texas Press.

Maddin, R., ed. 1988. *The beginning of the use of metals and alloys.* Cambridge: MIT Press.

Maddin, R., J. D. Muhly, and T. S. Wheeler. 1977. How the Iron Age began. *Scientific American* 237: (4):122–31.

Madry, S. L. H., and C. L. Crumley. 1990. An application of remote sensing and GIS in a regional archaeological settlement pattern analysis: The Arroux River valley, Burgundy, France. In *Interpreting space: GIS and archaeology,* edited by K. M. S. Allen, S. W. Green, and E. B. W. Zubrow, 364–80. Bristol, Pa.: Taylor & Francis.

Mallory, J. P. 2000. *The Arim mummies: Ancient China and the mystery of the earliest people from the West.* New York: Thames & Hudson.

Marquardt, W. H. 1978. Advances in archaeological seriation. In *Advances in archaeological method and theory.* Vol. 1, edited by M. B. Schiffer, 257–314. New York: Academic Press.

Marquardt, W. H., A. Montet-White, and S. C. Scholtz. 1982. Resolving the crisis in archaeological collections curation. *American Antiquity* 47:409–18.

Marshack, A. 1972a. *The roots of civilization.* New York: McGraw-Hill.

———. 1972b. Upper Paleolithic notation and symbol. *Science* 178:817–27.

Martin, P. S. 1971. The revolution in archaeology. *American Antiquity* 36:1–8.

Martin, W. A., J. E. Bruseth, and R. J. Huggins. 1991. Assessing feature function and spatial patterning of artifacts with geophysical remote-sensing data. *American Antiquity* 56:701–20.

Martlew, R., ed. 1984. *Information systems in archaeology.* Gloucester: Alan Sutton.

Mason, J. 1984. An unorthodox magnetic survey of a large forested historic site. *Historical Archaeology* 18:54–63.

Matson, F. R., ed. 1965. *Ceramics and man.* Chicago: Aldine.

Mazess, R. B., and D. W. Zimmerman. 1966. Pottery dating from thermoluminescence. *Science* 152:347–48.

McBryde, I., ed. 1985. *Who owns the past?* Melbourne: Oxford University Press.

McCauley, J. F., G. G. Schaber, C. S. Breed, M. J. Grolier, C. V. Haynes, B. Issaw, C. Elachi, and R. Blom. 1982. Subsurface valleys and geoarchaeology of the eastern Sahara revealed by shuttle radar. *Science* 218: 1004–20.

McConnell, D. 1962. Dating of fossil bone by the fluorine method. *Science* 136:241–44.

McGimsey, C. R., III. 1972. *Public archaeology.* New York: Seminar Press.

McGuire, R. H., and R. Paynter, eds. 1991. *The archaeology of inequality.* Oxford: Blackwell.

McIntosh, J. 1986. *The practical archaeologist.* London: Facts on File.

McKern, W. C. 1939. The Midwestern Taxonomic Methods as an aid to archaeological study. *American Antiquity* 4:301–13.

McKinley, J. R., and G. J. Henderson. 1985. The protection of historic shipwrecks: A New Zealand case study. *Archaeology* 38 (6):48–51.

McKusick, M. 1982. Psychic archaeology: Theory, method and mythology. *Journal of Field Archaeology* 9:99–118.

———. 1984. Psychic archaeology from Atlantis to Oz. *Archaeology* 37 (6):48–52.

McManamon, F. P. 1984. Discovering sites unseen. In *Advances in archaeological method and theory.* Vol. 7, edited by M. B. Schiffer, 223–92. Orlando, Fla.: Academic Press.

———. 2000a. Abandoned Shipwreck Act. In *Archaeological method and theory: An encyclopedia,* edited by L. Ellis, 1–2. New York: Garland.

———. 2000b. Antiquities Act of 1906. In *Archaeological method and theory: An encyclopedia,* edited by L. Ellis, 33–35. New York: Garland.

———. 2000c. Archeological and Historical Preservation Act. In *Archaeological method and theory: An encyclopedia,* edited by L. Ellis, 60–62. New York: Garland.

———. 2000d. Archaeological Resource Protection Act. In *Archaeological method and theory: An encyclopedia,* edited by L. Ellis, 62–64. New York: Garland.

———. 2000e. National Historic Preservation Act. In *Archaeological method and theory: An encyclopedia,* edited by L. Ellis, 385–86. New York: Garland.

———. 2000f. Native American Graves Protection and Repatriation Act. In *Archaeological method and theory: An encyclopedia,* edited by L. Ellis, 386–88. New York: Garland.

———. 2000g. Surveying and site examination, manual methods. In *Archaeological method and theory: An encyclopedia,* edited by L. Ellis, 605–10. New York: Garland.

McWeeney, L. 1984. Wood identification and archaeology in the Northeast. *North American Archaeologist* 5:183–95.

Meeks, N. D., G. de G. Sieveking, M. S. Tite, and J. Cook. 1982. Gloss and use-wear traces on flint sickles and similar phenomena. *Journal of Archaeological Science* 9:317–40.

Meggers, B. J., C. Evans, and E. Estrada. 1965. *Early formative period of coastal Ecuador: The Valdivia and Machalilla phases.* Smithsonian Contributions to Anthropology. Vol. 1. Washington, D.C.: Smithsonian Institution.

Meighan, C. W. 1959. A new method for the seriation of archaeological collections. *American Antiquity* 25: 203–11.

Meltzer, D. J. 1979. Paradigms and the nature of change in American archaeology. *American Antiquity* 44: 644–57.

———. 1983. The antiquity of man and the development of archaeology. In *Advances in archaeological method and theory.* Vol. 6, edited by M. B. Schiffer, 1–51. New York: Academic Press.

Meltzer, D. J., D. D. Fowler, and J. A. Sabloff, eds. 1986. *American archaeology past and future: A celebration of the Society for American Archaeology 1935–1985.* Washington, D.C.: Smithsonian Institution Press.

Meyer, K. E. 1977. *The plundered past.* New York: Atheneum.

Michael, H. N. 1985. Correcting radiocarbon dates with tree ring dates at MASCA. *University Museum Newsletter* (University of Pennsylvania) 23 (3):1–2.

Michel, M. 1981. Preserving America's prehistoric heritage. *Archaeology* 34 (2):61–63.

Michels, J. W., and I. S. T. Tsong. 1980. Obsidian hydration dating: A coming of age. In *Advances in archaeological method and theory.* Vol. 3, edited by M. B. Schiffer, 405–44. New York: Academic Press.

Miller, D. 1980 Archaeology and development. *Current Anthropology* 21:709–826.

Miller, D., and C. Tilley, eds. 1984. *Ideology, power and prehistory.* Cambridge: Cambridge University Press.

Minchinton, W. 1983. World industrial archaeology: A survey. *World Archaeology* 15:125–36.

Mitchen, S. 1989. Evolutionary theory and post-processual archaeology. *Antiquity* 63:483–94.

Monks, G. G. 1981. Seasonality studies. In *Advances in archaeological method and theory.* Vol. 4, edited by M. B. Schiffer, 177–240. New York: Academic Press.

Morgan, L. H. 1877. *Ancient society.* New York: Holt.

Mori, J. L. 1970. Procedures for establishing a faunal collection to aid in archaeological analysis. *American Antiquity* 35:387–89.

Moseley, M. E., and C. J. Mackey. 1974. *Twenty-four architectural plans of Chan Chan, Peru: Structure and form at the capital of Chimor.* Cambridge: Harvard University, Peabody Museum Press.

Moss, E. H. 1983. Some comments on edge damage as a factor in funcitonal analysis of stone artifacts. *Journal of Archaeological Science* 10:231–42.

Muckelroy, K, ed., 1980. *Archaeology underwater: An atlas of the world's submerged sites.* New York: McGraw-Hill.

Mueller, J. W. 1974. *The uses of sampling in archaeological survey.* Memoir no. 28. Washington, D.C.: Society for American Archaeology.

———. ed. 1975. *Sampling in archaeology.* Tucson: University of Arizona Press.

———. 1978. A reply to Plog and Thomas. *American Antiquity* 43:286–87.

Muller, R. A. 1977. Radioisotope dating with a cyclotron. *Science* 196:489–94.

Müller-Beck, H. 1961. Prehistoric Swiss lake dwellers. *Scientific American* 205 (6):138–47.

Munsen, P. J. 1969. Comments on Binford's "Smudge pits and hide smoking: The use of analogy in archaeological reasoning." *American Antiquity* 34:83–85.

Murray, T. M., ed. 1999a. *Encyclopedia of archaeology: The great archaeologists.* 2 vols. Santa Barbara: ABC-CLIO.

———. 1999b. Howard Carter. In *Encyclopedia of archaeology: The great archaeologists.* Vol. 1, edited by T. Murray, 289–300. Santa Barbara: ABC-CLIO.

———. 1999c. Sir Arthur Evans. In *Encyclopedia of archaeology: The great archaeologists.* Vol. 1, edited by T. Murray, 211–20. Santa Barbara: ABC-CLIO.

Muscarella, O. W. 1984. On publishing unexcavated artifacts. *Journal of Field Archaeology* 11:61–66.

Nance, J. D. 1979. Regional subsampling and statistical inference in forested habitats. *American Antiquity* 44:172–76.

———. 1981. Statistical fact and archaeological faith: Two models in small site sampling. *Journal of Field Archaeology* 8:151–65.

———. 1983. Regional sampling in archaeological survey: The statistical perspective. In *Advances in archaeological method and theory.* Vol. 6, edited by M. B. Schiffer, 289–356. New York: Academic Press.

Nance, J. D., and B. F. Ball. 1986. No surprises? The reliability and validity of test pit sampling. *American Antiquity* 51:457–83.

———. 1989. A shot in the dark: Shott's comments on Nance and Ball. *American Antiquity* 54:405–12.

Napton, L. K. 1975. Site mapping and layout. In *Field methods in archaeology.* 6th ed., edited by T. R. Hester, R. F. Heizer, and J. A. Graham, 37–63. Mountain View, Calif.: Mayfield.

Naroll, R. 1962. Floor area and settlement population. *American Antiquity* 27:587–88.

Nelson, B., ed. 1985. *Decoding prehistoric ceramics.* Carbondale: Southern Illinois University Press.

Nelson, D. E., R. G. Korteling, and W. R. Stott. 1977. Carbon-14: Direct detection at natural concentrations. *Science* 198:507–08.

Nelson, M. C. 1991. The study of technological organization. In *Advances in archaeological method and theory.* Vol. 3, edited by M. B. Schiffer, 57–100. Tucson: University of Arizona Press.

Nelson, S. M., and A. B. Kehoe, eds. 1990. *Powers of observation: Alternative views in archaeology.* Archaeological Papers of the American Anthropological Association, no. 2. Washington D.C.: American Anthropological Association.

Netting, R. M. 1977. *Cultural ecology.* Menlo Park, Calif.: Cummings.

———. 1982. Some home truths on household size and wealth. In *Archaeology of the household: Building a prehistory of domestic life,* edited by R. R. Wilk and W. L. Rathje, special issue of *American Behavioral Scientist* 25:641–62.

Newcomer, M. H., and L. H. Keeley. 1979. Testing a method of microwear analysis with experimental fling tools. In *Lithic use-wear analysis,* edited by B. Hayden, 195–205. New York: Academic Press.

Noël Hume, I. 1969. *Historical archaeology.* New York: Knopf.

———. 1979. *Martin's hundred: The discovery of a lost colonial Virginia settlement.* New York: Knopf.

Odell, G. H. 1994. Prehistoric hafting and mobility in the North American midcontinent: Examples from Illinois. *Journal of Anthropological Archaeology* 13: 51–73.

———. 2000. Use-wear analysis. In *Archaeological method and theory: An encyclopedia,* edited by L. Ellis, 651–55. New York: Garland.

Odell, G. H., and F. Cowan. 1987. Estimating tillage effects on artifact distributions. *American Antiquity* 52:456–84.

Olsen, S. J. 1964. *Mammal remains from archaeological sites.* Papers of the Peabody Museum, no. 56. Cambridge: Harvard University Press.

———. 1971. *Zooarchaeology: Animal bones in archaeology and their interpretation.* Modules in Anthropology, no. 2. Reading, Mass.: Addison-Wesley.

———. 1979. Archaeologically, what constitutes an early domestic animal? In *Advances in archaeological method and theory.* Vol. 2, edited by M. B. Schiffer, 175–97. New York: Academic Press.

———. 1985. *Origins of the domestic dog: The fossil record.* Tucson: University of Arizona Press.

Organ, R. M. 1968. *Design for scientific conservation of antiquities.* Washington, D.C.: Smithsonian Institution Press.

Orser, C. E., and B. M. Fagan. 1995. *Historical archaeology.* New York: HarperCollins.

Ortner, D. J., and W. G. J. Putschar. 1987. *Identification of pathological conditions in human skeletal remains.* Rev. ed. Washington, D.C.: Smithsonian Institution Press.

Orton, C. 1980. *Mathematics in archaeology.* Cambridge: Cambridge University Press.

———. 2000. Sampling. In *Archaeological method and theory: An encyclopedia,* edited by L. Ellis, 539–42. New York: Garland.

O'Shea, J. M. 1984. *Mortuary variability: An archaeological investigation.* Orlando, Fla.: Academic Press.

Ottaway, P. 1992. *Archaeology in British towns: From the Emperor Claudius to the Black Death.* London: Routledge.

Palmer, R. 1977. A computer method for transcribing information graphically from oblique aerial photographs to maps. *Journal of Archaeological Science* 4:283–90.

Parrington, M. 1983. Remote sensing. *Annual Review of Anthropology* 12:105–24.

Parsons, E. C. 1939. *Pueblo Indian religion.* 2 vols. Chicago: University of Chicago Press.

Parsons, J. R. 1972. Archaeological settlement patterns. *Annual Review of Anthropology* 1:127–50.

Patrik, L. S. 1985. Is there an archaeological record? In *Advances in archaeological method and theory.* Vol. 8, edited by M. B. Schiffer, 27–62. Orlando, Fla.: Academic Press.

Patterson, T. C. 1963. Contemporaneity and cross-dating in archaeological interpretation. *American Antiquity* 28:129–37.

———. 1986. The last sixty years: Toward a social history of Americanist archaeology in the United States. *American Anthropologist* 88:7–26.

Pearce, S. M. 1990. *Archaeological curatorship.* Washington, D.C.: Smithsonian Institution Press.

Pearsall, D. M. 1989. *Paleoethnobotany: A handbook of procedures.* San Diego: Academic Press.

———. 1992. The origin of plant cultivation in South America. In *The origins of agriculture,* edited by C. W. Cowan and P. J. Watson, 173–206. Washington, D.C.: Smithsonian Institution Press.

Peebles, C. S., and S. M. Kus. 1977. Some archaeological correlates of ranked societies. *American Antiquity* 42:421–48.

Peterson, W. 1975. A demographer's view of prehistoric demography. *Current Anthropology* 16:227–45.

Petrie, W. M. F. 1901. *Diospolis Parva.* Memoir no. 20. London: Egyptian Exploration Fund.

Pickersgill, B. 1972. Cultivated plants as evidence for cultural contracts. *American Antiquity* 37:97–104.

Piggott, S. 1952. *Prehistoric India.* Baltimore: Penguin Books.

———. 1959. The discipline of archaeology. In *Approach to archaeology,* by S. Piggott. Cambridge: Harvard University Press.

———. 1965. Archaeological draughtsmanship: Principles and practice. Part I, Principles and retrospect. *Antiquity* 39:165–76.

Pinsky, V., and A. Wylie, eds. 1900. *Critical traditions in contemporary archaeology.* Cambridge: Cambridge University Press.

Piperno, D. R. 1988. *Phytolith analysis: An archaeological and geological perspective.* San Diego: Academic Press.

Platt, C., ed. 1976. Archaeology and history. *World Archaeology* 7 (whole no. 3).

Plog, F. T. 1974. *The study of prehistoric change.* New York: Academic Press.

———. 1975. Systems theory in archaeological research. *Annual Review of Anthropology* 4:207–24.

Plog, S. 1978a. Sampling in archaeological surveys: A critique. *American Antiquity* 43:280–85.

———. 1978b. Social interaction and stylistic similarity: A reanalysis. In *Advances in archaeological method and theory.* Vol. 1, edited by M. B. Schiffer, 143–82. New York: Academic Press.

———. 1980. *Stylistic variation in prehistoric ceramics.* Cambridge: Cambridge University Press.

———. 1983. Analysis of style in artifacts. *Annual Review of Anthropology* 12:125–42.

Plog, S., F. Plog, and W. Wait. 1978. Decision making in modern surveys. In *Advances in archaeological method and theory.* Vol. 1, edited by M. B. Schiffer, 383–421. New York: Academic Press.

Polanyi, K., C. M. Arensburg, and H. W. Pearson, eds. 1957. *Trade and market in the early empires.* Glencoe, Ill.: Free Press.

Poole, L., and G. J. Poole. 1966. *One passion, two loves: The story of Heinrich and Sophia Schliemann, discoverers of Troy.* New York: Crowell.

Potts, R. 1984. Home bases and early hominids. *American Scientist* 72:338–47.

————. 1986. Temporal span of bone accumulation at Olduvai Gorge and implications for early hominid foraging behavior. *Paleobiology* 12:25–31.

Potts, R., and P. Shipman. 1981. Cutmarks made by stone tools on bones from Olduvai Gorge, Tanzania. *Nature* 291:577–80.

Preucel, R. W., ed. 1991. *Processual and postprocessual archaeologies: Multiple ways of knowing the past.* Occasional Paper no. 16. Carbondale: Southern Illinois University, Center for Archaeological Investigations.

Price, T. D., ed. 1989. *The chemistry of prehistoric human bone.* Cambridge: Cambridge University Press.

Price, T. D., M. J. Schoeninger, and G. J. Armelagos. 1985. Bone chemistry and past behavior: An overview. *Journal of Human Evolution* 14:419–47.

Pulak, C., and D. A. Frey. 1985. The search for a Bronze Age shipwreck. *Archaeology* 38 (4):18–24.

Purdy, B. A., ed. 1990. *Wet site archaeology.* Boca Raton, Fla.: CRC Press.

Quimby, G. I. 1979. A brief history of WPA archaeology. In *The uses of anthropology,* edited by W. Goldschmidt, 110–23. Washington, D.C.: American Anthropological Association.

Raab, L. M., and A. C. Goodyear. 1984. Middle-range theory in archaeology: A critical review of origins and applications. *American Antiquity* 49:255–68.

Raab, L. M., and T. C. Klinger, 1977. A critical appraisal of "significance" in contract archaeology. *American Antiquity* 42:629–34.

Ralph, E. K., and H. N. Michael. 1974. Twenty-five years of radiocarbon dating. *American Scientist* 62:553–60.

Ralph, E. K., H. N. Michael, and M. C. Han. 1973. Radiocarbon dates and reality. *MASCA Newsletter* 9 (whole no. 1).

Rapoport, Amos. 1982. *The meaning of the built environment: A nonverbal communication approach.* Beverly Hills: Sage.

Rapoport, Aratol. 1968. Foreword. In *Modern systems research for the behavioral scientist,* edited by W. Buckley, xiii–xxii. Chicago: Aldine.

Rapp, G., Jr. 1975. The archaeological field staff: The geologist. *Journal of Field Archaeology* 2:229–37.

————. 2000. Metals, characterization. In *Archaeological method and theory: An encyclopedia,* edited by L. Ellis, 364–67. New York: Garland.

Rapp, G., Jr., and J. A. Gifford, eds. 1985. *Archaeological geology.* New Haven: Yale University Press.

Rathje, W. L. 1978. The ancient astronaut myth. *Archaeology* 31:4–7.

Read, D. W. 1986. Sampling procedures for regional surveys: A problem of representativeness and effectiveness. *Journal of Field Archaeology* 13:479–91.

Read-Martin, C. E., and D. W. Read, 1975. Australopithecine scavenging and human evolution: An approach from faunal analysis. *Current Archaeology* 16:359–68.

Redman, C. L. 1973. Multistage fieldwork and analytical techniques. *American Antiquity* 38:61–79.

————. 1974. *Archaeological sampling strategies.* Modules in Anthropology, no. 55. Reading, Mass: Addison-Wesley.

————. 1982. Archaeological survey and the study of Mesopotamian urban systems. *Journal of Field Archaeology* 9:375–82.

————. 1987. Surface collection, sampling, and research design: A retrospective. *American Antiquity* 52:249–65.

Redman, C. L., M. J. Berman, E. V. Curtin, W. T. Langhorne, Jr., N. M. Versaggi, and J. C. Wanser, eds. 1978. *Social archaeology: Beyond subsistence and dating.* New York: Academic Press.

Redman, C. L., and P. J. Watson. 1970. Systemic, intensive surface collection. *American Antiquity* 35:279–91.

Reed, C. A., ed. 1977. *Origins of agriculture.* The Hague: Mouton.

Reed, N. A., J. W. Bennett, and J. W. Porter. 1968. Solid core drilling of Monks Mound: Technique and findings. *American Antiquity* 33:137–48.

Reinhard, K. 2000a. Archaeoparasitology. In *Archaeological method and theory: An encyclopedia,* edited by L. Ellis, 52–60. New York: Garland.

————. 2000b. Coprolite analysis. In *Archaeological method and theory: An encyclopedia,* edited by L. Ellis, 124–32. New York: Garland.

————. 2000c. Reburial, international perspectives. In *Archaeological method and theory: An encyclopedia,* edited by L. Ellis, 512–18. New York: Garland.

Reitz, E. J., and E. S. Wing. 1999. *Zooarchaeology.* Cambridge: Cambridge University Press.

Renfrew, C. 1969. Trade and culture process in European prehistory. *Current Anthropology* 10:151–69.

————. 1971. Carbon 14 and the prehistory of Europe. *Scientific American* 225 (4):63–72.

———. 1973a. *Before civilization: The radiocarbon revolution and prehistoric Europe.* New York: Knopf.

———. 1973b. Monuments, mobilization and social organization in Neolithic Wessex. In *The explanation of culture change: Models in prehistory,* edited by C. Renfrew, 539–58. Pittsburgh: University of Pittsburgh Press.

———. 1975. Trade as action at a distance: Questions of integration and communication. In *Ancient civilization and trade,* edited by J. A. Sabloff and C. C. Lamberg-Karlovsky, 3–59. School of American Research Advanced Seminar Series. Albuquerque: University of New Mexico Press.

———. 1980. The great tradition versus the great divide: Archaeology as anthropology. *American Journal of Archaeology* 84:287–98.

———. 1983a. Divided we stand: Aspects of archaeology and information. *American Antiquity* 48:3–16.

———. 1983b. The social archaeology of megalithic monuments. *Scientific American* 249 (5):152–63.

———. 1984. Social archaeology, societal change and generalization. In *Approaches to social archaeology,* by C. Renfrew, 3–21. Cambridge: Harvard University Press.

Renfrew, C., M. J. Rowlands, and B. A. Segraves, eds. 1982. *Theory and explanation in archaeology: The Southampton conference.* New York: Academic Press.

Renfrew, J. M. 1973. *Palaeoethnobotany.* New York: Columbia University Press.

Reyman, J. E. 1999. Walter W. Taylor. In *Encyclopedia of archaeology: The great archaeologists.* Vol. 2, edited by T. Murray, 681–700. Santa Barbara: ABC-CLIO.

Rice, P. M. 1987. *Pottery analysis: A sourcebook.* Chicago: University of Chicago Press.

Richards, J. D., and N. S. Ryan. 1985. *Data processing in archaeology.* Cambridge: Cambridge University Press.

Rick, J. W. 1976. Downslope movement and archaeological intrasite spatial analysis. *American Antiquity* 41:133–44.

Robertson, M. G. 1972. Monument thievery in Mesoamerica. *American Antiquity* 37:147–55.

Robinson, W. S. 1951. A method for chronologically ordering archaeological deposits. *American Antiquity* 16:293–301.

Roe, D., ed. 1971. Subsistence. *World Archaeology* 2 (whole no. 3).

———. ed. 1985. Studying stones. *World Archaeology* 17 (whole no. 1).

Rogers, J., and T. Waldron. 1989. Infections in paleopathology: The basis of classification according to most probable cause. *Journal of Archaeological Science* 16:611–25.

Roper, D. C. 1976. Lateral displacement of artifacts due to plowing. *American Antiquity* 41:372–75.

———. 1979. The method and theory of site catchment analysis: A review. In *Advances in archaeological method and theory.* Vol. 2, edited by M. B. Schiffer, 119–140. New York: Academic Press.

Rothenberg, B., ed. 1990. *The ancient metallurgy of copper.* London: Institute for Archaeo-Metallurgical Studies.

Rothschild, N. A. 1979. Mortuary behavior and social organization at Indian Knoll and Dickson Mounds. *American Antiquity* 25:313–23.

Rouse, I. 1953. The strategy of culture history. In *Anthropology today,* edited by A. L. Kroeber, 57–76. Chicago: University of Chicago Press.

———. 1960. The classification of artifacts in archaeology. *American Antiquity* 25:313–23.

———. 1986. *Migrations in prehistory.* New Haven: Yale University Press.

Rovner, I. 1983. Plant opal phytolith analysis: Major advances in archaeobotanical research. In *Advances in archaeological method and theory.* Vol. 6, edited by M. B. Schiffer, 225–66. New York: Academic Press.

Rowe, J. H. 1961a. Archaeology as a career. *Archaeology* 14:48–55.

———. 1961b. Stratigraphy and seriation. *American Antiquity* 26:324–30.

———. 1965. The Renaissance foundations of anthropology. *American Anthropologist* 67:1–20.

———. 1966. Diffusionism and archaeology. *American Antiquity* 31:34–38.

Rowell, R. M., and J. Barbour, eds. 1990. *Archaeological wood.* Advances in Chemistry Series, no. 225. Washington, D.C.: American Chemical Society.

Rowlands, M. J. 1971. The archaeological interpretation of prehistoric metalworking. *World Archaeology* 3:210–24.

Rudenko, S. I. 1953. *Kul'tura Naseleniia Gornogo Altaia v Skifskie Vremia.* Moscow: Akademii Nauk.

Rule, M. 1994. *The Mary Rose: The excavation and raising of Henry VIII's flagship.* London: Conway Maritime.

Ryder, M. L. 1983. *Sheep and man.* London: Duckworth.

———. 1984. Wools from textiles in the *Mary Rose,* a sixteenth-century English warship. *Journal of Archaeological Science* 11:337–43.

Rye, O. S. 1981. *Pottery technology: Principles and reconstruction.* Washington, D.C.: Taraxacum.

Sabloff, J. A., and C. C. Lamberg-Karlovsky, eds. 1975. *Ancient civilizations and trade.* School of American

Research Advanced Seminar Series. Albuquerque: University of New Mexico Press.

———. 1982. Introduction. In *Archaeology: Myth and reality: Readings from Scientific American,* edited by J. A. Sabloff, 1–26. San Francisco: Freeman.

Sabloff, J. A., and R. E. Smith. 1969. The importance of both analytic and taxonomic classification in the type-variety system. *American Antiquity* 34:278–85.

Sackett, J. R. 1966. Quantitative analysis of Upper Paleolithic stone tools. In *Recent studies in paleoanthropology,* edited by J. D. Clark and F. C. Howell, *American Anthropologist* 68 (special issue 2, pt. 2):356–94.

———. 1977. The meaning of style in archaeology: A general model. *American Antiquity* 42:369–80.

———. 1982. Approaches to style in lithic technology. *Journal of Anthropological Archaeology* 1:59–112.

Sahlins, M. D., and E. R. Service, eds. 1960. *Evolution and culture.* Ann Arbor: University of Michigan Press.

Salmon, M. 1982. *Philosophy and archaeology.* New York: Academic Press.

Salwen, B. 1962. Sea levels and archaeology in the Long Island Sound area. *American Antiquity* 28:46–55.

Sanders, W. T., and B. J. Price. 1968. *Mesoamerica: The evolution of civilization.* New York: Random House.

Saraydar, S., and I. Shimada. 1973. Experimental archaeology: A new outlook. *American Antiquity* 38:344–50.

Satterthwaite, L., Jr., and E. K. Ralph. 1960. New radiocarbon dates and the Maya correlation problem. *American Antiquity* 26:165–84.

Saxe, A. A. 1971. Social dimensions of mortuary practices in a Mesolithic population form Wadi Halfa, Sudan. In *Approaches to the social dimensions of mortuary practices,* edited by J. A. Brown, 39–57. Memoir no. 25. Washington, D.C.: Society for American Archaeology.

Schacht, R. M. 1981. Estimating past population trends. *Annual Review of Anthropology* 10:119–40.

Schele, L., and D. A. Freidel. 1990. *A forest of kings: The untold story of the ancient Maya.* New York: William Morrow.

Schele, L., and M. E. Miller. 1986. *The blood of kings: Dynasty and ritual in Maya art.* Fort Worth, Tex.: Kimbell Art Museum.

Schiffer, M. B. 1972. Archaeological context and systemic context. *American Antiquity* 37: 156–65.

———. 1976. *Behavioral archaeology.* New York: Academic Press.

———. 1978. Taking the pulse of method and theory in American archaeology. *American Antiquity* 43:153–58.

———. 1985. Is there a "Pompeii premise" in archaeology? *Journal of Anthropological Research* 41:18–41.

———. 1987. *Formation processes of the archaeological record.* Albuquerque: University of New Mexico Press.

———. 1988. The structure of archaeological theory. *American Antiquity* 53:461–85.

Schiffer, M. B., and G. J. Gumerman, eds. 1977. *Conservational archaeology: A guide for cultural resource management studies.* New York: Academic Press.

Schiffer, M. B., and J. H. House. 1977. Cultural resource management and archaeological research: The Cache Project. *Current Anthropology* 18:43–68.

Schiffer, M. B., A. P. Sullivan, and T. C. Klinger. 1978. The design of archaeological surveys. *World Archaeology* 10:1–28.

Schliemann, H. [1881] 1968. *Ilios, the city and country of the Trojans.* Reprint. New York: Blom.

Schmandt-Besserat, D. 1978. The earliest precursors of writing. *Scientific American* 238 (6):50–59.

———. 1992. *Before writing.* 2 vols. Austin: University of Texas Press.

Schrire, C., ed. 1984. *Past and present in hunter-gatherer studies.* Orlando, Fla.: Academic Press.

Schrire, C., J. Deetz, D. Lubinsky, and C. Poggenpoel. 1990. The chronology of Oudepost I, Cape, as inferred from an analysis of clay pipes. *Journal of Archaeological Science* 17:269–300.

Schuyler, R. L. 1971. The history of American archaeology: An examination of procedure. *American Antiquity* 36:383–409.

———. 1976. Images of America: The contribution of historical archaeology to the national identity. *Southwestern Lore* 42 (4):27–39.

———. ed. 1978. *Historical archaeology: A guide to substantive and theoretical contributions.* Farmingdale, N.Y.: Baywood.

Scollar, I., A. Tabbagh, A. Hesse, and I. Herzog. 1990. *Image processing in archaeology.* Cambridge: Cambridge University Press.

Sealy, J. C., and N. van der Merwe. 1986. Isotope assessment and the seasonal-mobility hypothesis in the southwestern cape of South Africa. *Current Anthropology* 27:135–50.

Sears, W. H. 1961. The study of social and religious systems in North American archaeology. *Current Anthropology* 2:223–46.

Sease, C. 1987. *Conservation for the field archaeologist.* Archaeological Research Tools 4. Los Angeles: UCLA Institute of Archaeology.

Semenov, S. A. 1964. *Prehistoric technology.* New York: Barnes & Noble.

Service, E. R. 1962. *Primitive social organizations: An evolutionary perspective.* New York: Random House.

———. 1975. *Origins of the state and civilization: The process of cultural evolution.* New York: Norton.

Sever, T., and J. Wiseman. 1985. *Remote sensing and archaeology: Potential for the future.* National Space Technology Laboratories, Miss.: National Aeronautics and Space Administration, Earth Resources Laboratory.

Shackley, M. L. 1975. *Archaeological sediments.* New York: Wiley/Halsted.

———. 1981. *Environmental archaeology.* London: Allen & Unwin.

———. 1985. *Using environmental archaeology.* London: Batsford.

Shafer, H. J., and R. G. Holloway. 1979. Organic residue analysis in determining stone tool function. In *Lithic use-wear analysis,* edited by B. Hayden, 385–99. New York: Academic Press.

Shanks, M., and C. Tilley. 1992. *Re-constructing archaeology.* 2d London: Routledge.

Shapiro, G. 1984. A soil resistivity survey of 15th-century Puerto Real, Haiti. *Journal of Field Archaeology* 11:101–10.

Sharer, R. J., and W. Ashmore. 1987. *Archaeology: Discovering our past.* Mountain View, Calif.: Mayfield.

Shaw, J. 2000. Archaeomagnetic dating. In *Archaeological method and theory: An encyclopedia,* edited by L. Ellis, 44–47. New York: Garland.

Sheets, P. D. 1971. An ancient natural disaster. *Expedition* 14 (1):24–31.

———. 1973. The pillage of prehistory. *American Antiquity* 38:317–20.

———. 1975. Behavioral analysis and the structure of a prehistoric industry. *Current Anthropology* 16:369–91.

Shelton, D. 1986. Law and looting. *Archaeology* 39 (4):80.

Shennan, S. J., ed. 1988. *Quantifying archaeology.* San Diego: Academic Press.

———. 1989. *Archaeological approaches to cultural identity.* London: Unwin Hyman.

Shepard, A. O. 1971. *Ceramics for the archaeologist.* Publication no. 609. Washington, D.C.: Carnegie Institution.

Shimada, I., and J. F. Merkel. 1991. Copper-alloy metallurgy in ancient Peru. *Scientific American* 265 (1):80–86.

Shipman, P. 1981. *Life history of a fossil: An introduction to taphonomy and paleoecology.* Cambridge: Harvard University Press.

———. 1986. Scavenging or hunting in early hominids: Theoretical framework and tests. *American Anthropologist* 88:27–43.

Shipman, P., A. Walker, and D. Bichell. 1985. *The human skeleton.* Cambridge: Harvard University Press.

Shott, M. 1985. Shovel-test sampling as a site discovery technique: A case study from Michigan. *Journal of Field Archaeology* 12:457–68.

———. 1989. Shovel-test sampling in archaeological survey: Comments on Nance and Ball, and Lightfoot. *American Antiquity* 54:396–404.

Sieveking, A. 1979. *The cave artists.* London: Thames & Hudson.

Sillen, A., J. C. Sealy, and N. J. van der Merwe. 1989. Chemistry and paleodietary research: No more easy answers. *American Antiquity* 54:504–12.

Sjoberg, A. 1976. Phosphate analysis of anthropic soils. *Journal of Field Archaeology* 3:447–54.

Skowronek, R. K. 1985. Sport divers and archaeology: The case of the Legare Anchorage ship site. *Archaeology* 38 (3):22–27.

Smith, B. D. 1974. Middle Mississippi exploitation of animal populations: A predictive model. *American Antiquity* 39:274–91.

———. 1987. The independent domestication of the indigenous seed-bearing plants in eastern North America. In *Emergent horticultural economics of the eastern woodlands,* edited by W. Keegan, 3–47. Occasional Paper no. 7. Carbondale: Southern Illinois University, Center for Archaeological Investigations.

Smith, G. E. 1928. *In the beginning: The origin of civilization.* New York: Morrow.

Smith, G. S., and J. E. Ehrenhard, eds. 1991. *Protecting the past.* Boca Raton, Fla.: CRC Press.

Smith, N. 1978. Roman hydraulic technology: *Scientific American* 238 (5):154–61.

Smith, P., and L. K. Horwitz. 1984. Radiographic evidence for changing patterns of animal exploitation in the Southern Levant. *Journal of Archaeological Science* 11:467–75.

Smith, P. E. L. 1976. *Food production and its consequences.* Menlo Park, Calif.: Cummings.

Smith, R. E., G. R. Willey, and J. C. Gifford. 1960. The type-variety concept as a basis for the analysis of Maya pottery. *American Antiquity* 25:330–40.

Smith, R. H. 1974. Ethics in field archaeology. *Journal of Field Archaeology* 1:375–83.

Solecki, R. S. 1975. Shanidar IV, a Neanderthal flower burial in northern Iraq. *Science* 190:880–81.

South, S. A. 1977. *Method and theory in historical archeology.* New York: Academic Press.

Spaulding, A. C. 1953. Statistical techniques for the discovery of artifact types. *American Antiquity* 18:305–13.

———. 1960. The dimensions of archaeology. In *Essays in the science of culture in honor of Leslie A. White,* edited by G. E. Dole and R. L. Carneiro, 437–56. New York: Crowell.

———. 1977. On growth and form in archaeology. *Journal of Anthropological Research* 33:1–15.

Spector, J. D. 1991. What this awl means: Toward a feminist archaeology. In *Engendering archaeology: Women and prehistory,* edited by J. M. Gero and M. W. Conkey, 388–406. Oxford: Blackwell.

Spector, J. D., and M. K. Whelan. 1989. Incorporating gender into archaeology courses. In *Gender and anthropology: Critical reviews for research and teaching,* edited by S. Morgen, 65–94. Washington, D.C.: American Anthropological Association.

Speser, P., K. Reinburg, A. Porsche, S. Arter, and P. Bienenfeld. 1986. *The politics of archaeology.* Archaeology and the Federal Government Publication Series. Washington, D.C.: Foresight Science and Technology.

Squier, E. G., and E. H. Davis. 1848. *Ancient monuments of the Mississippi Valley.* Smithsonian Contributions to Knowledge, no. 1. Washington, D.C.: Smithsonian Institution Press.

Stahle, D. W., and D. Wolfman. 1985. The potential for archaeological tree-ring dating eastern North America. In *Advances in archaeological method and theory.* Vol. 8, edited by M. B. Schiffer, 279–302. Orlando, Fla.: Academic Press.

Stallings, W. S., Jr. 1949. *Dating prehistoric ruins by tree-rings.* Rev. ed. Tucson: University of Arizona, Laboratory of Tree-Ring Research.

Stanford, D., R. Bonnichsen, and R. E. Morlan. 1981. The Ginsberg experiment: Modern and prehistoric evidence of a bone-flaking technology. *Science* 212: 438–40.

Stanislawski, M. B. 1973. Review of *Archaeology as Anthropology: A Case Study,* by W. A. Longacre. *American Antiquity* 38:117–21.

Stark, B. L. 1986. Origins of food production in the New World. In *American archaeology past and future: A celebration of the Society for American Archaeology 1935–1985,* edited by D. J. Meltzer, D. D. Fowler, and J. A. Sabloff, 277–321. Washington, D.C.: Smithsonian Institution Press.

Staski, E. 1982. Advances in urban archaeology. In *Advances in archaeological method and theory.* Vol. 5, edited by M. B. Schiffer, 97–149. New York: Academic Press.

Stein, J. K. 1983. Earthworm activity: A source of potential disturbance of archaeological sediments. *American Antiquity* 48:277–89.

———. 1987. Deposits for archaeologists. In *Advances in archaeological method and theory.* Vol. 11, edited by M. B. Schiffer, 337–95. New York: Academic Press.

Stein, J. K., and W. R. Farrand, eds. 1985. *Archaeological sediments in context.* Orono, Maine: Center for the Study of Early Man.

Stephen, D. V. M., and D. B. Craig. 1984. Recovering the past bit by bit with microcomputers. *Archaeology* 37 (4):20–26.

Stephens, J. L. [1841] 1969. *Incidents of travel in Central America, Chiapas, and Yucatan.* 2 vols. Reprint. New York: Dover.

———. [1843] 1963. *Incidents of travel in Yucatan.* 2 vols. Reprint. New York: Dover.

Steponaitis, V. P., and J. P. Brain. 1976. A portable differential proton magnetometer. *Journal of Field Archaeology* 3:455–63.

Sterud, E. L. 1978. Changing aims of Americanist archaeology: A citations analysis of *American Antiquity*—1946–1975. *American Antiquity* 43:294–302.

Sterud, E. L., and P. P. Pratt. 1975. Archaeological intrasite recording with photography. *Journal of Field Archaeology* 2:151–67.

Steward, J. H. 1938. *Basin-Plateau aboriginal sociopolitical groups.* Bureau of American Ethnology, Bulletin no. 120. Washington, D.C.: Smithsonian Institution Press.

———. 1942. The direct historical approach to archaeology. *American Antiquity* 7:337–43.

———. 1955. *Theory of culture change.* Urbana: University of Illinois Press.

Steward, J. H., and F. M. Setzler. 1938. Function and configuration in archaeology. *American Antiquity* 1:4–10.

Stiles, D. 1977. Ethnoarchaeology: A discussion of methods and applications. *Man* 12:87–103.

Stirland, A. 1999. *Human bones in archaeology.* 2d ed. Princes Risborough, England: Shire Archaeology.

———. 2000. *Raising the dead: The skeleton crew of Henry VIII's Great Ship, the Mary Rose.* New York: Wiley.

Stoltman, J. B. 1989. A quantitative approach to the petrographic analysis of ceramic thin-sections. *American Antiquity* 54:147–160.

Stone, P., and R. MacKenzie, eds. 1989. *The excluded past: Archaeology in education.* London: Unwin Hyman.

Stover, L. E., and H. Harrison. 1970. *Apeman, spaceman: Anthropological science fiction.* New York: Berkley.

Struever, S. 1968. Flotation techniques for the recovery of small-scale archaeological remains. *American Antiquity* 33:353–62.

———. 1971. Comments on archaeological data requirements and research design. *American Antiquity* 36: 9–19.

Struever, S., and J. Carlson. 1977. Koster site: The new archaeology in action. *Archaeology* 30:93–101.

Stuart, G. E. 1976. *Your career in archaeology*. Washington, D.C.: Society for American Archaeology.

Stuiver, M. 1982. A high-precision calibration of the A.D. radiocarbon time scale. *Radiocarbon* 24:1–26.

Sullivan, G. 1980. *Discover archaeology: An introduction to the tools and techniques of archaeological fieldwork*. New York: Penguin Books.

Sutton, M. Q., and B. S. Arkush. 1998. *Archaeological laboratory methods*. 2d ed. Dubuque, Iowa: Kendall/Hunt.

Swanson, E., ed. 1975. *Lithic technology: Making and using stone tools*. Chicago: Aldine.

Swart, P., and B. D. Till. 1984. Bronze carriages from the tomb of China's first emperor. *Archaeology* 37 (6): 18–25.

Tainter, J. A. 1978. Mortuary practices and the study of prehistoric social systems. In *Advances in archaeological method and theory*. Vol 1, edited by M. B. Schiffer, 105–41. New York: Academic Press.

Tarling, D. H. 1985. Archaeomagnetism. In *Archaeological geology*, edited by G. Rapp, Jr., and J. A. Gifford, 237–63. New Haven: Yale University Press.

Taylor, R. E. 1987. *Radiocarbon dating*. San Diego: Academic Press.

Taylor, R. E., and I. Longworth, eds. 1975. Dating: New methods and new results. *World Archaeology* 7 (whole no. 2).

Taylor, R. E., and C. W. Meighan, eds. 1978. *Chronologies in New World archaeology*. New York: Academic Press.

Taylor, R. E., P. J. Slota, Jr., W. Henning, W. Kutschera, and M. Paul. 1989. Radiocalcium dating: Potential applications in archaeology and paleoanthropology. In *Archaeological chemistry IV*, edited by R. O. Allen, 321–35, Advances in Chemistry Series, no. 220. Washington, D.C.: American Chemical Society.

Taylor, W. W. [1948] 1964–1967. *A study of archaeology*. American Anthropological Association, Memoir 69. Reprint. Carbondale: Southern Illinois University Press.

Thomas, C. 1894. *Report of the mound explorations of the Bureau of Ethnology*. Washington, D.C.: Smithsonian Institution Press.

Thomas, D. H. 1973. An empirical test for Steward's model of Great Basin settlement patterns. *American Antiquity* 38:155–76.

———. 1975. Non-site sampling: Up the creek without a site? In *Sampling in archaeology*, edited by James Mueller, 61–81. Tucson: University of Arizona Press.

———. 1978. The awful truth about statistics in archaeology. *American Antiquity* 43:231–44.

———. 1983. *The archaeology of Monitor Valley*. Vol. 1, *Epistemology*. Anthropological Papers, vol. 58, no. 1. New York: American Museum of Natural History.

———. 1986a. Contemporary hunter-gatherer archaeology in America. In *American archaeology past and future: A celebration of the Society for American Archaeology 1935–1985*, edited by D. J. Meltzer, D. D. Fowler, and J. A. Sabloff, 237–76. Washington, D.C.: Smithsonian Institution Press.

———. 1986b. *Refiguring anthropology: First principle of probability and statistics*. Prospect Heights, Ill.: Waveland Press.

Thompson, D. E., and J. V. Murra. 1966. The Inca bridges in the Huánuco area. *American Antiquity* 31:632–39.

Thompson, F. C. 1970. Microscopic studies of ancient metals. In *Science in archaeology*, edited by D. Brothwell and E. S. Higgs, 555–63. New York: Praeger.

Throckmorton, P. ed. 1987. *The sea remembers: Shipwrecks and archaeology from Homer's Greece to the rediscovery of the Titanic*. New York: Smithmark.

Tilley, C. 1990. *Reading material culture*. Oxford: Blackwell.

Topping, A. 1978. China's incredible find. *National Geographic* 153:440–59.

Torrence, R., ed. 1989. *Time, energy and stone tools*. Cambridge: Cambridge University Press.

Toth, N. 1985. The Oldowan reassessed: A close look at early stone artifacts. *Journal of Archaeological Science* 12:101–20.

Toth, N., and K. D. Schick. 1986. The first million years: The archaeology of protohuman culture. In *Advances in archaeological method and theory*. Vol. 9, edited by M. B. Schiffer, 1–96. Orlando, Fla.: Academic Press.

Toulmin, S., and J. Goodfield. 1965. *The discovery of time*. New York: Harper & Row.

Trigger, B. G. 1968a. *Beyond history: The methods of prehistory*. New York: Holt, Rinehart & Winston.

———. 1968b. The determination of settlement patterns. In *Settlement archaeology*, edited by K. C. Chang, 53–78. Palo Alto, Calif.: National Press.

———. 1970. Aims in prehistoric archaeology. *Antiquity* 44:26–37.

———. 1980. *Gordon Childe: Revolutions in archaeology*. London: Thames & Hudson.

———. 1984. Archaeology at the crossroads: What's new? *Annual Review of Anthropology* 13:275–300.

———. 1989. *A history of archaeological thought*. Cambridge: Cambridge University Press.

———. 1999. Vere Gordon Childe. In *Encyclopedia of archaeology: The great archaeologists*. Vol. 1, edited by T. Murray, 385–400. Santa Barbara, Calif.: ABC-CLIO.

Trigger, B. G., and I. Glover, eds. 1981. Regional traditions of archaeological research. 1. *World Archaeology* 13 (whole no. 2).

————, eds. 1982. Regional traditions of archaeological research. 2. *World Archaeology* 13 (whole no. 3).

Trigger, B. G., and I. Longworth, eds. 1974. Political systems. *World Archaeology* 6 (whole no. 1).

Tringham, R. 1983. V. Gordon Childe 25 years after: His relevance for the archaeology of the eighties. *Journal of Field Archaeology* 1:171–96.

Trinkaus, K. M., ed. 1986. *Politics and partitions: Human boundaries and the growth of complex societies.* Tempe, Ariz.: Anthropological Research Papers.

Tuggle, H. D., A. H. Townsend, and T. J. Riley. 1972. Laws, systems and research designs. *American Antiquity* 37:3–12.

Turnbaugh, W. A., C. L. Vanderbrock, and J. S. Jones. 1983. The professionalism of amateurs in archaeology. *Archaeology* 36 (6):24–29.

Turner, B. L., and P. D. Harrison, 1983. *Pulltrouser Swamp.* Austin: University of Texas Press.

Tylor, E. B. 1871. *Primitive culture.* London: Murray.

Ubelaker, D. H. 1989. *Human skeletal remains: Excavation, analysis, interpretation.* 2d ed. Washington, D.C.: Taraxacum.

Ucko, P. J. 1968. *Anthropomorphic figurines of predynastic Egypt and Neolithic Crete with comparative material from the prehistoric Near East and mainland Greece.* Royal Anthropological Institute, Occasional Paper 24. London: Szmidla.

————. 1969. Ethnography and archaeological interpretation of funerary remains. *World Archaeology* 1: 262–80.

Ucko, P. J., and G. W. Dimbleby, eds. 1969. *The domestication and exploitation of plants and animals.* London: Duckworth.

Ucko, P. J., and A. Rosenfeld. 1967. *Palaeolithic cave art.* New York: McGraw-Hill.

Ucko, P. J., R. Tringham, and G. W. Dimbleby, eds. 1972. *Man, settlement and urbanism.* London: Duckworth.

United Nations Educational, Scientific, and Cultural Organization (UNESCO). 1968. *The conservation of cultural property.* N.p.: UNESCO Press.

van der Merwe, N. J. 1982. Carbon isotopes, photosynthesis, and archaeology. *American Scientist* 70:596–606.

van der Merwe, N. J., and D. H. Avery. 1982. Pathways to steel. *American Scientist* 70:146–55.

van der Veen, M., and N. Fiedler. 1982. Sampling seeds. *Journal of Archaeological Science* 9:287–98.

Veit, U. 1989. Ethnic concepts in German prehistory: A case study on the relationship between cultural identity and archaeological objectivity. In *Archaeological approaches to cultural identity,* edited by Stephen Shennan, 35–56. London: Unwin Hyman.

Villa, P. 1982. Conjoinable pieces and site formation processes. *American Antiquity* 27:276–90.

Villa, P., and J. Courtin. 1983. The interpretation of stratified sites: A view from underground. *Journal of Archaeological Science* 10:267–82.

Vita-Finzi, C., and E. S. Higgs. 1970. Prehistoric economy in the Mount Carmel area of Palestine. *Proceedings of the Prehistoric Society* 36:1–37.

Vitelli, K. D. 1983. To remove the double standard: Historic shipwreck legislation. *Journal of Field Archaeology* 10:105–6.

Vogt, E. Z., ed. 1974. *Aerial photography in anthropological field research.* Cambridge: Harvard University Press.

von Däniken, E. 1969. *Chariots of the gods?* New York: Bantam.

————. 1970. *Gods from outer space.* New York: Bantam.

von den Driesch, A. 1976. *A guide to the measurement of animal bones from archaeological sites.* Bulletin 1. Cambridge: Harvard University, Peabody Museum of Archaeology and Ethnology.

Wagner, G. 2000. Fission-track dating. In *Archaeological method and theory: An encyclopedia,* edited by L. Ellis, 211–15. New York: Garland.

Walker, W. 2000. Behavioral archaeology. In *Archaeological method and theory: An encyclopedia,* edited by L. Ellis, 69–73. New York: Garland.

Ward, R. H., and K. M. Weiss. 1976. *The demographic evolution of human populations.* London: Academic Press.

Waselkov, G. A. 1987. Shellfish gathering and shell midden archaeology. In *Advances in archaeological method and theory.* Vol. 10, edited by M. B. Schiffer, 93–210. San Diego: Academic Press.

Watson, P. J. 1973. The future of archaeology in anthropology: Cultural history and social science. In *Research and theory in current archaeology,* edited by C. L. Redman, 113–24. New York: Wiley-Interscience.

————. 1977. Design analysis of painted pottery. *American Antiquity* 42:381–93.

————. 1986. Archaeological interpretation, 1985. In *American archaeology past and future: A celebration of the Society for American Archaeology 1935–1985,* edited by D. J. Meltzer, D. D. Fowler, and J. A. Sabloff, 439–57. Washington, D.C.: Smithsonian Institution Press.

Watson, P. J., and M. C. Kennedy. 1991. The development of horticulture in the Eastern Woodlands of North America: Women's role. In *Engendering archaeology: Women and prehistory,* edited by J. M. Gero and M. W. Conkey, 255–75. Oxford: Blackwell.

Watson, P. J., S. A. LeBlanc, and C. L. Redman. 1971. *Explanation in archaeology: An explicitly scientific approach.* New York: Columbia University Press.

———. 1984. *Archaeological explanation: The scientific method in archaeology.* New York: Columbia University Press.

Watson, R. A. 1990. Ozymandias, king of kings: Postprocessual radical archaeology as critique. *American Antiquity* 55:673–89.

———. 1991. What the New Archaeology has accomplished. *Current Anthropology* 32:275–91.

Wauchope, R. 1962. *Lost tribes and sunken continents.* Chicago: University of Chicago Press.

———. 1965. *They found the buried cities.* Chicago: University of Chicago Press.

Weiner, J. S. 1955. *The Piltdown forgery.* London: Oxford University Press.

Weiss, K. M. 1976. Demographic theory and anthropological inference. *Annual Review of Anthropology* 5:351–81.

Wendorf, F. 1973. "Rescue" archaeology along the Nile. In *In search of man: Readings in archaeology,* edited by E. L. Green, 39–42. Boston: Little, Brown.

Wenke, R. J. 1982. Explaining the evolution of cultural complexity: A review. In *Advances in archaeological method and theory.* Vol. 4, edited by M. B. Schiffer, 79–127. New York: Academic Press.

Wertime, T. A. 1973. The beginnings of metallurgy: A new look. *Science* 182:875–87.

———. 1983. The furnace vs. the goat: The pyrotechnologic industries and Mediterranean deforestation in antiquity. *Journal of Field Archaeology* 10:445–52.

Wertime, T., and J. Muhly, eds. 1980. *The coming of the Age of Iron.* New Haven: Yale University Press.

Wertime, T., and S. Wertime, eds. 1982. *Early pyrotechnology.* Washington, D.C.: Smithsonian Institution Press.

Weymouth, J. M. 1986. Geophysical methods of archaeological site surveying. In *Advances in archaeological method and theory.* Vol. 9, edited by M. B. Schiffer, 311–95. Orlando, Fla.: Academic Press.

Whallon, R., Jr. 1968. Investigations of late prehistoric social organization in New York State. In *New perspectives in archaeology,* edited by S. R. Binford and L. R. Binford, 223–44. Chicago: Aldine.

———. 1972. A new approaches to pottery typology. *American Antiquity* 37:13–33.

———. 1973. Spatial analysis of occupation floors. Part 1, Application of dimensional analysis of variance. *American Antiquity* 38:266–78.

———. 1974. Spatial analysis of occupation floors. Part 2, The application of nearest neighbor analysis. *American Antiquity* 39:16–34.

———. 1984. Unconstrained clustering for the analysis of spatial distributions in archaeology. In *Intrasite spatial analysis in archaeology,* edited by H. J. Hietala, 242–77. Cambridge: Cambridge University Press.

Whallon, R., and J. A. Brown, eds. 1982. *Essays on archaeological typology.* Evanston, Ill.: Center for American Archaeology Press.

Wheeler, A., and A. K. G. Jones. 1989. *Fishes.* Cambridge: Cambridge University Press.

Wheeler, M. 1943. *Maiden Castle, Dorset.* London: Society of Antiquaries of London.

———. 1954. *Archaeology from the earth.* Harmondsworth, England: Penguin Books.

———. 1955. *Still digging.* London: Joseph.

White, L. A. 1949. *The science of culture.* New York: Grove Press.

White, P. 1974. *The past is human.* New York: Taplinger.

White, T. D. 1990. *Human osteology.* San Diego: Academic Press.

Whiting, J. W. M., and B. Ayres. 1968. Inferences from the shape of dwellings. In *Settlement archaeology,* edited by K. C. Chang, 117–33. Palo Alto, Calif.: National Press.

Whittaker, J. 1994. *Flintknapping: Making and understanding stone tools.* Austin: University of Texas.

Wiessner, P. 1974. A functional estimator of population from floor area. *American Antiquity* 39:313–50.

———. 1983. Style and social information in Kalahari San projectile points. *American Antiquity* 48:253–76.

———. 1984. Reconsidering the behavior basis for style: A case study among the Kalahari San. *Journal of Anthropological Archaeology* 3:190–234.

Wilk, R. R., and W. Ashmore, eds. 1988. *Household and community in the Mesoamerican past.* Albuquerque: University of New Mexico Press.

Wilk, R. R., and W. L. Rathje, eds. 1982. Archaeology of the household: Building a prehistory of domestic life. *American Behavioral Scientist* 25 (whole no. 6).

Willey, G. R. 1953. *Prehistoric settlement patterns in the Virú Valley, Peru.* Bureau of American Ethnology, Bulletin no. 155. Washington, D.C.: Smithsonian Institution Press.

———, ed. 1956. *Prehistoric settlement patterns in the New World.* Viking Fund Publications in Anthropology, no. 23. New York: Wenner-Gren Foundation for Anthropological Research.

———. 1966. *An introduction to American archaeology.* Vol. 1, *North and Middle America.* Englewood Cliffs, N.J.: Prentice-Hall.

———. 1971. *An introduction to American archaeology.* Vol. 2, *South America.* Englewood Cliffs, N.J.: Prentice-Hall.

———, ed. 1974. *Archaeological researches in retrospect.* Cambridge, Mass.: Winthrop.

———. 1983. Settlement patterns and archaeology: Some comments. In *Prehistoric settlement patterns: Essays in honor of Gordon R. Willey,* edited by E. Z. Vogt and R. M. Leventhal, 445–62. Albuquerque and Cambridge: University of New Mexico Press and Harvard University.

Willey, G. R., and P. Phillips. 1958. *Method and theory in American archaeology.* Chicago: University of Chicago Press.

Willey, G. R., and J. A. Sabloff. 1980. *A history of American archaeology.* 2d ed. San Francisco: Freeman.

Williams, S. 1991. *Fantastic archaeology: The wild side of North American prehistory.* Philadelphia: University of Pennsylvania Press.

Williamson, R. A. 1979. Field report: Hovenweep National Monument. *Archaeoastronomy* 2 (3):11–12.

———, ed. 1981. *Archaeoastronomy in the Americas.* Los Altos, Calif., and College Park, Md.: Ballena Press and the Center for Archaeoastronomy.

Williamson, R. A., H. J. Fisher, and D. O'Flynn. 1977. Anasazi solar observations. In *Native American astronomy,* edited by A. F. Aveni, 203–17. Austin: University of Texas Press.

Wilmsen, E. N. 1970. *Lithic analysis and cultural inference: A Paleo-Indian case.* Anthropological Paper no. 16. Tucson: University of Arizona Press.

———. 1974. *Lindermeier: A Pleistocene hunting society.* New York: Harper & Row.

Wilshusen, R. H., and G. D. Stone. 1990. An ethnoarchaeological perspective on soils. *World Archaeology* 22:104–14.

Wilson, B., C. Grigson, and S. Payne, eds. 1982. *Ageing and sexing animal bones from archaeological sites.* British Archaeological Reports, British Series 109. Oxford: British Archaeological Reports.

Wilson, D. R. 1982. *Air photo interpretation for archaeologists.* New York: St. Martin's Press.

Wing, E. S., and A. R. Brown. 1980. *Paleonutrition: Method and theory in prehistoric foodways.* New York: Academic Press.

Winterhalder, B., and E. A. Smith. 1981. *Hunter-gatherer foraging strategies: Ethnographic and archaeological analysis.* Chicago: University of Chicago Press.

Winters, H. D. 1968. Value systems and trade cycles of the Late Archaic in the Midwest. In *New perspectives in archaeology,* edited by S. R. Binford and L. R. Binford, 175–221. Chicago: Aldine.

Wiseman, J. 1980. Archaeology as archaeology. *Journal of Field Archaeology* 7:149–51.

———. 1984. Scholarship and provenience in the study of artifacts. *Journal of Field Archaeology* 11:67–77.

———. 1985. Odds and ends: Multimedia documentation in archaeology. *Journal of Field Archaeology* 12: 389.

Wittry, W. L. 1977. The American Woodhenge. In *Explorations in Cahokia archaeology,* edited by M. L. Fowler, 43–48. Illinois Archaeology Survey Bulletin 7. Urbana: University of Illinois.

Wobst, H. M. 1977. Stylistic behavior and information exchange. In *For the director: Essays in honor of James B. Griffin,* edited by C. E. Cleland, 317–42. Anthropological Paper no. 61. Ann Arbor: University of Michigan, Museum of Anthropology.

———. 1983. We can't see the forest for the trees: Sampling and the shapes of archaeological distributions. In *Archaeological hammers and theories,* edited by J. A. Moore and A. S. Keene, 37–85. New York: Academic Press.

Wolf, E. R. 1982. *Europe and the people without history.* Berkeley and Los Angeles: University of California Press.

Wolfman, D. 1984. Geomagnetic dating methods in archaeology. In *Advances in archaeological method and theory.* Vol. 7, edited by M. B. Schiffer, 363–458. Orlando, Fla.: Academic Press.

Wood, M. 1985. *In search of the Trojan War.* New York: Facts on File.

Wood, W. R., and D. L. Johnson. 1978. A survey of disturbance processes in archaeological site formation. In *Advances in archaeological method and theory.* Vol. 1, edited by M. B. Schiffer, 315–81. New York: Academic Press.

Woodbury, R. B. 1973. *Alfred V. Kidder.* New York: Columbia University Press.

Woolley, C. L. 1934. *Ur excavations.* Vol. 2, *The royal cemetery.* Oxford and Philadelphia: British Museum and University Museum, University of Pennsylvania.

———. 1961. *Digging up the past.* Baltimore: Penguin Books.

Wright, H. T. 1986. The evolution of civilizations. In *American archaeology past and future: A celebration of the Society for American Archaeology 1935–1985,* edited by D. J. Meltzer, D. D. Fowler, and J. A. Sabloff, 323–65. Washington, D.C.: Smithsonian Institution Press.

Wright, R. V. S., ed. 1977. *Stone tools as cultural markers.* Canberra: Australian Institute of Aboriginal Studies.

Wylie, A. 1985. The reaction against analogy. In *Advances in archaeological method and theory.* Vol. 8, edited by M. B. Schiffer, 63–111. Orlando, Fla.: Academic Press.

Yellen, J. E. 1977. *Archaeological approaches to the present: Models for reconstructing the past.* New York: Academic Press.

Young, D., and R. Bonnichsen. 1984. *Understanding stone tools.* Peopling of the Americas Series, no. 1. Orono: University of Maine.

Young, P., ed. 1989. Archaeology in the 21st century. *Archaeology* 42 (whole no. 1).

Young, T. C. 1988. Since Herodotus, has history been a valid concept? *American Antiquity* 53:7–12.

Zeilik, M. 1984. Archaeoastronomy at Chaco Canyon: The historic-prehistoric connection. In *New light on Chaco Canyon,* edited by D. G. Noble, 65–72. Santa Fe: School of American Research Press.

Zeuner, F. E. 1958. *Dating the past: An introduction to geochronology.* London: Methuen.

Zimmerman, D. W. 1971. Uranium distributions in archaeological ceramics. *Science* 174:818–19.

Zubrow, E. 1975. *Prehistoric carrying capacity: A model.* Menlo Park, Calif.: Cummings.

———, ed. 1976. *Demographic anthropology: Quantitative approaches.* School of American Research Advanced Seminar Series. Albuquerque: University of New Mexico Press.

CREDITS

361

INDEX

Page references in italics refer to figures or tables.

impact fractures, 27
Incan civilization, 280–281
incision, in ceramics, 204–205, *205,* 212, *212*
inclusions, 188–189, 192–193, 245
index elements, 267
Indiana Jones, 21, 23
Indian Knoll site (Kentucky), 273–274
indirect dating, 139–140, *140*
indirect percussion, *171,* 172
inferences, 110
inlay, 225
in situ, definition, 132
Internet, sale of artifacts on, 311–315
intuitive sampling, 117
Inuit mummies (Greenland), 277–278
iron
    in the ancient world, 225–230
    characteristics, 225–229
    definition, 225
    in the historic era, 230–232
iron deficiency anemia, 275

Jamali, Zawar Amir Bux, 157
Jefferson, Thomas, 125
Jelderks, John, 314
Jericho site (Jordan), 16–17
Jorvik Viking Center (England), 279, 282
Journal of Field Archaeology, 94
journals, archaeological, 93, *94*

Karlsburg Castle (Czech Republic), *294*
Kelly, John, 298
Kennewick Man, 312–314, *313*
Kenyon, Dame Kathleen Mary, 16–17, *17*
Kidder, Alfred Vincent, 15, 48, 62–63
kiln firing, 196, 206, *207,* 221
Kirchner Marsh, Minnesota, *262*
Kirthar Mountains, 153–160, *154, 155*
Kistas, Harry, 253
KMT: Journal of Ancient Egypt, 94
knapping. *See* flintknapping
Kossinna, Gustaf, 62–63
Kremela I (Czech Republic), 255
Kroeber, Alfred, 35–36
Kubiena samples, 86
KV 62, 5
Kyrenia vessel, 251–253, *252, 253*

Lagenaria siceraria, 263
Lake Huleh site, 180–181
Lakehurst Railroad Roundhouse (New Jersey), 128
landfills, 65–66
Lascaux Cave paintings (France), 177–178, *178, 179*

Late Woodland tradition, *49,* 275. *See also* Mississippian cultures
Latin American Inquiry, 94
Law of Superposition, 42, 141
Leakey, Louis, 108
Leakey, Mary, 108, 164–165
leather tanning, 33
legislation
    Antiquities Act of 1906, 302–305, *305*
    Archaeological Resource Protection Act of 1979, 304, *305,* 312, 316–317
    Federal Abandoned Shipwreck Act of 1988, 307
    Historic Sites Act of 1935, 304, *305*
    National Environmental Protection Act of 1969, 304, *305*
    Native American Graves Protection and Repatriation Act of 1990, 269–270, *305,* 307–314
Leighton, William, 235
leopards, hunting by, *288*
Lepper, Brad, 192
Levallois technology, 172
lichens, in dyes, 256
light fraction, 136
limestone tools, 179
linguistic anthropology, 3–6
Lion Gate (Mycenae, Greece), *11*
lions, hunting by, 288
literature searches, 92–94
lithics, 161–162. *See also* tools, stone
Little Big Horn (Montana), *236,* 236–238
Lloyd's Bank Turd, *279*
logical positivism, 58, 60–61
Lohmann ceramics, *28*
looting
    armed conflict, 294
    ceramics, 315–316
    legislation against, 304–306, *305*
    Moche site of Sipán, Peru, 308–310
    Native American graves, 307–311
    sale of artifacts on the Internet, 311–315
    shipwrecks, 21–22, 306–307
lost-wax casting, 228
Lower Indus Valley, 153–160
Lubbock, Sir John (Lord Avebury), 46, 69
luminescence dating techniques, 149
Lyell, Charles, 42, 141, 287

macrobotanical remains, 250–257, *251*
Magdelanian period, 138, *175,* 177
magnetometers, 101–102
maille, 229
maize, 262, *263,* 275

Majumdar, Nani Gopal, 159
mammals, small, 284
Manihot esculenta, 263
Man Makes Himself (Childe), 180
manos, 182
mapping, 130
Marcey Creek pottery, *194,* 198
maritime foundations hypothesis, 258
market exchange, 252, 255
Marshack, Alexander, 176
Marx, Karl, 79
Marxist archaeology, *79,* 79–80, 180–181
Mary Rose, 226, 226–227, *227*
material culture
    behavioral archaeology and, 64–66, 72–73
    Binford classification, 182–183
    definition, 2
    distribution, 213–214
    Marxist interpretations, 79–80
    See also artifacts
matrilocal residence, 215
matrix, 76, 78
matting, 225
Mayan civilization
    collapse of, 261–262
    contact with Egyptians, 35
    intuitive sampling of sites, 117
    nutritional stress, 275
    warfare, 118
McKee, Alexander, 226
McKern, W. C., 36, 48–49
megalithic monuments, 53–55
Mellaart, Arlette, 76
Mellaart, James, 76–78
mescaline, 259
Mesolithic period, 46, *47,* 283
metal detectors, 102
metals, 220–232
    brass and bronze, 221–225
    copper, 220–221, 228
    gold, 228, *228*
    iron and steel, 225–232
    munitions, *226,* 226–227, 233–234
metamorphic rocks, 165
metates, 182
mica, in ceramics, 192–193
microbotanical remains, 257–263, *260, 263*
middens, 133–134
middle range theory, 58–59, *59,* 162, 182, 287–292
Midwest Taxonomic System, 36, 48–49
migrations, exchange systems and, 67
Miller, Christopher, 75
minerals, 164–165